Marketing Strategy
The Thinking Involved

For those who are curious about how two plus two equals six.

Marketing Strategy
The Thinking Involved

Mark E. Hill
Montclair State University

Los Angeles | London | New Delhi
Singapore | Washington DC

Los Angeles | London | New Delhi
Singapore | Washington DC

FOR INFORMATION:

SAGE Publications, Inc.
2455 Teller Road
Thousand Oaks, California 91320
E-mail: order@sagepub.com

SAGE Publications Ltd.
1 Oliver's Yard
55 City Road
London EC1Y 1SP
United Kingdom

SAGE Publications India Pvt. Ltd.
B 1/I 1 Mohan Cooperative Industrial Area
Mathura Road, New Delhi 110 044
India

SAGE Publications Asia-Pacific Pte. Ltd.
3 Church Street
#10-04 Samsung Hub
Singapore 049483

Acquisitions Editor: Patricia Quinlin
Associate Editor: Maggie Stanley
Editorial Assistant: Katie Guarino
Production Editor: Brittany Bauhaus
Copy Editor: Kim Husband
Typesetter: C&M Digitals (P) Ltd.
Proofreader: Theresa Kay
Indexer: Kathy Paparchontis
Cover Designer: Anupama Krishnan
Marketing Manager: Liz Thornton

Printed in the United States of America

Library of Congress Cataloging-in-Publication Data

Hill, Mark E., 1957-
Marketing strategy : the thinking involved / Mark E. Hill.

p. cm.
Includes bibliographical references and index.

ISBN 978-1-4129-8730-1 (pbk.)

1. Marketing—Management. 2. Strategic planning. I. Title.

HF5415.13.H546 2013
658.8′02—dc23   2011050631

This book is printed on acid-free paper.

12 13 14 15 16 10 9 8 7 6 5 4 3 2 1

Brief Contents

DETAILED CONTENTS

ABOUT THE AUTHOR

Mark E. Hill is an Associate Professor of Marketing at Montclair State University with more than 20 years of academic and professional experience. He has taught graduate and undergraduate courses in marketing strategy, marketing research, and consumer behavior and has published numerous articles on subjects related to marketing thinking. In 2011, Dr. Hill authored *Marketing Strategy in Play: Questioning to Create Difference*. In 2006, he was honored with the Best Article for 2001 award by *Marketing Education Review* for "Teaching and Effectiveness: Another Look," at the 2006 Society for Marketing Advances Annual Conference. His works also include titles such as "The Curiosity in Marketing Thinking," "The Obstacles to Marketing Thinking," "A Marketing Paradox," "That Which Is 'Not:' Forgetting," and "An Indefinite Consumer(s)," each contributing to this present work, *Marketing Strategy: The Thinking Involved.*

While Dr. Hill's research provides the academic foundation of *Marketing Strategy: The Thinking Involved*, it is a culmination of his years of teaching, observing students, and listening to what employers are looking for from graduating marketing students that led to his interest in developing a different approach to teaching marketing. It is the thinking side of marketing that is of interest to those who are curious and forward-looking as well as those who have dedicated their professional lives to being successful in the profession of marketing.

He received his Doctorate in Business specializing in Marketing from Southern Illinois University and has an MBA and a Bachelor's degree in Mechanical Engineering. Prior to his academic career, Dr. Hill worked as an aerospace engineer for General Electric, a technical manager for American Airlines, and a marketing representative for Unison Industries. He has been a consultant to companies across the United States, providing services in the areas of marketing research and marketing strategy.

PREFACE

Companies worldwide are experiencing an ever-increasing rate of change, from new forms of communications via the Internet to advances in technology. The challenges confronting businesses today and, in the future, will be about developing the capabilities to stay ahead. Navigating a constantly changing business landscape demands new ways of thinking about the marketplace and marketing strategy. Behind any marketing strategy is the thinking that went into creating it, and fundamental to any good strategy is good thinking. While other marketing strategy textbooks have focused on the dissemination of marketing concepts and theories that could be used for strategy purposes, *Marketing Strategy: The Thinking Involved* offers a different approach. Its focus is on developing thinking skills that lead to effective strategies for dynamic business environments. The reader will find that the text is written less like a dictionary and more like a thinking experience. Marketing concepts and theories are discussed, but from the perspective of the thinking behind them. In doing so, the limits of each are revealed while opening the doors for emerging marketing thinking that leads to new concepts, new theories, new perspectives, and, ultimately, to new strategies.

The Difference—Becoming a Marketing Strategist

The text begins with an exploration into what marketing thinking looks like and its dimensions—that is, creative thinking, critical thinking, reflective thinking, and thinking in time. No other marketing or marketing strategy textbook explicitly offers this very fundamental feature. Central to this perspective is that thinking and questioning go hand in hand with each dimension, providing the strategist different lines of questioning culminating in unique perspectives. With the focus on thinking, the emphasis is reversed from a traditional text for learning answers to learning the skills for good questioning that lead to better answers and more effective strategies. The thinking theme permeates the chapters and is elevated in the last chapter to thinking about thinking organizations and the types of environments that promote a thinking culture.

Marketing Strategy: The Thinking Involved utilizes a unique thinking agility design that offers Marketing Thinking Challenges after the different forms of marketing thinking have been discussed. Each of the Marketing Thinking (MT) Challenges asks the reader to try on a different form of thinking. The skill of thinking agility can be learned by exposure to many different forms of thinking, enabling the strategist to be much more effective in navigating the changing business landscape. For the strategist, thinking agility is a critical skill that enables one to possess a keen ability to sense and proactively respond to changes in the environment as they are developing. The diversity of more than 45 challenges that involve traditional and contemporary forms of marketing thinking lay out a course for the reader to develop his or her own thinking agility. In addition, for the purpose of developing a more comprehensive level of marketing thinking, mini cases are offered throughout the text that can be used to apply the thinking being developed through the MT Challenges. However, the primary development takes place through the various MT Challenges that are placed along a designed thinking path in the book.

Many of the chapters provide a contrast between traditional versus more contemporary forms of marketing thinking. This is done as a means to illustrate the differences in thinking behind their concepts and theories while also recognizing their limitations. From a thinking perspective, a prescriptive approach is not offered but, instead, the contrasts simply illustrate different forms of thinking, allowing the reader to consider his or her applicability for different situations that might arise. Examples and Marketing Thinking in Practice are also provided to illustrate the different forms of thinking being applied by businesses.

Several additional noteworthy differences include various visual images that are meant to be a part of the thinking experience along with pauses or white spaces to encourage the reader to stop and engage in his or her own thinking. Instead of going on and on with disseminating information, the text breaks up the delivery of information in a more parsimonious way. This is done so as not to obscure the true task with information overload but to develop the reader's thinking. The reader is also asked to consider various questions throughout the text as a means of encouraging active participation and of directing their thinking. In addition, there is an ongoing dialogue with a character figure and the teacher throughout in which the character takes on a reader's perspective.

Another departure from other textbooks is the inclusion of what are referred to as decompression exercises. As with any task, it's important to prepare for what is to be required. To prepare for thinking, the physiology and psychology of the brain must work together.

Decompression Exercises—Preparing the Way for Thinking

Decompression exercises are offered at the beginning of each chapter as a means to pause before getting started. They are provided for the purpose of preparing the way to be more effective at the task at hand, *thinking*, which hopefully will lead to more learning. Give them a try to see if they have the desired benefit.

When discussing thinking, there is often a tendency to focus on one level versus the other—either the physiology or the psychology. It is important to recognize that both are involved in the thinking phenomenon. The brain is an electrical-chemical processing organ that is producing our awareness, thoughts, and feelings. Like any other electrical-chemical mechanism, for example a car battery, if overutilized, it wouldn't be able to operate at its peak capacity and may not even start. The brain is the same way. If you feel sluggish or aren't interested in learning, these may be signs that you need to recharge before taking on the new task.

All of us lead very busy lives. It is this busyness and our environments that draw down the daily capacity of the brain and decrease our ability to think at peak capacity and fully comprehend new material—to learn something new. To learn more effectively, it is important to prepare the brain for the task—to afford the brain an opportunity to rejuvenate its chemistry or to be in a state in which learning can take place. *Decompression exercises* refer to a general category of exercises that are meant to relax the brain and provide an opportunity to shift from a very active state (busy, compressed) to a less active (relaxed, decompressed) state. A series of exercises could be used for this purpose, including listening to music, meditating, going to a spa, taking a walk in nature, joking around, playing, doodling, and/or engaging in projective imaginary tasks. Each offers different ways to relax and allow the brain to shift from a compressed to a decompressed state—similar to shifting from high to low gear in a car to slow down.

Decompression exercises have been designed to serve the following purposes: (1) to provide a moment to pause from your busyness to allow for the transition to a preferred state for thinking, (2) to relax and alleviate stress, and (3) to prepare the brain for more meaningful learning. Whether coming into a class or reading a text at home, it's important to be in the best possible state to get the most out of the learning experience. Before meaningful learning can occur, stress must be relieved, and the primary strategy is relaxation.[1]

The Marketing Terrain Coverage

Marketing Strategy: The Thinking Involved provides much more in-depth and expanded coverage of marketing's concepts, theories, and strategies than other marketing strategy textbooks currently available in the following ways. From an aggregate view, the text offers a contrast between traditional marketing and its contemporary, co-marketing (collaborative or participatory marketing). This allows for explorations, for example, into the differences between traditional forms of marketing communications and social media tools. Expanding on customer relationship management (CRM), customer interface management (CIM), and customer experience management (CEM) are also discussed within the same context for comparison purposes. Changes in technology have opened up a host of new strategy options that are considered as well including developing listening strategies via dashboards or using software such as Voicescape; using predictive analytics to offer real-time marketing to customers when shopping; using new forms of forward-looking metrics to navigate strategy; and utilizing emerging technology for coordination purposes within logistical value nets. Even the marketing mix (4 Ps) is expanded upon by presenting 33 additional mixes to illustrate the advances occurring in this form of thinking in terms of considering different mixes for different situations (e.g., e-commerce vs. retail). Thinking is also influenced by one's environment. To understand the significance of this, an examination of thinking organizations and their characteristics is provided as well. Today, organizations such as Google and Apple are developing their capabilities by developing thinking cultures to stay ahead of the changing business landscape. The thinking capabilities of an organization represent its future.

References

1. Howard, Pierce J. (2006), *The Owner's Manual for the Brain: Everyday Applications From Mind-Brain Research,* 3rd edition, Austin, TX: Bard Press.

ACKNOWLEDGMENTS

The ideas behind *Marketing Strategy: The Thinking Involved* benefited from many different interactions and experiences over the years with students, colleagues, and professionals. There are so many it would fill a directory. As such, I would like to offer a big thanks to all of you. The book wouldn't have been possible without your contributions, large and small.

SAGE provided an extensive peer review process for this book from the proposal through the development of each of the chapters. Each of the reviewers offered many constructive comments which was appreciated and have strengthened the text. While the following is a partial list of the numerous reviewers involved in the process, I'd like to extend a sincere thank you to each.

Jane Cromartie, *University of New Orleans*

John C. Crawford, *University of North Texas*

Hugh Daubek, *Purdue University–Calumet*

Giles D'Souza, *University of Alabama*

Stephen Garrott, *Troy University–Troy*

Tarique Hossain, *California State Polytechnic University, Pomona*

Brian Jorgensen, *Westminster College*

Debi P. Mishra, *State University of New York at Binghamton*

Jifeng Mu, *Alabama A & M University*

Don Price, *Metropolitan State College of Denver*

Also to the SAGE editors vital to the process from Deya (Saoud) Jacob, Acquisition Editor, for taking an initial interest in the project and for providing guidance through the proposal process; to Lisa Cuevas Shaw, Senior Executive Editor, for facilitating the review process and providing constructive comments and suggestions throughout; to Katie Guarino, Editorial Assistant, for handling all of the permissions and details to take it to production; and finally, to all of the team at SAGE who have played a critical part in the production of the text. Many thanks to all. Your efforts are greatly appreciated.

I also thank my colleagues at Montclair State University (MSU) for their encouragement and support for the project. Two colleagues stand out which I would like to especially recognize. The Chair of the Marketing Department Avinandan Mukherjee, Professor, was always willing to listen and to provide encouragement. He also understood the time commitment for such a project and provided a teaching schedule to accommodate my needs. Sometimes simply airing ideas with someone can be especially helpful. Professor John McGinnis was always willing to listen over numerous lunches and offered many ideas and suggestions for the text. To my MSU colleagues, your encouragement and support is truly appreciated. Thank you.

Finally, but not least, to my wife, Janice F. Hill, to whom I have been married for fifteen years and going. She has always been there, willing to read my materials and offer her insights, comments, and suggestions. Many of which are contained within the text. She also has been extremely patient through this prolonged process giving me the space and time needed to work on the project all the while offering encouragement and her love. To write a textbook, family support is critical. To Janice, I offer a special thank you!

Thanks to all!

—*Mark E. Hill*

The Role Marketing Thinking Plays in Strategy

CHAPTER 1 Marketing Thinking

Have you ever experienced being stressed out or anxious before having to tackle a challenging task that required you to think? The stress could be from being in heavy traffic before coming to work or school. Or you could simply be anxious about all of the tasks on your list of things to do. In either case, the stress or anxiety makes the thinking tasks at hand more difficult. In a perfect world, being stress free and doing things at your leisure, when you are ready, would be ideal. However, the world we live in, with its constant demands, isn't stress free and, hence, it's necessary to learn how to deal with it and still get things done. Knowing what state of mind you are in and when you work most effectively is the starting point. If you know you are anxious and your mind seems to be going in many directions, then it is time to stop and take a moment to allow your mind to settle. The mind is able to focus when in a more relaxed state, and it is in this state that you are able to think more clearly and effectively.

Each chapter begins with a decompression exercise. Their purpose is for the reader to take a moment to relax before engaging in the task of thinking. A decompression exercise can involve anything that leads to relaxation such as listening to music, going for a walk, taking a bath, or simply taking a moment to notice something simple. Those offered throughout the text can be experienced in a few moments in the classroom or before studying. Preparing for thinking is no different than when athletes stretch and warm up prior to an event. Developing the practice of preparing for the task of thinking will enable you to be that much more effective at it; it will seem easier and require less time. In today's busy world, this simple strategy of taking out time to relax before working on a challenging task can make your life that much more enjoyable while accomplishing what you to do. Give it a try. Before jumping into the chapter, try the following decompression exercise or simply take five or 10 minutes out to do something that relaxes you.

Decompression Exercise

Take a few moments and consider the following: When was the last time you noticed something simple? What was it? How did it make you feel?

| Figure 1.1 | A Flower |

Chapter Introduction

What is it that draws people to the marketing profession? It may have something to do with its ubiquity and high visibility throughout our everyday experiences. Marketing seems to be everywhere and hard to avoid. At the same time, it is a part of contemporary society and inherently possesses interesting qualities. It can grab our attention, make us laugh, affect our preferences, and, ultimately, get us to spend money. It is in these everyday experiences with marketing that the curiosity for marketing and wanting to find out more about this profession begins. How do marketers come up with those interesting advertisements? How does marketing generate money? What goes into becoming a good marketer? And why are some marketers better at marketing than others?

To become a marketing professional requires learning how to think like a marketer. It is similar to wanting to become an artist, which is to learn their particular way of thinking to be able to engage artistic activities. The same could be said for all professions. Within business, accounting, finance, management, and so forth, each involves different forms of skilled thinking.

What does marketing thinking involve? Take, for example, marketers like Steve Jobs of Apple, Jeff Bezos of Amazon, Pierre Omidyar of eBay, and A. G. Laftey of P&G. What made their thinking different from that of others? And could it be learned? The answer is a resounding *yes*. All have had a major impact on their markets, changing and redefining the nature of competition to the benefit of their organizations. In a recent *Harvard Business Review* (*HBR*) article, innovators such as these were studied to reveal their "innovator's DNA"[1] to understand how they develop "ground breaking new ideas." Several of the key "innovator's DNA" characteristics identified in the study were the ability to form associations and to continuously ask good questions.[2] Their questioning was a natural habit challenging the status quo, and this habit became infectious and an integral element of their companies' cultures. Within the challenging of the status quo is also the inclination toward change, which involves an interest toward adapting to unfolding situations and being agile in doing so. The agility here is a thinking agility that is in contrast to the status quo. It is through developing their questioning skills that they have been able to hone their thinking agility.

Marketers have to be resourceful and insightful to be able to navigate effectively across difficult landscapes. Today's markets are more dynamic than ever before. Financial upheavals, changing demographics, advances in technology, environmental concerns, and an increasing rate of innovations represent the landscape in which marketers conduct business. Each alone is challenging enough, but when combined, the task seems insurmountable. To be a skilled marketer today requires a particular type of thinking that isn't fixed, but agile. Developing marketing thinking based upon an agility perspective for strategy purposes is what this textbook explores.

What is a thinking agility perspective based upon? First, it recognizes that all thinking is limited in some form or another and, as such, the limitations must be recognized to have an eye for other possibilities. Second, everything is constantly in the process of change. So the marketer's thinking must also involve change. If the marketer's thinking remains fixed and the marketplace is changing, then the marketer, in essence, is becoming further and further removed from what is taking place within the marketplace, putting the organization's resources at risk. Thinking agility is consistent with a changing, dynamic marketplace. The more agile the marketer is in his or her thinking, the more able he or she would be to participate within the marketplace. Third, thinking agility is also about participating in the marketplace in ways that affect its nature, which requires new ways of understanding such changes. For example, the marketplace is transformed through new innovations with new forms of competition, practices, and/or consumption. As such, thinking agility involves understanding and developing new concepts, theories, and approaches leading to new strategies.

For example, consider the concept of *value*. Marketing involves marketing something. To pay for what the marketer is offering, there must be some form of value associated with it. Questions arise as to who is creating the value: the marketer, the consumer, or others? And where does the value reside? The answers to these questions have implications as to how you are thinking and their corresponding strategies.

If you assume the marketer is creating the value in the form of a product, then the value resides within the product (i.e., a *value-in-product* or *value-in-the-thing*) and the marketer is the one creating the value (an internal perspective). This view is consistent with a traditional perspective of marketing, leading to strategies based upon competition, persuasion, and targeting. On the other hand, if you assume an external perspective in which the consumer is creating the value in terms of how the product is to be used, that is, a *value-in-use,* or take into account brand communities via the Internet and social media where value is being created through the brand communities' practices, that is, a *value-in-practices,* or consider emerging organic collaborative channel configurations referred to as holonic value nets where value stems from the orchestration within to accommodate more effectively consumers' customized requests, that is, a *value-in-orchestration*, then in each case, who is creating the value is different, the concept of value has changed, and each involves a different form of thinking leading to different marketing strategies.

As we will see throughout the text, the value concept is changing with developments occurring within the marketplace as well as with marketing thinking. As the value moves around, this phenomenon can be described as chasing the *value tail,* which calls for greater marketing thinking agility to keep up with it. To get started, we'll need to examine what marketing thinking entails and to begin developing our thinking agility.

Marketing Thinking

Anyone with the ability to think and an interest in marketing can learn to think in a *marketing way* (the italics symbolize its dynamic nature). A thinking approach to learning marketing is different from simply learning about marketing. Instead of simply reading about it, a thinking approach to marketing requires you to actually try on the different forms of marketing thinking, to experience them. Through the act of experiencing them, your thinking is actually being affected (changed) in the process. If you have had the opportunity to read a number of marketing books or textbooks, you may have noticed that the focus was on marketing versus marketing thinking per se. The focus was on the content of marketing as a discipline in terms of concepts and theories. While we are interested in these elements of marketing, the primary focus here is on developing your marketing thinking, which can involve these elements, and how this skill or capability will help you develop more effective strategy.

A central premise is that marketing involves a particular way of thinking that is different from other forms of thinking such as thinking in an *accounting way* or in a *finance way.* Each has a particular perspective. Have you ever thought about what marketing thinking actually looks like? How is it different from other forms of thinking? And what is it about this form of thinking that can lead to more effective strategy?

To tell you the truth, I don't think I ever thought about it in that way.

Okay. What is *marketing* thinking?

All thinking involves questioning, and **marketing thinking** pertains to a particular type of questioning. It occurs when someone asks how to compete successfully by providing value (creating choice) as defined by some targeted market. It is an active, cognitive engagement centered on strategically out-thinking (or out-questioning) the competition.[3]

As we will see over the chapters, the nature of the questioning pertaining to marketing thinking will change when considering a more traditional view of marketing versus its more contemporary form. What stays the same is that there is always some form of questioning involved when engaged in marketing thinking. The above definition provides a good starting point for understanding what the questioning of marketing might involve.

> Let me see if I have this straight. What we are going to be learning are the questions or the questioning that marketers ask in the practice of marketing. Is this correct?
>
> So, it's not about memorizing concepts and theories? Wow, this seems different. But aren't the concepts and theories found in marketing the answers?
>
> And how can questions be more important than the concepts and the theories? Interesting!

With such questions, you are already starting to think and question the learning process. Hold on to these questions for a moment. They will be answered when we discuss what marketing thinking actually looks like and its various facets. But, before moving on, try the following short task and see what you can come up with.

Marketing Thinking Challenge 1.1: Interesting Marketing Questions

All of us have experiences with marketing, either professionally or as consumers. Therefore, this task shouldn't be too difficult. Put yourself in the marketer's position and generate 10 interesting marketing questions that you think would be useful to the marketer. Try not to evaluate your questions; simply list interesting ones. You'll use these questions later in the book to see how your questioning is changing.

Figure 1.2 Question Marks

Your list of 10 **interesting** marketing questions:

1. _____
2. _____
3. _____
4. _____
5. _____
6. _____
7. _____
8. _____
9. _____
10. _____

Marketing Thinking and Effective Strategy

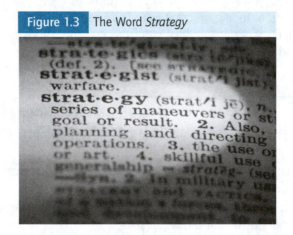

Figure 1.3 The Word *Strategy*

With this preliminary understanding of marketing thinking in mind, it is a good time to introduce what is generally meant by a strategy in a marketing context. In essence, *strategy* is a way to be meaningfully different in the marketplace. "It means deliberately choosing a different set of activities to deliver a unique mix of value."[4] "Choosing to perform activities differently than rivals do."[5] Or reconfiguring a company's value chain by changing its activities or sequence of activities.[6]

Here, a strategy is an organization's way to be different in terms of what is being provided and the manner in which it is provided in the marketplace via its configuration of activities. From this perspective, all organizations can be viewed as a composition of activities that include financial, accounting, operations, management, marketing, and so forth. The configuration of these activities in terms of which ones are selected, how they are interrelated, and how they are provided can be thought of as the organization's process for being different in the marketplace—that is, its strategy. For example, consider the differences between experiences with eating at McDonald's versus a fancy French restaurant. The experiences are different because of how these organizations configure their activities. They have different strategies for how they operate within the marketplace.

Strategy involves choices and decisions. Developing choices and the way in which the choices are to be decided upon is a matter of marketing thinking. The better your marketing thinking and the better the choices to choose from along the level of scrutiny given to the choices at hand, the better, ultimately, your strategy and, hence, a stronger position from which to compete.[7] As stated previously:

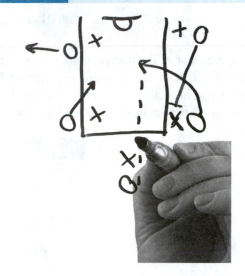

Figure 1.4 Strategy—A *Way* to Be Different

> All thinking involves questioning, and **marketing thinking** pertains to a particular type of questioning. It occurs when someone asks how to compete successfully by providing value [creating choice] as defined by some targeted market. It is an active, cognitive engagement centered on strategically out-thinking (or out-questioning) the competition.[8]

The focus of marketing thinking, the questioning, is on creating a **differential in value** (or choice) as defined (or understood) by the marketplace or those being pursued (the targeted market). The providing of value is done through a series of activities conducted by the organization. The configuration of these activities represents an organization's strategy—which activities, how the activities are to be done, the outcomes of the activities, and synergistic effects in combining the activities are all elements of strategy. In the end, the **effectiveness of a strategy** is determined by the marketplace—which is determined by what is being provided by the organization and whether it is received as a meaningful preferential difference in value and the degree to which the marketplace acts accordingly.

The larger the perceived differential in value—that is, the greater the contrast between an organization and its competition—the better it is for the organization. The degree of contrast is also an indication of the greater degree in effectiveness (i.e., preferential marketplace position or greater competiveness) of its strategy being employed. This also underscores the *playing field* in terms of where the competition is actually taking place—the competition occurs through *those targeted*. The playing field is the psychological landscape of the consumers being targeted. If those targeted do not perceive a differential in value or if they perceive your offering to be less than what others are providing, this would be due to an ineffective strategy that puts your organization into a less desirable market position. The remedy for this is marketing thinking. Later on in the text, this competitive view of marketing thinking is challenged and an alternative perspective is offered. However, what is central here is that the marketing strategy is directed toward having an influence or an effect on people in the marketplace in one form or another. Before moving on to explore at a deeper level what marketing thinking encompasses, try the following MT Challenge.

Figure 1.5	Identifying Strategy

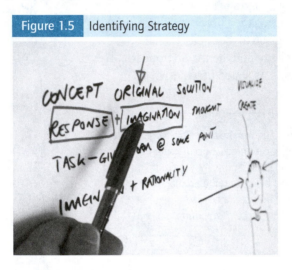

Marketing Thinking: 4-Dimensional Spherical (4-DS) Thinking

In the past, you may have seen thinking portrayed as being linear or one-dimensional (e.g., critical thinking), but these characterizations limit the scope of marketing thinking, which is much more spherical and multidimensional.[9] Figure 1.6 is a graphical representation of thinking.

Wow, it seems complicated. I think I like the earlier versions of thinking—linear and one-dimensional. Simpler. Less work.

Figure 1.6 4-Dimensional Spherical (4-DS) Thinking

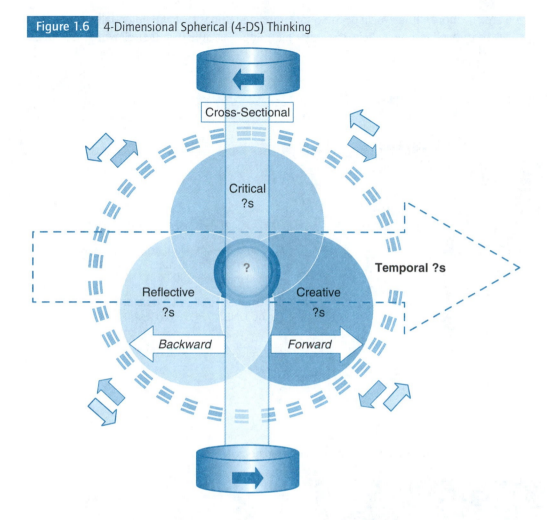

Given the dynamic nature of today's markets, it's important to be in a position to see changes as they are developing. Therefore, we need to consider more than one dimension. To be successful, like the innovators mentioned in the beginning of the chapter, we need the full range of thinking tools or skills to be able to be that much more resourceful and insightful. Once you understand what this view of thinking involves, it may not be as complicated as it first appears. Also, all unfamiliar things tend to seem complicated until they become familiar. This process involves effort. Thinking involves effort. Furthermore, thinking is like any other skill—with practice, it will become easier and you'll get better at it. It might actually be fun.

Being open or curious and willing to consider something new is a good starting point. Actually, curiosity is the fuel for thinking. The more curious

you are, the more willing you'll be to explore unrelated things that will potentially lead to new views or understandings. The 4-DS Thinking model basically has the following three main features:

| Figure 1.7 | Dimensions of Marketing Thinking |

Temporal — Thinking in Time

a. Change—The status quo is CHANGE, which should be integral to your thinking and strategy.

b. Expect CHANGE and be prepared for the UNEXPECTED (CHANCE).

First Feature: 4-Dimensional Perspective

Thinking can freely pivot in any direction within each of the four dimensions.

Second Feature: Spherical Perspective

(Continued)

Figure 1.7   (Continued)

The four dimensions interrelate to form a particular 4-DS view of the situation.

The particular 4-DS view represents a perspective.

Strategy is the marketer's way to be meaningfully different in the marketplace. To be different means to be innovative. This is where creative thinking comes into view. **Creative thinking** involves generating new ideas, innovations, and ways of doing things. It requires a type of questioning that looks forward in time and, hence, is a forward-looking form of differentiating.[10] Several of the key "innovator's DNA" characteristics identified in the *HBR* study were the ability to form associations and to continuously ask good questions.[11] Their questioning was a natural habit challenging the status quo, and this habit became infectious and an integral element of their companies' cultures. Creative thinking involves these aspects but also has an extension feature or orientation to it—it's about the new. In essence, the new is a function of the old but is more than the old. For example, 2 + 2 = 6 or old + old = new. When engaged in creative thinking, we are searching for associations to be formed that then become the platform for the new. The advances in technology or any innovation are based upon this process of leapfrogging from existing associations on to the next.

Figure 1.8   Using the Old to See the New

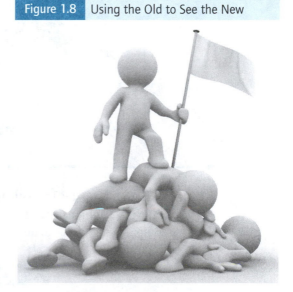

To see the new, to be in the position to ask the questions that lead to the new, requires rising above the old (what we know, the familiar)—and using the old as a platform from which to see the possibilities for the new. For example, what if you looked for two things that are typically not seen as being associated with each other; what new possibility could be seen in doing so? Looking at these two known, familiar things in this new way represents an opportunity to see a new association that could lead to a new possibility in the form of a new product and/or service category. Try the following exercises.

Marketing Thinking Challenge 1.3: Creative Thinking

For this challenge, see if you can create three new associations. Part A. Identify two unrelated things to form a new association. What are they?

1. _____

2. _____

3. _____

Part B. Then, from the above three new associations, what new possibilities can you see in terms of potentially new product or service categories? Also, explain the connections between Part A and Part B.

1. _____

2. _____

3. _____

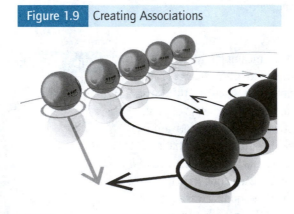

Figure 1.9   Creating Associations

How did you do? The path of success is driven by being able to generate a steady stream of innovative approaches, culminating in one's ongoing strategy. Apple is a good example of a company that is able to do this regularly, and this capability represents a vital component to its strategy.

Figure 1.10   Being on the Path of Success

Creative thinking is about generating new ideas. Deciding which ideas would be best given market conditions and the organization's objectives and capabilities requires critical thinking, the second dimensional point of view.

Critical thinking is a cross-sectional form of differentiating. It is about asking which of the alternatives is best given our current situation. Which course of action should we pursue?

Given the identified alternatives (through creative thinking), which unique way should we differentiate in the marketplace to be competitive? As will be discussed later, the evaluation of alternatives is situationally or contextually based. It involves idiosyncratic criteria based upon the organization's objectives and what is currently known about the situation the organization confronts.

Once the chosen alternative is operationalized, it then becomes a question of how well the strategy is working. This requires **reflective thinking** (the third dimensional point of view), which is a backward-looking form of differentiating in assessing differences across several points in time. The assessment would be based upon the objective(s) established at the time the alternative was being considered. An objective has three components: (1) a benchmark, (2) a goal, and (3) a timeframe. If the employed strategy isn't working, then a new one may need to be considered—again, calling upon your creative and critical thinking.

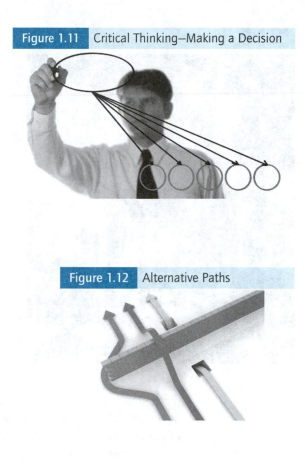

Figure 1.11   Critical Thinking—Making a Decision

Figure 1.12   Alternative Paths

Figure 1.13   Keeping Ahead—A Step at a Time

Of the three forms of thinking, creative thinking is the most challenging because of the extension aspect—that is, moving beyond the familiar into the new. Critical thinking is an easier form of thinking in that the alternatives have been identified, and it then simply becomes a matter of choosing which is the best. Reflective thinking would be the easiest form of thinking in simply seeing how things are working based upon the objective(s) established during the critical thinking stage.

Figure 1.14	Time

The fourth dimensional point of view is **time**. While all of the forms of thinking involve an element of time, the temporal dimension is drawn out separately to emphasize the importance of **change** and *chance*. The temporal point of view asks how things will change and in which ways they might change. The elements of time, change, and chance must be considered in any strategy. They are what drive the innovators to always be on the lookout for the new. What is on the horizon that I should be aware of? Can you see the beginnings of the changes starting to take place in the marketplace? What might the unexpected look like? Are you prepared for the unexpected?

Each of the four dimensions is spherical in nature in that the questioning within each perspective or point of view can pivot in any direction. For example, within the creative thinking perspective, you can look in any direction for new associations from which to leapfrog into the new. Similarly, there are an infinite number of criteria that could be used to evaluate alternatives within the critical thinking perspective. With reflective thinking, conditions or your thinking may have changed over time to a point at which you need to consider different ways to evaluate a strategy. Even the temporal dimension, while integral to the other three dimensions, also possesses a spherical quality. While we usually think of time in a linear way through its past, present, and future incremental positions, it also has a relative characteristic in that in any given moment, each of us is experiencing time differently—that is, the relativeness in which it is moving, fast or slowly. The relative characteristic of time perceptually is a function of its change and chance elements. As one experiences or sees more change occurring than someone else, time would seem to be moving faster. Likewise, with greater degrees of unexpected change through chance, time will appear to be moving through larger increments and, hence, feel like it is speeding up. The questioning in the time dimension is not only about moving forward but also about the rate at which change is occurring and the size of the increments being felt through unexpected change.[12] The chance element can pivot in any direction, setting the stage for the unexpected. Furthermore, the chance element could even pertain to a change that is unexpectedly reverting to some previous event, creating a feeling of nostalgia and, hence, a sense of traveling back in time.

Finally, four-dimensional spherical thinking, 4-DS thinking, is an integrated view or perspective used in developing strategy. The four dimensions come together to form a particular perspective of how you'll view the situation and, further, how you'll maneuver within this situation—your way of engagement.

Figure 1.15 is meant to symbolize the fluid, intermixing, and evolving nature of 4-DS thinking in motion. Nothing stands still, so don't let your thinking become static or stale. If you do, you'll be left behind, which is a too-common occurrence in business. All you have to do is look at the rate at which organizations go out of business.

Learning to Think in a *Marketing Way*

As stated in the introduction, anyone with the ability to think and an interest in marketing can learn to think in a *marketing way* (the italics symbolize its dynamic nature). Learning to think in a *marketing way* is really an exploration into contemporary societies with an eye to participate. The purpose of the exploration is to gain insights that can then be used to develop a strategy, a *way*, to participate by offering something meaningfully different than what is being offered by others. The *way* in which marketers conduct their exploration, thinking, is through varying their questioning to be able to see the nuances, the openings for new differences, and new ways to participate.

In an analogous way, the exploration into marketing thinking is similar to taking a road trip and getting off of the main highways and traveling the back roads, sightseeing along the way. To see (understand) the thinking behind marketing concepts and theories, we'll need to get off the highways, to slow down, to see the many forms of marketing thinking available, and there are many. Highways represent the well-traveled routes, the familiar, and the back roads represent the less-traveled roads, the unfamiliar. The exploration is about learning what you don't already know. Your route will be determined by the new questions you'll be acquiring along the way. Each form of marketing thinking involves different lines of questioning, and as you try them on, you'll experience the different forms of marketing thinking for yourself while developing your thinking agility. For each traveler (reader), there isn't a predetermined destination or route. There will be a lot of stops and starts, detours, rest stops, and unexpected events along the way—running out of gas, getting a flat tire, picking up an

| Figure 1.15 | 4-DS Thinking in Motion |

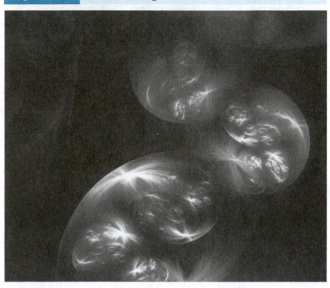

| Figure 1.16 | Contemporary Society |

additional passenger, bad weather. What you'll be seeing will be through the questions you ask, consider, or confront along the way. The questions are your tour guides, pointing out the sights to be seen (see Figure 1.17 on page 18.).

The Role Marketing Concepts and Theories Are to *Play*

Earlier in the chapter, the question was raised about whether the concepts and theories found in marketing are the answers, and shouldn't we be learning them as the answers? This is an important issue and deserves some thought. The problem with learning concepts and theories in this way, that is, learning them as *the* answers, is that it leads to a nonthinking orientation or situation. The rote form of learning (memorizing) is based on an answers perspective and

Figure 1.17   Seeing Through Your Questions

Figure 1.18   Marketing Concepts and Theories

doesn't have lasting effects. When learned in this way, things are easily forgotten. The reason for the forgetting is that we only remember things that we deem important enough to carry forward. If you don't see the significance of something, it will quickly be forgotten in time.

To understand an answer requires knowing the question it responds to—that is, the question represents the frame of reference for what the answer means. Without the frame of reference being provided, the significance of the answer is lost. What does it mean? Why is it important? How did it come about? How am I to use it? It's kind of like learning it as a thing or like being given a device of sorts—for example, a hammer—and simply using it for all repairs. At the same time, it doesn't promote utilizing and adapting the concepts and theories for varying situations—they are what they are, almost like statues or works of art to be studied from a distance. After all, they are someone else's thinking, not to be touched or played with. Right?

From a thinking perspective, if you had to guess, how might the concepts and theories found in marketing be viewed or used?

Along your marketing thinking travels, we will be experiencing the various concepts and theories by the questions they suggest. In other words, we'll be using their underlying questions as a perspective for what we might be able to see in the marketplace by way of their questions.

For example, what questioning is behind the concept of satisfaction? How might we use this line of questioning to create a strategy based upon satisfaction? We'll examine the satisfaction concept in Chapter 2.

How about considering the issues associated with all concepts in general in terms of how they affect thinking? In doing so, we are in a better position to recognize their limitations while having a keen eye for alternatives. In looking at the thinking behind the concept of a marketplace structure, we consider these concept issues in Chapter 3 and throughout the text.

In Chapter 4, we'll take up the question of who is segmenting the market (the marketer or the consumer). How you respond to this question will affect which strategies you'll consider.

Stepping back even further in Chapter 5, the question of what is really being consumed by consumers is examined to understand fundamentally that the marketplace is a marketplace of difference and to recognize the parameters of difference that all marketers confront. It also leads into a more contemporary form of marketing thinking that involves an understanding of marketing as a form of collaboration with others.

In Chapter 6, the marketing mix concept is examined; we consider multiple mixes, raising a situational question as to their appropriateness. In contrast, within a collaborative/participatory marketing form of thinking, the *contribution* concept is considered.

Chapter 7 raises the question of where the value resides—in the product (or service) or within the practices of a brand community?

The question of how social media are affecting the nature of marketing communications is raised in Chapter 8.

Chapter 9 examines the movement across the different marketing orientations and their thinking along the lines of customer relation management (CRM) to customer interface management (CIM) to customer experience management (CEM) and how technology is influencing these changes.

The contrast between the concepts of a value chain and value nets is considered in Chapter 10.

The question of price and the various pricing strategies are examined in Chapter 11.

The emerging perspective of forward-looking metrics is contrasted with the traditional rear-view metrics in Chapter 12.

And, finally, we examine what a thinking organization looks like, its characteristics, and organizational obstacles to thinking.

Returning to the questioning of the role of concepts and theories, each represents an answer to a line of questioning and, hence, is to be viewed as an outcome of its respective line of questioning. We will uncover (or dust off) the lines of questioning associated with marketing concepts and theories to use for our strategic purposes and will utilize and adapt them as needed. This will be explored in greater detail in Chapter 2 to facilitate your thinking on how to use the concepts and theories found in marketing based upon their intended use. Along the way, you'll hopefully acquire a deeper level and wider range of marketing questions, leading the *way* to your *marketing thinking*.

Marketing Thinking Challenge 1.4: Marketing Thinking—A Beginning

Choose a market in which you have an interest. Identify three different brands within the chosen market and the ways in which they are marketed (e.g., advertising, promotions, where they are available). All marketing in one way or another is soliciting our attention. Understanding what it is presenting to us requires us to question it. What is it? What does it mean to me? From the consumer's perspective and based upon how the brands are being marketed, what questions are they attempting to elicit from their consumers? How are the brands differing in the questions being elicited from the consumers? Based upon the differences in questioning across the brands, how might this affect their consumption experiences?

Figure 1.19 Shopping

Summary

- In this chapter, marketing thinking was initially defined as a type of questioning that pertains to issues of how to compete through providing value as interpreted by some targeted market or group of consumers.
- Strategy was defined as a *way* of being different in the marketplace for the purpose of obtaining particular marketing objectives.
- A marketer's perspective of the marketplace and/or competition is a function of the 4-dimensional (spherical) way of thinking.
- The four dimensions are creative, critical, reflective, and temporal. Each represents a different form or direction of questioning, and they come together to form a particular perspective at a point in time based upon the outcomes of the questioning engaged in by the marketer.
- Creative thinking was described as the form of thinking that represents the future for an organization, and while being a more difficult form of thinking as compared to the other dimensions, it is viewed as being perhaps the most important dimension, leading to new innovations.
- It was also discussed that it is more beneficial to understand concepts, theories, or perspectives from the questions by which they were generated than to simply learn them in a rote way. It is in the questions, the thinking behind the concepts, that their utility lies in terms of being applicable to effective marketing strategy.

References

1. Dyer, Jeffrey H., Hal B. Gregersen, and Clayton M. Christensen (2009), "The Innovator's DNA," *Harvard Business Review*, December, 61–66.
2. Dyer, Jeffrey H., Hal B. Gregersen, and Clayton M. Christensen (2009), "The Innovator's DNA," *Harvard Business Review*, December, 61–66.
3. Hill, Mark E., John McGinnis, and Jane Cromartie (2007), "The Obstacles to Marketing Thinking," *Marketing Intelligence and Planning*, 25 (3), 242.
4. Porter, Michael E. (2010), "What Is Strategy?" *Harvard Business Review—OnPoint*, February, 108.
5. Porter, Michael E. (2010), "What Is Strategy?" *Harvard Business Review—OnPoint*, February, 112.
6. Bryce, David J., and Jeffrey H. Dyer (2007), "Strategies to Crack Well-Guarded Markets," *Harvard Business Review*, May, 84–92.
7. Gavetti, Giovanni, and Jan Rivkin (2005), "How Strategists Really Think: Tapping the Power of Analogy," *Harvard Business Review*, April, 54–63.
8. Hill, Mark E., John McGinnis, and Jane Cromartie (2007), "The Obstacles to Marketing Thinking," *Marketing Intelligence and Planning*, 25 (3), 242.
9. Rickerl, Diane, and Charles Francis (2004), *Multi-Dimensional Thinking: A Prerequisite to Agroecology*, Madison, WI: American Society of Agronomy, 1–18.
10. Hill, Mark E. (2010), *Marketing Strategy in Play: Questioning to Create Difference*, New York: Business Expert Press.
11. Dyer, Jeffrey H., Hal B. Gregersen, and Clayton M. Christensen (2009), "The Innovator's DNA," *Harvard Business Review*, December, 61–66.
12. Camillus, John C. (2008), "Strategy as a Wicked Problem," *Harvard Business Review*, May, 99–106.

CHAPTER 2

Learning to Think in a Marketing *Way*

Decompression Exercise

Before getting started, pause for a moment and allow your mind to take a vacation. Where did you go?

Chapter Introduction

In Chapter 1, marketing thinking was explained along with its four integral, spherical dimensions (creative, critical, reflective, and temporal)—that is, 4-DS marketing thinking. Each of these dimensions represents a different form (or line) of questioning. Separately and when combined, they culminate in a particular perspective on a situation. Strategy as a *way* for an organization to be meaningfully different in a marketplace is a product of the marketer's 4-DS thinking. The more skilled the marketer is in questioning along the four dimensions, the greater the potential for better strategies. Within this skill is an openness toward challenging existing ways of thinking and a willingness to allow other perspectives to come into view and to change if an alternative is seen as being better. Openness and adaptiveness are characteristics of thinking agility.

This openness is also characterized by that which is less known. For example, being a strategic thinker involves being a visionary, thinking of a future that is different than the present. Within this thinking is a tension as described by a quote in an article titled "How to Think Like Steve Jobs":

> The visionary is a pattern hunter. And as the patterns begin to take shape, the visionary paces the hall anxiously, staring out the window. The cognitive dissonance builds between what is and what will be.[1]

The openness described above allows this tension, this cognitive dissonance or psychological discomfort. It is through this process of moving away from the familiar to the less familiar, looking for the new patterns that aren't readily apparent, that characterizes the visionary—the strategic thinker. The complacency associated with the familiar has to be overcome to see the new patterns. Being new, new patterns may at first appear odd, and as we'll see in this chapter, the familiar is only one of many obstacles that the thinker will have to deal with. Similar to running a gantlet of obstacles, the obstacles will need to be confronted and overcome for thinking to occur. The following are examples:

> Indeed, this is the secret of visionary ideas: Most earthshaking ideas look funny at first. They are not sensible. Think of the jokes that have been pulled: Jobs introducing the iMac—without a floppy disk! Branson, with no experience in it, starting an international airline. Disney (*DIS, Fortune 500*), at the depth of the Great Depression, proposing a full-length feature cartoon. "You have to have confidence in nonsense," says airplane designer Burt Rutan, whose aircraft have circled the globe on a single tank of gas, and have climbed to the edge of space as well.[2]

To think of a strategy other than as an answer to the marketer's question of how to proceed in the marketplace may seem odd as well. Traditionally, a strategy has been thought of as the answer. "This is the way we will be doing things. Our plan has been formalized and all we need to do is operationalize it." Yet this view of strategy possesses a static characteristic that reinstills the compliancy described above. The less counterintuitive view is to instead think of strategy as a question that is open and adaptive to a dynamic marketplace. As discussed in Chapter 1, it was important for the marketer to maintain an agile posture in terms of his or her thinking, and fixed (static) forms of thinking were counter to a constantly changing, dynamic marketplace. To have a fixed strategy is grounded in a fixed form of thinking. To free up this fixed thinking, a *thinking strategy* is called for that involves thinking of strategy as a question. As we'll see, viewing strategy as a question is a means of acquiring an agility thinking posture.

But what would strategy look like as a question? Later in the chapter, we will consider this question by reversing the thinking about strategy—not as an answer but instead as a question—and see the advantages in doing so.

To get started, and taking the lead from Chapter 1, we will utilize marketing concepts and theories by looking for their underlying questions—that is, the questions that may have generated them and other related ones. It is within the questions that the nuances for strategy lie and create visionary opportunities in the ability to see and create new patterns. To do this, we will look at marketing thinking through an understanding of the process of appropriation using the concept of satisfaction. Afterward, we'll examine the question of strategy not as an answer but as a question, and finally, we will discuss in general the obstacles that interfere with thinking.

The Process of Appropriation

Appropriation here refers to the process of empowering the reader, the student, the marketer, and/or the strategists with the authority or license to adopt and use any idea, concept, and/or theory in a manner that is beneficial to them. This means that you can use them in part or in full, in any combination or way, and modify them as you see fit. Throughout this book, examples will be used to illustrate how to adapt and apply marketing concepts for developing situations. It is through this process of appropriation that concepts and theories come to life and become useful in an applied context.

Figure 2.2	Thinking

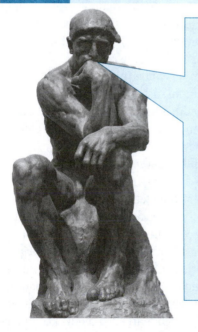

Through the process of appropriation, this prejudice toward answers is challenged and is shown as a blind spot in our thinking that needs to be recognized, corrected, and reversed. Lines of questioning, our questions, are our ways to see and navigate through a changing landscape. Without them, we would simply be responding to our environment, similarly to a single-celled organism, and not be able to effect change. For the innovators mentioned in Chapter 1, the keys for their success were the questions they were asking that challenged the accepted views—that is, the accepted answers of the day. Answers have a limited shelf life and need to be thought of in that way. How old are your answers? What is the expiration date on the answers you are using? When did they expire? Isn't it time to look for some new ones?

As discussed in Chapter 1, every concept and theory, whether from marketing or any other discipline, stems from a line of questioning and is a result of that line of questioning. Typically, through the presentation of a concept or a theory, the line of questioning isn't given front stage in its description or explanation. This has to do with a long prejudicial tradition in favor of answers over questions. After all, aren't we are in search of answers and not the questions?

Appropriation is a hands-on perspective to use any and all available conceptual ideas toward developing more effective strategy. It is okay to refashion existing concepts into new ones to serve different purposes. This is actually a natural process to be found associated with all words and concepts. Simply look in a dictionary of etymology, which provides the origin and chronology of words in terms of their changes in meanings or senses over time.

Any concept could be appropriated for the purposes at hand. Examples of typical consumer concepts that might be of interest to the marketer would include (dis)satisfaction, attitudes, values, lifestyles, involvement, memory, and so on. Each of these could be appropriated for the purposes of developing strategy. As an example, the concept of satisfaction will be used to illustrate the thinking involved in the appropriation process and how a strategy based upon the concept of satisfaction could be developed.

Appropriating the Concept of Satisfaction for Strategy Purposes

A series of coinfluences have driven the interest toward customer satisfaction. For example, the transition in capitalism from the 1930s to the present day is one of the influences. During the 1930s, there was a shift to *managerial capitalism* with a division between the management of an organization and its ownership. Then, in the 1970s, it shifted to *shareholder's value capitalism*. This was driven by the belief of owners that they weren't getting their full rate of return from the professional managers, who had their own interests.[3] However, businesses actually had a higher rate of return during the earlier managerial capitalism period than when pursuing shareholder's value capitalism.[4] The flaw in shareholder's value maximization lies in the cyclical nature of the future performance of organizations, realization of limits (e.g., growth), and the inherent short-term view of such pursuits in which the value of an organization can be temporarily pushed up but will eventually fall again, and so on. This has led to the shift toward *customer satisfaction capitalism*. Pursuing customer satisfaction not only affords an organization the opportunity to be more competitive in the marketplace but also possesses a longer-term view and can lead to a more sustainable valuation of shareholders' wealth. It also seems to accommodate the competing interests found with the earlier forms of capitalism—increasing the value for the customer leads to an increase in value for the organization and its owners, creating a win-win situation for all.

Parallel to the above transition, marketers' adoption of the concept of satisfaction occurred after going through an evolution of thought of their own, learning from the different orientations they had tried in conducting business. The different orientations or stages included a production orientation (emphasizing manufacturing and efficiencies); a sales orientation (a focus on selling as much product as possible regardless of consumer interests); a market orientation (engaging in marketing research, segmentation, positioning, and targeting for the purposes of effectiveness); and, today, a personal marketing orientation (emphasis on marketing to individuals versus segments through technology based upon customer relationship management—CRM).[5] It was with the later market orientations that satisfaction became a hallmark for strategy. As we will see in the later chapters, this evolution in marketing thought continues with the influences of technology and the Internet, where more contemporary marketing is starting to focus on what can be described as co-marketing (collaborative or participatory marketing). The beginnings of this form of thinking are developed through Chapters 3 through 5, and co-marketing is discussed in Chapter 6 and throughout the remaining chapters.

The above transition across the different orientations represents the ongoing appropriation process occurring in marketing, adopting new concepts and perspectives along the way, affecting marketing's direction and the way in which it is to be practiced. The things of the past were discarded for new ways and approaches through the acquisition of different beliefs about what works and what doesn't along with changing conditions as with new technology and so on. Through this process, marketers learned that the consumer played an important role to their success and, hence, customer satisfaction took up its pivotal position of interest.[6] Many marketing strategies are directed toward achieving customer satisfaction. One such logic is that with satisfaction comes a better position from which to compete. If satisfaction leads to customer loyalty, it could provide the organization with a more fortified, defendable position within the marketplace—hence, the interest in customer satisfaction.

Customers have higher expectations, and more buying power than ever. They have more options as well. Therefore, companies striving to be the best have made customer satisfaction and retention the cornerstone of their business strategy. To achieve *business success,* the *best companies* add to this cornerstone product innovation and quality, and a productive and responsive group of employees who are encouraged to *focus on customer service* in a vibrant corporate culture.

With radical, comprehensive, and pervasive changes in technologies and markets have come changes in the way salespeople achieve *customer satisfaction.* The days of "hit-and-run" selling are over. Salespeople must now act as account managers who are responsible for the ongoing quality of the company's relationships with customers.[7]

The significance of satisfaction is further highlighted by the various annual satisfaction reports rating companies. For example, Forbes reported in 2008 the following:

Industries generally scoring well [on customer satisfaction] were online retail (83 out of 100), led by Amazon.com (nasdaq: AMZN - news - people), and autos (82), thanks to a strong score from Toyota's (nyse: TM - news - people) Lexus division and a 3.9% improvement by Ford. Laggards include airlines (63), dragged down by big drops from United and Delta, and cellphone service (68), where Sprint-Nextel (nyse: S - news - people) saw its score drop more than 3% and AT&T (nyse: T - news - people) remained weak despite an improvement over 2006.

Retail stores came in very close to their year-earlier levels, as a big improvement at Macy's (nyse: M - news - people) was offset by falling scores at Wal-Mart and Best Buy (nyse: BBY - news - people). By tumbling 5.6%, Wal-Mart hit its lowest customer satisfaction rating since the ACSI began its survey in 1994.

Indeed, the solid fourth-quarter profit that Wal-Mart reported on Tuesday was driven by growth in its international business. Same-store sales edged up just 0.5% from last year, not a sign that customers are breaking the door down. Meanwhile, Home Depot, which recently made a strategic decision to replace knowledgeable store workers with clerks, suffered a 4.3% drop in its satisfaction rating to its lowest score since 2001.[8]

The above illustrates a kind of scorecard approach to how businesses are doing based upon changing consumer levels of (dis)satisfaction. The American Customer Satisfaction Index (ACSI) organization provides a "national index updated quarterly, factoring in ACSI scores from more than 225 companies in 47 industries and over 130 government agencies, departments, and websites."[9] As an example from the ACSI website, on a scale of 0 to 100, where 100 is the best possible ACSI score, Apple has been relatively consistent with its ratings—79 (2007), 85 (2008), 84 (2009), and 86 (2010). The average for other computer organizations was a 77 ACSI. With satisfaction being at the forefront for many organizations, what is the basis for a satisfaction strategy and how is one determined? This is where the appropriation process can be utilized.

The appropriation process can be thought of as kind of processor or mixer that takes what is at hand and, through the processing of mixing, produces something else. See Figure 2.3. The purpose of the appropriation process is to be able to see and consider things through your questioning that you might not have otherwise. The process is relatively straightforward. It involves three steps. The first step is to identify the main question the concept responds to. A concept is presented as a thing that is an answer to something. What is the question for which the concept is an answer? The second step is to identify other relevant questions. This is done to expand the scope outward to see other related aspects that might be important. The third step, with the interrelated questions at hand, is to ask what are the different ways in which you might respond to them given your situation? The second and third steps involve three of the 4-DS dimensions to various degrees—that is, the creative, the critical, and the temporal dimensions. Choosing the responses that will represent your strategy involves critical thinking.

According to the Appropriation Processor (Mixer) in Figure 2.3, the process starts by asking what something is responding to or what question(s) it stems from. This brings the frame of reference into view for what the concepts pertains to. Questions and answers go hand in hand. Understanding one requires knowing the other. What question does the satisfaction concept answer to? As with all conceptual ideas or concepts, they change over time through the natural process of appropriation, in which individuals adopt them for other purposes. Satisfaction is no exception to this, either.

Figure 2.3 The Appropriation Processor (Mixer)

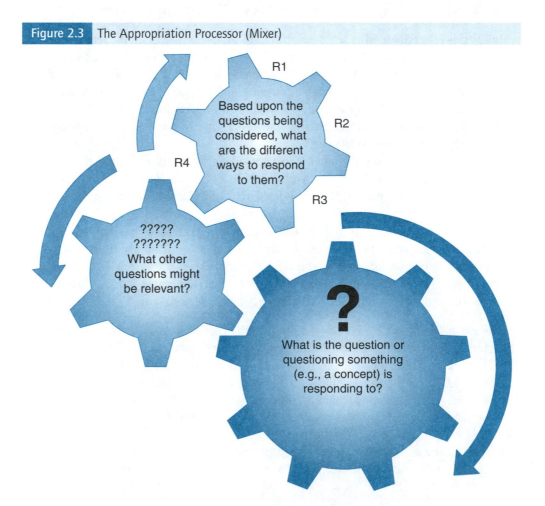

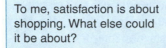

To me, satisfaction is about shopping. What else could it be about?

The concept of satisfaction actually originates from a religious context referring to penitence and atonement for sin. Later, it became associated with the payment of debt and subsequently, referred to some action leading to gratification. It was this latter association that was of interest to marketers, which they then appropriated for their own purposes.

From the above brief overview of the concept of satisfaction, we can now take up the original appropriation question of satisfaction—*What question does the satisfaction concept respond to in a marketing context?*

Based upon a gratification understanding of satisfaction, it seems to involve the marketer asking, What does the consumer want? With this in mind, an answer can be provided. In other words, *it is a question of fulfillment.*

According to the Appropriation Processor (Mixer) in Figure 2.3, the second step of the process asks what other questions might be relevant.

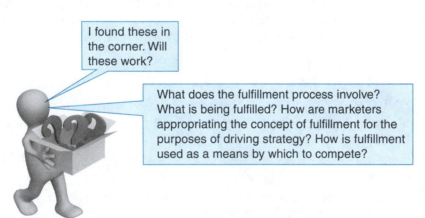

I found these in the corner. Will these work?

What does the fulfillment process involve? What is being fulfilled? How are marketers appropriating the concept of fulfillment for the purposes of driving strategy? How is fulfillment used as a means by which to compete?

The basic premise is that the more satisfied (fulfilled) customers are, the better it is for the organization, providing for a more defendable position in the marketplace from which to compete. In this sense, a marketing strategy is a question of whether what is to be offered will fulfill the requirements of the customers. As such, a strategy based upon satisfaction is a question of fulfillment. What is to be fulfilled? How is it to be fulfilled? And what are the possible degrees of fulfillment? It is at this stage that we need some assistance to get a better handle on what is involved with the issue of consumer fulfillment. Here, we'll need to bring into our discussion one of the theories on satisfaction to guide our questioning of our appropriation process.

According to the Expectancy Disconfirmation Model of Satisfaction,[10][11] satisfaction is an evaluation done by consumers of whether their expectations are being met and to what positive or negative extent. See Figure 2.4. Consumer requirements are based upon their expectations going into a situation. In other words, consumers use their expectations as a means for interpreting the experience that is to take place. Expectations become the consumer's frame of reference for the (dis)satisfaction interpretation.

Hence, fulfillment is driven by the consumers' expectations *acquired prior* to the consumption experience and used *subsequently, to judge* the experience. This suggests that satisfaction as a process actually plays out over a period of time.

With expectations being so important, what is an expectation? An *expectation* is an anticipating or looking forward to some coming or occurrence of something.[12] Understanding satisfaction and its fulfillment interpretation is understanding the significant role expectations play in this process and, as such, represents a vital area of consideration for the marketer in his or her strategy development. Expectations can come in many different forms. For example, expectations could pertain to product performance, service quality, aesthetics, overall experience, and so on.

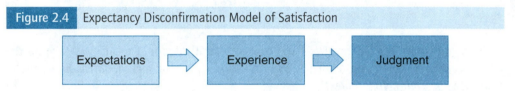

| Figure 2.4 | Expectancy Disconfirmation Model of Satisfaction |

Expectations ⇒ Experience ⇒ Judgment

From step one of our appropriation process, the main satisfaction question for the marketer is:

What consumer expectations are we going to try to fulfill?

With this main question in view, we can proceed now by being even more specific as to the second step of the appropriation process: identifying related questions. Some examples are provided in the following box. This is meant to fan out our strategic view via our questioning, to consider related things but also to do so at perhaps a deeper level of understanding.

Related possible questions:

1. What are consumers' expectations with similar products or services?

2. How can your strategy affect a different set of expectations and/or experiences than what is currently available?

3. How are you doing in terms of consumer expectations (the drivers of satisfaction)?

    a. Where do you need to improve?

4. What are the different ways in which you could configure your marketing activities (strategy) to affect consumers' expectations and experiences?

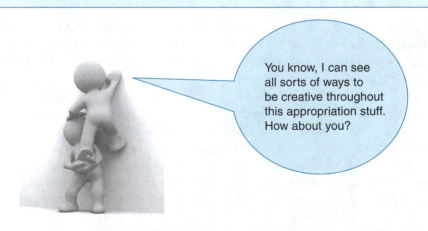

You know, I can see all sorts of ways to be creative throughout this appropriation stuff. How about you?

Following the Appropriation Processor (Mixer) in Figure 2.3, the third step of the process asks, "Based upon the questions identified and being considered, what are the different ways to respond to them?" The line of questioning associated with satisfaction suggests a number of questions that a marketer could use or respond to in strategy development. Figure 2.5 illustrates the multidimensional considerations involved in creating a satisfaction strategy.

Figure 2.5   Identifying Satisfaction Strategies Through Appropriation

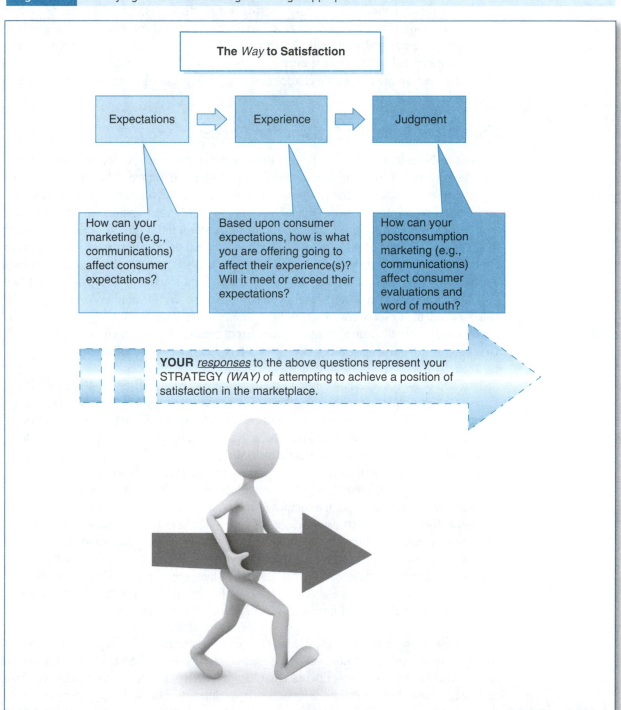

The underlying line of questioning suggested through the satisfaction concept concerns creating a situation of fulfillment in terms of consumer expectations. The questioning, the thinking, is driven in the direction of creating and achieving certain consumer expectations differently than what others in the marketplace are offering. A satisfaction strategy is a strategy motivated by consumers' expectations within the marketplace context.

Within this line of questioning, 4-DS thinking is employed. Creative thinking is used to develop different types of expectations and ways to associate them with the consumer experience through marketing (e.g., marketing communications). Critical thinking is then needed to decide which are to be pursued and orchestrated through one's strategy. Once the strategy is employed, then reflective thinking is called for to see if things are materializing as anticipated. At the same time, we are also talking about facilitating change in time while anticipating the element of chance that things may take place in unexpected ways.

Limitations With the Satisfaction Concept

One of the difficulties with a satisfaction strategy is that the consumption itself affects later expectations and subsequent satisfaction interpretations. If someone has an outstanding experience at a restaurant, the next time she goes back to the restaurant, her expectations have been elevated, and if the experience is simply similar to the previous one, the judgment of experience won't be as great, and, hence, the satisfaction interpretation will be less. Here, the marketer is in the position of always trying to exceed prior experiences in one form or another to stay on the consumer's constantly moving expectations treadmill. This also raises another problem with satisfaction. Measuring customer satisfaction is what can be described as a lagging indicator and not a leading one. In other words, it is similar to looking in the rear-view mirror to see where you have been or how you have done. But you can't drive forward by looking in the rear-view mirror. A different perspective is needed to have a forward-view or forward-thinking strategy. One approach is described in the following quote:

> Here's an unlikely suggestion from a customer strategist: Forget customer satisfaction. It's not a differentiator; it's table stakes for any company worth its salt. What's more, it's a lagging indicator, not a leading one. You can't build a forward-thinking strategy based on historical data like customer satisfaction. Instead, companies need to take satisfaction to the next level to create customer advocates. At the end of the day, improving advocacy leads to higher financial returns than improving customer satisfaction.
>
> …Advocacy is different than loyalty or satisfaction. It is a business strategy that places customers' interests ahead of the company's. It is built upon trust, and trust is an enduring competitive advantage that pays dividends today and long into the future. And, trust has become increasingly important as companies are losing control of the brand message to customers who can reach the masses in an anonymous, everlasting way. Advocacy, built on trust, is one of the single most powerful factors in influencing a customer's buying behavior.
>
> …Advocates are satisfied and loyal, but the opposite is not necessarily true. Companies need to determine the drivers of advocacy versus customer satisfaction.[13]

These issues are examined further in later chapters—for example, in Chapter 8, social media strategies are discussed pertaining to creating advocates, and the differences between rear-view and forward-looking metrics are discussed in Chapter 12. What the above quote points out is that all concepts have their limitations. Satisfaction is no different. From a thinking perspective, it's important to be aware of these limitations, to have an eye for other possibilities, which is consistent with a thinking agility perspective—to be open and poised to adapt as called for.

As part of the marketing thinking discussion in Chapter 1, 4-DS thinking characterizes the dimensions involved in the questioning of marketing thinking. The following examples illustrate how two companies, Muji and Sleep Squad, are engaging in their marketing thinking, appropriating the satisfaction concept to develop their strategies.

Marketing Thinking in Practice: Shifting Times—The Muji Experience

Muji, a Japanese company, is recognized as one of the largest retail brands in the world. "The Muji vision is not to be a brand. It is the no-brand. ...The philosophy of Muji is to deliver functional products that strive not to be the best, but 'enough.' Enough does not mean compromise and resignation but a feeling of satisfaction knowing that the product will deliver what is needed but no more."[14] Go to www.muji.us to read more about their philosophy and see images of their store layout and product line. The strategy is based upon a changing global economy in which consumers worldwide have been struggling through recessionary times. Here, the temporal dimension of the 4-DS thinking comes into view—that is, thinking in terms of change and the element of chance. For those experiencing the brunt of such financial difficulties, how do you think their focus has been shifting? What would be their concerns, and how would such concerns be translated into possible changes in expectations and consumption?

During financial difficulties, consumers naturally reassess their situations by asking themselves, What is really important? How can I stretch what money I have? With larger numbers of consumers worldwide finding themselves in such a situation, asking similar questions, the Muji philosophy had come into its time when a large number of consumers were interested in returning to the basics and were less interested in the superficiality associated with name brands as well as the costs that go with such consumption. The costs included paying more, financial debt, a self-concept driven by marketing images, and environmental concerns. For these consumers, expectations had changed along the lines that they wanted products that were functional, involved less marketing, and allowed them to return to a simpler life. Observing such changes, the Muji organization was in the position to ask, How do we market our business without it appearing that we are marketing?

How do you appear not to be doing marketing?

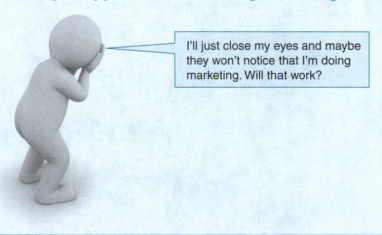

I'll just close my eyes and maybe they won't notice that I'm doing marketing. Will that work?

(Continued)

(Continued)

After all, there has to be some form of marketing involved or no one would know that you are there. The question actually is more straightforward than it may appear. It is simply a question of how to differentiate in a marketplace in which, in general, everyone else is engaged in heavy-handed marketing tactics and promoting excesses. It is a question of contrast.

To create the contrast, the Muji strategy involves appropriating the concept of satisfaction by shifting toward changing consumer expectations—that is, to be in the position to fulfill these consumers' changing expectations better than others. Muji customers' satisfaction stems from feelings (expectations) of doing what is right through consumption that involves "simplicity, moderation, humility, and self-restraint." It is about focusing on the more important things in life than consumption as portrayed through modern marketing. Drawing upon their creative and critical thinking, two dimensions of 4-DS thinking, they came up with store layouts consistent with this theme: plain, relaxing, no labels or brands, and offering functional products at low prices. There is marketing involved in their store layouts, as can be seen from their website, but it is purposely de-emphasized as a marketing strategy—that is, the marketing of less marketing. Their strategy creates value for these consumers through the changing satisfaction landscape, and in the process, Muji has established a satisfaction position in the marketplace from which to compete.

Marketing Thinking in Practice: Taking the Sleeping Business to a New Level—Sleep Squad Comes to You

Michael Cote, while working at T-Mobile running their B2B sales, was able to see the profitability in pursuing customer satisfaction. Based upon his experience, he decided to test the satisfaction to profitability theory to a new level by finding an industry associated with very high customer dissatisfaction and seeing if he could start a company that would turn the experience around while leading to profitability.[15] He started this experiment by asking, What industries have the worst customer experiences?

| Figure 2.6 | A Mattress Is Not Just a Mattress |

Using a list from the University of Michigan on people's worst customer purchase experience, he found purchasing mattresses to be near the top, below purchasing a used car.

In this case, Mr. Cote is appropriating the satisfaction concept by way of starting with a highly dissatisfying consumer situation and then asking, What is it that needs to be fixed in the mattress industry? "Based upon focus groups people hated lying on a mattress in public (men especially hated that); People hated that they couldn't effectively buy online; And people hated this sea of white. You walk into a mattress store and there's thirty-some mattresses, and it's overwhelming."[16] They also found that consumers would typically spend a day looking for a mattress, and they would have to wait for it to be delivered. With this information at hand, he started to brainstorm (creative thinking) what were the different ways to eliminate these issues from the mattress-purchasing experience to create a satisfying situation. Among his options, he decided that with the Internet and bringing the experience to the consumer, these issues could be avoided (critical thinking). Hence, a new business idea was realized and launched the Sleep Squad, which "reconfigures brick-and-mortar retail into a steel-and-rubber showroom."

The website allowed consumers to have access to more choices (150 vs. 30), and through the aid of online questions and customer service, the choice could be reduced to three or four in the convenience of the customer's home. Then, a no-obligation appointment can be scheduled within an hour. Sleep Squad offered free delivery, setup, and removal. A truck comes with the three or four options. It is set up like a showroom in which the consumer can actually try the mattresses privately. After introducing the mattresses to the consumer, the salesperson leaves until he or she is asked to come back. If a decision is made to purchase, the salesperson performs the setup for the customer and removes the old mattresses. The sales staff receives bonuses based upon ratings of customer satisfaction regardless of whether a sale is made. The online reviews have been very positive for the Sleep Squad experience.[17] Customers have commented about how quick and easy it is. Mr. Cote continues to monitor customer feedback, adjusting the business model as needed (reflective thinking and thinking in time).

Mr. Cote's approach illustrates 4-DS thinking through his appropriation of the satisfaction concept to develop a business strategy to maneuver within an established industry. He used the concept to find a market that was open or would be responsive to a different form of business. In the process, Sleep Squad created a position in the marketplace based upon satisfaction that has led to profitability.

To see if you understand the appropriation process previously discussed, try the following appropriation challenges.

Marketing Thinking Challenge 2.1:
Appropriating Satisfaction in a Consumer Situation

Find an industry other than the ones mentioned previously that is noted for consumer dissatisfaction. Using the concept of satisfaction, identify consumer expectations that aren't being met. Then, based upon the expectations that you have identified, how could you configure a business that would operate differently? Would it involve different expectations? How would the consumer experience be different based upon what you'd be offering?

Figure 2.7 A Consumer Situation

Marketing Thinking Challenge 2.2: Appropriating Satisfaction in a B2B Situation

Find a business-to-business (B2B) situation that is noted for dissatisfaction. Using the concept of satisfaction, identify the business customer's expectations that aren't being met. Then, based upon the expectations that you have identified, how could you configure a business that would operate differently? Would it involve different expectations? How would the business customer experience be different based upon what you'd be offering?

Figure 2.8 A Business-to-Business Situation

Marketing Thinking Challenge 2.3: Appropriating Concepts

Figure 2.9 Thinking About the Question(s) Behind the Concept

Take any concept you are familiar with from work or school and identify what you believe is the question it responds to. (1) What is the question for the concept? (2) Based upon what you identified as the question in part 1, what other related questions can you identify? And (3) What are some of the different ways in which you could respond to these questions?

Suggestion: Start by formally defining the concept. What theoretical explanations exists that could be used as your basis for understanding the concept at a deeper level? You'll find it easier to do the challenge if you start off in this way.

Strategy as a Question

As stated in Chapter 1, strategy is an organization's way of attempting to be different in a marketplace of difference. There are many different factors involved that play a role in affecting the outcome of one's strategy. The dynamics of the marketplace represent the challenge any strategy must work through to achieve its objectives. It is analogous to a chess game, in which your strategy needs to be flexible and adaptable to accommodate the different moves being played out by others in the marketplace. The dynamics of the marketplace stem from its constituents, each with its own varying interests and desires to have the marketplace play out in a certain way. In other words, you are not alone.

Figure 2.10	Thinking About the Different Moves

Developing strategy through 4-DS thinking is based upon a series of lines of questioning that culminate in your perspective of the situation and the ways you'll consider maneuvering through the dynamic marketplace landscape. With a dynamic marketplace, we'll need a strategy that is equally dynamic. Instead of thinking of strategy as an answer, we'll view it as a question. This will set up the thinking to be more aligned with the nature of the marketplace.

Okay. I understand that. Strategy comes from our questioning or this 4-DS thinking stuff. But why should we think of strategy as a question? Isn't it our answer to our questioning as to how we will be different in the marketplace?

Those are good questions that deserve our attention. Here, we'll need to look at how the different perspectives affect the nature of strategy. They represent important differences.

Strategy developed through 4-DS thinking is based upon an understanding that while we have *momentarily* come up with a way to participate in the marketplace, it is ultimately speculative as to whether it will work in the foreseen way. As such, by thinking of strategy as a question, we will be more agile, open, and responsive to the changes to occur through the interactions comprising the marketplace. In contrast, if we thought of our strategy as our answer to the marketplace, in essence, we would be taking a more fixed, closed-off, reactive posture, opening up the doors for others to lead through the ongoing changes taking place. Closure is associated with answers, but the marketplace is always open—open for business, open to change—and, hence, strategy must remain open as well. *A strategy should be thought of as a question, open to the will of the marketplace.*

Furthermore, whenever the marketer decides to place something in the marketplace, the marketer is soliciting some response. The act of soliciting involves an asking; it is a question to which a response is being requested. If a response manifests, many different forms are possible. Hence, the outcome of one's strategy is stochastically and not deterministically based.[18, 19] Strategy should be open-ended responding to consumers.

Responsiveness can also be thought of as an element of one's strategy operationalized through an organization's activities, processes, and structure. For example, Procter & Gamble provides data analysis to its retail customers to help it improve its responsiveness and costs.[20] Responsiveness as a focus for strategy will be discussed in a later chapter.

As discussed in Chapter 1, marketing thinking involves a type of questioning that is directed toward how to provide value (creating choice) as defined by a particular group of consumers or those being targeted (pursued). It is within this realm of consumer choices to be made that strategy operates, which continuously *plays* out over time. Strategy as a question also means that it is not a finished work but is a work in *progress* for this duration. It only becomes complete, finished, once it is removed from the marketplace. It is at this point that strategy can be thought of as an answer, but an answer to events that already took place.

To become more skilled at marketing thinking and thinking agility in general, it is important to recognize that thinking has its own difficulties that need to be overcome. These difficulties can be described as obstacles to thinking. We'll examine these next.

Obstacles to Marketing Thinking

Marketing thinking, as with any other form of thinking, requires effort. The notion of effort brings to the forefront the issue that if effort is required, then there must be obstacles that are hindering or interfering with the thinking phenomenon. At the same time, if these obstacles can be identified, then we might be able to do something about them to enhance our thinking. To start, try the following exercise.

Marketing Thinking Challenge 2.4:
Obstacles to Thinking

How many thinking obstacles can you identify? What are the things that you find interfering with your thinking? List them below.

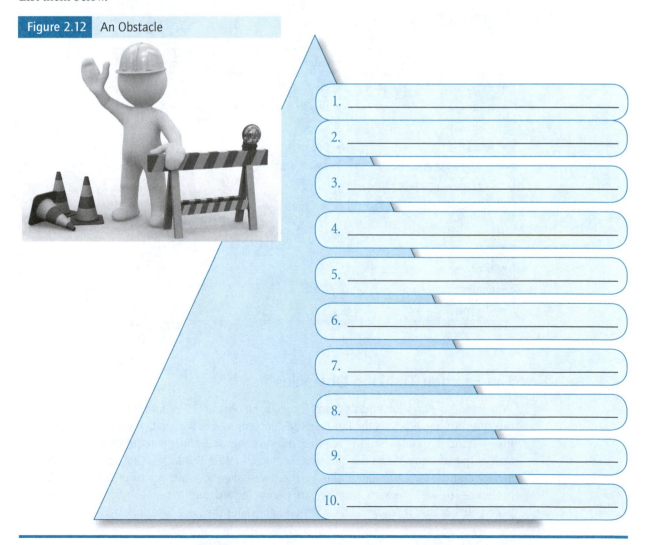

Figure 2.12   An Obstacle

1. _____

2. _____

3. _____

4. _____

5. _____

6. _____

7. _____

8. _____

9. _____

10. _____

| Figure 2.13 | Running Into an Obstacle |

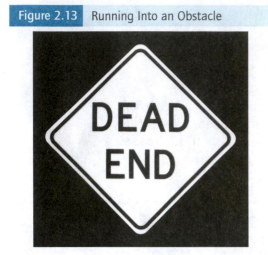

How did you do on the previous exercise? How many obstacles did you identify? If you couldn't think of any, that in itself suggests that you must have run into an obstacle.

To avoid obstacles first requires recognizing them and then taking some action to maneuver around them. Anything that could potentially hinder or interfere with your thinking can be thought of as an obstacle. Presented below are psychological and physiological examples of the typical obstacles affecting thinking.[21] Strategies for working around them are discussed as well.

| Table 2.1 | Obstacles to Thinking |

The Familar	Questioning	Physiological
• Knowledge	• Starting Point	• Dehydration
• Routines	• Direction (Perspective)	• Hunger
• Heuristics	• Scope	• Overeating
• Analogies	• Sequence	• Fatigue
○ Anchoring Effect	• Time Spent	• Stress
○ Confirmation Bias		• Information Overload
• Norms		• Sickness
○ Groupthink		• Depression
• Rules		
• Practices		
• Culture		
• The Past		

The Familiar Thinking Obstacles

Why would the familiar and its many forms be an obstacle? The familiar is a result of previous questioning, but with the familiar, the questioning has stopped. Thinking and questioning go hand in hand. Thinking requires questioning, and effort is required to engage in the task of questioning. When the questioning stops, so does thinking. What makes the familiar such a significant issue for thinking is that we have the tendency to gravitate toward the familiar—that is, it is something we are drawn toward, and the reason for this tendency is primarily because it requires less effort and alleviates the need for thinking.

| Figure 2.14 | When the Questioning Stops, So Does the Thinking |

The familiar shows up in many forms. For example, the accepted views within an organization are the familiar. The fact that they are accepted infers that they are *not* to be contested (questioned) and, hence, an obstacle has been erected. The accepted views come in many different forms, including knowledge, routines, heuristics, analogies (anchoring effects, confirmation biases),[22, 23] norms (groupthink[24]), rules, practices, culture (e.g., corporate culture, risk aversity), and our past.[25] Examples of analogies being used in business include Intel using a steel industry analogy in "referring to cheap PCs as 'digital rebar'"[26] or when Circuit City applied an electronic retail store analogy to the used-car industry in opening CarMax, a chain of used-car outlets. The analogical reasoning stems from some experience and identifying a similarity with a current situation and then applying the patterns of the past to a present situation. Problems arise with using analogies when superficial comparisons are made that lead to the analogical reasoning, channeling the thinking in making poor decisions.[27] The analogy is used as a means to simplify understanding of the present situation and to use the past as the guide for future courses of action. Each of the above promotes less- or nonthinking strategies.

The first step in breaking away from the familiar is to recognize it as an obstacle, at which point the process of unfreezing the familiar can begin by allowing questioning of the accepted views to start. This then allows for the movement in thinking to once again take up its advance and freely move in any direction through the 4-DS thinking spheres. As a caveat, and as previously mentioned, the familiar is very attractive because it is demanding less effort from those who have accepted it. Yet the familiar also represents a cost to an organization in the form of being less innovative and resulting in possible losses in the marketplace from becoming complacent.

Questioning Thinking Obstacles

Most might not think of questioning as an obstacle since it has already been stated that thinking and questioning go hand in hand. This would seem to be a contradiction. However, inherent in questioning are limiting characteristics that affect thinking. In other words, the characteristics of questioning inherently limit thinking in the process. Questioning is finite in that to start questioning, one would need to start somewhere and head in a certain direction. The starting point and the directionality of questioning both represent factors that could potentially impede or limit thinking and should be considered as such. For example, the practice of marketing per a *market orientation* follows a basic type of logic that typically starts with asking about who (a target market) we should pursue in the marketplace and then asks about how we should pursue them—two related but different lines of questioning. If you didn't follow this logic and you started with how (or the what) to market something without an understanding of who it is to be marketed to, this would take you back to one of the marketing orientations discussed earlier in the chapter (e.g., sales or production), which have been found to be faulty forms of marketing thinking. Hence, where one starts in the marketing questioning affects his or her orientation of marketing, which ultimately leads to different types of strategies—some good and some not so good.

Other related questioning issues include the scope, the sequence, and the time spent questioning. A narrow line of questioning will lead to less being considered, limiting thinking. Likewise, the less time spent questioning, the less thinking takes place. This is related to the familiar obstacle of using heuristics, alleviating the demands of thinking in shortening the time required and what is considered. Heuristics are a means by which to reduce or avoid thinking (e.g., higher price means higher quality). Furthermore, lines of questioning are composed of a series of questions corresponding to their line, scope, and direction. The sequence of the questions asked within the series will affect the line of questioning. This is similar to the starting point aspect of questioning as discussed above. As noted in the previous example, the sequence of the who and then the how questions will ultimately affect different strategies. Each of the questioning obstacles including the starting point, direction, scope, sequence, and time spent questioning affects our 4-DS marketing thinking and will be illustrated throughout the chapters to follow, along with ways to deal with them. For example, different starting points will be considered to illustrate how they lead to different strategies. One example comes from Chapter 4, which raises the question, Who is segmenting the market—the consumer or the marketer? How you respond to this question will lead to different perspectives of the marketplace and corresponding strategies. Also, one could step right or left of a line of questioning to potentially see other avenues for strategy. But first one needs to recognize the line of questioning as a line and recognize the limits that are associated with it.

Physiological Thinking Obstacles

The physiological obstacles tend to be more obvious in that all of us experience them regularly. For example, most would recognize that we don't do our best work when tired, sick, stressed, or depressed. Information overload can also contribute to stress and interfere with thinking. Additionally, when we are either hungry or if we overeat, leading to feeling lethargic, we have less energy and motivation to engage in a lot of thinking. Dehydration can have similar results. This basically means that each individual needs to know when and where he or she will be most effective with his or her thinking. Drinking plenty of water is important, as is being in good physical shape. Basic wellness leads to more effective thinking—getting your necessary rest, eating well, and avoiding getting sick. Also, certain environments lead to more productive thinking. For example, some think better when listening to music. Others prefer being outside. The key is to know what physical conditions will allow you to be more effective at thinking and, hence, to accomplish more in less time.

As mentioned previously, to be more skilled at thinking, obstacles need to be recognized and thinking strategies used to maneuver around them. But the first step is to recognize them, that is, to look for them. Try the following challenges to see if you can identify thinking obstacles that might be related to marketing problems and/or creating a new innovation.

Marketing Thinking Challenge 2.5: The First Step—Recognizing the Obstacles

Identify a marketing problem that you believe to be difficult or challenging. Identify the obstacles that seem to make it appear difficult. What are they? After identifying these difficulties, see if you can come up with ways to maneuver around them. What ways did you find? In thinking of ways to deal with the problem, does the problem now seem as difficult as it did initially? In general, what does this say about problems?

Figure 2.15   Maneuvering Around the Obstacles

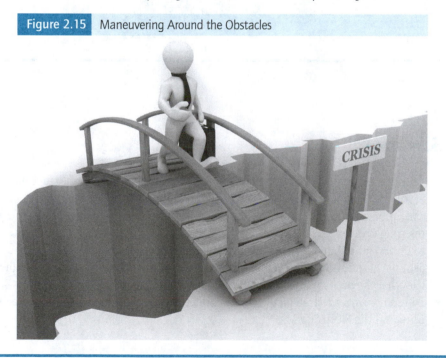

Marketing Thinking Challenge 2.6: Innovation and the Obstacles

Try imagining a truly innovative new product or service that would be marketable—that is, a new product or service category that doesn't already exist in the marketplace. Did you find this to be difficult? Why? What obstacles might you run into that prevent you from thinking of a truly innovative idea? How can you overcome or maneuver around the obstacles?

Suggestion: You might want to look at Marketing Thinking Challenge 1.3 to help with this challenge.

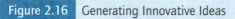

Figure 2.16	Generating Innovative Ideas

Summary

- Through the process of appropriation, the thinking behind the satisfaction concept was revealed, along with identifying ways to develop satisfaction strategies.
- The appropriation process can be used with any concept or theory for the purpose of opening up avenues for marketing thinking and strategy. It is a way to empower marketers to understand that marketing concepts and theories are not to be thought of as things but as lines of questions that can be adapted for differing situations. It is through appropriation that they obtain their value through use.
- Different *ways* or strategies were illustrated by the Thinking in Practice companies—Muji and the Sleep Squad.

- Reversing the thinking behind the concept of a strategy—that is, by not thinking of a strategy as an answer but instead as a question—changes the thinking and strategy to be agile, open, and responsive to the changes occurring within a marketplace.
- In addition, to get the most out of thinking requires an understanding of the obstacles that can interfere, and once you recognize them, they can be resolved.

References

1. Calonius, Eric (2011), "How to Think Like Steve Jobs," CNNMoney.com, March 15, http://money.cnn.com/2011/03/15/news/companies/steve_jobs_thought_process.fortune/index.htm
2. Calonius, Eric (2011), "How to Think Like Steve Jobs," CNNMoney.com, March 15, http://money.cnn.com/2011/03/15/news/companies/steve_jobs_thought_process.fortune/index.htm
3. Martin, Roger (2010), "The Age of Customer Capitalism," *Harvard Business Review*, January–February, 58–65.
4. Martin, Roger (2010), "The Age of Customer Capitalism," *Harvard Business Review*, January–February, 60.
5. "Evolution of Marketing," NOWSELL.com, www.nowsell.com/marketing-guide/evolution-of-marketing.html
6. Brown, Tim (2008), "Design Thinking," *Harvard Business Review*, June, 84–92.
7. (2009), "Make Customer Satisfaction and Retention the Cornerstone of Your Business Strategy," Topline Leadership—Custom Sales & Sales Management Training, July 19, www.toplineleadership.com/_blog/Inside_Our_Head/post/Make_Customer_Satisfaction_and_Retention_the_Cornerstone_of_your_Business_Strategy/
8. Van Riper, Tom (2008), "The Best and Worst Companies for Customer Satisfaction," Forbes.com, February 20, www.forbes.com/2008/02/20/service-consumers-retail-biz-cx_tvr_0220service.html
9. The American Customer Satisfaction Index (ACSI), www.theacsi.org/index.php?option=com_content&view=article&id=63&Itemid=101
10. Swan, John E., and I. Frederick Trawick (1981), "Disconfirmation of Expectations and Satisfaction with a Retail Service," *Journal of Retailing*, 57 (Fall), 49–67.
11. Wilton, Peter C., and David K. Tse (1988), "Models of Consumer Satisfaction Formation: An Extension," *Journal of Marketing Research*, 25 (May), 204–12.
12. Merriam-Webster, A. (1974), *Webster's New Collegiate Dictionary*, Springfield, MA: G. & C. Merriam Company.
13. Peppers, Don (2011), "Customer Strategist Matthew Rhoden: Stop Satisfying Your Customers," Peppers & Rogers Group, April 19, www.peppersandrogersgroup.com/blog/2011/04/customer-strategist-matthew-rh-1.html
14. Aaker, David (2010), "Muji: The No-Brand Brand," *Marketing News*, 13.
15. Prais, Thomas A. (2008), "Thomas 2.0: Reinventing Retail," *Furniture Style*, January (website now defunct).
16. Prais, Thomas A. (2008), "Thomas 2.0: Reinventing Retail," *Furniture Style*, January (website now defunct).
17. Sleep Squad, yelp.com, www.yelp.com/biz/sleep-squad-chicago
18. Moyer, Don (2008), "Strategy Paradox," *Harvard Business Review*, June, 144.
19. Camillus, John C. (2008), "Strategy as a Wicked Problem," *Harvard Business Review*, May, 99–106.

20. Davenport, Thomas H. (2006), "Competing on Analytics," *Harvard Business Review*, January, 98–107.
21. Hill, Mark E., John McGinnis, and Jane Cromartie (2007), "The Obstacles to Marketing Thinking," *Marketing Intelligence & Planning*, 25 (3), 241–51.
22. Day, George S., and Paul J. H. Schoemaker (2005), "Scanning the Periphery," *Harvard Business Review*, November, 135–48.
23. Gavetti, Giovanni, and Jan Rivkin (2005), "How Strategists Really Think: Tapping the Power of Analogy," *Harvard Business Review*, April, 54–63.
24. Schoemaker, Paul J. H., and George S. Day (2009), "How to Make Sense of Weak Signals," *MIT Sloan Management Review*, 50 (3, Spring), 81–9.
25. Day, George S., and Paul J. H. Schoemaker (2005), "Scanning the Periphery," *Harvard Business Review*, November, 136.
26. Gavetti, Giovanni, and Jan Rivkin (2005), "How Strategists Really Think: Tapping the Power of Analogy," *Harvard Business Review*, April, 56.
27. Gavetti, Giovanni, and Jan Rivkin (2005), "How Strategists Really Think: Tapping the Power of Analogy," *Harvard Business Review*, April, 57.

SECTION 2

Thinking Through the Marketing Process

CHAPTER 3

The BIG Question(s)

Assessing the Situation

Decompression Exercise

Before starting, take a moment to watch the sun set.

Figure 3.1 A Sunset

Chapter Introduction

The first two chapters illustrated at a fundamental level what marketing thinking looks like and how it might be applied through an appropriation process for strategy purposes using the concept of satisfaction. This chapter moves a step further by considering different types of thinking that have been associated with different views of the marketplace. From a thinking agility perspective, exploring different ways to view the marketplace is a means of expanding the set of options to be considered that could be appropriated for different strategy purposes as well.

One approach—or *questioning strategy*—is to examine where a central concept originates and the meanings that have been associated with it. All concepts have their boundaries as to what they refer to, and it is within these boundaries that the channeling effects of concepts can occur. Strategy as a concept is no exception to this. How has the concept of strategy affected how marketers practice marketing?

This chapter will begin with one of the main sources of influence that has affected how marketers approach the marketplace by looking at where the word *strategy* originates and its associated inflections of meaning. The meaning of *strategy* will potentially have the effects of influencing how the marketer views the marketplace and what type of information he or she will look for in configuring a marketplace strategy. The information the marketer looks for in understanding the marketplace can be described as a *situation assessment*.

We'll come to see that there is more than one way to view what marketing strategy is. These different perspectives are interrelated with how the marketer views the purpose of strategy and its role to be played out in the marketplace. The different perspectives of strategy are interrelated with how the marketer views the structure of the marketplace, which also affects what is to be assessed through a situation assessment. Each of these aspects is discussed in the chapter.

Two main views of strategy are being utilized today. Strategy can be about either competition or consumers (by going it alone to create a new market and value). The two strategy perspectives involve two different forms of thinking about marketplace structure. A *competitive-oriented strategy perspective* views the marketplace structure as an already existing structure created by others (competitors), and strategy is developed from within this structure (a structure-*bound* perspective). In contrast, a *consumer-oriented strategy perspective* views the marketplace structure dynamically as a structure to be created (a *creating* structure perspective). Which form of thinking the marketer employs will not only affect how he or she will assess the current situation but will also affect the strategies to be considered.

At the core of this discussion is the question, What is a *structure* in a marketing context? The chapter examines how the different perspectives of strategy interrelate with their corresponding views on marketplace structure and what is important for a situation assessment of the marketplace. We'll start with the origins of strategy.

The Origins of Strategy—As a Starting Point

By looking at how strategy has been appropriated and how this appropriation has affected the intent of the analysis, we'll be able to see how the strategy concept can channel the marketer's thinking through a situation assessment. Since developing an understanding of the marketplace is for the purpose of developing strategy, perhaps a good starting point is to examine the concept of strategy.

An English dictionary of etymology provides a chronology of words and the development of each word's senses or meanings. As such, *strategy* originates from the word *stratagem,* which derived from a military context. *Stratagem* referred to an artifice, trick, or device to surprise an enemy.[1] Similarly, *strategeîn* meant *general, strategós* referred to *commander-in-chief,* and *stratós* was *army.* Similarly,

> The Greek word "strategy" (either as *strategía* or *strategiké*) was used in antiquity for the art or skills of the general (the *strategós*)—"the general is the one who practices strategy." By the sixth century at the latest, however, at the time of Emperor Justinian, in Byzantine usage, a difference was made between "strategy"—"strategy is the means by which the general may defend his own lands and defeat his enemy's"—and hierarchically subordinated to it, "tactics" (*taktiké*), the "science [*epistéme*] which enables one to organize and maneuver a body of armed men in an orderly manner"...[2]

Over time, businesses also adopted this military view of strategy for their own purposes. "The very language of corporate strategy is deeply imbued with military references— chief executive 'officers' in 'headquarters,' 'troops' on the 'front lines,' and fighting over a defined battlefield."[3] As such, strategy originates from a military context, which pertains to conflict and succeeding through warfare. Strategy involves developing ways or skills to overcome those you are in conflict with or those you are competing with for something. The land or turf to be fought over is a marketplace of consumers. The turf is delineated or squared off by market share. From a military perspective, strategy is a means to defend or gain market share. In either case, defending or advancing involves conflict, which pertains to some form of moving against others, to maintain one's position or to advance at the expense of others.

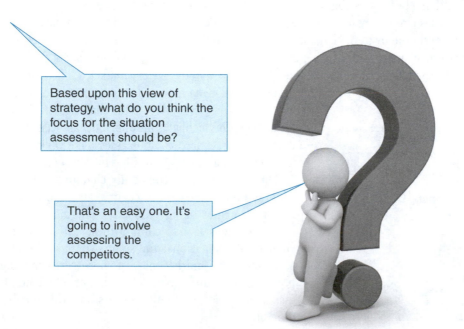

From the previous perspective of strategy, the focus will be on understanding the dynamics of the marketplace from a competitive perspective, how to secure a defensible position, and one that you can potentially advance from as well. This is one perspective, and one that is very entrenched in business today. Yet there is another perspective, a consumer perspective, that could also be pursued that we will discuss later in the chapter. Let's turn our attention to examining what is needed to understand these competitive dynamics. In other words, what should be the focus of a marketplace situation assessment based upon this competitive perspective of strategy?

The Significance of the Situation Assessment to Strategy

Good information is central to developing effective marketing strategy. The better the information, the better the potential for getting it right. Conducting a situation assessment of the marketplace is an important resource for obtaining information. A *situation assessment* is an attempt by the marketer to understand the topography of a market (or industry) and its various participating constituents. It is a study of the lay of the land to determine the best areas and means possible to maneuver around. Traditionally, the topography in this case involves identifying the competitive characteristics of the marketplace and their structural relationships. Some of these characteristics may be more dynamic (or stable) than others.

In other words, the situation assessment is an opportunity for the marketer to obtain a momentary bearing as to what exists in terms of opportunities and possible ways to navigate. The logic behind conducting a situation assessment is: The better the situation assessment, the better the marketplace information for the marketer to work from that can lead to identifying better possibilities for more effective strategies and greater returns.

It is also important to keep in mind that all markets and industries are dynamic compositions that are constantly in motion, moving in one direction versus another. While at times they may appear to be more stable, there is always the potential for change and the element of chance—to move in an unexpected direction. To participate in the advance of a market, it is necessary to have insight into its dynamics, and strategy needs to be designed that is capable of responding to the challenges it will confront across time. This highlights the difficulties associated with conducting a marketplace situation assessment while pointing to the true test of a strategy—which is *the test of time*.

The marketplace is constantly changing with the continuing influx of new products or services; different marketing strategies being pursued; changing technologies, laws, or regulations; competitors; the environment; changes in populations; and so on. All make the situation assessment of a market that isn't necessarily moving in a predetermined direction that much more challenging. The task is even more difficult and sets up a dilemma for the marketer.

| Figure 3.2 | Assessing the Situation |

The situation assessment dilemma: On the one hand, due to the complexity of a market, the information from a situation assessment will always be incomplete (i.e., it should be thought of as such), and with less-than-complete information, there is the potential for making wrong decisions. On the other hand, *not* to do an assessment of the situation is like shooting in the dark and perhaps raising the risks even higher. The general consensus is to conduct a situation assessment even with its limitations. Given this situation, where do you start?

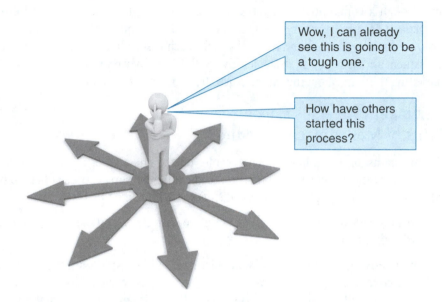

Wow, I can already see this is going to be a tough one.

How have others started this process?

Questioning Applied to the Situation Assessment

From our 4-DS thinking perspective, it's important to keep the different dimensions in mind along with the obstacles discussed in Chapter 2. Additionally, a thinking agility perspective views everything as being open to questioning and *not* accepted as a given. In essence, this suggests that we interrogate the concepts we are using to reveal their underlying assumptions and limitations. For example, the familiar (e.g., accepted view) needs to be questioned and interrogated as a questioning technique to work through this obstacle. Also, the interrogation concept can be applied to what we would be doing to conduct a situation analysis.

We will be using lines of questions as our means to interrogate the marketplace to understand what is going on. Keep in mind that the line aspect of questioning is itself an obstacle or limitation to our thinking. As such, we need to be nimble enough to step left and right of the questioning we are using—that is, multiple lines of questioning would potentially be better to allow for different perspectives to be a part of the situation assessment.

The starting point of your questioning is an important one because, as discussed in Chapter 2, it can also represent an obstacle or limitation to your thinking. Starting off on the wrong foot can be problematic and lead to poor decisions and ineffective strategy. Where one starts with this process will ultimately affect the types of strategies to be considered.

As also discussed in Chapter 2, in thinking of *strategy as a question,* it would be open to the will of the marketplace seeking its answers. Will your strategy be agile and adept at responding to a changing marketplace in pursuing its objectives? In general, a situation assessment might consider questions like, Why is the market moving in the direction it is headed? What is moving it? How long has it been on this path? Is there something beneath the surface that could potentially change its direction? Are there emerging markets? If you had this type of information, how might it affect your strategy?

Possessing dynamic views of strategy and of the marketplace is important, yet the marketer still needs to be aware of the effects of how he or she conceptually thinks about strategy. To illustrate these effects of strategy, we'll start with a brief contrast between viewing strategy through a competitive lens versus a consumer-oriented one. Then we'll examine the *competitive perspective strategy* in more detail. A discussion on the *consumer-oriented perspective of strategy* will follow. As we'll see, for each case, what is conducted for a situation assessment and its resulting strategies is very different. They represent two different forms of marketing thinking about the marketplace structure and strategy.

A Competitor Versus Consumer Focus of Marketplace Structure

The two paths, or currents of thought, center on the question of market structure and its relationship with strategy. Or, in other words, the different perspectives adhere to two different views of the marketplace structure. It runs something like this:

> Instead of letting your environment define your strategy, craft a strategy that defines your environment.[4]

The underlying question of this statement is: Should we start with the market structure and then create strategy or vice versa, where strategy is to create its own new structure? Which is supposed to come first? This seems to be a chicken-and-egg situation but actually translates into two very distinct approaches (as illustrated in Table 3.1) as to what is to be the focus of the analysis and resulting strategies.

On the one hand, there are those who advocate analyzing the structure of the market first and then developing strategies that will be effective within the identified structure. This is the *structure shapes strategy* approach. The other approach, *strategy shapes structure*, moves in a direction other than what others are currently offering to create a new market per se. The two approaches have been referred to as the **Red Ocean** versus the **Blue Ocean** strategy.[5]

The **Red Ocean** strategy is focused on competing in a crowded market with established competitors. It is to take existing market space, territory, or profits away from other competitors. The driving question behind this thinking is, How can I beat the competition? In contrast, the **Blue Ocean** strategy is focused on creating a new market that is open, ideally without direct competitors.

While the *competitor-focused* view operationalized through **Red Ocean** strategies is well entrenched in the practice of business today, stemming from strategy's origins, the more recent *consumer-oriented* view operationalized through **Blue Ocean** strategies offers an alternative to consider. This is to orient toward creating new markets based upon providing something meaningfully different (a differential in value) than what is currently available. It concerns creating consumer value through innovation. The focus is on consumers and *not* on how to compete against competitors.

As such, strategy's focus could be about consumers or competitors. Which view you adhere to will ultimately affect your thinking in terms of the types of strategies you'll potentially develop. The two different views are presented in Table 3.1 as a synthesis of the currents of thought.

| Table 3.1 | Two Different Paths for Assessment and Strategy |

Competitor Focused	Consumer Focused
Red Ocean Strategy	**Blue Ocean Strategy**
Structuralist view or environmental determinism	Reconstructuralist view
The structure shapes strategy approach The basis for strategy is to identify the existing structure in the market based upon others (potential competitors) and then develop a strategy to compete against them.	***The strategy shapes structure approach*** The basis for strategy is that the rules and boundaries, that is, the structure created by others, *isn't* to be accepted. New rules, boundaries, and structure can be created with the intent of making competition irrelevant. Identify potential segments in the market for creating new demand (consumer value).
There is a strategy trade-off between differentiation *"or"* costs.	There is no trade-off between differentiation and costs. Differentiation *"and"* costs can be the basis for strategy.
Supply oriented. Hierarchical disciplined[1]—*exploitation* oriented in which an existing innovation is exploited throughout the value chain.	Demand oriented. Market disciplined[2]—*exploration*-oriented through innovation.

Source: Kim, Chan W., and Renee Mauborgne (2005), "The Blue Ocean Strategy: From Theory to Practice," *California Management Review, 47* (3), 105–21.
[1] Wasden, Christopher (2009), "Hit and Miss," *Communications Review*, 15 (1), PricewaterhouseCoopers, 15–28.
[2] Wasden, Christopher (2009), "Hit and Miss," *Communications Review*, 15 (1), PricewaterhouseCoopers, 15–28.

These two approaches are based upon different ways of thinking and lead to different types of market analysis. Let's take a closer look at both and see what we might be able to appropriate from them for strategy purposes.

| Figure 3.3 | Red vs. Blue Strategies—Which *Way*? |

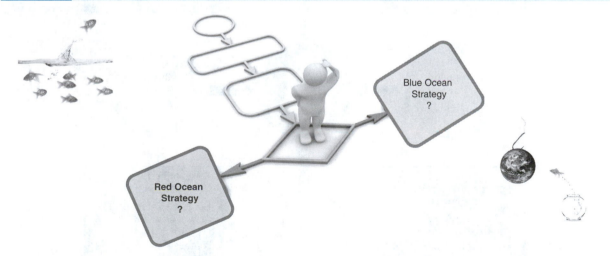

Structure Shapes Strategy vs. *Strategy Shapes Structure*

Structure Shapes Strategy

The *structure shapes strategy* approach suggests that we start with understanding the structure of the market. It assumes there is a structure already in place to be assessed that is an established structure created by others in the marketplace. Let's stop here for a moment and consider what a structure means or represents.

Understanding Structure

What is a **structure**?

Structure can refer to many different things and depends on the context in which the structure question is being raised. In general, a structure refers to some form of construction, a pattern of organization, or an arrangement (interrelationship) of parts into a whole. From this perspective and pertaining to a marketplace, we should begin by looking for how the market is constructed in terms of its parts and how they are interrelated. This assumes that the marketplace structure can be defined with its parts and their interrelationships. It also implies that there is some degree of stability in terms of their form. Hence, this assumes a static view of marketplace.

What kind of parts should we be looking for? Porter's Five Forces Model[7] has been used for this purpose to analyze industries and competition. It suggests that there are five main components (forces) to the structure of an industry that interrelate, forming the basis for competition. From this perspective, the structure of the marketplace—that is, its parts—is in the form of competitive forces, and there are five of them that need to be identified before a strategy can be developed. The Five Forces Model is presented below.

Figure 3.4	Forces Driving Industry Competition

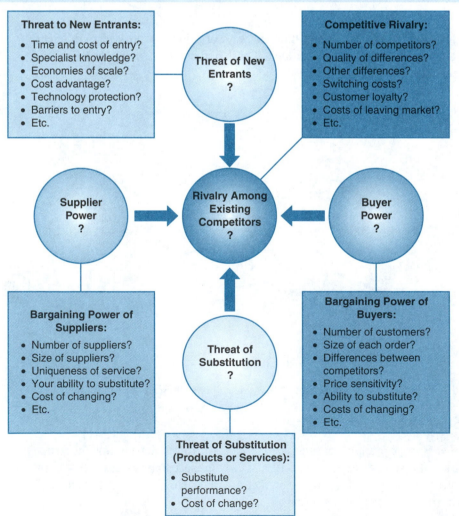

Threat to New Entrants:
- Time and cost of entry?
- Specialist knowledge?
- Economies of scale?
- Cost advantage?
- Technology protection?
- Barriers to entry?
- Etc.

Threat of New Entrants ?

Competitive Rivalry:
- Number of competitors?
- Quality of differences?
- Other differences?
- Switching costs?
- Customer loyalty?
- Costs of leaving market?
- Etc.

Supplier Power ?

Rivalry Among Existing Competitors ?

Buyer Power ?

Bargaining Power of Suppliers:
- Number of suppliers?
- Size of suppliers?
- Uniqueness of service?
- Your ability to substitute?
- Cost of changing?
- Etc.

Threat of Substitution ?

Bargaining Power of Buyers:
- Number of customers?
- Size of each order?
- Differences between competitors?
- Price sensitivity?
- Ability to substitute?
- Costs of changing?
- Etc.

Threat of Substitution (Products or Services):
- Substitute performance?
- Cost of change?

Thinking About the Five Forces Model

The Five Forces represent different vantage points for examining the nature of competition within a market. Using our appropriation process discussed in Chapter 2, we could use the Five Forces model in its entirety, or we could use part of it as indicated by the suggested questions. For example, from Figure 3.4, we could examine the marketplace by asking questions about potential new entrants, the degree of competitive rivalry and what the rivalry is based upon, the nature of bargaining power of suppliers, and so forth. Each question represents a lens through which to see what might be taking place in the marketplace from a competitive perspective.

As with all models or concepts, they themselves are based upon an underlying view. This model is no exception. How is the Five Forces model channeling the marketer's thinking and approach to viewing the marketplace?

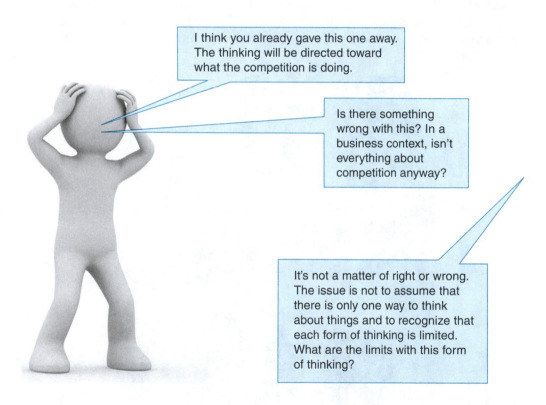

I think you already gave this one away. The thinking will be directed toward what the competition is doing.

Is there something wrong with this? In a business context, isn't everything about competition anyway?

It's not a matter of right or wrong. The issue is not to assume that there is only one way to think about things and to recognize that each form of thinking is limited. What are the limits with this form of thinking?

The *competitive analogy* is in *play* here, which represents a potentially limiting factor in your thinking if you don't recognize it as such. As discussed in Chapter 2, analogies are a form of an obstacle to thinking. In this case, all things tend to be viewed as some form of competition.

The Five Forces Model provides a series of questions that is used for the purpose of analyzing the market from a competitive perspective. The questioning, the thinking, is grounded in a competition orientation. "In essence, the job of the strategist is to understand and cope with competition. [That is the]...rivalry that results from all five forces defines an industry's structure and shapes the nature of competitive interaction within an industry."[8]

The Five Forces Model is used in creating **Red Ocean Strategies** based upon the competition in terms of focusing on developing strategies to maneuver in an ocean of incumbents. Everything is a competition, whether you are talking about competing directly with other companies, buyers, channel members, or substitutes. And the different competitions each have different bases from which the competition takes place. For example, supplier power or supplier competition is a function of the number of suppliers, the size of the supplier, and so on, and your company's position in relationship with the supplier (e.g., costs of changing and your ability to substitute). Similarly, competitive rivalry is driven by the number of competitors, differences in what is being offered, customer relationships, and costs of leaving a market.

Limitations of the Competitive View of Strategy

This is not to say that the competitive view isn't to be considered, but from our thinking agility perspective utilizing our 4-DS thinking, it is necessary to consider things for what they are and what they offer, with an understanding that all things have limitations. The competitive analogy is limiting as well. Each of the questions individually is worthy in and of itself, yet collectively, they will channel your thinking and strategy toward viewing everything as a competition.

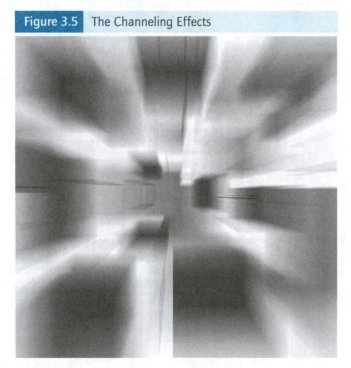

| Figure 3.5 | The Channeling Effects |

Consequently, the competitive orientation originating out of the military perspective was appropriated in business into a "make-and-sell"[9] view that leads to a more entrenching posture in terms of investing in structure (market and organizational, e.g., the value chain), which, in kind, results in a more rigid psychological mindset (individually and/or organizationally), impeding innovation and the like. The focus becomes one of exploitation of an existing innovation (product or service) throughout the value chain for competitive purposes versus exploration oriented through innovation. The competitive perspective focuses on "what is" versus "what could be." These are two very different forms of thinking that head in different directions. As such, one might ask, Does the consumer benefit from this competitive view of strategy and the marketplace?

Even with these caveats, many large companies pursue this perspective and have done quite well. This can be seen by the reported profits of industries such as software, cosmetics, distilled spirits, and pharmaceuticals.[10] For an example of the Five Forces Model, go to www.mindtools .com/pages/article/newTMC_08.htm. When conducting an industry analysis using the Five Forces Model to create a **Red Ocean Strategy**, some suggestions are provided in Figure 3.6.[11]

Figure 3.6	Industry Analysis Suggestions

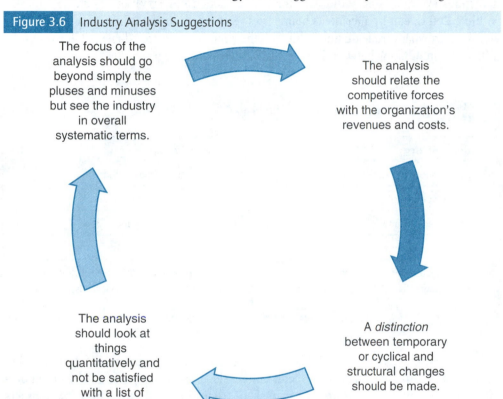

The focus of the analysis should go beyond simply the pluses and minuses but see the industry in overall systematic terms.

The analysis should relate the competitive forces with the organization's revenues and costs.

The analysis should look at things quantitatively and not be satisfied with a list of qualitative factors.

A *distinction* between temporary or cyclical and structural changes should be made.

Marketing Thinking Challenge 3.1: A Five Forces Industry Analysis

In this challenge, you'll use your critical and creative dimensions of 4-DS thinking. Choose an industry of interest. Use Porter's Five Forces Model to analyze your industry. Answer as many questions in the Five Forces Model as you can. From your answers, what is the primary basis of competition in this industry? If you were considering entering this market, how might you do it? In other words, where are the openings to enter? What is your *Red Ocean Strategy*?

Figure 3.7	Looking for a Way In

Strategy Shapes *Structure*

In contrast, we'll now consider the *strategy shapes structure* perspective and its counterpart, the **Blue Ocean Strategy**, to see the difference in thinking and the resulting strategies. The "Blue oceans denote all the industries not in existence today—the unknown market space, untainted by competition. In blue oceans, demand is created rather than fought over."[12] Accordingly, there are *two ways* in which Blue Oceans can be created: (1) create a completely new industry (e.g., as eBay did with the online auction industry); or (2) create a market within a **Red Ocean** by altering its boundaries (e.g., redefining a traditional product or service, such as what Cirque du Soleil did with the circus experience). Table 3.2 illustrates the differences in thinking between **Red** versus **Blue Ocean** strategies.[13]

Table 3.2 Red vs. Blue Strategies—The Differences

Red Ocean Strategy	Blue Ocean Strategy
Compete in existing market space.	Create uncontested market space.
Beat the competition.	Make competition irrelevant.
Exploit existing demand.	Create and capture new demand.
Make the value/cost trade-off.	Break the value/cost trade-off.
Align the whole system of a company's activities with its strategic choice of differentiation *or* low costs.	Align the whole system of a company's activities in pursuit of differentiation *and* low cost.

What we can see from Table 3.2 is that both strategies are pursuing differentiation but going about it differently. The **Red Ocean** *thinking* is differentiating within already-known forms of differentiation (within the established structure), that is, in terms of what others are already doing, and then differentiating within this frame of reference. The **Blue Ocean** *thinking* is directed toward creating new forms of differentiating and creating a new frame of reference outside of what others are doing, thereby making the competition null and void.

How is the **Blue Ocean** market analysis different? The analysis follows two basic steps.[14] This analysis has to do with moving away from what others are offering. The *first step* involves capturing the current state of affairs in a particular market. In essence, you have to start somewhere to have a sense of direction of what to move away from. This step involves creating a *Strategy Canvas* on which the current state of affairs is mapped out.

For the *second step*, using the information depicted in the *Strategy Canvas*, a *Four Actions Framework* is employed to reconstruct buyer value. Through this step, the accepted value lines are challenged to see new possibilities. It is interrogating the current state of affairs to find new areas for consumer value. The accepted rules, boundaries, and offerings all can be challenged in the process. As such, the familiar doesn't necessarily have safe ground to hide. It becomes a subject of attention. The second step in the analysis represents the stepping away point or the strategy for how to move away from the current state of affairs into new a direction to create a new market.

Figure 3.8   Moving in a New Direction

We'll start with the *Strategy Canvas*. The questions used to create the *Strategy Canvas* concern what is currently being offered, and how, to consumers in the market. While examining the competitive offerings, it is ultimately a consumer assessment in terms of what they have available to them and then using this information as a basis from which to step into a new market. This is done through the *Four Actions Framework*.

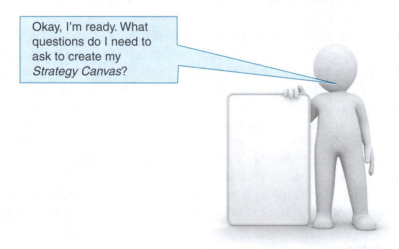

Okay, I'm ready. What questions do I need to ask to create my *Strategy Canvas*?

In mathematical terms, the *strategic canvas* is two dimensional in an X-Y configuration. However, this doesn't mean it couldn't be expanded to more dimensions, but doing so would make the analysis more difficult. The X axis represents the various ways the offerings are being made available in the market in terms of their means of differentiating (e.g., quality, prestige, convenience, services, pricing). The Y axis indicates where each of the offerings in the market is positioned along the various X axis factors. If two brands or more have the same vertical position on a factor, it indicates that they are doing the same thing.

| Figure 3.9 | An Example of a *Strategy Canvas* |

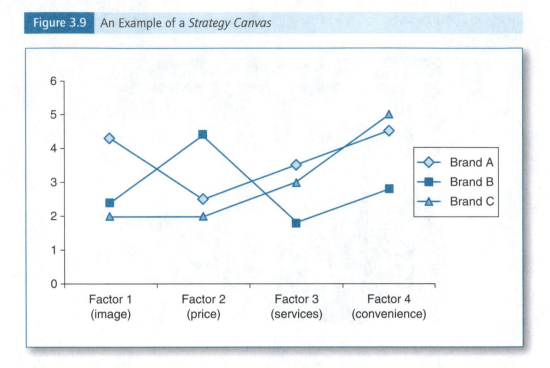

From these examples, it looks like Brands A and C are following similar strategies and would potentially be viewed similarly by consumers in the marketplace, whereas Brand B has taken a different path. The next step in the process is to use the *Four Actions Framework* to consider the following options.

Using the *strategic canvas* as backdrop from which to work, you can then use the *Four Actions Framework*'s questions (Figure 3.10) to create a new market. For example, the Eliminate question asks, Which aspects are ones that have long been competed on and no longer have value or may even detract from the value? These should be considered for elimination. The Reduce question asks, Which aspects were added for competition purposes or are being overdone? These aspects add to the cost structure, and reducing them should be considered. The Raise question asks, Which aspects have been compromised that are important to consumers? Raising them should be considered. Finally, the Create question asks, Which aspects are important to consumers that have never been offered? Creating and adding these new aspects represents a shift away from what is currently being offered, offsetting existing means of competition and, hence, indicating a **Blue Ocean**.

An Example of a Blue Ocean Strategy—Sleep Squad

Sleep Squad, discussed in Chapter 2, represents a Blue Ocean strategy. Any industry in which consumer expectations aren't being met is an opportunity for a Blue Ocean strategy. In essence, they created a *Strategy Canvas* based upon an understanding of what was making consumers dissatisfied, such as having to lie on a mattress in public, not being able to buy online, and disliking the retail setting in which mattresses were presented.

Based upon this information, Sleep Squad considered different options for dealing with these issues. They identified those aspects of purchasing a mattress that needed to be

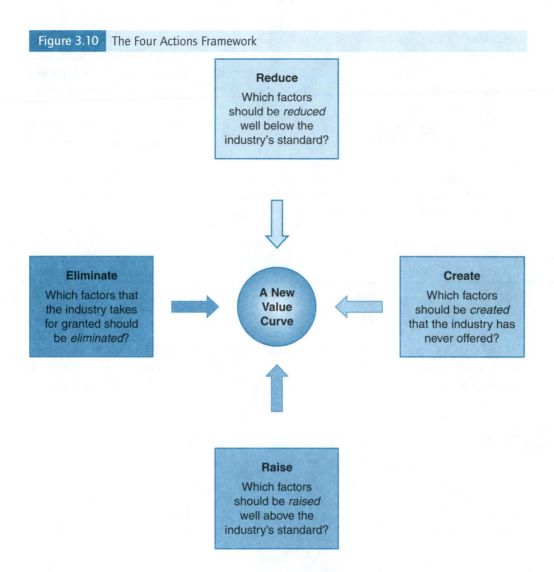

Figure 3.10   The Four Actions Framework

eliminated (e.g., the stationary retail store) or reduced (e.g., customer shopping time). They looked for ways to create a more satisfying mattress-purchasing experience. This was accomplished by offering an online ordering system tied to a mobile retail setting that made purchasing easy and convenient. Through the online ordering system and with online sales assistance, they were able to raise the amount of options and information for consumers to choose a better mattress. In doing so, they changed the rules and boundaries for what it meant to purchase a mattress and created their own market structure and Blue Ocean in a Red Ocean in the process.

Limitations of the Consumer View of Strategy

As with the *competitive* view of strategy, the *consumer* view of strategy has its limitations or caveats. If you actually created a Blue Ocean market that was large enough with plenty of potential, it would eventually attract other businesses (competitors) and could turn into a Red Ocean. Here, peripheral vision is called for.

Another potential limitation to this thinking is that the strategy ends with the creation of the new market. The thinking obstacle comes in the form of being satisfied with your accomplishments and, hence, you let your guard down. With the creation of a new market, it's just the beginning. To guard against this very alluring obstacle, you need to be wary of what might just be around the corner. Keep in mind that with time, change and chance are involved. A change-readiness mentality is needed.[15] Since this perspective is grounded in innovation, you'd need to stay on the innovation path to create consumer value quicker than what others can copy.

As previously discussed, one problem with the *competitive* view of strategy was with innovation being impeded. In contrast, the problem with the *consumer* view of strategy is with keeping up with innovation—staying on the innovation treadmill.

Marketing Thinking Challenge 3.2: Creating a Blue Ocean in a Red Ocean

In this challenge, you will use your critical and creative dimensions of 4-DS thinking. In MT Challenge 3.1, you were to approach an industry from a Red Ocean perspective. In this exercise, use the same industry, but now use the *Strategy Canvas* and *Four Actions Framework* to see if you can identify a **Blue Ocean** within the **Red Ocean**. What does your **Blue Ocean** look like?

Figure 3.11   Looking for a **Blue Ocean** in a **Red Ocean**—Can you find one?

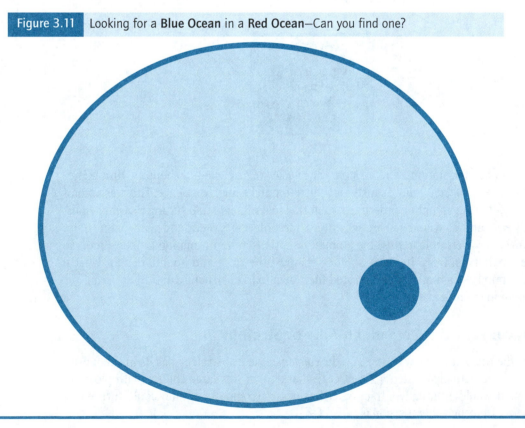

Marketing Thinking Challenge 3.3: Entering a Blue Ocean

Research Cirque du Soleil. Is it still in a **Blue Ocean**? Conduct a situation assessment using the **Red Ocean** approach (Porter's Five Forces). Based upon your situation assessment, how would you recommend entering this market?

Figure 3.12   A Blue Ocean

Other Related Considerations— Changes in Information

Changing technologies have significantly affected the flow of and access to market information. The Internet has, in essence, created the opportunity for equal access to the creation and dissemination of information worldwide through websites, blogs, Twitter, and social networks. This has also accelerated the rate and the volume at which information is being made available and, as a consequence, it makes the situation assessment more challenging.

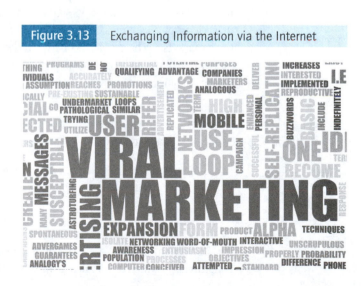

Figure 3.13   Exchanging Information via the Internet

Furthermore, when information was primarily available through traditional modes of communication, such as the trade journals, published research, and the news, it was assessed by criteria as its source (credibility), timeliness, relevance, level of specificity, and so on. These criteria are based upon a search for the factual basis of the information. It is a search for truth. It is also grounded in the logic that

> market change was usually gradual enough to make incremental organizational change as an effective way to cope with it. Phrases such as "plan your work, work your plan," "we control our destiny," "optimization," "supervision," "supply *chains*," "value *chains*," and "*chains* of command" are examples of make-and-sell vocabulary that reveal how deeply the concepts of stability, efficiency and predictability are embedded in today's corporate mindset—even those that proclaim responsiveness, speed, agility, resilience, variability and adaptiveness to be the institutional qualities they seek.[16]

However, with the explosive accessibility of information via the Internet, truth or fact may not be the basis on which information needs to be assessed. The Internet has changed the nature of information from being objective (grounded in fact) and stable to being more subjective, more local on a global basis, and more dynamic. As a result, new ways of thinking about what and how market information is to be assessed are emerging. Examples include detecting weak signals, sensing and responding, organizational peripheral vision, signals of value, and whispers.

From an information volume perspective, the Internet may appear as noise or chaos. But organizations are developing technologies to separate the apparent noise or clutter from the first indications for potential change—weak signals. "Strong signals are what we already know" and weak signals are what we don't know but would like to.[17]

Different questions are being asked and, as a result, they are looking for a new kind of information that isn't well established but may eventually become temporarily established. The implications can be described as follows: Organizations that were and are about making and selling can be described as "bus companies" that follow a predetermined schedule. On the other hand, organizations that are moving toward a sense-and-respond business structure can be described as "taxis" in which the organization's capabilities are dispatched in response to changing consumer directions.[18] "Hierarchical discipline perpetuates and causes massive overinvestment in failure; market discipline actively seeks signals of value and eliminates those activities that fail to measure up."[19] Market discipline companies get their directions by actively searching for the tensions in their markets.[20] The differences between these two orientations can be described as being internally versus externally oriented or exploitation versus exploration oriented. Again, these are different forms of thinking leading to different ways of doing things or strategies.

> "Sense making or interpretation is usually the weakest link in the process of capturing weak signals and eventually making a sound decision."[21]

> "Consumers are in the midst of a conversation that isn't ours. The race is on to grow ears large enough to learn what they are saying."[22]

> John Hayes, CMO, American Express

"Conversation is the new source of consumer intelligence."[23] Marketers are listening in on consumers' online conversations and using software like Voicescape to analyze the landscape of consumer voices—volume of words, common phrases and tags (e.g., products and issues), frequency (how often they occur), and clustering (how closely they are grouped together). …Then conduct deeper analysis, such as on sentiment (positive, negative, or neutral), tonality (which words and phrases appear most often in the positive or negative conversations), spread (how widespread is the discussion), and volume over time (around a specific phrase, word, or concept).[24]

They are using this technology and information to identify "shouts (obvious red flags) and whispers (patterns of interest with uncertain meaning that need further investigation)."[25]

Another method, bibliometric analysis, has been used for identifying weak signals associated with new technology innovations. In the case of the introduction of DVD technology, for example, by researching trade publications and the general press, the number of articles referring to DVD technology can be mapped, indicating its rising status over time.[26]

Several implications can be drawn from these points. As a result of the growth of the Internet, the shelf life of information has changed from months and weeks to perhaps days and hours. Also, rumors and misinformation can be promoted and propagated as they gain momentum and take on their own reality that can significantly affect today's organizations. The marketer has been put into the position of having to learn to be a better listener and strategically learn how to participate with consumers in their conversations. Conversation has become a new element for marketing strategy. The discussion on social media in Chapter 8 explores additional ways to listen to consumers.

All the while, the changes taking place in the marketplace require the marketer to be that much more agile and adept in his or her thinking and strategy.

Marketing Thinking Challenge 3.4:
The Listening Challenge—Listening for *Weak Signals*

Choose any industry of interest. Identify industry-related blogs and listen in to what they are discussing. What is the current conversation? How widespread is it? What was it that started the conversation? Do you hear any potential *weak signals*?

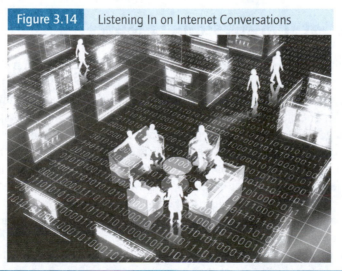

Figure 3.14   Listening In on Internet Conversations

Summary

- This chapter highlighted the channeling effects stemming from the concept of *strategy* and how it initially acquired its meaning from a military context.
- Two different perspectives of strategy were discussed—the *competitive perspective of strategy* and the *consumer-oriented perspective of strategy*. What view of strategy the marketer adheres to will influence how he or she will view the marketplace structurally and the subsequent strategies that will be considered.
- The *competitive perspective of strategy* views the marketplace structure (a structure-bound perspective) based upon Porter's Five Forces model. The marketplace structure's parts involved these five competitive forces that could be used to describe the nature of competition, and the task for the marketer is to develop strategy to effectively outmaneuver these forces.
- The *consumer perspective of strategy* views the marketplace structure as one that is to be created through strategy (a *creating* structure perspective). The objective is to create a marketplace that provides unique value to consumers and one that is competition free. To accomplish this, the Strategy Canvas and Four Actions Framework were used in combination as a method to create unique value.
- The differences in these views of strategy were captured in the following contrast: *structure shapes strategy* versus *strategy shapes structure*. They represent different forms of thinking and resulted in different strategies. Their corresponding strategies were **Red Ocean** versus **Blue Ocean** strategy. The **Red Ocean** strategy was competitively oriented, while the **Blue Ocean** strategy was consumer oriented.
- There is also an ongoing conversation taking place via the Internet in real time that can be a vital source of marketing information. The Internet is also forcing organizations to move toward a real-time marketing posture. This is highlighted through the *sense-and-respond* view leading to a more adaptive mode of operations. Technologies are being developed and already exist that allow organizations to "sense" changes, to listen in on conversations, and be more prone to respond accordingly.

Case: JetBlue—Customers Matter

JetBlue airline was launched in the winter of 2000 by David Neeleman at the age of 46. He was entering the airline scene at a time when the full effects of airline deregulations of the 1970s had become materialized with consolidation down to a smaller number of airlines (e.g., United, American, and Continental), intense competition, and hub-spoke–designed flight scheduling. With fewer airlines along with increasing fuel and maintenance costs, the strategy became one of reducing costs (e.g., cutting back on nonessentials), filling flights (e.g., eliminating less popular flights and designations), and capitalizing on yield management techniques (or value pricing). Value pricing involves pricing customer amenities based on product differentiation (e.g., access to lounge, meal service, seating preference—first class and availability—escalating pricing based upon occupancy, and time to departure). None of these tactics was directed toward increasing customer satisfaction. The hub-spoke design is based on pooling travelers to fill planes and typically increases the number of stops involved and time traveling. As part of the strategy, airlines would purchase smaller airplanes that were more fuel efficient for shorter trips (e.g., MD-80s). To get more out of these smaller airplanes, the seating was condensed to accommodate more seats in less space. On the cost-cutting side, airlines were reducing the number of employees in both maintenance and service areas of the business while increasing their responsibilities. In essence, employees were seen as an expense and were treated accordingly.

With this scene set, JetBlue entered this environment. From the onset, JetBlue was to be a "challenger brand" to be based upon differentiation.[27] As JetBlue's VP of corporate communications, Gareth Edmondson-Jones, says, "We wanted to bring the humanity back to airline travel. It's not enough just to launch a low-fare airline that can be undersold by the big carrier."[28] He also describes the situation as follows:

> When asked what the greatest offense of the large carriers is Edmondson-Jones hit the nail on the head by saying "Indifference. Indifference directed at the passenger. It's easy to feel that you've lost your dignity flying the big guys. You are a number and a boarding pass. It's like a cattle call. …Everyone's trying to shave three or four cents off a passenger. Passenger expectations are so low that when you help them with their baggage, it's a real shock from what they're used to." He went on to add: "It's amazing that the level of expectations for airlines in general and especially for discount entrants is so low that if you set your standards high, it's easy to create a reputation for customer service."[29]

The JetBlue strategy is to offer low fares, provide amenities that other airlines don't, and provide excellent service.

> The flights are probably the most comfortable of all of the airlines with leather seats, more leg room than most passengers are accustomed to on other airlines, great in-flight entertainment, and with people who are the most helpful in the industry. JetBlue is one of the few airlines that offer free Direct TV as well as XM satellite radio providing passengers with 100 channels of largely commercial free programming, from all sorts of different styles of music, and talk. From the company's inception, JetBlue's founders were aware that its seemingly contradictory goals—the internal mantra is "high touch, low cost"—were achievable only through aggressive and strategic use of technology. They are aggressive where it makes sense—that's why they have Direct TV in every seat, and why they're ahead of the pack on Web services. At the same time, they standardize where it makes sense, from their PCs right up to the airplanes. As JetBlue continues to conquer the odds, their repeated choice of Airbus aircraft proves that efficiency on all levels, including equipment and operations, is a must for an airline's continuing health. JetBlue demonstrates that with the right people, the right product and the right cost structure, airlines can grow, even in this current, challenging, environment.[30]

They are also trying offering wireless Internet connections to attract younger travelers, and for the business customer, their loyalty program is based on how much you spend, not on how much you travel in terms of miles, along with all seats being available for redemption.[31] (The other carriers block a certain number of seats that can only be used and the times they are available.) They have also been remodeling their waiting areas to be more contemporary and comfortable, which can be seen on their website (www.jetblue.com/experience/). While they do use regular advertising and recently switched advertising agencies (the new agency offered a better fit and greater integration, which they felt was needed), they also incorporate social media into their marketing including twitter (@JetBlueCheeps) and Facebook. Twitter has been used to send out promotion deals such as $9 tickets from New York to Massachusetts.[32] They also ran a parody advertising campaign called the "The Flyer's Collection" of a series of fictional products to be used if you had to fly on one of the other airlines.[33] One example was a "knee jockey" to keep your knees up so they don't get smashed by the seat in front of you.

The central part to their strategy still remains with their employees. JetBlue is very selective with who they hire and puts potential hires through a series of hypothetical situations to see how they would handle them. If hired, the employees are treated well with respect along with a good work environment, potential for rapid advancement, contribution of 15% to their profit-sharing plan, and stock options.[34] Through training, incentives, and recognition of good behavior, employees understand the values of the company, treating customers as they should be with respect and courtesy. The company values still involve safety, caring, integrity, fun, and passion and are expressed through employees in the form of what has been described as "Jetitude" (JetBlue attitude), which is: "Be in Blue always, Be personal, Be the answer, Be engaging, and Be thankful to every customer."[35]

JetBlue has had its setbacks in the past as well. In February 14, 2007, a fast-moving storm over the East Coast affected thousands of travelers. Many of JetBlue's customers were stranded on the tarmac, some up to 11 hours. While on the plane, trapped customers were using their cell phones contacting friends, colleagues, and families about their ongoing experience. Some even sent pictures of overflowing toilets and the like. The event clearly caught JetBlue off guard. They quickly tried to communicate the mistakes they made and how they were going to correct them so this would never happen again. But through social media, the negative effects had already taken hold and are lasting even today as a part of JetBlue's legacy. Shortly after the event, they posted a Customer Bill of Rights and Tarmac Contingency Plan on their website at www.jetblue.com/about/ourcompany/promise/index.html. This example perhaps illustrates how fast a story can travel and how companies need to be much more proactive than in the past.

Is JetBlue pursuing a **Red** or **Blue Ocean** strategy? What makes its marketing strategy different than that of the traditional consumer-targeting approach? Is the strategy based upon quality or something else? Explain your positions for each of these questions with examples.

References

1. Onions, C. T. (1995), *The Oxford Dictionary of English Etymology*, New York: Oxford Press, 874.
2. Heuser, Beatrice (2010), *The Evolution of Strategy: Thinking War From Antiquity to the Present*, New York: Cambridge University Press, 4.
3. Kim, Chan W., and Renee Mauborgne (2005), "The Blue Ocean Strategy: From Theory to Practice," *California Management Review*, 47 (3), 105.
4. Kim, Chan W., and Renee Mauborgne (2009), "How Strategy Shapes Structure," *Harvard Business Review*, September, 73.
5. Kim, Chan W., and Renee Mauborgne (2004), "Blue Ocean Strategy," *Harvard Business Review*, October, 76–84.
6. Kim, Chan W., and Renee Mauborgne (2005), "The Blue Ocean Strategy: From Theory to Practice," *California Management Review*, 47 (3), 105–21.

7. Porter, Michael E. (1980), *Competitive Strategy: Techniques for Analyzing Industries and Competitors*, New York: The Free Press.
8. Porter, Michael E. (2008), "The Five Competitive Forces That Shape Strategy," *Harvard Business Review*, January, 79–93.
9. Haeckel, Stephan H. (2004), "Peripheral Vision: Sensing and Acting on Weak Signals Making Meaning out of Apparent Noise: The Need for a New Managerial Framework," *Long Range Planning*, 37, 183.
10. Porter, Michael E. (2008), "The Five Competitive Forces That Shape Strategy," *Harvard Business Review*, January, 83.
11. Porter, Michael E. (2008), "The Five Competitive Forces That Shape Strategy," *Harvard Business Review*, January, 87.
12. Kim, Chan W., and Renee Mauborgne (2004), "Blue Ocean Strategy," *Harvard Business Review*, October, 77–8.
13. Kim, Chan W., and Renee Mauborgne (2004), "Blue Ocean Strategy," *Harvard Business Review*, October, 81.
14. Kim, Chan W., and Renee Mauborgne (2005), "The Blue Ocean Strategy: From Theory to Practice," *California Management Review*, 47 (3), 105–21.
15. Browning, Randy, Joe Duffy, and Karen Vander Linde (2008), "How to Build an Agile Foundation for Change," *Achieving Operational Excellence Series*, February, PricewaterhouseCooper, 28.
16. Haechel, Stephan H. (2004), "Peripheral Vision: Sensing and Acting on Weak Signals Making Meaning out of Apparent Noise: The Need for a New Managerial Framework," *Long Range Planning*, 37, 182.
17. Zeisler, Steven, and Dyer Harris (2000), "Order From Chaos Part Two," *Scenario & Strategy Planning*, 2 (2), 15.
18. Haechel, Stephan H. (2004), "Peripheral Vision: Sensing and Acting on Weak Signals Making Meaning out of Apparent Noise: The Need for a New Managerial Framework," *Long Range Planning*, 37, 183.
19. Wasden, Christopher (2009), "Hit and Miss," *Communications Review*, 15 (1), PricewaterhouseCoopers, 20.
20. Wasden, Christopher (2009), "Hit and Miss," *Communications Review*, 15 (1), PricewaterhouseCoopers, 20.
21. Schoemaker, Paul J. H., and George S. Day (2009), "How to Make Sense of Weak Signals," *MIT Sloan Management Review*, 50 (3), 83.
22. Bothun, Deborah, Randy Browning, Jason Wagner, and Herb Walter (2008), "How Consumer Conversation Will Transform Business," *Achieving Operational Excellence Series*, January, PricewaterhouseCoopers, 20.
23. Bothun, Deborah, Randy Browning, Jason Wagner, and Herb Walter (2008), "How Consumer Conversation Will Transform Business," *Achieving Operational Excellence Series*, January, PricewaterhouseCoopers, 14.
24. Bothun, Deborah, Randy Browning, Jason Wagner, and Herb Walter (2008), "How Consumer Conversation Will Transform Business," *Achieving Operational Excellence Series*, January, PricewaterhouseCoopers, 14.
25. Bothun, Deborah, Randy Browning, Jason Wagner, and Herb Walter (2008), "How Consumer Conversation Will Transform Business," *Achieving Operational Excellence Series*, January, PricewaterhouseCoopers, 16.
26. Makinen, Saku, Heini M. Jarvenpaa, Turo Uskali, and Jari Ojale (2007), "Spotting Weak Signals Considering New Technology Innovations: An Empirical Search for Appropriate Sources," www.innovationjournalism.org/conference/ij4presentations/m%C3%A4kinenj%C3%A4rvenp%C3%A4%C3%A4uskaliojala.pdf

27. Parekh, Rupal (2010), "How JetBlue Became One of the Hottest Brands in America," *Advertising Age*, July 6, http://adage.com/cmostrategy/article?article_id=144799

28. Rusch, Robin D. (2001), "Blue Skies Ahead," brandchannel, June 18, www.brandchannel.com/features_effect.asp?id=41

29. Rusch, Robin D. (2001), "Blue Skies Ahead," brandchannel, June 18, www.brandchannel.com/features_effect.asp?id=41

30. Dodds, Bill (2007), "JetBlue Airways: Service Quality as a Competitive Advantage," *Journal of Business Case Studies*, 3 (4), 33.

31. Parekh, Rupal (2010), "How JetBlue Became One of the Hottest Brands in America," *Advertising Age*, July 6, http://adage.com/cmostrategy/article?article_id=144799

32. "Successful Strategies of JetBlue in Online Marketing," Libardo & Lambrando's Blog, http://syndikomm.com/blog/2010/01/successful-strategies-of-jetblue-in-online-marketing/

33. "Successful Strategies of JetBlue in Online Marketing," Libardo & Lambrando's Blog, http://syndikomm.com/blog/2010/01/successful-strategies-of-jetblue-in-online-marketing/

34. Dodds, Bill (2007), "JetBlue Airways: Service Quality as a Competitive Advantage," *Journal of Business Case Studies*, 3 (4), 33.

35. "The Who and What of JetBlue," Customer Experience Matters, http://experiencematters.wordpress.com/2010/06/01/the-who-and-what-of-jetblue/

CHAPTER 4

Thinking Further About Marketplace Structure and Strategy

Decompression Exercise

Before beginning the chapter, picture yourself sitting at the edge of the fountain listening to the frogs play.

Figure 4.1	Imagine Frogs Playing in a Fountain

Chapter Introduction

The thinking agility issues surrounding the concept of marketplace structure are significant in terms of recognizing that this very concept sets the stage for many other influential marketing concepts, and to not explore this very fundamental concept would preclude the opportunity to expand our strategic options. Perhaps the problem with the marketplace structure is that is typically taken as a given and doesn't undergo the scrutiny it deserves. The strategist has to be willing to put everything on the table, conceptually and otherwise, to explore what it **means**, the directions in which they channel thinking, what other ways could also be considered, and so on.

As we saw in Chapter 3, the marketer can either assume an already existing marketplace structure and then develop strategy within this structure (a structure-*bound* perspective, a **Red Ocean** strategy), or, based upon what is already being provided within the marketplace, proceed to move in a different direction, creating a new marketplace in the process. This means creating a new structure through strategy (a *creating* structure perspective, a **Blue Ocean** strategy). The view you adhere to leads to a different perspective of the marketplace situation and the role of strategy. As you may recall, in Chapter 3, the main question was:

Structure **Shapes Strategy or Strategy Shapes** *Structure?*

| Figure 4.2 | Heading in Different Directions |

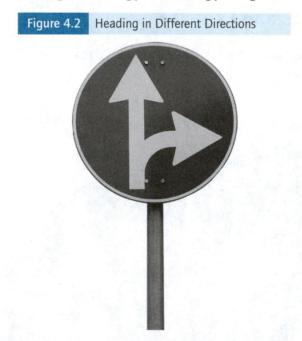

Yet what else could there be with the marketplace structure? Either we view it in an existing way or we view it as something to be created. Right? But there is more. For example, if you assume an existing marketplace structure, other issues might pertain to whether it is to be viewed as one solid, homogeneous mass or as a composition of different entities and therefore heterogeneous. Another related issue could involve who is actually doing the structuring, the marketer, the consumer, or others? Each perspective leads to different views of the marketplace and stems from different forms of thinking that lead to different strategy alternatives. By examining and considering these various forms of thinking about how we are approaching the marketplace structure, numerous thinking corridors open up that could potentially lead to even more strategic options in the process. All the while, our thinking agility is also building up by taking on these very fundamental marketing concepts for the purposes of plumbing them for all that we can gleam from them.

This chapter continues with the development of our marketing thinking by expanding the marketplace structure discussion developed in Chapter 3. We will first start with the question of viewing the marketplace homogeneously or heterogeneously and which marketing concepts are related to which view of the marketplace structure. Then we will take up the second main question of who is doing the structuring of the marketplace. This question leads to the separation in views between traditional marketing and emerging perspectives that involve marketing taking on more of a compatibility orientation with consumers and being less about competition. The traditional marketing concepts of segmenting, positioning, the marketing mix, targeting, and so forth are discussed in the chapter as well.

The following question is related to the structure-*bound* perspective discussed in Chapter 3 but explores it even more explicitly. The implications of the question are that which view you adhere to will affect the direction of your marketing thinking and, ultimately, your strategy. The structure-related question in its simplest form is basically:

Is the marketplace homogenous or heterogeneous?

Marketplace Structure Orientations

This structural question considers the composition of the marketplace. Is the marketplace one group, multiple groups, a composition of individuals, or none of these? Depending upon which way you choose to view the marketplace, the corresponding marketing strategies you'll consider will be affected. The marketplace structure orientations to be discussed are mass marketing, segmentation, self-selection segmenting, and one-to-one marketing.

A Homogeneous Marketplace Structure—Mass Marketing Orientation

The view of the marketplace as a homogenous group based upon common needs is a mass-marketing orientation. The classic example of an organization adhering to this view was the Ford Motor Company in the 1920s with Henry Ford's Model T. The marketplace was viewed as one large, homogenous group based upon the common need for transportation. The Model T was to be a "universal vehicle" in the sense that it was simply a means to provide a mode of transportation and not much more. All the cars were to be the same, black in color, and all with the same features. To be able to do this, Henry Ford transformed the assembly line to produce the Model T more efficiently, so each car rolling off the line was manufactured the same way. In the process, he was able to transform the automobile from a luxury item to an everyday necessity. The mass-production assembly line also allowed for all of the Model Ts to be offered at the same affordable price of the time. This *standardized marketing strategy*—one strategy for the entire marketplace—was based upon a mass-marketing orientation.

A Heterogeneous Marketplace Structure—Segmentation Orientation

To counter Ford's strategy, Alfred P. Sloan, president of General Motors (GM), viewed the marketplace not as being homogenous but instead as heterogeneous based upon differences in ability to purchase and, accordingly, proceeded to segment the automobile market in the United States. Pursuing a segmentation orientation, Sloan recognized that there might be cause to believe that there were differences in the ability to purchase an automobile. The marketing strategy involved a pricing scheme based upon different segments (groups) with different needs in the marketplace.

Instead of the standardized marketing strategy as with the Model T, Sloan's marketing strategy involved *customizing* GM's marketing for the different segments identified to be pursued.

While this market segmentation view was initiated in the 1920s, it really doesn't appear formally in the market literature until 1950s.[1] Accordingly, "Segmentation is based upon developments on the demand side of the market and represents a rational and more precise adjustment of product and marketing effort to consumer or user requirements."[2] *Segmentation* involves an analysis of the marketplace to identify groupings of individuals or businesses based upon the potential of behaving similarly. As markets become more fragmented, segmentation can lead to *microsegmentation,* which involves identifying smaller and smaller groupings.

Not Based Upon a Marketplace Structure—Self-Selection Segmenting Orientation

Recently, the process of segmenting the market has been called into question, leading to the emergence of the self-selection segmenting orientation.[3] There are numerous problems with the segmentation determination process, from an infinite number of ways of segmenting the market to many different mathematical methods for conducting the analysis to a marketplace that is constantly changing. And, perhaps, the structure the marketer is trying to identify can be thought of as an elusive structure that is in process and, hence, difficult to quantify. By recognizing these difficulties, the self-selection segmenting orientation has begun appearing in the marketing literature.

> …although the ability to segment is a necessary element to be able to practice revenue management, the segmentation does not have to be performed by the firm. With an increasing amount of data available about customers, firms could provide a menu of choices that could be less costly than the traditional costs of targeting, coordinating and erecting rate fences.[4]

According to the self-selection segmenting orientation, there are two strategic elements. The first is to provide an array of choice options that would be available to all segments and in which each choice is seen as being clearly different, along with a different price. Second, within each choice set, there would be options for consumers to choose from, adding a dynamic means of differentiation within and across the choices.

> To discern consumer preferences, …self-selection segmentation [is offered], whereby all product choices are accessible to all segments, yet each segment willingly pays a different price because they have no interest in mimicking the other segment.[5]

Not Based Upon a Marketplace Structure— One-to-One Marketing Orientation

A concept similar and related to self-selection segmenting is one-to-one marketing. With advances in technology, this alternative orientation of the marketplace has become possible. With the Internet and new database management technology, companies like Amazon.com can utilize customers' past purchases to develop individual profiles and then market directly to them. For example, if you have purchased anything on Amazon's website lately and provided an e-mail address, you may periodically receive recommendations for new purchases based upon items you have purchased in the past.

Issues With the Different Structural Orientations

These different orientations—mass marketing, segmentation, self-selection segmenting, and one-to-one marketing—are a result of how one views the structure of the marketplace (homogenous or heterogeneous), the recognition of the limits the marketer has to work within to understand the marketplace (e.g., marketing research difficulties and a dynamic marketplace), and advances in technology (the Internet and database-management software). Returning to Chapter 3's question of *Structure Shapes Strategy or Strategy Shapes Structure*, we saw that the **Red Ocean** strategies were structure *bound* whereas the **Blue Ocean** strategies were about *creating* structure. A similar distinction occurs here with the different orientations. Mass marketing and segmentation assume a known marketplace structure (e.g., a homogenous market with a common need or a heterogeneous market made up of segments with distinctive needs or wants), which is used in developing strategy (i.e., structure *bound*). In contrast, self-selection segmenting and one-to-one marketing aren't based upon a presumption of marketplace structure in advance per se.

Furthermore, mass marketing and segmenting are based upon a *post hoc* marketer's view for strategy development, whereas self-selection segmenting and one-to-one marketing are driven or directed by consumers in real time. Additionally, mass marketing and segmentation, as *post hoc* orientations, would tend to be static due to the rigidity of working (thinking) within what the marketer believes to be the way the market is structured (a kind of conceptual "box"), whereas this particular thinking obstacle isn't present with the latter two orientations and, hence, allows for a more dynamic marketing strategy.

As we'll see later, the presumption of a marketplace structure has had a major influence on how marketing is practiced and strategized. To examine the influence the different views on marketplace structure have had on marketing, we'll need to bring into the discussion the second question mentioned in the introduction as well. Related to the structure *bound* versus *creating* structure orientations examined in Chapter 3 is the underlying structuring issue that is captured in the following question:

Who is it that is segmenting the market—the marketer or the consumer?

If you take the marketer's position, it assumes that a structure can be correctly identified and that it will stay that way for a certain duration. As such, from our 4-DS thinking perspective, the time dimension of the marketer's thinking is being quelled. And, as we saw in Chapter 3, the structure **bound** to *strategy* perspective is grounded in a <u>competitive orientation</u> where strategy focuses on competing within a structure being created by others.

If you take the consumer's position, then the *TIME* dimension of the market's thinking has been reinstated and becomes active in strategy development. Additionally, the consumer's position to the question leads to a different orientation to strategy than the competitive one.

I guess I've never thought about it that way. Does it matter?

If it's not grounded in competition, then it must be something consumer oriented. Right?

Yes, that's correct. The consumer perspective is based on a *compatibility orientation*, which we will explore later in the chapter.

The difference between the *creating* structure orientation discussed in Chapter 3 and the consumer perspective to be presented in this chapter has to do with who is doing the structuring—the marketer or the consumer. For the *creating* structure orientation, the marketer is doing the structuring by *creating* a new structure based upon unique value, whereas with the consumer perspective, it is the consumer that is doing the marketplace structuring. While both are consumer oriented, the structuring assumptions head off into different directions.

We will look the differences between when the marketer is doing the structuring versus when the consumer is and the thinking that accompanies each. The more traditional segmenting, positioning to targeting logic, will be discussed first, and the self-selection segmenting and one-to-one marketing will follow.

Traditional Marketing Logics and Their Sequential Role to Developing Strategy

While we have addressed what marketing thinking looks like in Chapter 1, we haven't formally defined marketing.

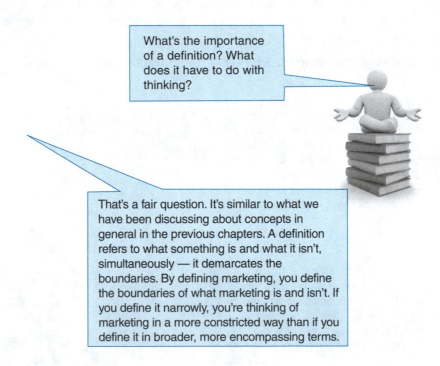

How do you define marketing? In 2007, the American Marketing Association (AMA) offered a new definition of marketing:

Marketing is the activity, set of institutions, and processes for creating, communicating, delivering, and exchanging offerings that have value for customers, clients, partners, and society at large.[6]

Definitions provide the basis for the logics that are associated with any discipline. To understand marketing is to understand the logics behind the practice of marketing. *Logic* refers to the formal principles of a branch of knowledge or a particular mode of reasoning viewed as being valid or faulty.[7] As a branch of knowledge, marketing has its own logics.

The AMA's definition has been influenced over the years by pivotal marketing concepts such as the marketing concept (or its more current form, the market orientation), segmentation, positioning, and targeting, which also lead to other concepts, for example, relationships (relationship marketing), integration (to be more effective and efficient), and alignment (to be better aligned in the market and, hence, more effective and competitive). To understand the logics driving the practice of marketing, we'll examine these influential concepts next.

Influential Marketing Concepts

The *marketing concept* was introduced in the 1950s to offer an alternative orientation to organizations pursuing a production or sales perspective: one that considers consumers' needs in making marketing decisions. For example, in the late '50s to early '60s, Pillsbury made the transition to a marketing orientation:

> The company's purpose was no longer to mill flour, nor to manufacturer a wide variety of products, but to satisfy the needs and desires, both actual and potential, of our customers.[8]

The *marketing concept/market orientation* is a philosophy guiding how marketing is to be practiced (Figure 4.3). Even with the more recent developments of the marketing concept, which include considering competition, market factors, and technology in conjunction with consumer interests—hence, the more expanded view of the *market orientation*—the basic guiding principles are inherent in how marketing is taught and practiced today. In essence, by shifting attention toward what is going on in the marketplace in terms of consumers, the marketer began to recognize that the marketplace wasn't homogenous as in a mass-marketing perspective but, instead, could be better described as a composite of differing interests of consumer needs and wants and, accordingly, potentially lead to more effective marketing strategy.

As mentioned earlier, at about the same time the marketing concept appeared on the scene, so did the concepts of segmentation and their related concepts of product differentiation, positioning, and the marketing mix.[9, 10] *Product differentiation* refers to modifying the offering to be more suited to different segments. The concept of *positioning* has two aspects. The first involves identifying the relative perceptual consumer understandings of the products, services, or brands in a particular product or service category. This involves marketing research and analytical techniques such as multidimensional scaling. Second, as a strategy consideration, the various ways to actively affect one's brand's perceptual position in the marketplace needed to be considered, which is where the marketing mix comes into view.

The *marketing mix* was offered as a conceptual tool to organize the various aspects that could be configured in varying ways for the purpose of what a marketer might offer to consumers. Since its introduction in the United States in the 1950s, the marketing mix has centered around the four Ps: price, promotion, place, and product.[11, 12] As one might expect, there are other marketing mix versions also available, which are discussed in Chapter 6.

All of these concepts stemming from the marketing concept come together under the umbrella concept of targeting. *Targeting* refers to actively pursuing certain consumers through the processes of segmentation and positioning that inform the configuring of a particular marketing offering via the marketing mix to facilitate particular relationships in the marketplace that benefit the organization.

The Marketing Concept—A Guiding Philosophy of Marketing

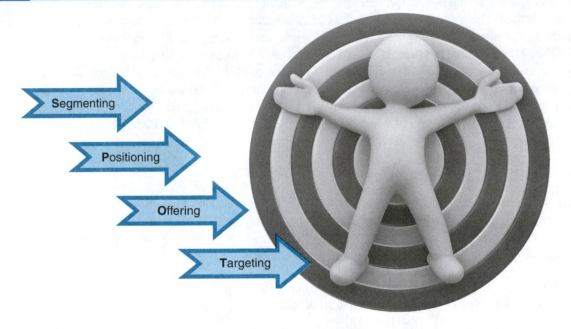

The marketing logics of segmentation, positioning, configuring an offering, and targeting (SPOT) stem from the marketing concept philosophy—guiding what type of information is needed to practice marketing effectively and efficiently, which is the role *marketing research* serves. The *sequential ordering of information* is also suggested through these marketing logics in that segmentation should be conducted first, followed by positioning, then configuring the offering and, ultimately, explaining the targeting of the *who?* and *how?* they are to be pursued by the marketer. These logics are formally presented next.

Traditional (SPOT) Marketing Logics

The following are some of the current marketing logics being used in practicing marketing.

Marketing Logic 1 (Segmenting): Segmentation analysis is used to identify the most attractive segment(s) from the organization's perspective. A segment(s) selected as being attractive enough to pursue then becomes known as the target market(s).

Marketing Logic 2 (Positioning): Once a target market has been chosen, positioning can be conducted, which includes identifying the relative perceptual positions of products/services within the minds of the target market. This type of analysis also provides competitive information from the target market's perspective.

Marketing Logic 3 (Configuring an Offering/Marketing Mix): With the target market and positioning information at hand, a marketer has information available to determine what the marketing mix needs to accomplish. It is at this point that the marketer has the information to start thinking about developing an appropriate offering through configuring an integrated marketing mix. In this context, the marketer can also assess the likelihood of achieving certain marketing objectives.

Marketing Logic 4 (Targeting): Developing particular types of relationships by *aligning* with a targeted market (e.g., brand loyalty), the marketer has the potential to develop a *competitive advantage* whereby the target market would be resistant to competitive actions.

As discussed in Chapter 1, strategy is a way to be meaningfully different in the marketplace by choosing different means to provide unique value. *These marketing logics lay out a process for determining such unique value in the marketplace.* Accordingly, *marketing strategy* is the process of first choosing a *target market* and, secondly, *creating and maintaining a satisfying/competitive offering* (i.e., marketing mix—product, price, promotion, and place) for a constantly changing business environment. It is a dynamic and ongoing process. The marketing strategy maps out the *Way* the marketing objectives are to be obtained. See Figure 4.4.

Figure 4.4	The Elements of a Marketing Plan

The Way

Strategy

Target Market (the Why? and the Who?)

The Offering via the Marketing Mix (the How?)

Marketing Objectives (Benchmark, Goal, and Time Frame)

The Problems of Not Recognizing the Position of the Questions Being Considered (Up- vs. Downstream Marketing Questions)

The above logics explain a sequential process to the practice of marketing. Accordingly, if one steps outside of the sequence, it would potentially lead to less effective strategy. Conceptually, you can think of it as a *flowing river* of marketing questioning and decisions that need to be made in strategy development.

At the same time, as discussed in Chapter 2, questioning itself in terms of its sequencing, starting points, scope, and so forth need to also be recognized as potential obstacles to marketing thinking. While we'll examine the difficulties related to not adhering to the logics associated with the SPOT perspective of marketing, the sequencing itself is an issue in terms of challenging the thinking in a particular direction and should be recognized as such.

Figure 4.5	Marketing Thinking—As a *Flowing River* of Marketing Questioning

Upstream Marketing Questions—Segmenting Questions

The upstream questions start out with the very basic questions about understanding the nature of the marketplace *before actually deciding to enter it.* What is the structure of the marketplace? How diverse is it? From a strategy perspective, can this diversity be beneficial? Who is in the marketplace that might be interested in what could be offered by the organization? Are there enough of them to warrant pursuing in terms of obtaining a certain rate of return on the investment? The upstream questions involve learning about the composition of differences comprising the marketplace. These questions represent the basis to conducting a segmentation analysis.

Midstream Marketing Questions—Positioning Questions

Once these differences are identified, then the marketer's questions move further downstream to a more midstream point in the *flowing river* of marketing questioning. The midstream marketing questions *ask about the relative relationships* among the identified differences. These are questions about the different positions that already exist in the marketplace (e.g., available brands). Then the questioning proceeds to ask about how to enter and what the best position(s) would be to attempt to take up as a defendable position relative to what is already available in the marketplace. These questions represent the basis for a positioning analysis.

With the answers to the upstream and midstream questions in view, a decision can be made whether to enter at this time. If a negative decision is made, then the process would need to start over to look at a different marketplace or to go through the process at another time. *Time changes all,* which means the *flowing river* of marketing questioning is continuous and the marketer is always in the position of having to keep going back upstream in his or her questioning to stay current. If a decision is made to enter the market and attempt to create a defendable position, then the more downstream questions can begin.

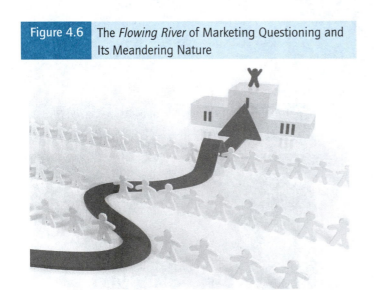

| Figure 4.6 | The *Flowing River* of Marketing Questioning and Its Meandering Nature |

Downstream Marketing Questions—Targeting Questions

The downstream marketing questions are about the details of the *"how to."* The *"how to"* questions involve using the information available from the segmentation and positioning analyses to *creatively* and *critically* decide what is to be offered. Hence, the *flowing river* of marketing questioning isn't necessarily a straight line but can meander as the marketer considers different creative options. At this point, strategic thinking can begin when the information of knowing who is to be pursued is available and the landscape of the marketplace in which the marketer has determined the best inroads and position(s) to take. Prior to this point, the questioning focused on acquiring information that is needed to direct the strategic choices to be made.

To understand the information that is needed to answer this stream of questioning, we'll first look at what information comes from a segmentation analysis and the inherent logic of this type of analysis. Then, in a likewise fashion, we will examine the information from a positioning analysis.

Segmentation Questions

Keep in mind that from this segmenting-positioning-offering-targeting (SPOT) perspective, it is the marketer that is doing the segmenting of the market, which goes to the question raised in the beginning of the chapter: Why would the marketer want to segment the market? What would he or she gain from going through this process?

Segmentation from this perspective is an analysis that tries to reveal some structural characteristics of the market in terms of its composition of constituents and, based upon this information, the marketer hopes to identify better choices and, consequentially, make better strategy decisions. The *purpose* of a segmentation analysis for the marketer is to ideally identify a segment or segments from the marketplace composition of constituents that may be deemed worthy or attractive enough to pursue as their target market(s). So a segmentation analysis focuses on identifying a potential target market. This involves marketing research and analytical techniques such as multidimensional scaling, clustering, artificial neural networks, latent class models, or occasion-based segmentation. For more information on these techniques, refer to a marketing research textbook.

One of the main problems the marketer has in conducting a segmentation analysis is similar to what is depicted in Figure 4.7. How do you know how to do the groupings? What should the groups be based upon? What separates one group from another? Are they mutually exclusive? And does the manner in which they are placed into groups actually match how those in the market perceive things? In other words, does the marketer's superimposed structuring match how the market is actually structured via those in it? As in the above figure, it is like starting out in a situation in which all of the balls look identical and the marketer, in some sense, is using an arbitrary means to sort them into groups. Once groups or segments have been formed, then the marketer has to decide which to pursue.

Even so, segmentation analysis is an analysis of determining the relative attractiveness across the identified segments. Here, as depicted in Figure 4.8, the marketer now has to decide how to evaluate them in terms of attractiveness. Criteria are needed.

Figure 4.7   Segmentation—Dividing Up the Market

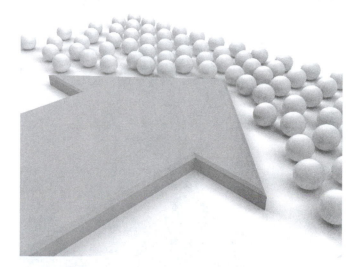

Figure 4.8   Which Segment(s) to Target?

Marketing Thinking Challenge 4.1:
Identifying a Target Market

Figure 4.9 | Identifying a Target Market

Before getting into any technical discussion on segmentation, see what you can come up with for the following: Choose any market of your choice. Now, how would you identify a target market within this marketplace? Explain the process of how you would reveal the *relative attractivenesses* across the potential groups (segments) to be identified.

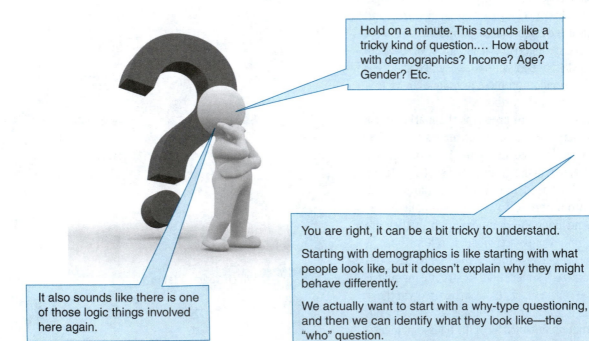

As a marketer, where would you start in segmenting a market?

Hold on a minute. This sounds like a tricky kind of question.... How about with demographics? Income? Age? Gender? Etc.

You are right, it can be a bit tricky to understand.

Starting with demographics is like starting with what people look like, but it doesn't explain why they might behave differently.

We actually want to start with a why-type questioning, and then we can identify what they look like—the "who" question.

It also sounds like there is one of those logic things involved here again.

The process of segmentation (and the logic within the process) is discussed next. Keep in mind the questions being asked within this process and what it means from a thinking perspective.

Generally, the basic segmentation analysis involves five different criteria. Each represents lines of questioning and is used to relatively rate the attractiveness of the identified segments.[13, 14] The criteria are listed in Table 4.1.

Table 4.1   Segmentation Criteria

Segmenting Criteria	Explanation
1. Measurability	Used to determine the relative ease of identifying the segments. Which segments are more discernable and easier to identify as to who they are?
2. Accessibility	Used to determine the differences in accessing, communicating with the segments. For example, which segments would be easier to communicate with? Which segments utilize preferred media that are consistent with the organization's marketing?
3. Substantiality	Used to determine the relative potentials across the segments. Which segments possess the greater potential? Which segments would provide the greatest rate of return?
4. Unique Responsiveness	Used to determine the differences in responsiveness across the segments in terms of what might be marketed. Which segments would respond more favorably to what the marketer might offer?
5. Actionable	Used to determine the relative degree of the organization's ability to effectively orchestrate suitable marketing programs across the segments. Which segments could the organization develop more effective marketing programs for?

The segmentation criteria are used to evaluate each segment relative to the others in terms of their attractiveness along each criterion's dimension from the organization's perspective. They are used to judge the worthiness of each segment. *But they are NOT actually used to do the segmenting.* Other variables are required to do the segmenting. In generic form, the segmentation analysis would look like Table 4.2.

Table 4.2   Generic Segmentation Analysis Matrix

Criteria Variable(s)	Segment 1 (Label)	Segment 2 (Label)	Segment 3 (Label)	Segment N (Label)
Measurability Demographics				
Accessibility Media Types				
Substantiality Size Disposable Income Costs				
Unique Responsiveness (Dis)Satisfaction Attitudes				
Actionable Current Marketing				

Hold on! I have a question. You had asked me before about where I'd start the segmenting process, and you said that we would start with the "why" question. I don't see that in what's been presented so far. Where in the matrix does it indicate where you start the process?

That's a good question. There is a built in logic into this type of analysis. You want to separate out the apples from the oranges into their respective groups. Instead of starting out with the demographics which would lead to getting the apples mixed in with the oranges, <u>we start with the Unique Responsive criterion and its variable(s) for segmenting the market</u>. This important criterion and its variables are about **Why** one segment would respond differently, uniquely, from another. Those indicating more favorable responses to what the marketer could market would be considered more attractive.

The segmentation process begins with the Unique Responsiveness criterion and its variables. *It is the variables within this criterion that are used to actually segment the market.* The segmenting variables fall into three general categories, which are presented in Table 4.3.

Table 4.3 The Unique Responsiveness Criterion's Variables for Segmenting

Variable Type	Examples
Psychological	Attitudes
	(Dis)Satisfaction
	Involvement—high vs. low
	Lifestyle—VALS II; activities, interests, and opinions (AIO)
	Needs
	Wants
	Etc.
Social	Norms—motivation to comply
	Culture—values, practices, etc.
	Subculture
	Etc.
Behavioral	Occasion—special, weekly, etc.
	Loyalty—hardcore, switchers, etc.
	Usage rate—light, medium, heavy; 20/80 rule
	Etc.

Any consumer behavior text will provide an extensive array of variables that could be used to help explain *why* people might respond differently in differing situations. As such, the marketer is still in the position of having to know something beforehand about the consumer's situation to be able to choose which of these variables would be appropriate as a starting point. Each of the variables represents a particular perspective that could be applied to see if that perspective would be evidenced in the market and potentially provide insights into the market composition.

For example, is it a high- or low-involvement situation? This will affect which variables would be applicable. Some variables/concepts characterize high-involvement situations, whereas others pertain to low-involvement situations. For example, with the attitude concept, consumer attitudes that are formed in a high-involvement situation typically involve some compensating cognitive processing around the consequences of the purchasing behavior. In a low-involvement situation, consumer attitudes could form based upon an association being formed through the process of repetition and contiguity using peripheral cues (e.g., advertising using favorable music or attractive people). The first view of an attitude is based upon the Theory of Reasoned Action perspective,[15] and the latter view utilizes a Classical Conditioning perspective.[16] For more explanation on these perspectives or theories, see a consumer behavior text.

Once the segments have been identified via the Unique Responsiveness variables (**the Why?**) then:

1. The segments can be identified from a demographics perspective (**the Who?**),

2. Their media or communications patterns can be identified (**the How to Access Them?**),

3. Their potential can also be determined at this time (**the How Much?**), and

4. Finally, the organization's marketing capabilities can be assessed in relationship to each of the segments (**the Marketing Suitability?**).

From the analysis, all segments would now possess profiles based upon why they would respond uniquely, who they are, how to reach them, the potential in pursuing them, and what marketing programs would be needed to effectively target them. All of this information would be helpful to develop appropriate strategy, which explains the purpose for the SPOT perspective and marketing being practiced in this manner. Once a segment or segments become(s) a likely candidate(s) for an organization's target market, then a positioning analysis can be conducted, which is discussed next.

Positioning Questions

Positioning is a concept that has two aspects associated with it. The *first* involves assessing the relative perceptions within the target market for the brands found within a product or service category. To be clear here, the positioning analysis pertains exclusively to analyzing the target market's perceptions and *not* the entire marketplace. If it were done involving the entire marketplace, it would tend to muddy the results with the views of others, which aren't of interest at this time. Therefore, it is logical to conduct a segmentation analysis before a positioning analysis. It is a type of analysis involving marketing research to identify the relative perceptions of the existing brands within a particular market defined as the target market.

This perceptual mapping can be thought of as identifying the ongoing structuring occurring within the marketplace by consumers—that is, how they differentiate one brand from another. The marketer is interested in knowing what these relative psychological maps of the brands look like for strategy purposes.

This leads into the *second* aspect of positioning, which concerns strategy. Once these perceptual maps are available, the marketer can then use them to decide how to enter the market, the positioning

Figure 4.10   Perceptual Map of Beer Brands

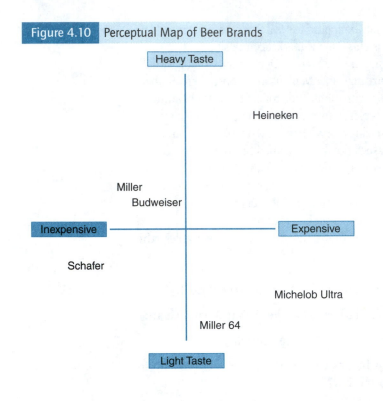

Heavy Taste

Heineken

Miller
Budweiser

Inexpensive ———————— Expensive

Schafer

Michelob Ultra

Miller 64

Light Taste

to take up relative to the other brands' positions, or whether to change one's position in the market for a better one that is more suitable with the organization's evolving marketing objectives.

Positioning as an analysis utilizes multi-dimensional scaling, which typically produces a two-dimensional mathematical space for illustrating the relative positions of brands using different variables measured with semantic differential-type scales—for example, a two-dimensional space based upon the dimensions of expensive to inexpensive and high quality to low quality. A perceptual map of beer might look something like Figure 4.10.

These perceptual maps provide a view of the brands in the marketplace as viewed by those in the target market. In this sense, they provide competitive information in terms of how the competition has ultimately been positioned relatively from the consumer's perspective. This frame of reference also provides an understanding of how other brands are being interpreted and how any new introductions in the marketplace will initially be compared. This can be very valuable information for strategy purposes where *creative*, *critical*, and *reflective* marketing thinking will be required by the marketer.

Marketing Thinking Challenge 4.2: The Multiplicity of Differentiating Within a Market

This challenge is about determining how consumers might be differentiating in a market. Choose a particular market and then pick a relevant product or service category of interest. Proceed to identify the different ways those within the market could potentially be differentiating the brands. Based upon what you have determined, explain the nature of competition that is leading to the different brand perceptions.

Figure 4.11   Perception

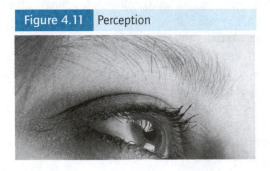

Issues With the SPOT Marketing Perspective

Nonetheless, there are problems with the segmenting-positioning-offering-targeting (SPOT) perspective. There are an infinite number of ways to conduct both segmenting and positioning in terms of available variables and concepts. With positioning and its two-dimensional space representation, it should be kept in mind that this is a simplification of something that may actually be far more involving and complicated than is being presented and, hence, may misdirect those using them. Again, it is the marketer in these cases that is attempting to do the segmenting and mapping.

The other aspect of this SPOT perspective is that it is grounded in a competitive view and is used inherently in developing **Red Ocean** strategies. The implications are that there is a tendency for "herding" in which all of the competitors are flocking together trying to keep ahead of one another but ultimately all heading in the same direction.[17] In essence, if you buy into the competitive landscape, you'll be influenced by the ways of others versus going it alone. Ultimately, it becomes a moving-against orientation, as depicted in Figure 4.13.

The two-dimensional positioning maps provide a basis for comparison but, at the same time, it is difficult not to project yourself into the map. Hence, the influence has already begun.[18] The herding phenomenon can be seen with the automobile, television/audio, airline, toothpaste, and food industries, to name a few. Over the years, it has become more and more difficult to say how one brand is really that different from another. Over this course of time, when one offers a new aspect, the others follow suit quickly afterward. It simply is a notching-up game in which the marketer believes he or she is creating meaningful difference, whereas the consumer knows otherwise.

The resulting strategies come in the form of *augmentation by addition* and *augmentation by multiplication*.[19] Toothpaste is a great example of *augmentation by addition*. In the beginning, toothpaste was simply an abrasive material like crushed bone to clean teeth. Then, around the year 1824, soap was added, and it wasn't until 1874 that it was first mass produced with a nice smell and in a jar.[20] Skipping ahead, in the 1960s came fluoride,

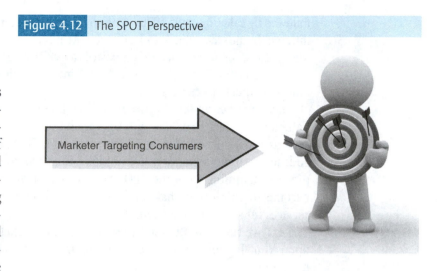

Figure 4.12 The SPOT Perspective

Marketer Targeting Consumers

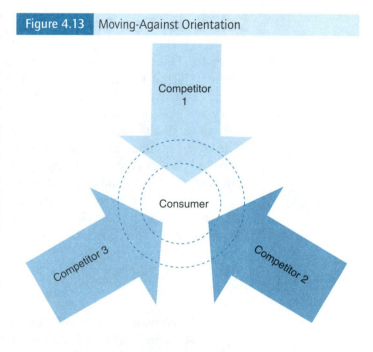

Figure 4.13 Moving-Against Orientation

Competitor 1

Consumer

Competitor 3

Competitor 2

followed by calcium in the 1980s. Over the years, the additives kept coming, along with many different brands available—Colgate, Crest, Arm & Hammer, Sensodyne, Close-up, Aim, Tom's Main, Jason, and so on. Today, toothpaste is about fresh breath, fighting tooth and gum decay, whitening, tartar control, and so on. Every time a brand comes out with something new, the others are quick to offer the same.

Augmentation by multiplication involves line extensions such as Coke with Diet Coke, Caffeine Free Coke, Diet Coke with Lemon, and so on. Other brands in the soft drink category such as Pepsi offer similar, matching extensions. These are exemplars of augmentation by addition and augmentation by multiplication, illustrating the herding phenomenon in process stemming from the SPOT perspective of marketing. The SPOT perspective has become so entrenched that you can see its effects in most if not all mature product or services categories in today's markets.

Next, we turn our attention to looking at the marketing orientations that aren't based upon knowing an a priori market structure: self-selection segmenting and one-on-one marketing.

Self-Selection Segmenting Questions

The critics of the SPOT view of marketing argue that segmentation is flawed for the following reasons: (1) It provides a static view of consumer segments in a constantly changing(volatile) society and economic climate; (2) *mutually exclusive segments* is a misnomer in that consumers are never just part of one segment and may cross back and forth to different segments in varying situations; and (3) with the advances of the Internet and communications technology, consumers are gaining more control or have greater influence with marketing activities.[21] Others have argued that segmentation typically leads to an oversimplification with too few segments and ones that are too heterogeneous to be of practical value, raising the questions of segmentation as a useful marketing strategy, and with the advent of large databases, perhaps there are alternative ways.[22] The issue may simply come down to the fact that segmentation "may not be useful in suggesting real differences in consumer behavior— differences that a firm could use"[23]

An alternative that has been suggested is *self-selection segmenting* as a marketing strategy. It stems

> from the economic concept of a "design contract" for compensating an agent who possesses more information than the agent who offers the contract. By choosing a contract, agents with more information reveal the truth about their preferences. In marketing, this "designed contract" can be deemed to be a product-price pair and the product-price line as an array of contracts offered by the firm who does not know the identity of the consumers in his market…From that array, consumers choose to buy different pairs, thus revealing what they truly value.[24]

The suggested market strategy here recognizes the *asymmetrical relationship* between the consumer and the marketer in which the consumer possesses more information than the marketer could ever determine through a segmentation analysis.

Figure 4.14   Self-Selection Segmenting Orientation

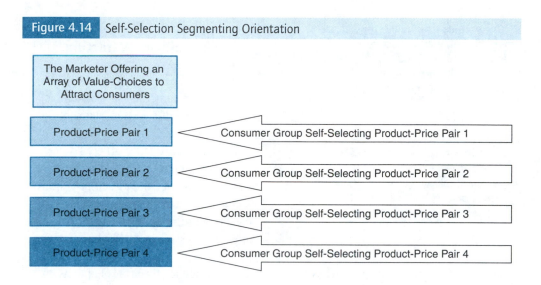

Returning to the question in the beginning of the chapter: Who is it that is segmenting the market—the marketer or the consumer? along with the corresponding question of the presumption or lack of one in terms of a market structure. By not assuming a market structure per se, a *reversal* with the primary marketing concept of *targeting* emerges.

Figure 4.15   Questioning the Reversal of Targeting—A Main Marketing Concept

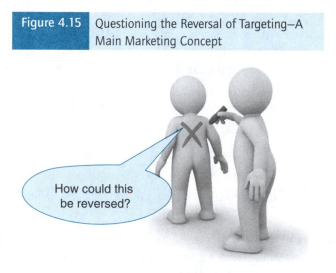

What a self-selection segmenting strategy is based upon is putting the value in the array of product or service choices versus the seeking and persuasion of consumers.

By providing valued choices, the firm could well spend less money—seeking and persuading customers. In other words, firms should closely weigh the cost of reaching out to customers against the cost of producing an array of products such that each consumer's choice is truth revealing, market-separating and that could draw the customer to the firm…[25]

> This sounds like the theme—"If you build it, they will come"—from the movie *Field of Dreams* and the building of a baseball field. Is that what this is about?

> Yes, in a similar way. It's about creating clear options offering different value. It's about accessibility. It's also about consumer empowerment.

The difference is in:

Pursuing vs. Attracting

The SPOT perspective invests in the pursuing or targeting of consumers, whereas the self-selection segmenting strategy is based upon investing in developing an attractive array of value-choices that consumers would seek out. A simple example of a self-selection segmenting strategy has been offered in the literature based upon garlic. Most grocery stores sell garlic. It comes in four basic forms—loose, preselected packets, peeled, and diced. Consumers purchasing garlic may choose among the array of options for various different reasons.

Some may not know how to choose garlic and prefer the pre-packaged option, while others may not like the smell of garlic on their hands and will choose the diced option. Still others have high time costs and do not want to waste their efforts on making a choice. Whatever the reason, the product choices have performed a major marketing function.[26]

They have effectively led to self-selection segmenting by each option possessing a distinct value and price. This strategy also allows for re–self-selection segmenting for other situations that might arise and, hence, less potential for marketing waste. This is also an example of thinking in *time* (via our 4-DS thinking)—by creating an array of value-choice options that would be appealing in different situations. The focus is on developing the array of value-choices.

The consumer accessibility and empowerment aspects are highlighted in the following strategy recommendations:

1. "Build correlation clusters between purchased products and services, and serve them up as recommendations (Amazon, Apple's Genius feature).

2. Offer networking opportunities based on self-acclaimed interests (Facebook, LinkedIn).

3. Design and provide content or a deal-alert function that automatically informs consumers about something new or interesting in the 'opted-in' interest domain of a consumer (Google Alert, Orbitz Fare Alert).

4. Enable sharing of consumer-generated content or feedback in the context of your brand (BlueCross' 'Power of the Human Voice' campaign)."[27]

In summary, the SPOT perspective is about competitors pursuing (targeting) the consumer through augmentation and so forth, and it's about a battle of persuasion with the potential for high marketing waste.[28] The self-selection segmenting option is driven by consumers seeking out the firm based upon it offering clear distinctive choices (attracting) and becomes a battle of perception, value, and accessibility. Ultimately, one's views of the marketplace structure will conceptually influence one's marketing thinking and the corresponding strategies.

Marketing Thinking Challenge 4.3: Self-Selection Segmenting

Identify three different companies that you believe to be using a self-selection segmenting strategy. Describe their strategies and explain some of their similarities and differences. Also, explain which you think would be most effective and why.

Figure 4.16   Offering a Choice

One-on-One Marketing Questions

We've seen that mass marketing and the SPOT orientation have their own strategies and logics that are based upon a particular view of the market structure (homogenous or heterogeneous). The self-selection segmenting orientation doesn't assume a market structure primarily because of the difficulties in attempting to identify such a structure but also because the strategy suggested through the self-selection segmenting doesn't require such information. In focusing on providing an array of value-choice options, the market will naturally do its own segmenting through the selection process. However, in creating and maintaining the array of value-choice options, the marketer is still in the position of learning from consumers and, as time goes on, continuing to learn from them in an effort to serve them better.

This is where we are able to see the alternative perspective, from the competitive orientation, come into view. The alternative perspective is the *compatibility orientation*. As consumers engage in their self-selection-segmenting consumption, the marketer still relies on marketing research. However, it has more to do with *who* is buying which option and *why* they are buying that particular option. This sounds similar to the questions raised in segmentation research, but the difference is that the information is being acquired during or after a purchase and not before, as with segmentation studies in general. The research

Figure 4.17   One-to-One Marketing

Accessibility

Aligning Directly

Consumer

Compatibility

Marketer

Relevance

Real Time

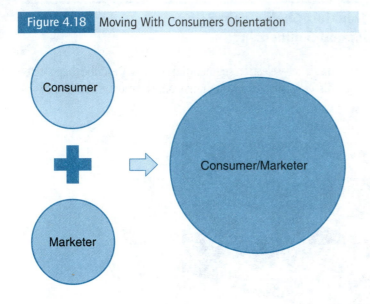

Figure 4.18 Moving With Consumers Orientation

and subsequent strategies are already *aligning* with the consumers' practices as they are occurring and, hence, are grounded in a compatibility orientation from the onset. This is highlighted to an even greater degree with *one-to-one marketing*.

One-to-one marketing has emerged primarily as a consequence of advances in technology. In essence, the marketer is able to market directly to individuals and tailor offerings in real time. As consumers make purchases, the information is stored in databases and processed for marketing purposes. The *compatibility* orientation is founded on the marketer aligning more directly with individuals through developing a reciprocal relationship with the consumer based upon accessibility (via technology), aligning (through the exchange of information, real-time individualized marketing, and predictive analytics), and relevance. See Figure 4.17.

In contrast, *targeting* is grounded in a competitive perspective and operationalized through the SPOT logics. While the traditional SPOT perspective is well entrenched in the practice of marketing today, there appears to be a shift toward alternative orientations that opens the doors for new forms and practices of marketing. In a general sense, the earlier views grounded in a competitive orientation involve marketing that is directed toward *moving against* others in the market place as illustrated through the augmentation strategies, whereas emerging orientations seem to be based on a type of marketing oriented toward *moving with* consumers and less about competition. See Figure 4.18. *Attracting* implicitly is a *moving with* consumer perspective involving value creation, accessibility, and empowerment. *Compatibility* explicitly is *moving with* consumers through aligning, relevance, and accessibility, all in real time. The potential implications are that those who are able to truly move continuously with consumers will be the market leaders of tomorrow.

Marketing Thinking in Practice:
Predictive Analytics

The field of *predictive analytics* is involved with developing software to analyze the vast amount of consumer information to facilitate one-to-one marketing. While traditional marketing at the retail level had been offering across-the-board discounts or deals aimed at categories of customers, with the advent of this technology, industry experts are expecting more retailers to move toward more individualized offerings.[29] Examples include Sam's Club eValues program offering bargains tailored to members.

On a recent evening, for instance, Angela Otero stopped by the Sam's Club in Secaucus and printed out four pages of eValues offers at a bright green kiosk near the front door, including $50 off a plasma television, $3 off a 30-pack toilet paper and $2.50 off a box of meatless burgers. Ms. Otero said she had used eValues since it started in August and found that the discounts covered "the majority of things I want. It's basically my own grocery list."

Linda Vytlacil, vice president for member insights and innovation at Sam's Club, said coupons normally had a response rate of 1 percent or 2 percent. With eValue, she said, as many as 20 percent to 30 percent of eligible customers collect the discount they offered.

…"There's no clipping coupons," Ms. Vytlacil said, adding that eValues offered "highly individualized relevant offers specific to each Plus member. All they have to do is purchase the product, and the savings are automatically applied at checkout." Like other membership clubs, shoppers must present a card at checkout.

The eValues program is the latest iteration in the fast-growing field known as predictive analytics, which uses vast amounts of data to spot trends and anticipate consumer behavior.[30]

Some other examples include eHarmony for matchmaking; eLoyalty analyzes customer calls to predict which customers might cancel and then tailors a call-back message to attempt to keep them from canceling; and CVS Caremark uses its ExtraCare loyalty program to individualize discounts. Sam's Club eValues has even incorporated FICO scores to aid in the prediction of the time-frame within which customers will buy. Anticipating consumer behavior through predictive analytics is an example of the *sensing and responding* concept discussed in Chapter 3, which will be examined further in Chapter 6. The strategy logic being employed is:

"If you get more relevant to shoppers, you get more loyalty, you get more business," said Dave Carlson, chief executive of Relevance Partners, which provides software to retailers to glean consumer insight from shopping data.[31]

| Figure 4.19 | Predictive Analytics |

The compatibility orientation through technology is about aligning with customers more directly along the lines of being relevant in real time. For organizations that don't have the predictive analytics technology capabilities to fully capitalize on one-to-one marketing, self-selection segmenting is a step toward the one-to-one option but wouldn't be as effective in that predictive analytics enable the marketer to offer more on-point, individualized, flexible (adaptive) marketing in real time. Further, it is being done under the competitive radar since the marketing is done at the individual level.

Marketing Thinking Challenge 4.4: Predictive Analytics

Research the topic of predictive analytics and identify what its capability and use are currently. Based upon what you find, what new marketing strategies does it suggest and when would it be applicable?

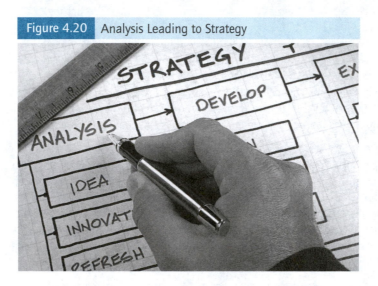

| Figure 4.20 | Analysis Leading to Strategy |

Summary

- This chapter extended the marketplace structure discussion developed in Chapter 3 by examining the two related questions of (1) Is the marketplace homogenous or heterogeneous? and (2) Who is structuring the marketplace—the marketer or the consumer? The *bound* structure perspective discussed in Chapter 3 relates to the first question and to the marketer doing the structuring in the second question. These perspectives of the marketplace structure are being operationalized through a competitive, SPOT perspective of marketing.

- The influential concepts of segmenting, positioning, configuring a marketing mix, and targeting are all related to the *bound* structure perspective, with the marketer doing the structuring. Segmentation and positioning were discussed, along with their associated logics representing the practice of traditional marketing via the SPOT perspective and their related difficulties.

- The strategies of *augmentation by addition* and *augmentation by multiplication* were a result of the *bound* structure perspective, leading to the means for competition. These strategies were characterized as being based upon a *moving-against* orientation.

- If one doesn't assume an a priori marketplace structure, the strategies of *self-selection segmenting* and *one-to-one marketing* are plausible options. Self-selection as a strategy is based upon creating an array of value options such that the consumer, in making a choice, is also engaging in a self-selection segmenting process. One-to-one marketing as a strategy involves aligning, relevance, and accessibility, all in real time. Both self-selection and one-to-one marketing were based upon a compatibility perspective with consumers and, hence, were characterized as a *moving-with* consumer orientation.

- Predictive analytics were being used in conjunction with a one-to-one marketing strategy for the purposes of being able to be relevant in a real-time capacity. Examples were provided.

Case: Red Bull—What Does the Future Hold?

As the story goes, while on a business trip to Thailand in 1982, Dietrich Mateschitz, an Austrian working as an international marketing director for Blendax (a toothpaste company), tried an energy drink called Krating Daeng to combat the effects of jet lag. The translation for Krating Daeng is "Red Bull," and it was developed by Thailand resident Chaleo Yoovidhya. Mateschitz saw the potential for the drink and entered into an agreement with Yoovidhya to launch the Red Bull company in 1984. The European version of the product wasn't made available until 1987 after being modified by TC Pharmaceutical (a Blendax licensee) for a European market and being approved by the health ministries.[32] It was first introduced to an Austrian market and then made its way to Germany, the United Kingdom, and the United States in 1997.[33]

What is Red Bull? It is an energy drink, which represents a niche in the global soft drink market. Its ingredients include taurine, glucuronlactone, caffeine, B vitamins, sucrose, and glucose, and the sugar-free version contains phenylalanine instead of the sucrose and glucose.[34] Red Bull Cola contains coca leaves, which show up in the drink as traces of cocaine. As an energy drink, a caffeine drink, it is promoted with the slogans "Red Bull vitalizes body and mind" and "Red Bull gives you wiiings!"[35] The description from the Red Bull website describes the drink as follows:

> Red Bull® Energy Drink is a functional beverage with a unique combination of ingredients. It has been specially developed for times of increased mental and physical exertion.
>
> Red Bull® Energy Drink vitalizes body and mind.
>
> Red Bull® Energy Drink
> —increases performance
> —increases concentration and reaction speed
> —improves vigilance
> —improves the emotional status
> —stimulates metabolism
>
> Red Bull's effects are appreciated throughout the world by top athletes, busy professionals, active students and drivers on long journeys.

The criticisms for the drink include: Energy drinks should not be used for hydration (e.g., by athletes);[36] they may cause cardiovascular problems, especially with those with coronary artery disease; they shouldn't be used by those under stress, with high blood pressure, or established atherosclerotic disease; there is potential for overdose, causing postural orthostatic tachycardia syndrome (e.g., in young athletes); they may cause death; and, in the case of Red Bull Cola, they may have traces of cocaine.[37] Red Bull has been banned in several countries, including France and Denmark, and is considered a medicine in Norway.[38] Some have referred to Red Bull as "Liquid Cocaine"[39] or "Liquid Viagra."[40] Red Bull has countered by stating that the product is safe for healthy individuals and if used in moderation. It also has stated that the level of caffeine is similar to the amount in a regular cup of coffee. To justify the safety claims, the company states, "Red Bull must be safe, as it was felt the only way Red Bull could have such substantial global sales is if various health authorities had concluded the drink safe to consumer."[41]

The primary market is the 14- to 29-year-old group, males and females, worldwide.[42, 43] To appeal to this global group, the marketing has been to associate the brand with events that the company believes the target market would view as being "cool," trendy, and on the edge. At the same time, the Red Bull slogan and the events it sponsors are meant to associate the brand with energy, danger, the youth culture (e.g., being rebellious), and escapism.[44, 45] "For Red Bull's target audience, being authentic means being a bit irreverent, a bit antiestablishment, and every bit different from your parents"[46] References to "liquid cocaine" and "liquid Viagra" may actually be enhancing the Red Bull's image with the target market.

The marketing includes student brand managers (using student trendsetters to put on Red Bull parties with free samples); identifying and being a part of hot spots (e.g., bars, parties); sponsoring or putting on extreme sporting events (e.g., cliff diving, surfing, Formula 1 racing, skateboarding, Red Bull Flugtag); sponsoring high-performance athletes; quirky ads (e.g., advertising on TV shows like *T.F.I. Friday* and in magazines like *Time Out* and *Men's Health*; advertising on campaign cars (e.g., a Formula 1 car and a Cobra helicopter); creating videogames and product placement in videogames; developing followings on YouTube, Facebook, and Twitter; posting events on the company website; sports clothing; team ownerships (e.g., New York Red Bulls, Red Bull Racing Teams, RB Leipzig soccer, EC Red Bull Salzburg Austrian hockey team); and using "consumer educators" (roaming the streets looking for people with "low energy" to give them free samples and to educate them about Red Bull).[47, 48, 49, 50] All are meant to be where the action is taking place and to keep the "buzz" and "viral" marketing going. Red Bull also uses premium pricing to convey the quality of the product.

While the company has used and continues to use a full-court-press marketing strategy, using a basketball figure of speech, there are issues that may cause problems ahead for Red Bull. These problems exist in several forms: (1) While Red Bull has the lead in the energy drink category with a 60% to 70% market share,[51] Coca Cola, Pepsi, and others are in pursuit with their own energy drinks (e.g., think V Energy Drink and Coke's version, Mother). Can Red Bull maintain its lead? (2) With more options available in the market, there may be a blurring effect in which all energy drinks start to look the same, and Red Bull could lose its "point of difference." Or the brand may simply lose its edge and become "stale." (3) The health concerns are still out there and may become amplified if bloggers start to take issue with these drinks and become more concerned with health in general and, more particularly, with childhood obesity and diabetes. (4) The target audience may move on as it ages. (5) A limited product line could be a risky strategy if things change.[52]

What do you see as the most likely changes to occur in the market for energy drinks? Provide examples and an explanation. What marketing advice would you offer to Red Bull for now and the future? Explain why?

References

1. Smith, Wendall R. (1956), "Product Differentiation and Market Segmentation as Alternative Marketing Strategies," *Journal of Marketing*, 21 (July), 3–8.
2. Smith, Wendall R. (1956), "Product Differentiation and Market Segmentation as Alternative Marketing Strategies," *Journal of Marketing*, 21 (July), p. 5.
3. Moorthy, K. Sridhar (1984), "Market Segmentation, Self-Selection, and Product Line Design," *Marketing Science*, 3 (4, Fall), 288–307.
4. Ng, Irene C. L. (2005), "Differentiation, Self-Selection and Revenue Management," *Journal of Revenue and Pricing*, July, 7.
5. Ng, Irene C. L. (2005), "Differentiation, Self-Selection and Revenue Management," *Journal of Revenue and Pricing*, July, p. 9.
6. AMA Definition of Marketing, American Marketing Association, www.marketingpower.com/Community/ARC/Pages/Additional/Definition/default.aspx
7. Webster, A. Merriam (1974), *New Collegiate Dictionary*, Springfield, MA: G. & C. Merriam Company.
8. Keith, Robert J. (1960), "The Marketing Revolution," *Journal of Marketing*, 24 (July–August), 37.
9. Smith, Wendall R. (1956), "Product Differentiation and Market Segmentation as Alternative Marketing Strategies," *Journal of Marketing*, 21 (July), 3–8.
10. Borden, Neil H. (1964), "The Concept of the Marketing Mix," *Journal of Advertising Research*, 4 (June), 2–7.
11. Frey, Albert W. (1956), *The Effective Marketing Mix*, Hanover, NH: Amos Tuck Business School.
12. Borden, Neil H. (1964), "The Concept of the Marketing Mix," *Journal of Advertising Research*, June, 2–7.
13. Kotler, Philip, and Kevin Lane (2009), *Marketing Management*, Upper Saddle River, NJ: Pearson Prentice Hall, 228.
14. www.netmba.com/marketing/market/segmentation/
15. Shrimp, Terence A., and Alican Kavas (1984), "The Theory of Reasoned Action Applied to Coupon Usage," *Journal of Consumer Research*, 11 (December), 795–809.
16. Gorn, Gerald J. (1982), "The Effects of Advertising on Choice Behavior: A Classical Conditioning Approach," *Journal of Marketing*, 46 (Winter), 94–101.
17. Moon, Youngme (2010), *Different: Escaping the Competitive Herd—Succeeding in a World Where Conformity Reigns But Exceptions Rule*, New York: Crown Publishing.
18. Moon, Youngme (2010), *Different: Escaping the Competitive Herd—Succeeding in a World Where Conformity Reigns But Exceptions Rule*, New York: Crown Publishing, 25.
19. Moon, Youngme (2010), *Different: Escaping the Competitive Herd—Succeeding in a World Where Conformity Reigns But Exceptions Rule*, New York: Crown Publishing, 54.
20. www.parentingtoddlers.com/toothpaste-history.html
21. Fassnacht, Michael (2009), "The Death of Consumer Segmentation? Rethinking a Traditional Marketing Tool," *Advertising Age*, April, 13.
22. Stewart, David W. (1991), "Consumer Self-Selection and Segments of One: The Growing Role of Consumers in Segmentation," in *Advances in Consumer Research*, Vol. 18, ed. Rebecca H. Holman and Michael R. Solomon, Provo, UT: Association for Consumer Research, 179–86.

23. Moorthy, K. Sridhar (1984), "Market Segmentation, Self-Selection, and Product Line Design," *Marketing Science*, 3 (4, Fall), 288–307.

24. Ng, Irene, C. L. (2005), "Does Direct Marketing Need to Have a Direction?," *Marketing Intelligence & Planning*, 23 (6/7), 631.

25. Ng, Irene, C. L. (2005), "Does Direct Marketing Need to Have a Direction?," *Marketing Intelligence & Planning*, 23 (6/7), 632.

26. Ng, Irene, C. L. (2005), "Does Direct Marketing Need to Have a Direction?," *Marketing Intelligence & Planning*, 23 (6/7), 630.

27. Fassnacht, Michael (2009), "The Death of Consumer Segmentation? Rethinking a Traditional Marketing Tool," *Advertising Age*, April, 13.

28. Ng, Irene, C. L. (2005), "Does Direct Marketing Need to Have a Direction?," *Marketing Intelligence & Planning*, 23 (6/7), 634.

29. Martin, Andrew (2010), "Sam's Club Personalizes Discounts for Buyers," *New York Times*, May 20, www.nytimes.com/2010/05/31/business/31loyalty.html?pagewanted=all

30. Martin, Andrew (2010), "Sam's Club Personalizes Discounts for Buyers," *The New York Times*, May 20, www.nytimes.com/2010/05/31/business/31loyalty.html?pagewanted=all

31. Martin, Andrew (2010), "Sam's Club Personalizes Discounts for Buyers," *The New York Times*, May 20, www.nytimes.com/2010/05/31/business/31loyalty.html?pagewanted=all

32. http://en.wikipedia.org/wiki/Red_Bull

33. www.scribd.com/doc/19489027/Red-Bulls-Marketing-Mix

34. "Position Statement and Recommendations for the Use of Energy Drinks by Young Athletes," *National Federation of State High School Associations*, http://en.wikipedia.org/wiki/Red_Bull

35. www.redbullusa.com/cs/Satellite/en_US/Products/Company-021242755317296

36. www.nfhs.org/search.aspx?searchtext=energy%20drinks

37. http://en.wikipedia.org/wiki/Red_Bull

38. www.trcb.com/business/marketing/redbull-marketing-strategy-7375.htm

39. www.trcb.com/business/marketing/redbull-marketing-strategy-7375.htm

40. http://findarticles.com/p/articles/mi_m0BDW/is_22_42/ai_75286777/

41. http://en.wikipedia.org/wiki/Red_Bull

42. www.utalkmarketing.com/Pages/Article.aspx?ArticleID=4274&Title=How_Red_Bull_invented_the_%E2%80%98cool%E2%80%99_factor

43. www.sosemarketing.com/?p=351

44. www.drawert.com/red_bull_7.php

45. www.scribd.com/doc/19489027/Red-Bulls-Marketing-Mix

46. Rodgers, Anni Layne (2001), "It's a (Red) Bull Market After All," *Fast Company*, September 30, www.fastcompany.com/articles/2001/10/redbull.html

47. www.sosemarketing.com/?p=351

48. http://marketingpractice.blogspot.com/2008/08/red-bull-it-gives-you-wiings.html

49. www.drawert.com/red_bull_7.php

50. http://en.wikipedia.org/wiki/Red_Bull

51. www.trcb.com/business/marketing/redbull-marketing-strategy-7375.htm

52. www.scribd.com/doc/19489027/Red-Bulls-Marketing-Mix

CHAPTER 5

Thinking Through Difference

The Nature of the Marketplace and Consumption

Decompression Exercise

Before beginning the chapter, focus on Figure 5.1. Water has a very soothing effect. How does the image make you feel?

Figure 5.1 A Ripple

Chapter Introduction

In pursuing thinking agility by utilizing and developing our 4-DS thinking across the chapters, we have opened up our spectrum for different forms of marketing thinking that can be employed for strategy purposes. Chapters 3 and 4 raised questions to consider about marketplace structure and how different forms of thinking result in different strategies. For example, in Chapter 3, the structure-*bound* perspective of the marketplace led to a **Red Ocean** strategy, grounded in a competitive orientation. Conversely, the *creating* structure perspective of the marketplace led to a **Blue Ocean** strategy based on creating unique value, potentially resulting in a competition-free marketplace. Chapter 4 continued the inquiry into marketplace structure by considering how one views who is segmenting or structuring the marketplace—the marketer, the consumer, or others (as we will see later). Assuming the marketer is doing the segmenting or structuring led to the traditional SPOT way of marketing thinking, involving strategies of competing for target markets (targeting) through forms of persuasion (e.g., advertising). In contrast, assuming the consumer is segmenting or structuring the marketplace led to self-selection segmenting strategies. From this perspective, the marketer attracts consumers by creating an array of value choices from which the consumer engages in self-selection segmenting. These different forms of thinking benefit our thinking agility by keeping us open to recognizing and considering them along with instilling a willingness to appropriate from them as called for.

To constantly be open and expanding our view requires effort and an inclination toward questioning things, even at a very fundamental level. In contrast, our natural tendency is toward closure and accepted views of things in the form of the familiar, which requires less effort and no questioning. One of the issues marketers have to deal with is that there is a tendency to jump onto a narrow view of what is going on in the marketplace and to develop strategy from this constricted perspective. Constricted, narrow views are characteristic of fixed thinking or fixedness. In contrast, thinking agility requires developing a more open, expanded view to be in the position to have the means by which to be agile in strategy within the marketplace. To counter the tendency toward closure requires a thinking agility strategy—a questioning strategy. One such questioning strategy is to simply *step back and ask very fundamental questions* about (1) how we think about things, (2) what we are doing based upon these views, and then, (3) to look for other views and means that might also be considered to accomplish the tasks at hand. It is a means to *unfreeze* the familiar, to open new forms of thinking, to move from what is known to what is unknown, and to be able to see other possibilities for new strategies.

Asking Fundamental Questions to Create Openings for New Views

Returning to our discussion of marketplace structure, what do we really know about this structure? The discussions in Chapters 3 and 4 suggest that there may be much more going on with this structuring than we are aware of, and without questioning our assumptions, we would still not be open to the possibility for other views that could very well lead to interesting strategic insights. In this chapter, we will apply the thinking agility strategy to step back even further than what we have done so far to ask about the structuring of the marketplace. What is being structured? How is the structuring occurring? Are there certain parameters with the structuring of the marketplace? And how do these parameters affect strategy?

To do so, let's look at the issue from an aggregate level by considering the degree of consumption occurring worldwide and the rate at which it is increasing.

The estimated one billion people who live in developed countries have a relative per capita consumption rate of 32. Most of the world's other 5.5 billion people constitute the developing world, with relative per capita consumption rates below 32, mostly down toward 1.

…People who consume little want to enjoy the high-consumption lifestyle. Governments of developing countries make an increase in living standards a primary goal of national policy. And tens of millions of people in the developing world seek the first-world lifestyle on their own, by emigrating, especially to the United States and Western Europe, Japan and Australia. Each such transfer of a person to a high-consumption country raises world consumption rates, even though most immigrants don't succeed immediately in multiplying their consumption by 32.

Among the developing countries that are seeking to increase per capita consumption rates at home, China stands out. It has the world's fastest growing economy, and there are 1.3 billion Chinese, four times the United States population. The world is already running out of resources, and it will do so even sooner if China achieves American-level consumption rates. Already, China is competing with us for oil and metals on world markets.

Per capita consumption rates in China are still about 11 times below ours, but let's suppose they rise to our level. Let's also make things easy by imagining that nothing else happens to increase world consumption—that is, no other country increases its consumption, all national populations (including China's) remain unchanged and immigration ceases. China's catching up alone would roughly double world consumption rates. Oil consumption would increase by 106 percent, for instance, and world metal consumption by 94 percent.[1]

Fundamentally, what is being consumed with all products and/or services?

Wow, that's a big one! So, it would be something common to all things. Right?

Yes, but give it some thought. It has strategic implications in understanding the nature of the marketplace, marketing, consumers, and competition.

The above discourse indicates that there is a lot of consumption occurring worldwide and at an increasing rate, all of which is putting a strain on world resources. What is driving the accelerating rate of consumption beyond simply population growth? What is behind the need to pursue a high-consumption lifestyle? And, at a very fundamental level, have you ever thought about what is actually being consumed through all of this consumption? Consider the question asked by the character on the previous page.

As a marketing student or professional, have you ever thought about this fundamental question? If not, you have been utilizing a transcendent perspective of what is occurring by circumscribing the issue without explicitly addressing it—it is what it is, without saying what it is. The transcendent view suggests that it is beyond comprehension. But is it? We all engage in consumption in one form or another constantly. Certainly, we should know what we are consuming and why we are compelled to engage in this behavior. To understand the nature of this behavior might also help explain where marketing fits in. Perhaps the problem we are experiencing with this question is that it is about something familiar.

The Familiarity Paradox

It may be difficult to answer the consumption question right away is because it is obscured to some degree by the familiarity obstacle discussed in Chapter 2. You have run up against a thinking obstacle. There's a paradox associated with the familiar. The *familiarity paradox*—while we gravitate to the familiar, we also tend to overlook it because of it being familiar. This suggests that we gravitate to that which we know, and yet once it becomes accepted as the known, it receives less scrutiny or none at all and, hence, gets overlooked. To answer the question, we are looking for something we are all very familiar with, something that is fundamental to all of us. What is fundamental to all of us?

| Figure 5.2 | Taking a Moment to Reflect on the Question |

All things are of *difference*.

Stop and think about this. What does this really mean?

A Disciplinary Perspective to the Question

Taking a wider view of the question, whether you want to think about it at a metaphysical, onto-logical, epistemological, methodological, meteorological, psychological, physiological, sociological, anthropological, biological, scientific, or other level, everything is of difference. All disciplines are attempting to map out differences from their perspective—for example, psychology concerns the study of the mind and behavior, which may involve differences held in beliefs or differences in memory that can affect behavior. With meteorology, the science that deals with the study of the atmosphere and its phenomena of weather, the meteorologist is attempting to understand and explain weather or changes in the atmosphere in all of its forms or differences. Examples include tornados, rain, wind, clouds, sunshine, temperatures, atmospheric pressures, and so on. Similarly, consumer behavior as a discipline related to marketing has appropriated many other disciplinary perspectives such as psychology, sociology, economics, history, anthropology, statistics, and more for the purposes of explaining differences in consumer behavior.

What is fundamental to all of these disciplines is that they are all attempting to understand difference as it unfolds—that is, they are all studying difference creation from their unique vantage points. Even if they don't refer to it as a study of difference, what they are studying is difference and its creation process. Yet there is a paradoxical aspect to these efforts in that as they study difference, they are participating in the process of difference creation at the same time, creating new differences along the way—in terms of new understandings, concepts, theories, methods, and/or strategies. We are all a part of the phenomenon of difference, and to study it in all of its forms is a study of us in terms of understanding what we are made up of and our nature.

A Consumer Perspective to the Question

People are a product of this process of difference creation and, as such, represent different forms of difference themselves. Being a part of this process means that we are all becoming different in time (e.g., going from being young to becoming old, getting a new haircut). Difference is what we know; it is familiar and therefore easily overlooked. From the very beginnings of time, everything has always involved difference creation. What's unique to our times is that the forms of difference creation we seek involve products and services and their marketing. These differences could involve simply satisfying a hunger need with the purchase of food, facilitating an aspiration to be more like the images seen in advertisements, or solving a pressing problem at hand with the purchase of a product. All of these pertain to going from one state to another—that is, creating a difference and the process is ongoing. What this means is that at a very fundamental level, consumers are seeking, creating, and consuming difference constantly in its many forms, utilizing products and services in their difference-creation process.

A Thinking Perspective to the Question

As you may recall, discussed in Chapter 1 was the relationship between thinking and questioning. When you are questioning, thinking is underway. When you stop questioning, you've stopped thinking. Chapter 1 characterized the following situation:

> Today's markets are more dynamic than ever before. Financial upheavals, changing demographics, advances in technology, environmental concerns, and an increasing rate of innovations represent the landscape in which marketers conduct business. Each alone is challenging enough, but when combined, the task seems insurmountable. ... Instead, what appears on the scene is a different type of marketer, ... resourceful, insightful, and able to navigate effectively across difficult landscapes. Exemplars include Steve Jobs of Apple, Jeff Bezos of Amazon, Pierre Omidyar of eBay, and A. G. Laffey of P&G. Each has had a major impact on their markets, changing and

redefining the nature of competition to the benefit of their organizations. ... innovators such as these were studied to reveal their "Innovator's DNA"[2] to understand how they develop "ground breaking new ideas."[3] What made their thinking different from others? And could it be learned? The answer is a resounding *yes*. ... To be a skilled marketer today requires a particular type of thinking, which is what this textbook explores.

These innovators have tapped into an understanding of difference, a thinking that's akin to the nature of difference and, hence, are able to participate more effectively in their markets as a result. How the innovators have tapped into the process of difference is through their questioning nature and the constant search for new associations or new forms of difference. The searching for new associations is also a form of questioning and, as discussed in Chapter 1, involves creative thinking. It is a question of what could be. Ironically, thinking is about understanding difference while also being involved in the difference-creation process itself in terms of creating new understandings, new concepts, new practices, and/or new strategies.

The Significant Role Questions Play in the Process

This next question is a question about *thinking about thinking*. What are questions about?

Difference?

Questions lead to answers. Answers are another form of difference. Is it this or is it that. But there's a funny thing about questions. They are open and closed at the same time—closed in the sense that questions are about something—an issue, a concern, or something else—but open to possibilities that could momentarily address the issue or the concern. The funny part of questioning is that the answers don't satisfy the questions completely and, therefore, the questions remain open for further exploration and new answers. Our questions are never completely satisfied. They are to be used again to take up their difference-creation role. Questions can be used over and over, and therein lies their utility. Each time different answers are possible, different differences are possible. What this means is that the phenomenon of difference creation repeats over and over through our questioning, producing new differences every moment, day in and day out. This is the way of difference in that it is continuing.

Yet difference occurs not only through our questioning. In reading this, you have changed, and you're different, a little older. It may have started to rain while you read this chapter, or perhaps it just got windy. Or the stock market went up or down. Or you just received a text message. In each instance, difference has occurred. The marketplace is also a composition of difference and a dynamic one at that—continuing, through the difference-creation process involving constant change, reconfiguring its composition each step of the way. In gaining a better understanding of this process of difference, perhaps, we'd be able to think more like the innovators previously mentioned and be better at developing strategy.

Returning to our initial chapter questions of What is being structured? How is the structuring occurring? Are there certain parameters with the structuring of the marketplace? And how do these parameters affect strategy? At this point, we can say that what is being structured are the differences being created through the difference-creation process and that this process is ongoing in that it is constantly repeating, creating new differences every moment. In contrast, think about how things would be if this process were to stop. For one, time would stop. Consequently and relatively speaking, with each new difference created, subsequently all other forms of existing differences are changed in the process as well, through the ongoing structuring of the difference process. This will be elaborated on later in the chapter.

We can also identify the dynamic source of the marketplace, which comes from the difference-creation process, operationalized through its *repetition*. In other words, what makes the marketplace dynamic is the repetition of the ongoing difference-creation process. As we'll see later on in the chapter, the repetition of difference is critical to understanding the nature of the difference-creation process and what it means to consumers and to marketing strategy.

Now let us address the question of who is structuring the marketplace—the marketer, the consumer, or others? All things, including each of us, play a part in its structuring, being elements within. So the answer is all things affect the marketplace structuring—people, weather, cosmic events, and so forth. Similarly, if there are more than 7 billion people in the world, this suggests the vast scope of ongoing structuring occurring, which also raises the question of the role marketing strategy plays in affecting the structuring of the marketplace. This is also examined further later in the chapter. Next, we'll examine the marketplace parameters stemming from the difference-creation process.

A Difference Perspective of the Marketplace

The landscape the marketer confronts is a challenging one, and it is important for the marketer to possess the best possible view of the lay of the land. But what makes the marketplace so challenging? There are certain parameters of difference that contribute to the challenge, which the marketer should be aware of to be in the position of thinking through the issues to be confronted and to develop new ways of thinking as a consequence.[4] They are presented in Figure 5.3.

Figure 5.3 Parameters of Difference Shaping the Marketplace

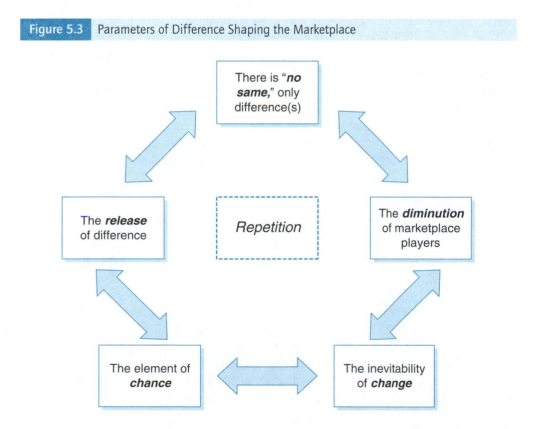

The *Repetition*...of Difference Creation

The significance in understanding the nature of difference or this difference-creation process is to recognize that the phenomenon is repeating constantly.[5] Through its *repetition*, the other parameters appear—that is, there is *"no same,"* there is a *diminution* of marketplace players, there is *change*, there is an element of *chance*, and there is a *release* of difference as well. All of the parameters are interrelated and are outcomes of the repetition of the difference-creation process. Each of these will be explained in turn.

But first, let's look at the *repetition* parameter to see what it means to the marketer. The only constant is the repetition of difference creation. All other things are in flux, meaning they are not permanent or static in any sense. Take, for example, consumer satisfaction, which we discussed in Chapter 2. One of the issues raised in our previous discussion was that satisfaction as a concept is based upon a rear-view perspective, meaning that the vantage point is on what has already occurred—Did we satisfy our customers? This is what is referred to as a *post hoc* perspective. As such, it doesn't explicitly recognize that the consumption itself has changed the consumer, potentially affecting future such experiences. Each consumer event is a form of difference while causing a new form of difference to materialize in the process—that is, the consumer is a different consumer as result of a (dis)satisfactory consumption experience.

Using another example, target market profiles that were discussed in Chapter 4, these profiles are static in nature, characterizing consumers with surrogate forms of representations. As previously discussed, these characterizations tend to be from the marketer's perspective in terms of which variables are chosen to profile the target market. They mask the dynamic nature of consumers through their overly simplified presentation, and ultimately, they turn the marketer's attention and thinking toward the competition versus focusing on the consumer. The SPOT approach to marketing is not based an understanding of the repetition occurring within the marketplace and, as such, can be misleading to practitioners.

What is needed is to first recognize the repetition occurring in the marketplace. Then, conceive of ways of thinking about this phenomenon and ways in which to participate. In general, a thinking agility perspective is consistent with the repetition of difference because the thinking is open to the new forms of difference as they are developing or occurring. In particular, the *co-marketing* perspective discussed across the chapters is one such way of thinking about this repetition by centering the thinking externally, where the difference creation is occurring, which should be a concern to the marketer. This perspective will be elaborated over the chapters. Let's next consider the "*no same*" parameter and how this is an outcome of the repetition of difference.

The *"No Same"* Parameter

It has been stated before that all things are of difference. This is highlighted through the parameters and, more particularly, with the parameter that states that there is "*no same*," only difference(s). Each repetition of difference involves a new permutation of the difference-creation process, which involves creating new space and time, which creates the division or separation between things. In the land of difference, which the marketplace is, everything is different.

The notion of the *same* stems from language but isn't empirically evidenced in the same way as with difference. The word *same* simply is used to help in understanding what we mean by the word *difference*. But it should be understood that everything is different, and this is an absolute. For example, two blank sheets of paper may look the *same*, but in fact they are different, separated by time, space, and material. No two sheets of paper are identical and, hence, all things are different or of difference.

Now, this doesn't say that the *same* can't be a marketing concept used in marketing, such as through the notions of quality control or marketing to confuse consumers that two brands are the *same*, but the *same* as an empirical entity doesn't exist other than as a concept or notion. It is important to separate what is tangible (difference[s]) from the intangible (the *same*) so we're not misleading ourselves.

From a thinking agility perspective, this infers that all marketing strategies are to be viewed as being different and that thinking in terms of differentiation or the process of differentiation is more consistent with the repetition of difference occurring in the marketplace.

The *Diminution* Parameter

At the same time, the marketer isn't alone in the marketplace. There are many, many interrelated constituents, some direct and others indirect. Each has its unique perspective and interests or points of difference(s). If you were to start from the very beginning to build up to a marketplace and started with some singular element (a singular form of difference) and built it up to the level of differences found in the marketplace, it would be unfathomable. The direct effects that one marketer can have on a marketplace become potentially fewer and fewer as the market size increases and, hence, we see the diminution of the marketplace *players* parameter.

This view is compounded even further when the *difference-creation process* and its *repetition* are factored in. With each repetition permutation, the outcome is not knowable. This suggests that marketers shouldn't assume control of the direction of the marketplace but should be more active participants in trying to nudge the market, consumers, in certain directions in their difference-creation processes where the outcome isn't predetermined. Here, the marketer needs to think in terms of an ongoing process with a moving target. The marketer can be a part of the process, not to think it in terms of controlling it but in terms of participating and developing a more agile understanding of what the process is about. This is where a *co-marketing* (collaborative and participative marketing) perspective gains it sensibilities and is developed throughout the chapters. Instead of thinking in terms of the here and now, that is, the present forms of difference, the marketer needs to be thinking about being a part of creating the new associations, the new forms of difference, because the movement is always toward something different from the present.

In this way, the marketer is always mindful that the market could turn in an unexpected way (a different form of differentiating), and the marketer would be more prone to take additional actions. Also, to assume control over something like a marketplace is a thinking obstacle that creates a blind spot for unexpected change that the marketer does not look for or anticipate.

The *Change* and *Chance* Parameters

As a marketplace of difference, difference is repeating, creating new differences continuously. These new differences are in the form of *change*, and with change, there is always the element of chance. *Chance* is a result of the repetition permutations involving the interrelationships of all other forms of existing differences as they are in their difference-creation process. As such, all are interrelated, causing a cascading effect throughout the marketplace. Think about the events that lead up to the financial crisis in 2008 through 2009 that affected the banks, automobile manufacturers, mortgages, and unemployment. There may have been signs of trouble on the horizon, but the unfolding outcomes were not knowable. Such signs represent the beginnings of new forms of difference unfolding.

Both change and chance play into the diminution aspect of the marketplace as well. As discussed in Chapter 1, change and chance are also elements involved in thinking in time.

Time is a form of difference as well. What this suggests is that *the marketer should anticipate change and expect the unexpected (i.e., the element of chance).* Here, thinking agility is vital to being open to the horizon of change and having a wide enough view to possess an understanding of some of the possibilities.

The *Release* Parameter

Through the repetition of difference, new differences come about through change and chance but also through the release of difference (undifferentiation). With change comes new forms of difference in which existing forms are transformed through the process of differentiating and undifferentiating—which occurs simultaneously. Several things are occurring within the difference-creation process. The difference-creation process is repeating and creating new differences constantly while creating a frame of reference for the differences being created.

For example, with each new innovation introduced into the marketplace, a new form of difference is being introduced that simultaneously changes the positions (or meanings) of all others products in the marketplace. Consider how something (e.g., a product) goes from being new to old. It could be based on how long it has been in the marketplace or on the number of new products being introduced, thereby relatively displacing the previously new item to one that is now being differentiated as less recent (new) or as old. In either case, as a new form of difference is introduced into the marketplace, either as in time or new products, the existing differences are being undifferentiated at the same time.

What this means is that with each new form of difference created or added to the overall frame of reference, all other forms of existing differences will simultaneously be relatively displaced or undifferentiated—to be differentiated anew, as different differences. For the new to become old, it has to be undifferentiated in the process to become a new difference—the old. This differentiating/undifferentiating (the release) process is a function of the ongoing repetition of the difference-creation process, contributing to the "no same," the diminution, the change, and the chance parameters. The difference parameters are all related, affecting what the marketer has to confront in the practice of marketing.

Figure 5.4 Difference—Creating an Un-Relentless Marketplace

As mentioned previously, the dynamic nature of the marketplace is attributed to this repetition occurring with the difference-creation process. Here, the marketer needs to understand that you can't rely on past accomplishments or successes, because even if your brand is doing well today, as new brands enter the marketplace, your brand is being displaced with each new entry, along with all of the other brands. The release of difference suggests that the marketer must constantly think in terms of creating new differences or meanings with the brand to stay abreast of the changes occurring.

In other words, the marketer is to think in terms of the *repetition* occurring in the marketplace and develop strategies that can participate with its movement. Thinking in repetition is similar to thinking in *time*, but the difference is to explicitly think in terms of the difference-creation process and ways to participate that go beyond thinking in a temporal way. Again, thinking agility is called for here.

Marketing Thinking in Practice: The Global Crisis

At the 53rd CIES World Food Business Summit, June 2009, Nielsen Chairman and CEO David Calhoun provided retailers and manufacturers with an overview of the shifts taking place among consumers stemming from the global financial crisis. His comments are presented as follows:

New Rules: The Crisis Has Changed Consumer Behavior

The free fall of the economy may be coming to an end, but new rules are in play:

- There has been a fundamental shift in consumer spending patterns, as restraint has become the new mantra. Over the next 18 months to two years, consumers will make critical decisions about discretionary spending, saving, or paying down debt, which will have long-term bottom line implications.
- Increased consolidation has meant a shift from an emphasis on pricing and assortment of retailers to a merchandising advantage based on value, branding, and store equity.
- Brand offers that are strong—whether store brands or national/manufacturer brands—win at the expense of secondary, under-invested brands.
- But this is not a zero-sum game. When strong manufacturer brands meet strong retail brands, and the focus is on the consumer, this strategy always wins.
- To engage the new consumer, players need to reach across three screens: TV, online, and mobile. Ads across multiple media win consistently against ads in a single medium.
- Social networks belong in the marketers' playbook: Consumers trust recommendations from friends far more than any form of engagement. "What you learn and how you interact with this digitally powered consumer is truly an amazing phenomenon," Calhoun concluded. "All of us have to embrace it in ways we never conceived before."[6]

Mr. Calhoun's comments characterize the unexpected changes that are always just around the corner of any market while illustrating that no one individual or entity has control over the outcomes. It underscores that the marketer needs to follow or be a part of the consumer's lead and that marketing's role is a collaborative one with consumers in their difference creation and not the other way around. His comments also highlight the parameters of difference in *play*.

Marketing Thinking Challenge 5.1: The Changing Marketplace—The Twists and Turns

Choose a marketplace of interest. All marketplaces are undergoing change in one form or another. It's simply a matter of looking for change. Identify what changes you believe are occurring. What is causing the changes? Are the changes moving the market into unexpected directions? What makes them unexpected? How will the changes affect marketing in this market?

Figure 5.5   Observing Change—Observing Difference Unfold

Difference Perspective of Consumers

From a difference perspective, consumers are constantly *becoming* different. As previously discussed, consumers change as a result of their consumption and become different through the consumption of difference. They are of difference and are participating in the process of difference. What this means is that the marketer should attempt to understand consumers in their *becoming* and not what they are but where they are headed. What is also suggested here is that from the outset, consumers are not knowable in the way a SPOT perspective would imply, which is about what they were. In other words, the SPOT perspective would focus on a consumer that no longer exists because he or she has already moved on—that is, has already changed. What a difference perspective tells us is that consumers are seeking difference for the purposes of creating their own new differences. They are on a path of *becoming* and not seeking some static end point.

4-DS Consumer Thinking—Creating a Path of Difference

Consumers are also utilizing their 4-DS thinking in their difference-creation process. Each of the 4-DS thinking dimensions is about difference, illustrated as follows.

As you may recall from Chapter 1, the four spherical thinking dimensions were creative, critical, reflective, and time. It is not only the marketer that engages in these forms of thinking but also the consumer. Creative thinking involves questioning, that is, a forward-looking form of differentiating. Consumers use *creative thinking* in their *becoming*. For example, say a male consumer is interested creating a new image. He might consider a number of clothing lines or brands, projecting into the future the relative impact each might have on his image. Creative thinking, the questioning, is about generating new ideas, new options, new paths to pursue. All are about new differences.

Critical thinking pertains to a cross-sectional form of differentiating. Continuing with the new image example, a decision among the identified options would need to be made and a choice made. Is he going to go with Armani, IZOD, Hanes, Tommy Bahama, or prAna Lyndon, or some other brand? Critical thinking is also used in the consumer *becoming* in terms of choosing an option that fits in with where he is headed.

After making his choice and having a chance to wear the clothing, he would want to see if it had the desired effect. This involves *reflective thinking*, which is a backward-looking form of differentiating. Are the people he is interacting with reacting to him in the desired way? Did it work? How did the new clothes make him feel? Perhaps the change did materialize in a way that was satisfactory. A change was created and then it served a particular purpose. Therefore, the created change, the created difference, is being lived through and, as such, consumed. Consumers use reflective thinking in their *becoming* as a way of gauging whether their choice(s) are producing the desired effects in terms of where they are headed.

The time dimension is also a part of or integral to the other three dimensions in that all four are interrelated where they come together to form a unique perspective, but the time dimension, that is, *thinking in time,* is characterized with the elements of *change* and *chance*. The consumer knows that his choice is speculative in terms of the outcomes, but the thinking is about change and understands that there is always an element of chance involved with all things.

Figure 5.6 The Four Dimensions Forming a Unique Perspective

Each of the thinking dimensions can be a part of the consumer difference-creation process. Through their utilization, differences are created and consumed along the way. What is important to recognize is that these differences are being created not for some static purpose, but for the purposes of moving along some path of difference creation—that is, a path of *becoming*, like a new image. With the repetition of difference and its permutations, this path is not linear and is constantly changing directions. Yet what is central here is that it is a moving path of difference creation, and the movement is through the repetition of difference, which is creating it.

Consumer Behavior Concepts and Difference

Concepts that have attempted to explain consumers, such as perceptions, beliefs, attitudes, preferences, memory, values, motives, satisfaction, lifestyles, or norms, are all forms of differentiating and are a result of the ongoing process of difference. The psychological concepts possess a latent quality and are speculative yet fundamentally serve a difference purpose. They also stem from a kind of questioning in which each is an outcome from some form of questioning—whether the questioning was involving or casual in nature. Every event changes consumers. Whenever a consumer buys something new, he or she is changed through the experience.

Returning to the *satisfaction* discussion of Chapter 2, as consumers develop expectations prior to a consumption experience, the expectations are a change, and a new form of differentiating has come into view. During the consumption experience, change is occurring—the consumer is evaluating the experience through the expectations as it is taking place. When a judgment is made as to whether or not he or she is satisfied by the experience, the judgment is a change as well. If the person was satisfied by the experience, this then becomes a part of that individual's perspective of things affecting future choices. The change is indicative of the realization, utilization, and consumption of difference.

Similarly, with the concept of *value*—value doesn't reside in the thing itself. This is a common fallacy of marketers in which they believe value is a characteristic of the product or service and

Figure 5.7	The Changing Consumer of Difference

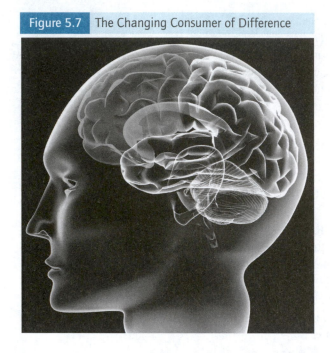

that they have control over the value. Rather, value is a form of differentiating being done by the consumer. For something to become of value, the consumer would have to be moving in the direction of differentiating in a particular way in which the thing is acquiring its relative meaning through the emerging form of differentiation. It is also to be understood that the consumer is changing through the process as well. Just as quickly as something acquires value, a form of differentiating, it can be undifferentiated and no longer of value when the consumer has changed again and becomes different through the process. Yet at the same time, this process doesn't preclude the possibility for collaboration with the consumer. The marketer can potentially affect consumers' differentiating processes by being a part of consumers' difference-creation process in which some form of value is implicated. However, it is to be understood that the marketer doesn't have control over the process or the outcome.

Consumer Implications From a Difference Perspective

The consumer can be described as being on the move, a more nomadic consumer that is *creating a unique path of difference creation* while potentially being affected by others pursuing their paths.[7] The nomadic characterization pertains to the changing nature of consumers through which they are able to leave behind earlier forms of differentiating and move on to other forms that would be beneficial as future situations develop. Less useful perspectives can be discharged to make room for new ones based upon new and changing experiences.

Products and services are consumed along the way in creating these unique paths of differences. They are a form of difference and are differentiated idiosyncratically by each consumer. As such, products can go quickly from being new and exciting to being old and familiar. As the consumer's process of difference speeds up due to more and more unique experiences, the likelihood increases for purchased products to lose their luster and fade into the realm of the old and to be eventually discarded.

A part of the process of difference is the undifferentiating that occurs simultaneously with new forms of differentiating. There is a kind of forgetting, release, or letting go associated with the process of differentiating.[8,9] This allows for change and the element of chance. It also explains how something can go from being *"new"* to being "old." The *"new"* would have to be undifferentiated to be redifferentiated as the "old."

To understand the resulting differences (e.g., attitudes, satisfaction, preferences), the questioning generating them would need to be revealed. The questions are the means or the frame of reference for understanding the meaning for the differences or differentiating taking place.

From this difference perspective, consumers are constantly *becoming* different and, hence, they are of difference, participating in the process of difference creation. Consumers aren't things in a static sense but instead are differentiators involved in an ongoing process of differentiating in an ever-changing environment. A difference perspective is dynamic in its characterization of things, which sets the stage for what the marketer confronts.

As consumers move about, differentiating difference can be thought of as a process of *structuring* that creates not only the differences but also the frame of reference for their relationships and meanings of things found in the marketplace. This *structuring* is dynamic, open, and continuing as difference repeats. Every time a new product is introduced into the marketplace, the structure of the marketplace changes, shifting all of the other products relatively. Hence, the *structuring* relentlessly continues through new differences, new relationships, new meanings, and so on. *Change* and *chance* are forms of difference and, as such, are natural outcomes of its *structuring* process. Through the constant reshuffling of the deck, new products and services of tomorrow are dealt into the marketplace.

The previous difference characterization of consumers suggests the opportunity for the marketer to *move with* consumers through some form of collaboration. It also points toward an understanding of what this collaboration might involve—that is, *a collaboration of difference creation*. This suggests that marketers should focus their efforts on difference creation through collaboration with consumers and others (e.g., employees, suppliers, channel members, or allies).

This characterization is applicable not only to consumers but also to businesses. The process of difference is occurring collectively within an organization and is an even more involving, complicated process of difference than that at an individual level.[10]

Marketing Thinking Challenge 5.2: Consumers and Difference

Choose a product or services category of interest and identify some of the ways in which they are being differentiated by consumers in the marketplace. Then offer what you think might have been the lines of questioning that led up to these forms of differentiation. What might be some of the strategic implications to what you have revealed?

Figure 5.8   Identifying the Lines-of-Questioning Leading to Differentiation

From a Difference Perspective— The Role of Strategy

A difference perspective of the marketplace suggests that strategy needs to be just as dynamic as the marketplace. Thinking of *strategy as a question,* as discussed in Chapter 2, complements this perspective. Strategy has to be open to the changes that are to come in the marketplace as the difference-creation process unfolds. Thinking agility utilizing 4-DS thinking is called for to accomplish this. Additionally, strategy should also focus on the difference-creation process taking place. This certainly has at its pinnacle the consumer, but a more expanded collaborative view of the difference-creation process will need to be strategically considered. As such, we'll examine the beginnings of the collaborative orientation that marketing is moving toward.

In moving across the different marketing orientations of SPOT, self-selection segmenting, and one-to-one marketing, the strategy question that comes into view is to ask about the type of collaboration that marketing is gravitating toward. Several elements come together to shape the emerging collaboration understanding. They include technology, an empowered consumer, aspects of the other marketing orientations, and a multidimensional pursuit of collaboration.

What comes into view is an orientation labeled *collaborative marketing (CM)*, which has been developing over the years. In 2001, a definition appeared.

> Collaborative marketing can be defined as: the relationship between a company and its customers that maximizes their long-term mutual benefit. This approach incorporates the most basic concept of marketing—a customer-driven orientation.[11]

In essence, the shift across the marketing orientations involves going from a "push" to a "pull" strategy that involves a combination of tasks such as developing customer relationships, product innovation, and building an infrastructure to handle the operational logistics and to be responsive.[12] The self-selection segmentation strategy discussed in Chapter 4 emphasizes the "pull" strategy through an understanding of developing an attractive array of value-choices that consumers would want to seek out. The attraction notion is developed further with a collaborative marketing orientation.

> **In essence, collaboration marketing focuses on attracting customers rather than intercepting them with traditional advertising.** It attracts customers by becoming more and more helpful to them, both in terms of evaluating potential new products and services and getting more value from products and services once they have been purchased. In part, collaboration marketing programs seek to become more helpful by mobilizing a broad range of relevant, specialized third parties to add value to the customer relationship. **Collaboration marketing challenges the current mantra of "one to one marketing" and instead views the opportunity as "many to one"**, connecting each customer with as many entities (including other customers) as may be required to maximize value for the customer. Collaboration marketing represents a "pull" approach where the marketer becomes so helpful to customers that they seek the marketer out, rather than a conventional "push" approach blasting marketing messages out in an effort to find customers that might be receptive to the marketer's offering.
>
> Rather than "owning the customer," collaboration marketing strives to give each customer the perception that they own the vendor. To do this well, companies will also need to master the skills required to capture and analyze detailed information about individual customers. By serving as the orchestrator, helping to connect customers

with other entities, collaboration marketers develop richer profiles of customers and their needs and they learn much more deeply and rapidly about their customers than traditional marketers who focus on narrow "one to one" relationships. The good news is that powerful new platforms and tools, ranging from the internet to web services technology and powerful analytic tools, are available to help vendors implement these new marketing programs and deliver on this new brand promise.[13]

| Figure 5.9 | Collaborative Marketing: The Collaborative Constituents |

Figure 5.9 illustrates that a collaborative marketing strategy needs to consider not only collaboration between the marketer and the consumer but also collaborating with suppliers and channel members in terms of logistics, technology, and expertise (vertical collaboration); alliances with other related companies to form a wider marketing net through complementary marketing activities (cross-sectional collaboration); employees as a resource for innovative and organizational development (internal collaboration); and social networks as a part of consumers' ongoing referent basis for products and services information (external Internet collaboration).

| Figure 5.10 | Collaborating Together |

The following Marketing Thinking in Practice illustrates an example of Nestlé's initial collaborative efforts and the beginnings of where they are strategically headed.

Marketing Thinking in Practice: Nestlé

Nestlé executive Bernard Teiling explains how the company developed a collaborative marketing strategy by working with a distributor, UK supermarket chain Sainsbury, to mutually adapt to consumer responses in real time in the marketplace. Using shared promotional information via an extranet, they were able to communicate collaboratively to respond to consumer demand. The excerpts are presented as follows:

> Nestlé, the $50 billion consumer goods giant, is at the forefront of thinking in collaborative commerce. The company is embracing the model right across its operations. Moreover, it is encouraging its vast network of partners to do likewise.
>
> For the past two years, Nestlé has been working with UK supermarket chain Sainsbury's on its Easter egg campaigns to assess just how effective collaborative marketing technologies can be. At this stage, the technology that Nestlé and Sainsbury's use to collaborate is nothing too sophisticated—essentially, the two companies share promotional information on an extranet. The different departments in each organisation are able to see each others' data on how the campaign is progressing, and where products sit in the supply chain.
>
> Within hours of Sainsbury's stocking its shelves with a certain Easter egg, it is able to tell from early sales data if the product is likely to sell well. That information is fed into the extranet and Nestlé can react swiftly. So if there is a poor consumer response to, say, a Harry Potter Easter egg, then Nestlé may quickly repackage the same chocolate in a Lord of the Rings packaging, hopefully ensuring that neither company ends up with a huge inventory of unsold chocolate eggs the day after Easter.
>
> In the scope of what some companies are planning—or indeed have already implemented—for collaborative commerce, this is a relatively simple collaboration. But the benefits to Nestlé have been substantial. "Such collaborative promotional activity can dramatically reduce cost and increase efficiency, with a return on investment of more than 1,000%," says Teiling.[1]

Getting all of the different constituents to collaborate could theoretically lead to greater real-time value for all and potentially create a sustainable collaborative relationship between the marketer and consumer. Instead of a win-lose stance (a competitive view) as in a traditional marketing perspective (SPOT), collaborative marketing is a win-win situation for all involved. It's a "we" versus a "me" perspective. What is interesting about collaborative marketing is that competition among other rivals isn't central to this orientation/strategy. Researching competitive activities simply becomes a resource for potential ideas that could be employed in the collaborative process, but the focus is on being a part of the consumer's value-creation process.

From a collaborative marketing (CM) orientation, marketing is focused on being on the path with consumers in their unique difference creation. It describes a much more expansive view of the difference or differentiation process involved, along with the sources for collaboration. It involves creating a collaborative network with the consumer at the pinnacle or hub of the collaboration. The more tapped into the various collaborative sources the marketer is, the more the marketer will be able to stay on this path, which can be a potential path for continued success. This goes beyond the notion of a *sustainable advantage* but moves on to *sustainable collaborative differentiating.* The former is based upon a static view, whereas the latter is dynamically oriented. In the process, the marketer becomes the organization's collaborative differentiator (CD). Next, we'll examine some of the means available to the marketer to consider in collaborating directly with consumers.

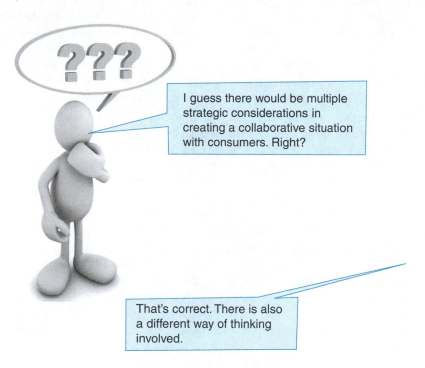

I guess there would be multiple strategic considerations in creating a collaborative situation with consumers. Right?

That's correct. There is also a different way of thinking involved.

The following Marketing Thinking in Practice describes some of these collaborative strategic considerations for the marketer.

Marketing Thinking in Practice: Strategic Collaboration Options

There are numerous examples of companies developing ways to collaborate with consumers. However, a reversal of thinking from the traditional "inside-out" to an "outside-in" perspective is required.[15] It involves creating ways in which consumers can contribute but also creating choices for consumers to differentiate on their own. Please refer to the examples listed on pages 118 and 119.

Collaborative Pricing allows customers to become active participants in defining the prices that they want to pay and adapting prices and services to their changing needs. For instance, computer manufacturer Hewlett-Packard has introduced a new pricing program, called "partition pricing," for its high-end servers. In this program, customers pay incrementally for capacity as they need it instead of paying upfront for hardware. This flexible pricing approach allows customers to align the timing and amount of their payments with their forecasted growth. By introducing capacity on demand, pay-per-use financing programs, and flexible service offerings, firms can allow customers to better manage their cash flow by aligning costs to their evolving needs.

Collaborative Segmentation allows customers to configure offerings to suit their preferences and to self-select into segments. Firms like Herman Miller, Dell, and General Motors allow customers to configure, price, and order products, saving time for customers as well...Instead of the firm deciding what segments to target with what offerings, customers...choose from a flexible menu of offerings that they can configure to suit their needs. By making customers active participants in the segmentation process, firms can make segmentation more accurate and more efficient, because customers know their needs better than marketers do.

Collaborative Communication lets firms work with customers to create "just-in-time" marketing communications that are relevant to customers. Automobile companies like GM and Toyota are partnering with Edmunds.com, an online automobile information provider, to create contextual messages that are triggered by customer activity and facilitate customer decision-making. Contextual messaging turns conventional advertising on its head. Instead of "just-in-case" marketing communications that characterize traditional advertising, contextual messaging becomes "just-in-time" communication, because it is initiated by customers, and it is relevant to their context.

Collaborative Support allows firms to reduce support costs while increasing customer satisfaction by allowing customers to dialogue with the firm and among themselves to solve support problems. For instance, Cisco's Networking Professionals Connection is an online community that allows customers to get answers to support questions from peers and experts. By making customers a part of the support operation, Cisco is able to decrease customer support costs while increasing customer satisfaction. While the community originally started out as a customer support initiative, it is also becoming a valuable source of new product ideas and competitive intelligence.

While the benefits of collaborative marketing are compelling, it is not easy for firms to make the transition from the "command-and-control" mentality that characterized the age of information asymmetry to the "connect-and-collaborate" mentality that will be needed in the age of information democracy. It will require a fresh approach to designing processes, platforms, products, and pricing. Here are the key steps firms need to take on this journey:

Reverse Your Thinking—Firms need to think "outside-in" instead of "inside-out" about their customers and markets. Instead of thinking about finding customers for their products, they need to think about finding products for their customers. They need to understand what customers really buy from them in terms of the business outcomes, solutions, and experiences they seek. They need to understand what activities customers perform as they evaluate, buy, and use their products and services. They need to think deeply about when and where they hand off products, services, and information to their customers. They need to ask which activities they can perform better than customers. Conversely, they need to ask what activities customers can perform better than the firm. To take the first step forward to designing collaborative processes, firms first need to think backward from customer activities and customer processes.

Create Collaboration Platforms—To enable collaborative processes, firms need to build technology platforms that allow customers to connect to their business processes. They need to harness the power of collaborative design tools like National Semiconductor does, community management platforms like Cisco uses, collaborative ideation platforms like Eli Lilly uses, and collaborative configuration tools like the one Herman Miller uses on its Web site for configuring office furniture. These collaborative tools are essential to connect customers to the firm's design process, sales process, order management process, and customer support process. To facilitate customer integration, firms need to map out all the business processes that connect to customers and then think about redesigning these processes so that they interface seamlessly with the customer operations.

Embrace Modularity—To allow customers to self-configure offerings, firms need to make their offerings more modular and their pricing more granular. Dell and Herman Miller are able to exploit the power of "customerization"— customer-driven mass customization, because they create modular products that are highly configurable. On the other hand, General Motors is limited to being able to offer its customers a "locate-to-order" capability because they cannot create automobiles that can be "built to order." By thinking deeply about the possibilities of modularity, firms can involve their customers much more meaningfully in the segmentation and product configuration process.

Align Incentives—Collaboration will not succeed unless both parties in the collaborative exchange have the appropriate incentives. A key challenge in involving customers in the firm's marketing activities is the reluctance of customers to contribute time and effort to the collaboration. Firms need to think strategically about incentives for customers to share expertise. These incentives can be monetary rewards. For instance, Eli Lilly offers bounties for scientists to solve problems, and P&G offers free samples to its volunteer customers. Incentives can also be social recognition, like Cisco's approach to certifying network engineers who are well-qualified to answer support questions. And incentives can be improved efficiency and effectiveness of the customer's operation because of better process integration. The key is to create a compelling value proposition for collaboration so that customers and the firm are motivated to engage in collaborative interactions.[16]

These examples illustrate some of the ways to be a part of the consumer's process. The result is more effective marketing through strategy built around collaborating or participating with consumers in their unique differentiation-creation process. It's no longer one shoe fits all, but working with consumers to create the right shoes at particular points in time that are to be a part of where they are headed in their process of *becoming*.

Marketing Thinking Challenge 5.3:
Collaborative Marketing in Practice

Go online and find companies that are utilizing collaborative marketing through their websites. What features or aspects are being provided that involve consumer collaboration? How are they using them in their marketing? How effective do you think they are? What other collaborative means could they utilize?

Figure 5.11   Collaborating With Consumers

Summary

In this chapter, we examined the following:

- For thinking agility purposes, the questioning strategy of stepping back even further to ask more fundamental questions about the marketplace structure was utilized. The questions considered included: (1) What is being structured? (2) How is the structuring occurring? (3) Are there certain parameters with the structuring of the marketplace? (4) How do these parameters affect strategy? and (5) Fundamentally, what is being consumed by consumers?
- Ultimately, the structuring pertained to the *difference-creation process* that involves all things, and what is being consumed by consumers is difference in their difference-creation process.
- The difference parameters shaping the marketplace included its *repetition*, there is "*no same,*" there is a *diminution* of marketplace players, there is *change*, there is an element of *chance*, and there is a *release* of difference occurring within the process. The repetition of the difference-creation process is producing the other interrelated parameters.
- It was suggested that the marketing thinking shift from a static view of the marketplace to a type of thinking that involves thinking within the repetition of difference occurring.
- Consumers were portrayed as being in a state of *becoming,* and it was suggested that the marketer look for where consumers are headed and not where they have been. In other words, it describes a consumer on the move, a nomadic consumer that is *creating a unique path of difference creation* while potentially being affected by others similarly pursuing their paths.
- A difference perspective of the marketplace suggests that strategy needs to be just as dynamic as the marketplace. Thinking of *strategy as a question* complements this perspective. Strategy has to be open to the changes that are occurring in the marketplace as

the difference-creation process unfolds. Thinking agility utilizing 4-DS thinking is called for to accomplish this. Additionally, strategy should also focus on the difference-creation process taking place. The consumer is at the pinnacle of this collaboration, but other participants need to be considered as well, and that requires a more expanded collaborative view of the difference-creation process.

- The collaborative network can potentially lead to a *sustainable form of collaborative differentiating* that is mutually beneficial to all within the network (e.g., consumers, marketer, suppliers and channel members, alliances, and social network participants).
- The collaborative view of marketing was contrasted with traditional marketing. The primary differences included a "pull" vs. a "push" approach, a "many-to-one" vs. a "one-to-one" perspective, and an orientation of the "customer owns the vendor" vs. "owning the customer."
- Strategic collaboration options were discussed, including collaborative pricing, collaborative segmenting, collaborative communications, and collaborative support.

Case: Apple, Inc.—The Need to Be *Different*

The Apple Computer company was started on April Fool's Day 1976 by Steven Jobs, Steve Wozniak, and Ronald Wayne in the Jobs family garage in Los Altos, California, to build and market a computer design by Wozniak. It was to be a different computer and company. Their inauguration day of April 1, April Fool's Day, was a way of saying "we want to be different," with a little tongue in cheek going on from the onset. They soon were challenged on their company name by the Apple Recording label, owned by the Beatles, which was founded in 1968. A lawsuit by the Apple Corps (Records) against Apple, Inc. (Computer) was filed in 1978 and settled in 1981, with an undisclosed amount being paid to Apple Corps and Apple Computer agreeing not to enter the music business. Of course as their history goes, Apple Computer had other ideas and so the peace didn't last long—a problem that would plague the two companies for decades to come through multiple lawsuits. However, in 2006, Apple Computer prevailed by obtaining a favorable court ruling on the restrictions contested, which cleared the way for iTunes and other developments.

While Apple Computer, Inc., was the company's name for 30 years, it dropped the computer part in 2007 to reflect its expansion into the electronics market. From this point forward, it has been simply referred to as Apple. The company has an interesting history from beginning in a garage to having more than 36,800 employees in 2009[17] and reported annual sales of $42.91 billion.[18] What is perhaps most important is how Apple has continued to create meaningful differences that set it apart from other platforms, devices, and ways of doing things. Examples include Apple II (1977), with its color graphics and open architecture; Macintosh (1984), with its advanced graphics capabilities and LaserWriter along with the introduction of the first PostScript laser printer (some have said that these three products led to desktop publishing); PowerBook (1991), establishing the modern form of a laptop computer; PowerPC Reference Platform (1994), a platform developed through an alliance with IBM and Motorola (the AIM alliance) that was meant to be an advancement over the PC platform; iMac (1998), an all-in-one computer (over time to include iMovie, Final Cut, GarageBand, iPhoto, and iLife); Apple Retail Stores (2001); iPod (2001), a portable digital audio player; Apple's iTunes Store (2003), offering online music downloads; Intel-based Mac computers (2006), that allowed users to install Windows XP or Windows Vista alongside MAC OS X; iPhone and the Apple TV (2007); App Store (2008), selling third-party applications for the iPhone and iPod Touch; and the iPad (2010), a large-screen media device that runs same apps as the iPhone.[19]

This chronology maps out a company that is always striving for the next thing and doesn't appear to rest on its successes. A YouTube video titled "Being Meaningful" at www.you tube.com/watch?v=Jvwf-VOW8dg&feature=related shows Jobs speaking to his employees in 1997 about the company. In essence, he explains the company is not about creating things per se—"it's not about boxes to get the job done. ...The company's core value is about people with passion to change the world." Given the long lineage of innovations made through Apple's advances, Jobs does appear to be fulfilling his vision for the company and the role it is to play in changing the world in terms of changing the way things are done. The vision permeates the organization as well as the marketplace with a steadfast cult-like consumer base.

According to author Simon Sinek, Apple's success can be attributed to a reversal of thinking.

If Apple communicated like most of us, their message would sound something like this, Sinek says: "We make great computers. They're beautifully designed, simple to use, and user friendly. Want to buy one?"

Instead, according to Sinek, here's what Apple is actually telling us:

Everything we do, we believe in challenging the status quo. We believe in thinking differently. The way we challenge the status quo is by making our products beautifully designed, simple to use and user friendly. We just happen to make great computers. Want to buy one?[20]

This quote, along with Jobs's speech, suggests that Apple is constantly creating meaningful differences with the understanding that these differences will only last so long. The question then becomes—to be different from what? Perhaps this ties back to starting the business on April Fool's Day. But some have questioned whether this radical perspective can endure when Apple may actually have already become what it was trying to be different from. Blogger Erik Sherman raises the issue in his blog on "Apple's Big Marketing Danger: Losing Its Identity":

Historically, Apple emphasized fine industrial design, both hardware and software, that appealed to the designers, artists, and other creatives in the company's core audience who appreciated aesthetics. As the famous 1984 commercial indicated, the company framed itself in opposition to corporate "stiffs," which also resonated with the group. Third, there were many art, graphic, and media work you could do on a Mac that was impossible on a Windows machine. Apple became the physical embodiment of the customers' self-identity. ...

Such a company eventually gets to a crossroad. It can try to expand use of the brand and increase its revenue and size, or it can stick with more moderate ambitions. Apple chose expansion. For a time, customers for product line extensions such as the iPod and iPhone could co-exist with the traditional core customers. The long-term buyers were among the first adopters of new products. But when a company expands enough, it necessarily dilutes the identity message because it now addresses broader audiences and, literally, cannot be all things to all people. There are too many conflicting images, characteristics, and qualities. It becomes an attempt to merge an opera company with a rodeo.[21]

Given Apple's history and its current situation, is it possible for Apple to stay on its path of creating meaningful differences in terms of changing the ways things are done and not becoming the established or status quo? State your position. How would you advise Apple? Be explicit and provide relevant examples.

References

1. Diamond, Jared (2008), "What's Your Consumption Factor," *New York Times*, January 2, www.nytimes.com/2008/01/02/opinion/02diamond.html

2. Dyer, Jeffrey H., Hal B. Gregersen, and Clayton M. Christensen (2009), "The Innovator's DNA," *Harvard Business Review*, December, 61–6.

3. Dyer, Jeffrey H., Hal B. Gregersen, and Clayton M. Christensen (2009), "The Innovator's DNA," *Harvard Business Review*, December, 61–6.

4. Hill, Mark, E. (2010), *Marketing Strategy in Play: Questioning to Create Difference*, New York: Business Expert Press, 12.

5. Deleuze, Gilles (1994), *Difference & Repetition*, Trans. Paul Patton, New York: Columbia University Press.

6. "New Rules: The Crisis Has Changed Consumer Behavior," nielsenwire, http://blog.nielsen.com/nielsenwire/consumer/new-rules-the-crisis-has-changed-consumer-behavior/

7. Hill, Mark, E. (2010), *Marketing Strategy in Play: Questioning to Create Difference*, New York: Business Expert Press, 9.

8. Hill, Mark E., and Jane Cromartie (2007), "That Which Is 'Not': Forgetting…," *Consumption, Markets & Culture*, 7 (1, March), 69–98.

9. Hill, Mark E. (2010), *Marketing Strategy in Play: Questioning to Create Difference*, New York: Business Expert Press, 41.

10. Hill, Mark, E. (2010), *Marketing Strategy in Play: Questioning to Create Difference*, New York: Business Expert Press, 12.

11. Rosenberg, Larry J., and James H. Van West (2001), "The Collaborative Approach to Marketing," *Business Horizon*, (November–December), 32.

12. Hagel, John, III, and Marc Singer (1999), "What Business Are You Really In? Chances Are, It's Not What You Think. Unbundling the Corporation," *Harvard Business Review*, (March–April), 133–41.

13. Restoring the Power of Brands, John Hagel III, www.johnhagel.com/view20050612.shtml

14. Collaborative Marketing, Information Age, www.information-age.com/article-archive/300441/collaborative-marketing.thtml

15. Sawhney, Mohanbir, "Beyond Relationship Marketing: The Rise of Collaborative Marketing," Kellog School of Management, http://mthink.com/revenue/sites/default/files/legacy/crmproject/content/pdf/CRM3_wp_sawhney.pdf

16. "Beyond Relationship Marketing: The Rise of Collaborative Marketing." April 11, 2003. http://www.crm2day.com/content/t6_librarynews_1.php?id=EpVppyEAAuvYLagcNF; Reprinted with permission of Internet.com. Copyright 2011 QuinStreet, Inc. All Rights Reserved.

17. "Cisco Touts Social CRM Call Center Success," enterpriseAPPStoday, www.numberof.net/number-of-apple-employees/

18. "Number of Apple Employees," #NumberOf.net, www.marketwatch.com/investing/stock/AAPL/financials

19. "Apple Inc.," Wikipedia, http://en.wikipedia.org/wiki/Apple_Inc

20. Bosker, Bianca (2010), "Apple's Secret to Success Explained by Simon Sinek," *Huntington Post*, July 10, www.huffingtonpost.com/2010/05/10/apples-secret-to-success_n_570604.html

21. Sherman, Erik (2010), "Apple's Big Marketing Danger: Losing Its Identity," *BNET*, May 17, http://industry.bnet.com/technology/10007937/apples-big-marketing-danger-losing-its-identity/

CHAPTER 6 Thinking Through the Marketing Mix

Decompression Exercise

Before beginning the chapter, visualize raking a pattern in the sand.

Figure 6.1 A Pattern in the Sand

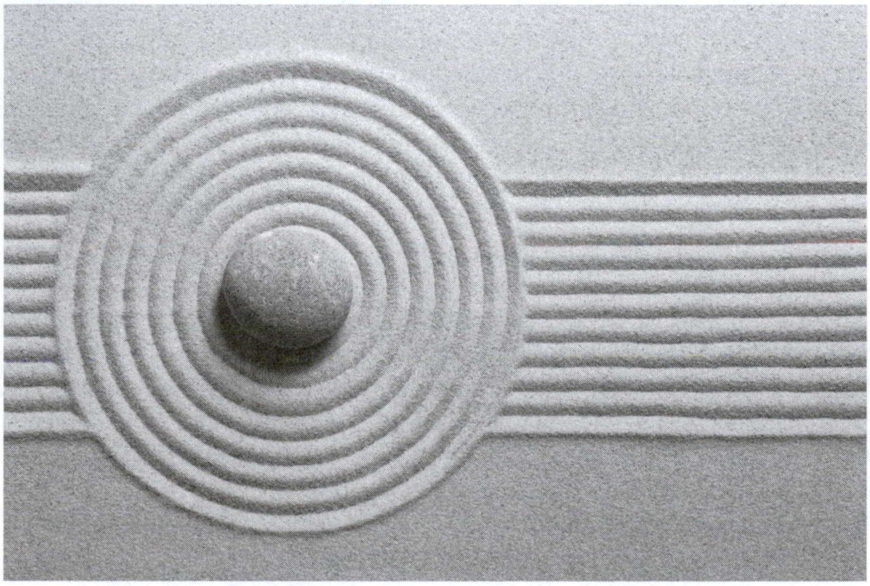

Chapter Introduction

The first five chapters have laid out a foundation for understanding marketing thinking and how the different forms of thinking lead to different orientations and strategies. Ultimately, the different forms of thinking stem from the marketer's differentiating process via his or her questioning. Changing lines of inquiry or questioning will potentially lead to different forms of differentiating, different answers, or different strategies. Differentiating in one way versus another affects how marketers see the marketplace, consumers, and the role of marketing. In this sense, the marketer consumes difference in the practice of marketing. This consumption is ongoing and requires the marketer always to be engaged in his or her 4-DS thinking to create beneficial differences (internal and external) on behalf of the organization.

At the same time, the marketer is dependent upon consumers to allow the marketer to participate in their *difference-creation process,* as discussed in Chapter 5. To be more effective in this collaborative process, the marketer must expand his or her view of collaboration to create a network in which the consumer is at the pinnacle of the network. The network can include suppliers, channel members, alliances, employees, and social network participants. In its basic form, it is a "*we*" strategy in which, in order for it to succeed, all must benefit from the network in one form or another. It is at this point that the role of the marketer appears as the organization's collaborative differentiator (CD), where the organization's objectives are to be accomplished through the collaborative network. A *sustainable collaborative differentiating* is possible and is a potential path for success. However, its success will depend in part on the marketer's ability to stay tapped into the ongoing differentiating occurring through the network by anticipating the *repetition* of difference through its temporal elements of *change* and *chance* along the way. *Thinking in time*, the temporal dimension, is required here.

The different orientations discussed in the previous chapters have affected how the marketer is to think about what he or she marketing. One concept that appeared in the mid-1950s that has had a major influence is the *marketing mix*.[1] The marketing mix was conceived as a conceptual tool to aid marketers in the decisions needed to configure an offering to consumers. As such, the marketing mix and its conceptual counterpart, the offering, were thought of as two expressions of the same thing. The original form of the marketing mix included decisions about product, price, promotion, and place (distribution), commonly referred to as the 4 Ps.

From a thinking agility perspective, given the marketing mix's influential standing in the marketing literature and its use in practice, we'll need to approach the concept with some degree of skepticism. With its stature within the practice of marketing, it assumes a preferred position of being integral to marketing. Traditionally, for many marketers, the 4 Ps have been the starting point for thinking in terms of what their marketing strategy consists of. But could there be other considerations than the 4 Ps? If so, and if they aren't considered, what implications might this have for strategy purposes? Perhaps there might be an underlying question(s) that needs to be asked that could start the marketing process off on a different footing.

This chapter examines the marketing mix concept and, in the process, reveals other lines-of-questioning that could be instrumental in developing more effective marketing strategy.

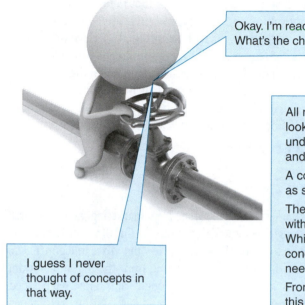

Okay. I'm ready to get things going. What's the chapter question?

All right. But we'll need to keep in mind the importance of looking behind marketing concepts and emerging ones to understand their directional influence on marketing thinking and strategy.

A concept is a form of differentiation (a perspective) and, as such, influences how you see and understand things.

The role of a concept with thinking is to guide the thinking within the parameters of the concept (a conceptual box). While it may seem counterintuitive, in essence, the utility of concepts is to lessen the need for thinking—that is, the need to think about fewer ideas, not more.

From our thinking perspective, it's important to recognize this about all concepts and to be prepared to challenge their applicability and limitations.

I guess I never thought of concepts in that way.

How does the concept of a *marketing mix* (e.g., the 4 Ps) affect marketing thinking and strategy?

There are various ways to look at these issues. We'll try to address the question by reviewing the changes offered in the literature to the original marketing mix concept. Since its inception, much has been written on this subject and many, many alternatives proposed, which suggests that there are problems with the nature of the concept, its role in strategy development, and its influence on the practice of marketing. But, as suggested above, perhaps the issue lies more fundamentally with the nature of a concept itself. If this is the case, how might we maneuver around this type of obstacle? Are there thinking or questioning strategies available to deal with this issue?

Before we can address these particular questions along with the chapter question, an overview of what has been offered in the marketing literature relating to the marketing mix concept needs to be provided. We'll start there.

The Marketing Mix(es)

Several comprehensive studies have identified six main areas in which numerous marketing mixes are being offered.[2, 3] These include consumer marketing, relationship marketing, services marketing, retail marketing, industrial marketing (B2B), and e-commerce marketing. With the existence of these six areas, what do you think might be the underlying issue suggested by them?

The six areas implicitly suggest that there is a situational factor involved in choosing among the various marketing mixes to find the most appropriate one to configure and, ultimately, what is going to be offered. Their presence indicates that the marketer needs to ask about the situation he or she is confronting and what type of mix would be best.

This also suggests that one-size-fits-all thinking, as with the original 4 Ps, doesn't seem to fit anymore or, perhaps, never did. As a consequence, a lot more thinking is called for by the marketer. The six areas and their respective marketing mixes are presented in the figures that follow. The mixes are representative of what has been offered in the literature but aren't meant to be a complete presentation due to new ones always being developed. We'll discuss each to see what insights can be drawn from within the areas and collectively across all six. We'll start with the consumer marketing area first.

Consumer Marketing Mixes

The marketing mixes in the consumer marketing area originate from marketing theory research. As such, the "consumer" part of the label might be somewhat of a mislabeling of whose perspective they pertain to, especially as you review the mixes in Figure 6.3. As you can see from the figure, starting from the top and working down across the rolls of mixes, 1 through 3 are an internal perspective (from the marketer's perspective), 4 and 5 are an external perspective (from the consumer's perspective), and the last two are a mix of internal and external perspectives (the marketer's, employees', consumers', and competitors' perspectives).

| Figure 6.2 | What Is the Marketer Offering Today? |

For the first mix, the original 4 Ps, as previously mentioned, the concept was developed to aid marketers in their decisions to configure an offering to consumers. It pertains to what the marketer has control over and, therefore, the perspective is from the marketer's point of view, explaining the Ps labeling—product, price, promotion, and place.

The *problems* raised with the 4 Ps in the literature and that explain the impetus behind the proliferation of newer versions include:[4]

1. it is an internal perspective,
2. it assumes a passive view of consumers,
3. it doesn't take into account consumer interaction,
4. it doesn't consider relationships,
5. it doesn't consider market opportunities and threats, and
6. it is viewed as an overly simplistic conceptual tool, narrowly restricting the marketer's thinking in strategy development.

The other marketing mixes (4–7) are a response to these criticisms. Mixes 4 and 5 are from the consumer's perspective but actually still retain some of the original understandings of the 4 Ps. For example, performance and value relate to the product; penalty and viability relate to price; perception and virtue relate to promotion (communications); and process, variety, and volume relate to place (distribution). So, while the conceptual movement has been toward the consumer's perspective, the mixes are still tied to the earlier 4 Ps perspective. The last two mixes (6 and 7) simply suggest that more than two perspectives need to be considered to make decisions as to what is to be offered but, as such, tend to be too general, limiting their prescriptive role while still retaining a mix conceptual perspective.

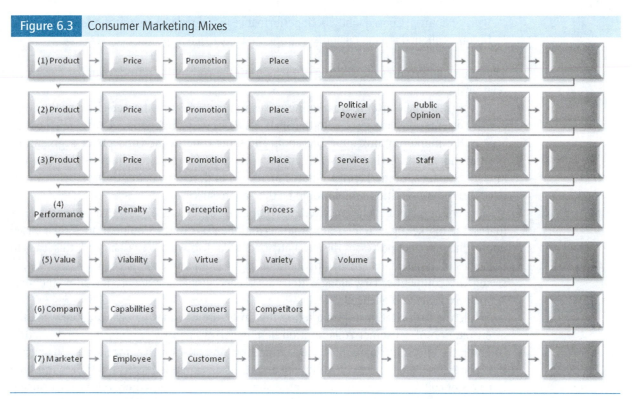

Figure 6.3 Consumer Marketing Mixes

(1) Product	Price	Promotion	Place				
(2) Product	Price	Promotion	Place	Political Power	Public Opinion		
(3) Product	Price	Promotion	Place	Services	Staff		
(4) Performance	Penalty	Perception	Process				
(5) Value	Viability	Virtue	Variety	Volume			
(6) Company	Capabilities	Customers	Competitors				
(7) Marketer	Employee	Customer					

Sources: (1),[5] (2),[6] (3),[7] (4),[8] (5),[9] (6),[10] (7)[11]

Relationship Marketing Mixes

The relationship marketing mixes are presented in Figure 6.5. In comparison with the consumer marketing mixes in Figure 6.3, there is a clear shift toward considering customer needs, personalization or customization, interaction, and communications with the focus on creating relationships with consumers. Mix 5 moves beyond the others, being based upon creating "smart services." Here, the organization operates under a *sense and respond* (as opposed to *make and sell*) mode, recognizes that "value resides in processes and people ('the way we do things around here') as opposed to things," and customer buyer behavior evolves through changes with technology requiring an expanded "offering."[12]

As discussed in Chapter 3, the *sense and respond* form of thinking has become more of a reality as a result of the advances in technology. For example, the marketer has the ability to track consumers' online conversations to *sense* potential changes and then can proactively *respond* to the changes.

Focusing attention on the consumer has had the effect of changing or questioning the importance of the offering:

> Identifying the customer as an asset means that the focus of attention shifts away from offerings per se and that the customer, and not the product, is viewed as the real generator of wealth for the company. The source of competitive advantage is seen less in terms of having unique or superior products and more with respect to having special *relationships*

Figure 6.4 Creating a Relationship

with customers. Consequently, both performance measures and organizational structure becomes aligned around customers as opposed to particular products or services.[13]

The quote underscores the shifting of focus from the competition to developing consumer relationships.

In contrast, the consumer marketing mixes in Figure 6.3 are characteristic of the competitive orientation associated with the SPOT view discussed in Chapter 4. After all, the concept of the marketing mix appeared about the same time as the concepts of segmenting, positioning, and targeting. They all run along the same competitive lines of thinking (an antagonistic form of marketing), and the focus was to develop a better thing, a better product, than the competition, which would be the path to success.

Inherent in the originally conceived marketing mix concept is a "thing-like" perspective—that is, the marketing is to focus on products and their attributes. Competition is then based upon which product possesses the latest attribute(s) and, as we saw in Chapter 4, this leads to strategies of *augmentation by addition* and/or *augmentation by multiplication*. But, as we are seeing, this competitive view along with its SPOT conceptual components, including the marketing mix, is being challenged.

While the fifth relationship marketing mix in Figure 6.5 does involve collaboration, the interpretation of consumer collaboration here is narrower in scope than that presented in Chapter 5. The more expanded understanding of collaborative marketing discussed in Chapter 5 is a more recent development and offers an expanded interpretation in thinking in terms of collaborative networks. Relationship marketing focuses more on the relationship with the customer (a vertical collaboration *in time*, a symbiotic form of marketing), whereas collaborative marketing focuses on creating a collaborative network with the consumer at the pinnacle of the network (an all-directions collaboration *in time*). See Chapter 5 for more on collaborative marketing.

Figure 6.5	Relationship Marketing Mixes

Sources: (1),[14] (2),[15] (3),[16] (4),[17] (5)[18]

Services Marketing Mixes

The services marketing mixes are presented in Figure 6.7. In reviewing these mixes, we can see a conceptual inter-mixing with the original 4 Ps and SPOT view of marketing, along with some departure toward thinking of services as creating relationships or as an event similar to a theater performance. Mixes 1, 2, and 3 are more aligned with the original 4 Ps. Mix 4 is influenced by the SPOT view of marketing. Mixes 5 and 6 are influenced by relationship marketing. But, in Mix 6, the relationship is created experientially and based upon customer satisfaction. This is to be accomplished by viewing services as a theatrical performance in which employees are thought of as actors and customers as the audience (e.g., Disney World).

Perhaps what is central to the services marketing mixes is this: Rather than thinking primarily in terms of tangibles, as with products, marketers should consider the intangibles associated with the personal nature of services that are important to customer interaction, one-to-one communications, and relationship building. As such, services represent a different situation and require different thinking about what is to be offered or provided by the marketer.

Figure 6.6 In the Restaurant

Figure 6.7 Services Marketing Mixes

(1) Product	Price	Promotion	Place	Personnel			
(2) Concept Mix	Cost Mix	Communication Mix	Channel Mix				
(3) Participants	Physical Evidence	Process					
(4) Differentiation via SPOT	Customer Contact	Unique Vision on Quality					
(5) Relevance	Response	Relationships	Results				
(6) Participants	Physical Evidence	Process	Actors	Audience	Setting	Performance	

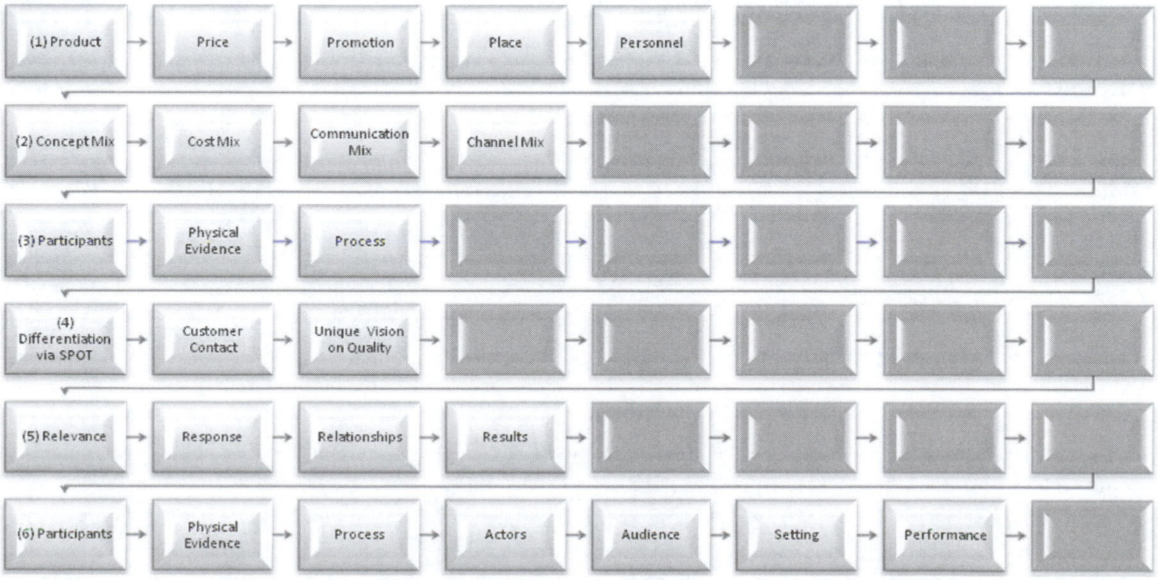

Sources: (1),[19] (2),[20] (3),[21] (4),[22] (5),[23] (6)[24]

| Figure 6.8 | In the Store |

Retailing Marketing Mixes

The retailing marketing mixes are presented in Figure 6.9. Several characteristics stand out with these mixes. The 4 Ps have had a major influence on the mixes, and the SPOT view is implicitly integral to the thinking behind them as well, if not explicitly. One mix that stands out as possessing a different orientation is the third mix, in which the mix elements are considered from the consumer's perspective and not from the marketer's (as a 4-Ps orientation would suggest). The consumer's perspective is underscored via the 4 Cs labeling.

Additionally, given the retail contexts, the mixes focus on the place aspect with a store environment interpretation. For example, the marketer in a retail situation needs to consider the services and store atmospherics as a part of the offering, taking into account the shopping experience side of consumption.

Creating a particular shopping experience is a way to differentiate and is similar to creating a unique consumer experience through a service performance. In comparing Figures 6.9 and 6.7, the difference in how the marketer in the retail context thinks about facilitating the particular experiences through what he or she is offering is based upon the *physical environment* (the store environment, atmospherics), whereas in the services context, the emphasis is on *personnel* (the employees, actors). In addition, in the retail context, the place itself becomes a competitive aspect of marketing in terms of store location, positioning, and image.

| Figure 6.9 | Retailing Marketing Mixes |

Sources: (1),[25] (2),[26] (3),[27] (4),[28] (5)[29]

Industrial (B2B) Marketing Mixes

The industrial (B2B) marketing mixes are presented in Figure 6.11. Several noteworthy observations can be made of these mixes. There are fewer of them, which indicates less attention has been devoted to this marketing context related to the marketing mix concept. While there is still some carryover from the 4 Ps, it's not as apparent which is due to the B2B context and the influence of relationship marketing on the thinking behind these mixes. Accordingly, the basis for B2B relationships will be empathy, mutual benefits, and cooperations, and through understanding and fulfilling customers' needs.[30]

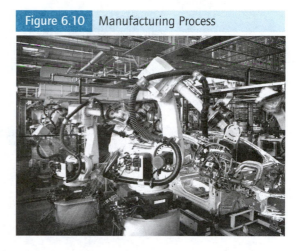

Figure 6.10 Manufacturing Process

The emphasis in these mixes is on the customer-interactions aspect. There are inflections of collaboration via networking (external), teamwork (internal), and codesign/production (external), but the collaboration understanding is narrower in scope, stemming from a relationship marketing perspective compared to that found within Collaborative Marketing discussed in Chapter 5.

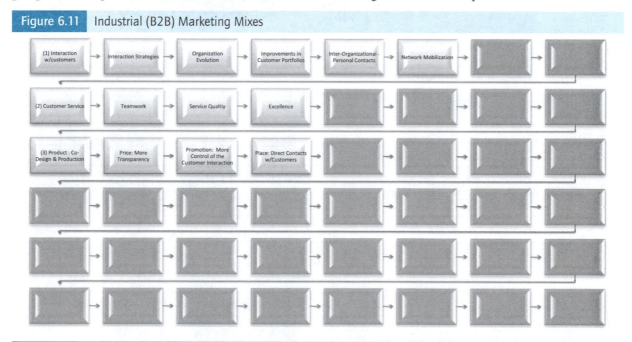

Figure 6.11 Industrial (B2B) Marketing Mixes

Sources: (1),[31] (2),[32] (3)[33]

E-Commerce Marketing Mixes

E-commerce marketing mixes are presented in Figure 6.13, in which several noteworthy observations can be made. There are more mixes to choose from in comparison to the other mix areas. This is probably a result of the pervasiveness of the Internet and how the Internet has dramatically affected businesses' practices. While there is still some carryover from the 4 Ps and the SPOT view with these mixes, the Internet context has resulted in greater consideration given to issues of connectivity, findability, site and content design, personalization and customization, privacy and security, and community building.

The mixes are also influenced by relationship marketing through elements such as convenience, personalization and customization, and customer service. Yet, at the same time, elements of collaborative marketing appear in these mixes as well. Examples of collaborative elements include community building (external), partnerships (external), operational synergies (internal), promotions that are action-oriented activities, and flexibility (external with consumers).

| Figure 6.12 | E-Commerce |

| Figure 6.13 | E-Commerce Mixes |

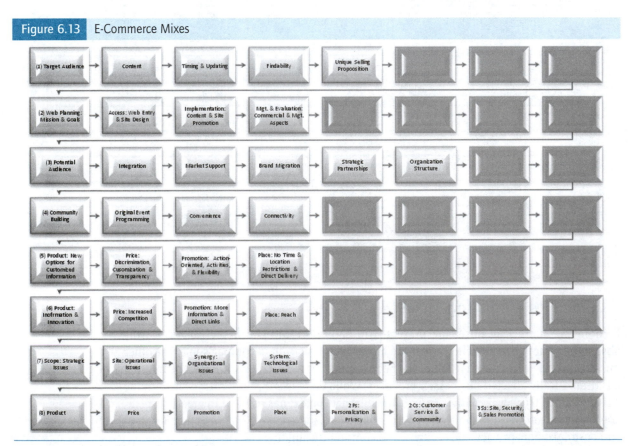

(1) Target Audience	Content	Timing & Updating	Findability	Unique Selling Proposition			
(2) Web Planning: Mission & Goals	Access: Web Entry & Site Design	Implementation: Content & Site Promotion	Mgt. & Evaluation: Commercial & Mgt. Aspects				
(3) Potential Audience	Integration	Market Support	Brand Migration	Strategic Partnerships	Organization Structure		
(4) Community Building	Original Event Programming	Convenience	Connectivity				
(5) Product: New Options for Customized Information	Price: Discrimination, Customization & Transparency	Promotion: Action-Oriented, Activities, & Flexibility	Place: No Time & Location Restrictions & Direct Delivery				
(6) Product: Inofrmation & Innovation	Price: Increased Competition	Promotion: More Information & Direct Links	Place: Reach				
(7) Scope: Strategic Issues	Site: Operational Issues	Synergy: Organizational Issues	System: Technological Issues				
(8) Product	Price	Promotion	Place	2 Ps: Personalization & Privacy	2 Cs: Customer Service & Community	3 Ss: Site, Security, & Sales Promotion	

Sources: (1),[34] (2),[35] (3),[36] (4),[37] (5),[38] (6),[39] (7),[40] (8)[41]

Marketing Thinking in Practice: Barnes & Noble's E-Commerce

Blogger Anton Shilvo describes the dynamic nature of the book industry and how e-commerce has become a pivotal strategic element for the book companies. William Lynch, CEO of Barnes & Noble, explains how they are pursuing a strategy capitalizing on the advantages of e-commerce while blending digital services with their retail store environment.

Barnes & Noble, the world's largest seller of books, on Thursday appointed its new chief executive officer William Lynch, a move that clearly indicates the direction of the company's future growth: various forms of electronic commerce.

"William came to us as a skillful leader in *e-commerce* who, in a short period of time, has done a superb job in quickly establishing Barnes & Noble as a major player in e-commerce and digital content," said Leonard Riggio, chairman of Barnes & Noble.

Since joining Barnes & Noble in February 2009 as president, Mr. Lynch has put Barnes & Noble's core e-commerce business on a high growth track and launched the company's digital commerce platform, including Nook, an *e-book reader* from B&N. It is not a secret that a lot of people acquire paper books via the Internet and there is growing number of readers buying electronic books wirelessly. Therefore, it is not surprising that Barnes & Noble is planning to focus on electronic business going forward.

"Given the dynamic nature of the book industry, William is uniquely qualified to lead the company's transition to multi-channel distribution and drive the continuing expansion of our e-commerce platform, eBooks and other *digital content* and products," added Mr. Riggio.

The new chief executive of B&N has a long experience in various e-commerce companies. Mr. Lynch came to Barnes & Noble from HSNi, where he was executive vice president of marketing and general manager of HSN.com. From 2004 to 2008, he was chief executive officer of gifts.com, an IAC subsidiary he co-founded. From 2000 to 2004, he was vice president and general manager of e-commerce for *Palm*, where he oversaw Palm's web properties, including Palm.com, the Palm online store, the Palm software connection and the Palm. Net wireless ISP. Earlier in his career, Mr. Lynch held senior positions at Seagram Universal and Guinness.

"Our commitment is to leverage our Barnes & Noble stores and leading e-commerce channels such as bn.com, to provide consumers convenient access to the physical and digital products they want virtually anytime, anywhere. I look forward to [...] deliver on this promise to our customers, and blend our digital services with our traditional retail store operations to provide compelling in-store experiences and unmatched purchasing options," said William Lynch, the new CEO of Barnes & Noble. [42]

Marketing Thinking Challenge 6.1: The Marketing Mix—Consumer vs. B2B

Choose a consumer and a business-to-business market and a product or service of interest for each. After reviewing the numerous marketing mixes presented in this chapter and other sources you might find relevant, develop what you believe would be the most appropriate mixes for each of the markets you have chosen. In each case, explain why you believe your marketing mixes are the best. How do they differ? How do the differences between mixes suggest different strategies? In each case, explain what it is you are fundamentally offering and provide a detailed explanation for each of the above questions.

| Figure 6.14 | Mixing an Offering Up |

Marketing Thinking
Challenge 6.2: E-Commerce Marketing Mix

Go online and conduct a search for "e-commerce examples." Identify several websites that you believe are well-designed sites from a marketing perspective and explain why you believe them to be well designed. Describe in detail what is being offered through the design of their websites and why you believe these aspects to be important to their marketing strategy.

| Figure 6.15 | Searching for E-Commerce |

In reading through the chapter, I found these keys that I think will unlock the chapter question. It seems that the *offering* concept operationalized through a mix understanding has at least two difficulties for marketing thinking and strategy. One is with the perspective originating from the marketer's vantage point. The second is also a perspective issue in that a mix understanding is really grounded in a "thing-like" view of what is being offered (e.g., a mix). What do you think?

That's very good. But we'll need to look at it in a bit more detail.

Issues With the Marketing Mix Concept

As has been discussed, the marketing mix as initially conceived in the form of the 4 Ps was meant to be a conceptual tool, to aid marketers in thinking through the decisions that should be made in configuring an offering to be presented to an identified target market. The marketing mix (e.g., the 4 Ps) and the SPOT view stem from the same line of thinking or logics. As with all concepts or conceptual tools, they represent a kind of conceptual box—that is, through defining a concept, a domain and its scope are demarcated in terms of what they pertain to and what they don't. And, *through the focusing aspect of a concept, it lessens the task of thinking by requiring us to think about less*—that is, to think within the designated boundaries of the concept. In using a concept, thinking is channeled within the parameters of the defined concept. The channeling that is occurring with the mix concept can be seen across the chapter figures. Some of these effects will be discussed next, along with identifying a possible alternative. Thinking strategies will also be offered to address in general how to maneuver around the *concept obstacle*.

The Channeling Effects of the Mix Concept

As previously observed, the proliferation of mixes is symptomatic of a problem with the concept. The problems identified previously in the chapter and in the literature include an internal perspective, assuming a passive view of consumers, not taking interaction into account, not being about relationships, and being overall simplification restricting the marketer's thinking. As a result of these difficulties, other mixes were offered that split off into their respective contextual areas: consumer, relationship, services, retailing, B2B, and e-commerce. At the same time, we saw that they were all, in some sense or another, still tied to a mix understanding, which, in effect, tied the hands of the architects' thinking (to be more correct) of the new forms of mixes in terms of setting limits on how far the new thinking would be allowed to go—it is to stay within a mix format perspective with its parts, and so forth. Some of the issues are as follows.

Marketer–Consumer Dualistic Thinking

The marketing mix is viewed from the perspective of what the marketer intends to offer to prospective customers. To *offer* is to present, to make available, or to recommend something to another. From the very beginning, the perspective starts from the marketer being the one doing or initiating the initial act, which is then operationalized through an internal perspective or, in other words, the act is constructed by the marketer for his or her purposes.

This leads to a kind of dualism (cf. to the body and mind form of dualism found in philosophy), that is, an artificial divide (or mindset) between the marketer and consumers, which has plagued marketing for many years. This *marketer–consumer dualism* can be tied back to the marketing mix concept (the *offering*). One such consequence with this form of thinking is that it originates out of one side of the divide, a kind of "one-sided" form of thinking, while the other side isn't given equal consideration and, hence, has led to inequalities with the marketer–consumer relationship. As such, marketing has sometimes been accused of acts of misrepresentation, deceptive tactics, and just being out for the buck. This can be attributed to this one-sided type of thinking. To attempt to bridge this divide, the movement has been in the direction of relationship and collaborative marketing.

"Thing-Like" Marketing Thinking

Another issue with the *offering* concept has been the way it has been operationalized via the mix concept, which perhaps is also associated with the marketer–consumer dualism problem. A mix begins with a *thing-like set of qualities,* similar to mixing the ingredients to make a cake. As a consequence, from the onset, the marketer is thinking in terms of attributes, thing-like qualities that are to be a part of what is to be offered. This again takes on the marketer's perspective as seen through the Ps labeling and, therefore, the consumer's perspective, if considered, becomes a secondary or aftermath form of information for the marketer. But it also obscures other aspects of what could be a part of the marketing—for example, collaboration that isn't based upon a thing-like perspective. Again, as seen through the various mixes, there has been movement in terms of adding Cs to the mixes—that is, adding the consumer's view to consideration—but the hangover affects from the Ps and the mix perspective are still inherent in such proposed changes. Furthermore, the thing-like view inherently places the value within the thing, the mix. With the movement toward the consumer's perspective, the value is relocated conceptually with the consumer and what the consumer is doing with products, services, and the marketing.

The question then becomes, How does the marketer mitigate these issues? The overviews from the chapter figures are already providing indications as to how to resolve these issues. For example, the marketer–consumer dualism problem can be avoided by, instead of thinking from a two-camps perspective, simply starting from the consumer's camps and *working from within* versus from the outside. And, as we'll see across the chapters, technology is making it easier for the marketer to do so. The working-within perspective is further elaborated in the next section. In addition, viewing marketing in terms of offering things needs to change to a view that is different and larger in scope. This is where an alternative perspective is needed. The question then is, If not the marketing mix concept, what other concept or conceptual means might represent the next generation of marketing thinking?

Marketing Thinking in Practice: Collaborative Marketing

Blogger Julian Gratton's description of collaborative marketing explains the many ways in which collaboration can take place, the benefits to collaboration, and that it may be easier than it might first appear.

Good old Yellow Pages. They don't just help with the nasty things in life, like a blocked drain—they're there to help you understand about **collaborative marketing** too. See, collaborative marketing is the practice of unifying lots of brands from a similar sector under one big marketing umbrella...and it's a practice that's really starting to take off.

Bringing companies together: Collaborative marketing, also called "horizontal" or "fusion" marketing, is the strategic alliance of two or more companies under a single marketing banner. In layman's terms, it's a case of "you scratch my back, I'll scratch yours".

Of course, this is nothing new. Companies have formed alliances for years to help promote each other's brands or sell each other's products. Think of James Bond films and Aston Martins, Disney and McDonald's, Pepsi and Brand Beckham. If you fly with Emirates they'll recommend you book your hotel with lastminute.com and hire your car from holidayautos.co.uk. But these are all examples of very different companies offering very different things, enjoying a mutual association that increases their exposure in a market they may otherwise not reach. So what happens when it's two companies that are in direct competition with each other?

Directories and comparisons: One of the pioneers of bringing competitors together is the Yellow Pages business directory, where companies are listed in categories based on the product or service provided. The idea was that putting a whole host of similar businesses in one place makes life easier for the consumer, as they can ringaround knowing they're in with a good chance of finding what they're looking for. *Fly Fishing* by J. R. Harley? No problem.

A newer development is the price comparison website, although the benefit to the consumer is much the same—save time by finding everything you're looking for in the same place. Why trudge around every high street insurer to compare prices when you can do it in seconds online?

The reason many companies sign up to these services is simply because they're afraid of missing out. If your competitors in the antique toy train business are all listed but you aren't, you are effectively waving goodbye to a load of potential customers. Surely it's better to have a stake in the market, even if it means advertising beside your competitors, than to completely miss out on it.

True collaboration: While directory listings may just be a way to equal the playing field with those who offer similar services to yours and share a target market, true collaborative marketing involves you consciously teaming up with them to produce a joint marketing campaign. Your competitors become your business partners. £12 million was spent on collaborative direct mail in the UK, and experts believe that will rise to a whopping £22 million by the end of 2009. The question is...why? Don't businesses want exclusive access to your custom? Why would they want to spend their marketing budgets jostling for your attention next to their competitors on a directory, DM, door-drop or website?

The benefits of collaboration: Well, there are many benefits to collaborative marketing. For the consumer it gives added value; a DM pack containing special offers from 5 top insurers offers more to the consumer than a single offer from one insurer, so is more likely to be read. The collaboration also represents a greater impartiality when compared to a solo DM in which one brand blows its own trumpet.

(Continued)

(Continued)

For the company, the main incentive is cost. A collaborative DM pack can cost as a little as a tenth that of a solo campaign...and it delivers a higher return on investment too. See, the conversion rates are generally lower but so is the cost per acquisition, so sending out ten collaborative packs will give you much better value for money than one single-branded DM.

It's good for your image too, especially if you're a small company. If you manage to squeeze onto a collaborative DM with one of your larger competitors you look like you're in the same league as them. Essentially, your brand gains kudos by piggybacking on the slick image of your more successful competitors, while the pack actually gives you equal billing to explain why your company is the better choice. That's one of the benefits of price comparison sites too; all the big players are there, but it's a level playing field and smaller businesses have equal opportunity to peddle their wares.

Integrating further: Collaborative marketing doesn't have to just mean sharing space on a mailing or website—it can be far more integrated than that. Take The Book Depository for example. It's difficult to imagine a start-up online book seller having much success with Amazon around, yet less than five years ago The Book Depository launched and was profitable from the very first month. Now it's the fastest-growing book distributor in Europe with over 1.8 million titles available for shipping. So how did they do it?

The key, according to their company statement, is that they don't see themselves as Amazon's competitors. "We complement Amazon by providing books which have poor availability and offering good discounts on certain titles which Amazon are unable to. On the other hand, we recognize that our customers want books quickly and so if we do not have stock or if Amazon is considerably cheaper, our customers are able to order direct from Amazon via a link from our website." You read it right—they actually post links that send their customers to Amazon. So the online book giant gets free links to its site plus access to The Book Depository's stock, allowing them to offer rare or out-of-print books they would otherwise not be able to. In short, it's a mutually beneficial collaboration.

Symbiotic marketing: Talking of mutually beneficial relationships, how about "symbiotic marketing"—collaboration between company and consumer. A good example of this is the Nike+ Human Race, which encouraged people everywhere to run a 10km race, upload their stats to Nike's website and see how they stack up against other runners around the globe. Which runner wouldn't want the opportunity to test themselves against their peers? To top it off, Nike even promised to donate to one of 3 charities of their choice if they completed a full 10km. With all this offered free of charge, participants didn't object a jot to the gentle nudges towards Nike's running trainers and sportswear.

The key to symbiotic marketing is that consumers feel they're getting something worthwhile from a company, and are therefore very happy to foster a relationship with them. Think of all those mobile phone companies who give away free handsets—it's because they know customers who feel they've been given something special by their provider are unlikely to change...even when the rates go up.

Walkers recently ran a campaign where customers could vote for a new flavour of crisps. If you voted by SMS you got a message from 02 offering you 2 SIM cards, absolutely free. All you had to do was provide your name and address. This is data capture with a difference—no underhand tactics or hidden catches, just the formation of a mutually beneficial relationship.

Collaborating is easy: Collaborative marketing doesn't have to be complicated...and it doesn't have to cost a penny. It can be as simple as two antique shop owners agreeing to recommend customers to each other if they are looking for something they don't have. Collaborative marketing is basically about fostering a positive, rather than combative, relationship with your competitors." [43]

Alternative Views to Consider

The chapter figures illustrate that alternative views are emerging through an understanding of collaborating or participating with consumers. What are emerging are new forms of marketing or marketing thinking in the forms of collaborative marketing (CM) and participatory marketing (PA). These are discussed next.

Collaborative Marketing

One alternative view that is emerging is collaborative marketing. This is where the marketer needs to think more in terms of creating collaborative networks with the consumer at the hub or pinnacle of the network so that all within the network are able to benefit from the network. At the same time, it is understood that those within the network would also be a part of other networks, and so on. A web of networks results in which all are interconnected in one form or another. *From this perspective, products and services take on a secondary or subsidiary role in that the primary focus is on what is taking place through the network.*

> Increasingly, we are going to see **businesses doing well by doing good, a philosophy that guides thinking and decision making at Unilever.** In a recent discussion, **Harish Manwani**—President Asia, Africa, Eastern and Central European Regions at Unilever—shared that for Unilever **value co-creation is not just collaborating with customers, it is collaborating with the interlinked ecosystems that the company operates in.** According to him, this passion and commitment to doing well by doing good, is the reason why the **Dow Jones Sustainability Index** has rated Unilever as the best company in its category for ten years running.[44]

In thinking through a collaborative network, it suggests that the marketer isn't the one who has control over the network. Actually, no one individual or party has control over it. It is similar to the market-diminution aspect discussed in Chapter 5. The network is a larger form of difference in which the directions of the network or those within it are indeterminate. In contrast, from the discussion in Chapter 4, the segmenting and positioning aspects of the SPOT perspective of marketing assume that the marketer is in control by utilizing the information obtained from the segmenting and positioning process to be used competitively to persuade consumers to acquire the marketer's products and/or services. However, if the marketer isn't in control in this collaborative context, then the marketer is in the position of reconsidering what role he or she is to play and how it is to be played. The question becomes, Which perspective of marketing fits best within a collaborative network—the SPOT perspective or some other?

Participatory Marketing—Taking It a Step Further

The question is, What elements are needed for the collaborative network to work? Well, there would need to be inclusion, social ability, and the ability to partake in what is being done through the network. In essence, we are talking about participation. In this sense, taking the lead from collaborative marketing and taking it to the next level, marketing would become more about participating in a more expanded way (participatory marketing) than simply trying to create the condition to relate with consumers via connecting with them through communication and relevance as in the relationship marketing (symbiotic marketing). Also, it would no longer simply concern competing in the marketplace among competitors over consumers via the things they persuasively put in the marketplace as with a SPOT view (antagonistic marketing). To think in a participatory way requires an understanding of being related to a larger whole that includes taking part or sharing in something. In this case, the marketer would be attempting to partake with consumers and network members in their *difference-creation process.*

At this juncture, thinking agility is called for. Here, we need to switch our thinking to thinking from within the perspective of not being in control and to ask what we can gain from doing so. What things have we not seen by assuming the control perspective?

The participatory perspective recognizes the vulnerability of the marketer and yet views this state of affairs as an opportunity and not as a disadvantage. To have a sense of being vulnerable, which we all are whether we recognize it or not, increases: the likelihood of being more vigilant, a greater sense of awareness beyond oneself, and being more prone for change. The participatory marketing (PM) perspective attempts to capitalize on the *vulnerability paradox*—that is, in the *sense of vulnerability*, there is strength. Within the sense of vulnerability is empathy, which leads to being more open to working with those upon which you rely. These characteristics—vigilance, awareness, proneness for change, empathy, openness, and working with others—are all strengths from which any business can draw as it takes on the future.

In essence, participatory marketing views marketing as involving *active participation* in the collaborative network of collaborative marketing with the emphasis on *active participation* by the marketer utilizing the above characteristics. Through the ongoing participation process, the marketer will have a greater sense of what the contributions will be. So, instead of thinking in terms of an offering (an internal perspective), in PM, the marketer thinks in terms of contributions that may be in the form of process, communications, and/or creating value. Instead of thinking through the "mix" concept, the *contribution concept* originates out of the participation (co-creation) process in which *the form the contribution is to take will be a function of those participating.* From the very beginning, the thinking originates (or resides) from *within* versus from the outside—thereby eliminating the marketer–consumer dualist thinking. This form of thinking is developed further throughout the later chapters.

Furthermore, future success for businesses may lie in being seen as contributors to society's needs versus simply pursuing profits. The new bottom line comes in the form of a triple bottom line in the following order: people, planet, and then profits.[45]

At the same time, it should be understood from this chapter discussion that the PM orientation and its *contribution concept,* if they become established, will be also challenged in time, making room for other orientations and concepts to emerge as needed. Again, this is part of the ongoing difference process discussed in Chapter 5.

Thinking Strategies to Maneuver Around the Concept Obstacle

The *concept obstacle* is a difficult one to completely avoid in that we tend to think conceptually. The following are some suggestions that might lessen its negative impact on your thinking:

1. Recognize that you are thinking conceptually and identify which concepts you are frequently utilizing.

2. Consider the limitations of the concepts you are using—think about their domains, scopes, directionalities, and the types of strategies that follow.

3. Look for other options, alternatives, or concepts. What do they suggest you consider?

4. Be creative with concepts, intermixing the best or most appropriate ideas and adapting them to your situation as needed.

5. Be reflective with what worked and what didn't. Sometimes what doesn't work is more informative than what does. Similarly, problems are really opportunities to learn, to think more about situations anew and, as such, are a resource for future strategies.

6. And, finally, be adaptable and flexible conceptually, as things change in time. This requires developing your thinking agility.

Marketing Thinking Challenge 6.3:
Thinking Through Participatory Marketing (PM)

Choose any product or service situation of interest. Research the situation and identify the various entities that might have a vested interest in the situation. Graphically map out a collaborative network, provide a description of each of the participants, and explain why your collaborative network would work best for this situation. As part of your description, explain how each of the members of the network would benefit from their participation. In what forms would the benefits come? Explain how you, as the marketer, could increase their benefits through your participatory role(s). What forms of participation could you *contribute* to the process? Be explicit.

Figure 6.16 Participating

Summary

- In this chapter, we look at how the *"mix" concept* and its counterpart, the marketing *"offering,"* affect marketers' thinking about what is to be provided. At a more fundamental level, issues associated with a concept in general were discussed. Two such issues involved the channeling effects of concepts and how concepts reduce versus increase thinking. Thinking strategies were suggested to avoid some of the negative aspects of conceptual thinking.

- As a consequence of the mix concept, there has been a proliferation of mixes developed that divides into six different contextual marketing areas: consumer, relationship, services, retailing, B2B, and e-commerce. The proliferation of mixes was found to be symptomatic of the problems associated with the concept.

- The different orientations of marketing as seen through the SPOT view (antagonistic marketing), relationship marketing (symbiotic marketing), and collaborative marketing were discussed. It appears that marketing as a discipline is moving in the direction of relationship and collaborative marketing, in which collaboration is becoming a more important aspect of marketing. The two different forms of collaboration were identified. The narrower interpretation of collaboration (symbiosis) associated with relationship marketing is between the marketer and the consumer. The more expanded version of collaboration is associated with *collaborative marketing*, which involves creating a collaborative network with the consumer at the pinnacle or hub of the network.

- Expanding upon collaborative marketing, another alternative orientation of marketing was offered based upon *participatory marketing*, which led to the *contribution concept*. This concept was presented in contrast to the *marketing mix concept*.

Case: Ally Bank—The Bank That Wants to Be Your "Trusted" Friend

Out of the banking government bailout ashes in 2009 comes what appears as a new bank—Ally Bank. In May 2009, GMAC Financial Services' retail banking subsidiary GMAC Bank changed its name to Ally Bank, a holding company.[46] The oversight panel overseeing the repayment of TARP monies reported that GMAC may not be able to fully pay back the monies owed, potentially costing taxpayers $6.3 billion. The government currently has a 56.3% ownership in the company.[47] Blogger Anthony Malakian explained the logic behind the transformation from GMAC Bank to Ally Bank is as follows:

Despite its ties to the beleaguered General Motors and its own capital concerns, GMAC Bank had little trouble attracting deposits after it established a bank holding company in December. Deposits surged 16 percent in the first quarter, to $22.5 billion.

With such a good start, why did the online bank abruptly shed the GMAC Bank brand in favor of new moniker, Ally Bank?

A recognition of independence, says the Midvale, Utah, bank. It didn't own the gmac. com domain name and with General Motors steadily decreasing its ownership stake in Ally Bank's parent, GMAC LLC, the bank wanted to send the message that it is not merely a financing arm for GM cars.

"As we've been making improvements to the GMAC Bank experience, we felt like at some point we wanted to be in a position where we're investing in a brand that we can grow with…and feel that this is the right time," says Vinoo Vijay, brand, advertising and product executive at the $36 billion-asset Ally Bank.

But some marketing experts believe the switch had more to do with the bank distancing itself from the bankrupt carmaker and GMAC LLC, which took in $13.5 billion in federal aid. GMAC Bank had also been hit hard by GM's woes, losing nearly $271 million in the six months that ended March 31.

"Rebranding itself as Ally does the major point of separating itself from the baggage that GM carries," says Bruce Clapp, president of the Dayton, Ohio, marketing consultancy MarketMatch.

That rebranding effort in mid-May with a new motto—"The world doesn't need another bank; it needs a better bank"—prime-time television spots, a major print buy (including a two-page spread in the first edition of a revamped *Newsweek*), and prominent Web placements on Yahoo!, among other major sites.

The campaign aims to win over consumers by promising no hidden fees, no balance restrictions and no minimum deposits.[48]

As a repositioning strategy, Ally Bank is promoting itself as a different kind of bank—"an honest bank," one that can be "trusted." "The campaign takes a three-pronged approach that includes outreach to current bank customers, building awareness among prospective customers, and communications to the employee base, according to Sue Mallino, executive director of global communications at GMAC."[49] The strategy involves an aggressive TV and print advertising campaign directed at illustrating how Ally Bank is different than other banks. Its advertising illustrates established banking practices through the eyes of children, making the point that even children know that such practices are wrong. Examples of the advertising themes are described below:

One TV spot, for example, shows a young boy playing with a toy truck that a banker gave him. But then the banker snatches the truck away and hands him a cardboard cutout of a truck because that was part of the deal. The child is not pleased. "Even kids know it's wrong to hide behind fine print," a voiceover says. "Why don't banks?"

Another ad shows a banker giving a young girl a bicycle but then says she can only "ride" it inside of a small, rectangular area that's taped off. A voiceover then asks, "Even kids know that an offer shouldn't come with ridiculous conditions. Why don't banks?"[50]

To back up the message, Ally Bank offers an interest-earning checking account with no fees, no minimum balances, free online bill-pay, and free use of any ATM nationwide. They also will refund fees charged by other banks using their ATMs and will charge a single $9 overdraft fee compared to the standard of $35 per transaction charge over.

"We've really done our research and listened to customers to develop a product that puts the customer first," says Ally Chief Marketing Officer Sanjay Gupta, a former marketing executive at Charlotte-based BofA. "Our interest checking account is another significant step as we evolve a new business model that we hope encourages customers to expect more from their bank," he says. "We're developing our products with the philosophy that we are a financial partner with our customers, and we're making money with them—not off them."[51]

They provide 24/7 customer service and make it easy to contact a person at the bank. All of the descriptions of their banking products are spelled out in plain, everyday language, and they don't use fine print. Ally Bank's interest rates on CDs and other financial products have been much higher than what competitors have been offering. However, their aggressive strategy has drawn critics, as seen below:

Ally has been criticized for hiding its affiliation with troubled parent GMAC, recipient of $13.5 billion in government aid, and for portraying bankers as dishonest in its ad campaign.

Last summer, the American Bankers Association even complained to regulators that Ally's interest rates were "inappropriate" and "risky" for a bank receiving taxpayer aid.[52]

Similar concerns have been raised by the Congressional Oversight Panel. A part of the report is presented below:

Although GMAC is cutting costs across the organization, its investment in Ally Bank is staying largely stable. GMAC has been engaged in an aggressive marketing campaign for Ally Bank. Among other things, Ally Bank has been attempting to interest depositors by offering CD rates that are nationally among the highest available. This strategy has been politically contentious regulators view unusually high rates as an indication of instability. In the summer of 2009, when Ally Bank's rates were more than double the national average, the rates prompted a letter of complaint from the American Bankers Association (ABA) to the FDIC. The ABA letter stated that the Ally Bank strategy—aggressive courting of deposits and extremely rapid growth in assets—was risky and required regulatory supervision. The ABA was particularly incensed by Ally Bank's strategy in light of the government bailout, arguing that Ally Bank was shielded from investor and market influences, and was therefore free to follow risky strategies. Citing the high interest rates paid by troubled financial institutions during the banking crisis of the 1980s, the ABA observed that such high rates and risky behavior can create a race to the bottom, in which other banks are also forced to raise their rates above the market rate.

In response, Ally Bank vigorously contested the ABA's characterization of Ally Bank as troubled, citing its capitalization ratio and protesting that its rates were supported by its relationship with the GM and Chrysler dealership network. Ally Bank's arguments, however, did not persuade the FDIC, which sent a letter conditioning Ally Bank's access to the TLGP on FDIC review of Ally Bank's CD rates and later adopted new regulations setting a variety of standards for the interest rates permissible for insured depository institutions that are not well capitalized. At present, Ally Bank still offers rates that are among the highest available, although Mr. Carpenter has said that Ally Bank hopes to move away from aggressive rates and toward a more traditional banking model, albeit an online one. According to one analyst, however, internet banks do not have a history of success. Among other things, overhead is high because in the absence of branches the banks depend on expensive advertising. In addition, at present Ally Bank has approximately 10 percent of its deposits in brokered deposits. One analyst considers Ally Bank's proportion of brokered deposits and lack of restrictions on deposit withdrawals to be a warning sign of bank instability. Finally, as the Federal Reserve discontinues the extraordinary measures it has been using to keep interest rates low, interest rates are likely to rise and with them Ally Bank's cost of funds. Although these shifts will affect the industry as a whole, Ally Bank already has high deposit costs and a high proportion of brokered deposits. Some commentators note Ally Bank's high costs for acquiring and retaining depositors and low core deposits and liken Ally Bank to the unstable S&Ls of the 1980s. Given that Ally Bank's deposits serve the same purpose for GMAC as commercial paper, GMAC instability affects not only GMAC and Ally Bank…but also brings to the fore the moral hazard of using government-insured deposits as the basis for monoline financing—Ally Bank's depositors. Ultimately, Ally Bank appears to be both critical to GMAC and very much a work in progress, and whether it will be a success remains to be seen.[53]

Another concern, from the marketing side of the strategy, raises the issue that advertisements casting Ally Bank against the villain (i.e., the banking industry) is that "the positive message of Ally is far less vivid than the negative message about the other banks."[54] In essence, the campaign may simply be reinforcing the message that banks can't be trusted and that Ally Bank is just another bank. What is also interesting is that the top chief officers of Ally Bank all come from the banking industry, the industry they are denouncing, and each of them had high-ranking roles at banks like Citi and Bank of America. Given the roles they had, it would seem very unlikely that they hadn't participated in the very banking practices that are being depicted in the Ally advertisements.

Do you think that Ally Bank's strategy will work? Explain your position. Given its financial situation with the government, do you think the strategy is a sound one? Explain your position. What strategic considerations do you think they need to consider and what recommendations would you offer?

References

1. Borden, Neil H. (1964), "The Concept of the Marketing Mix," *Journal of Advertising Research*, 4 (June), 2–7.
2. Constantinides, E. (2006), "The Marketing Mix Revisited: Towards the 21st Century Marketing," *Journal of Marketing Management*, 22, 407–38.
3. Goi, Chai Lee (2009), "A Review of Marketing Mix: 4 Ps or More?," *International Journal of Marketing Studies*, 1 (1), 2–15.
4. Goi, Chai Lee (2009), "A Review of Marketing Mix: 4 Ps or More?," *International Journal of Marketing Studies*, 1 (1), 4.

5. Borden, Neil H. (1964), "The Concept of the Marketing Mix," *Journal of Advertising Research*, 4 (June), 2–7.

6. Kotler, Phillip (1984), *Marketing Management: Analysis, Planning and Control*, 5th Edition, Englewood Cliffs, NJ: Prentice Hall.

7. Doyle, P. (1994), *Marketing Management and Strategy*, Englewood Cliffs, NJ: Prentice Hall.

8. Yudelson, J. (1999), "Adapting McCarthy's Four P's for the Twenty-First Century," *Journal of Marketing Education*, 21 (1), 60.

9. Bennett, A. R. (1997), "The Five Vs—A Buyer's Perspective of the Marketing Mix," *Marketing Intelligence & Planning*, 15 (3), 151–56.

10. Robins, F. (1991), "Four Ps or Four Cs or Four Ps and Four Cs," paper presented at the MEG Conference.

11. Shultz, D. E. (2001), "Marketers: Bid Farewell to Strategy Based on Old 4 Ps," *Marketing News*, 35 (2), 7.

12. Glazer, Rashi (2000), "Smart Services: Competitive Advantage Through Information-Intense Strategies," in *Handbook of Services Marketing & Management*, ed. Teresa A. Swartz and Dawn Iacobucci, Thousands Oaks, CA: Sage, 411.

13. Glazer, Rashi (2000), "Smart Services: Competitive Advantage Through Information-Intense Strategies," in *Handbook of Services Marketing & Management*, ed. Teresa A. Swartz and Dawn Iacobucci, Thousands Oaks, CA: Sage, 411.

14. Lauterborn, B. (1990), "New Marketing Litany: Four Ps Passé: C-words Take Over," *Advertising Age*, 61 (41), 26.

15. Rosenberg, L., and J. Czepiel (1992), "A Marketing Approach to Consumer Retention," *Journal of Consumer Marketing*, 59, 58–70.

16. Gummesson, E. (1994), "Making Relationship Marketing Operational," *International Journal of Service Industry Management*, 5 (5), 5–20.

17. Goldsmith, R. E. (1999), "The Personalised Marketplace: Beyond the 4 Ps," *Marketing Intelligence & Planning*, 17 (4), 178–85.

18. Glazer, Rashi (2000), "Smart Services: Competitive Advantage Through Information-Intense Strategies," in *Handbook of Services Marketing & Management*, ed. Teresa A. Swartz and Dawn Iacobucci, Thousands Oaks, CA: Sage, 409–20.

19. Heuvel, J. (1993), *Diensten Marketing* (Services Marketing), Groningen, The Netherlands: Wolters-Noordoff.

20. Brunner, G. C. (1989), "The Marketing Mix: Time for Reconceptualization," *Journal of Marketing Education*, 11, 72–7.

21. Booms, B. H., and M. J. Bitner (1981), "Marketing Strategies and Organization Structures for Services Firms," in *Marketing Services*, ed. J. H. Donnelly and W. R. George, Chicago, IL: American Marketing Association, 47–51.

22. Fryar, C. R. (1991), "What's Different About Services Marketing?" *Journal of Marketing Services*, 5 (4), 53–8.

23. English, J. (2000), "The Four 'P's of Marketing Are Dead," *Marketing Health Services*, 20 (2), 20–23.

24. Grove, S. J., R. P. Fisk, and J. John (2000), "Service as Theater, Guidelines and Implications," in *Handbook of Services Marketing & Management*, ed. Teresa A. Swartz and Dawn Iacobucci, Thousands Oaks, CA: Sage, 21–36.

25. Ster, van der W. (1993), *Marketing en Detailhandel* (Marketing and Retailing), Groningen, The Netherlands: Wolters-Noordoff, 328.

26. Boekema, J. J., E. B. Bueren van, S. Lobstein, A. Oosterhuis, and P. Schweitzer (1995), *Basisbook Marketing* (Basic Book of Marketing), Derde druk, Groningen, The Netherlands: Wolters-Noordhoff.

27. Rousey, S. P., and M. A. Morganosky (1996), "Retail Format Change in US Markets," *International Journal of Retail & Distribution Management*, 24 (3), 8–16.

28. Mulhern, F. J. (1997), "Retail Marketing: From Distribution to Integration," *International Journal of Research in Marketing*, 14, 103–24.

29. Kotler, Phillip (2003), *Marketing Management*, 11th edition, Upper Saddle River, NJ: Prentice Hall International Edition.

30. Constantinides, E. (2006), "The Marketing Mix Revisited: Towards the 21st Century Marketing," *Journal of Marketing Management*, 22, 423.

31. Turnbull, P., D. Ford, and M. Cunningham (1996), "Interaction, Relationships and Networks in Business Markets: An Evolving Perspective," *Journal of Business & Industrial Marketing*, 11, (3/4), 44–62.

32. Parasuraman, A. (1998), "Customer Service in Business-to-Business Markets: An Agenda for Research," *Journal of Business and Industrial Marketing*, 13 (4), 309–21.

33. Peattie, K. (1997), "The Marketing Mix in the Third Age of Computing," *Marketing Intelligence & Planning*, 15 (3), 142–50.

34. Mosley-Matchett, J. D. (1997), "Include the Internet in the Marketing Mix," *Marketing News*, 31 (25).

35. Evans, J. R., and V. E. King (1999), "Business-to-Business Marketing and the World Wide Web: Planning, Managing and Assessing Web Sites," *Industrial Marketing Management*, 28, 343–58.

36. Chaffey, D., R. Mayer, K. Johnston, and F. Ellis-Chadwick (2000), *Internet Marketing Strategy, Implementation and Practice*, Upper Saddle River, NJ: Prentice Hall, 158–68.

37. Kambil, A., and P. Nunes (2000), "Internet Marketing: Lessons From the Field," Research Note, *Accenture Institute for Strategic Change*, July 24, www.accenture.com/xd/xd.asp?it=enweb&xd=_isc/iscresearchnote_12.xml

38. Bhatt, G., and A. F. Emdad (2001), "An Analysis of the Virtual Chain in Electronic Commerce," *Logistic Information Management*, 14 (1/2), 78–85.

39. Allen, E., and J. Fjermestad (2001), "E-Commerce Marketing Strategies: An Integrated Framework and Case Analysis," *Logistics Information Management*, 14 (1/2), 14–23.

40. Constantinides, E. (2002), "The 4S Web-Marketing Mix Model: E-Commerce Research and Applications," *Elsevier Science*, 1/1 (July), 57–76.

41. Kalyanam, Kirthi, and Shelby McIntrye (2002), "The E-Marketing Mix: A Contribution of the E-Tailing Wars," *Journal of the Academy of Marketing Science*, 30 (4), 487–99.

42. Shilvo, Anton (2010), "World's Largest Book Seller Appoints E-Commerce Specialist as Chief Executive. Appointment of CEO May Point to Barnes & Noble's Future: Electronic Commerce," (March 3), www.xbitlabs.com/news/multimedia/display/20100318100401_World_s_Largest_Book_Seller_Appoints_E_Commerce_Specialist_as_Chief_Executive.html

43. Gratton, Julian (2009), "The Rise and Rise of Collaborative Marketing," June, www.redcmarketing.net/blog/marketing/collaborative-marketing/

44. Bhalla, Gaurav (2010), "Recently in Collaborative Marketing Category," www.gauravbhalla.com/collaborative-marketing/

45. Bhalla, Gaurav (2010), "Recently in Collaborative Marketing Category," www.gauravbhalla.com/collaborative-marketing/

46. Ally Bank, Bloomsberg Businessweek, http://investing.businessweek.com/research/stocks/private/snapshot.asp?privcapId=8752867

47. "Future of Ally Bank as GMAC Tries to Repay Its TARP Debt?," DEPOSITSACCOUNTS.com, March 17, 2010, www.depositaccounts.com/blog/2010/03/future-of-ally-bank-as-gmac-tries-to-repay-its-tarp-debt.html

48. Malakian, Anthony (2009), "New Ally, Big Splash," *US Banker*, July, www.americanbanker.com/usb_issues/119_7/-384026-1.html

49. Garcia, Tony (2009), "GMAC launches campaign to promote Ally Bank," PRWEEK, May 20, www.prweekus.com/pages/login.aspx?returl=/gmac-launches-campaign-to-promote-ally-bank/article/137162/&pagetypeid=28&articleid=137162&accesslevel=2&expireddays=0&accessAndPrice=0

50. Malakian, Anthony (2009), "New Ally, Big Splash," *US Banker*, July, www.americanbanker.com/usb_issues/119_7/-384026-1.html

51. O'Daniel, Adam (2010), "Ally Bank a Rising Player in Web World," *Charlotte Business Journal*, January 29, http://charlotte.bizjournals.com/charlotte/stories/2010/02/01/story2.html

52. O'Daniel, Adam (2010), "Ally Bank a Rising Player in Web World," *Charlotte Business Journal*, January 29, http://charlotte.bizjournals.com/charlotte/stories/2010/02/01/story2.html

53. Congressional Oversight Panel, *Oversight Report*, March 10, 2010, 106–7.

54. Dolliver, Mark (2009), "Ally Bank 'Pony,'" ADWEEK, May 21, www.adweek.com/news/advertising-branding/ally-bank-pony-130187

CHAPTER 7

Co-creating Meaningful Differences With Products and Services

Decompression Exercise

Before beginning the chapter, take a moment to release the balloons.

Chapter Introduction

Historically, a focus on products and services has always been at the core of marketing thinking. The various marketing functions of personal selling, promotion, distribution, pricing, and so forth all have been developed with the thinking about products and services in mind. The thinking has also been evolving or transforming through various orientations—from a production orientation to a sales orientation to a market orientation—and this transformation continues today, as we'll see throughout the chapters. But, foundationally, the thinking at its core has been about products and services.

Another way to think about marketing and its thinking is to ask, What would marketing be without products and services? Raising the question reveals a prejudice regarding the centricity of products and services for the marketer's focus or thinking. But how has the marketer's thinking been affected by this focus? How has using products and/or services as a starting point for the thinking affected the line(s) of questioning? In what direction has this starting point sent marketers off to, and if the starting point were to be changed, what would this mean for marketing?

So the question is, How do we think about products and services? And, based on our perspective of products and services, how is the marketer's focus affected in terms of his or her marketing thinking? For example, when you think about Apple marketing iPods and iPads, is their marketing about the products or does it pertain to something else?

This chapter is an extension of Chapter 6, which examined the thinking behind the marketing mix concept. Since product is one of the Ps found in the original marketing mix concept, and given the influential role products (and services) have had on marketing thinking, we'll examine at a deeper level the thinking associated with products and services and the implications for strategy.

Thinking about products and services involves conceptual forms of thinking. For example, as we saw in Chapter 6, applying a SPOT marketing perspective involves thinking of some form of product differentiation. It could pertain to differences in attributes (e.g., different features) or a difference in quality (e.g., better craftsmanship or materials). In the case of Apple, is the marketing based on a style differentiation (an attribute)? If so, then the thinking involves some thing-like characteristic. Yet, as discussed in Chapter 6, this represents an internal perspective along with a thing-like conceptualization of a product integrated into an offering being made by the marketer. And, as we saw, this type of thinking is associated with the marketing mix concept and is contributing to the marketer–consumer divide and its difficulties for the marketer.

On the other hand, what if you view products and services from the perspective of a contribution? The contribution concept was also discussed in Chapter 6. Here, the marketer would need to ask, *Contributing to what?* The difference conceptually between the SPOT view and a contribution perspective of a product has to do with *where* it acquires its meaning or where the contribution (the product) derives its sense of being a contribution. Does the product become a contribution during manufacturing, through the selling process, or from the participation process within the collaborative network as described in Chapter 6? If you subscribe to the later view, accordingly, for network participants to consider something a contribution, it would have to be seen as being of use, merit, importance, or worth *from their perspective* in some form or another. Here, it is to be noted that the marketer is *not* the one determining whether it is a contribution. Returning to the Apple case, in this context, the iPod's contribution(s) is to be understood within the collaborative network or brand community and the practices that have developed around the product (or brand). Brand communities are collaborative networks that may or may not involve the marketer. They will be discussed in detail later in the chapter.

As such, the marketer's contributions to the collaborative network could come in the form of process (e.g., making things more convenient), communications (e.g., listening and being more responsive), and/or creating value (e.g., providing unique benefits, enabling, and/or enhancing the practices within a brand community). Here, the marketer's focus or thinking involves the collaborative process underway and how to participate within this process, of which products and/or services may be a part. In this context, the centricity of the marketing thinking involves the collaborative process underway and, as such, products and/or services are relegated to a subsidiary position from which they derive their position and meaning.

To be explicit, the thinking behind the marketer's contributions originates out of the participation process *within* the collaborative network. Participatory marketing (PM), discussed in Chapter 6, involves a thinking from *within* (from the very beginning) and, as a consequence, the marketer–consumer divide is absent (or at least less apparent). PM conceptual counterparts included the collaborative network, a sense of vulnerability, *active participation*, and the contribution concept. In this regard, PM is about focusing on the ongoing process occurring within the collaborative network(s) and actively *contributing* to the process versus a thing-like view of marketing as seen through the SPOT perspective.

To understand these two different forms of marketing thinking, we will examine how products acquire their meaning(s) and then look at how the two different views of products (and services) above derive their relative meaning(s). To accomplish this, we'll examine the SPOT view of products (and services) through a quality perspective and then the PM orientation in discussing brand communities and their practices in which contributions obtain their meanings (or sensibilities).

The Meaning-Generation Process—
Creating Differences

It was stated in Chapter 5 that all things are of difference. This is still the case. In the introduction, we have actually been discussing different forms of thinking or differentiating through different line(s) of questioning. The differences stem from the context in which they originate their line of questioning, that is, their starting points are different. The SPOT view with its offering originates internally, whereas the PM orientation begins externally within the collaborative network. Yet in each case, they are creating meaningful differences. The primary differences lie within what is meant by whom the offering or contribution is to be meaningful for and where they acquire their meaning(s).

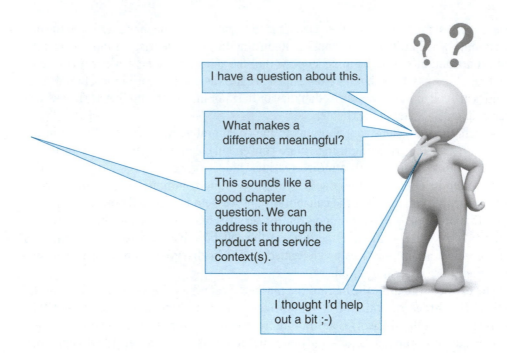

Meaning resides within the relativeness of differences. This involves understanding how differences form a frame of reference and how their relativeness becomes established. From a SPOT view, the differences lie within the characteristics or attributes of products and/or services, as in differences in quality. This frame of reference is based on things and their characteristics and, hence, this thing-like perspective is inherently static. For example, think about a positioning analysis (discussed in Chapter 4) and how it is mapping out brands relative to each other from the consumer's perspective. The focus is on how consumers perceive the different characteristics of the brands—e.g., high versus low quality. It should also be noted that this perspective doesn't take into account the ongoing repetition of difference occurring (as highlighted in Chapter 5).

In contrast, for the PM orientation, the frame of reference for meaningful differences is to be found within the collaborative network or brand community. Furthermore, it is not a static frame of reference but one that is constantly open to changes, with new differences being created along the way. This suggests that the relativeness or meaning is dynamic rather than static and it is not based upon things but, instead, pertains to the process of difference creation. As such, the PM orientation is based upon an understanding of difference and its *repetition*. Furthermore, as characterized in Chapter 5, it involves a nomadic consumer that is *creating a unique path of difference creation* while potentially being affected by others similarly pursuing their paths.

To get a better understanding of the roles products and services play in today's markets, we'll need to look at what is taking place within the collaborative network in which the (meaningful or otherwise) differences are being created. What is actually taking place within these networks? How are the differences being created?

Parallel to this discussion is the issue or concept of value. Which view you adhere to will affect where the value is to be located, its meaning, and, ultimately, your strategy. For example, does the value reside within the product (or service), as in a quality perspective, or does the value reside somewhere in what is taking place within the brand communities? Within each context, different strategies are suggested.

We'll begin with the traditional perspective of ways to differentiate products and services through the concept of quality. Then the discussion will bring in more recent research on brand communities to look at products and services through the concept of practices.

Transitional Thinking—From Quality to Innovation and Beyond

As mentioned previously, marketing—or more accurately, the thinking associated with marketing—has been on the move through its different orientations and their relative concepts. As discussed in Chapter 4, the SPOT concepts were developed early on during the 1950s and 1960s in a period during which the thinking was shifting toward developing an understanding of marketing from a consumer's perspective for the purposes of being more competitive. Marketing along the lines of differences in quality (products or services) and/or offering something new (an innovation) to the marketplace both stem from that type of marketing thinking. Yet within the thinking, in terms of quality and innovation, there are further differences in thinking that need to be brought about to understand these forms of marketing thinking and their strategies. We'll begin with examining the quality concept and then proceed to look at the transitional thinking from quality to innovation and within the innovation concept itself.

Quality as a Means for Differentiation

The concept of quality has received much attention in the marketing and management literature. Yet quality, as a concept, has been plagued with problems, primarily due to its level of abstraction. To understand this, ask two people what quality means to them. You'll most likely receive two different responses. So what is quality? The more abstract a concept becomes, the less concrete it is, making it that much more difficult to ascertain its meaning. With abstraction, thinking becomes less clear and more fuzzy. As discussed next, multiple definitions of quality for products and services exist.

Product Quality

Examples of definitions of product quality include transcendent ("even though quality can't be defined, you know what it is"); product-based (differences in ingredients or attributes); user-based (degree to which it satisfies consumer wants); manufacturing-based (conformance to requirements); and value-based ("excellence at an acceptable price and the control of variability at acceptable costs").[1] It has been observed of these definitions that "each are vague and imprecise when it comes to describing the basic elements of product quality."[2] To attempt to alleviate the situation, dimensions of quality have been suggested, as shown in Table 7.1.

Table 7.1	Product Quality Dimensions

Dimensions	Examples
Performance	How clear is the sound of your iPod?
Features	Does your iPod allow more than one person to listen to the music?
Reliability	Is the sound consistently good?
Conformance	Was the initial use of the iPod relatively easy to learn compared to what you had been using?
Serviceability	How easy is the iPod to maintain?
Aesthetics	Is the iPod pleasing to the eye?
Perceived Quality	Does the iPod brand project an image of high standards?

Sources: [3]

The importance of these dimensions is an attempt to be more concrete in defining quality in a product context. The strategic importance of defining quality in this way is to identify different ways to differentiate. However, several noteworthy observations can be made regarding this approach. The dimensions originate from an internal perspective and are thing-like or attribute based. Also, they are conceived to provide different ways in which to compete against other organizations in the market and other brands. As such, while they may give the appearance that they involve the consumer, in essence, they concern differentiating among products in the product category. Does this sound similar to the augmentation strategies discussed in Chapter 4? Now we'll bring service quality into the discussion.

Service Quality

As with product quality, service quality has also been defined dimensionally, whereby consumers judge the quality of a service. An example is presented in Table 7.2.

Table 7.2	Service Quality Dimensions

Dimensions	Examples
Tangibles	Is the restaurant clean?
Reliability	Was the service done well?
Responsiveness	How attentive was the wait staff?
Assurance	Did the staff give the impression they knew what they were talking about?
Empathy	Did they seem to care about your experience?

Sources: [4]

In both the product and service views of quality, a carryover effect can be seen from the offering or marketing mix concepts, similar to those discussed in Chapter 6. In other words, the thinking behind the views of quality inherently has a thing-like perspective and is internally oriented. Again, this creates the marketer–consumer gap and requires the marketer to bridge this gap, which causes difficulties along the way. Furthermore, this type of thinking sets up a situation that increases the likelihood of the marketer getting it wrong. This is a prevalent issue for those pursuing exclusively a quality strategy of differentiation and, as such, is problematic. In the context of services, while the issues of being responsive, having empathy, providing assurances, and so on are all good things for the marketer to be thinking about, if the thinking is thing-like or internally oriented, these aspects could very well be operationalized in ways that do not transcend the consumer's situation in a meaningful way and, as a consequence, a meaningful (beneficial) difference will not materialize in the marketplace. Before moving on to discuss the innovation concept, try the following Marketing Thinking Challenge on quality.

Marketing Thinking Challenge 7.1: Differentiating Through Quality

Choose a product or services category of your choice that uses quality in its marketing. Identify the competing brands and describe how they are using quality in their marketing and as a means for competition. From what you have identified, do you believe this to be an effective business strategy? Provide your rationale for your position. Offer an alternative strategy and explain how it would work.

| Figure 7.2 | Planning With Quality in Mind |

Innovation vs. Quality

As an alternative, it has been proposed that the focus should be on innovation rather than on quality. "Drucker proposed innovation, rather than quality or productivity, as the unique competitive approach to survive the ensuing complexities and uncertainties of the new era of discontinuity."[5] "The message for management is clear. New conditions continually emerging in a global economy lead to frequent changes in customer preferences for products and services makes it difficult to satisfy them with existing offerings (Drucker 1999). ...The only way for a firm competing in a changing environment to survive and grow is by introducing successful innovations which offer greater value than existing products or services."[6] The constantly changing conditions of the marketplace stem from the repetition of difference. This is also an example of thinking in time or thinking in difference, where nothing ever stays the same.

While innovations represent the future, several things can be said regarding this: (1) Implicit to this view is a thing-like perspective in that it suggests that success could come by continually offering a string of new things and (2) it offers an overly narrow view by implying that the value resides in the things (products and services), which would also have the effect of constricting the views for innovation in terms of what could be considered an innovation (that might not be a thing) and potential sources for innovation.

Innovation—A Process vs. "Thing" Orientation

However, a more recent innovation perspective is more customer centered and process oriented while being less about things. It is referred to as the jobs-to-be-done innovation theory that states that "people 'hire' products and services to get a job done."[7] Accordingly, companies can use the jobs-to-be-done perspective to map out consumption through a jobs orientation for the purposes of identifying ways to improve consumers' processes and reveal opportunities for innovations. It also suggests a way in which the marketer could identify ways to be a part of the consumers' value-creation process. While this is a step away from the thing-like perspective previously discussed and moves toward value creation and participation, the thinking behind it involves a narrower, more dyadic perspective between the marketer and the consumer and doesn't take into account the more expanded collaborative network view.

Expanding the Thinking

To avoid the above situation, an expanded, externally oriented form of thinking is called for. The marketer's thinking needs to begin from within the collaborative network and proceed accordingly, as with PM orientation. When considering products or services, this might seem counterintuitive, since the marketer is the one creating and/or providing the products and services. Right? This seems to be the question: Who is creating what? Or, more to the point, how should the marketer think about who is doing the creating?

The counterintuitive aspect can be traced back to earlier forms of marketing thinking, for example, with the production orientation discussed in Chapter 2, which is based on the perspective that the marketer is doing the creating. The marketing mix concept and the production orientation are part of marketing's lineage and its evolution in thinking and still have a major influence on how marketers think of marketing today. Both are grounded in a thing-like perspective, which ultimately leads to a mindset that, in essence, centers on building a better mousetrap. If one starts marketing thinking internally and views marketing as an activity of making and marketing things, then strategies will be developed that center around thing-like characteristics. This approach is overly simplistic and obscures other avenues for strategy. As previously discussed, conceiving of the situation about things leads to the marketer–consumer divide form of thinking with its one-sided or one-way characteristic.

However, more attention has recently been devoted to understanding how communities develop around brands, and these communities have been described in the form of a collaborative network. This focus on brand communities sheds light on how the co-creation process within these collaborative networks may be occurring, and it is the practices found within these networks (of which products and/or services may be a part) that create the value or meaning. This perspective places the creating process within the network, of which the marketer may or may not be a part. This would suggest that the marketer would need to become aware of the practices in the collaborative network, or, more generally, in the marketplace and then find ways to participate and contribute among them. This may involve marketing strategy that is directed toward enabling consumer practices and, therefore, marketing's focus becomes more about the consumer practices (where the value resides) and less about the things, products, and services per se. Again, this may seem counterintuitive because it is less familiar and involves a different orientation, a different form of thinking, and different strategies to conceive of and implement. Next, we'll examine brand communities and the practices that can be identified with them.

Creating Value Through Practices

A revolution in both marketing thought and practice is at hand. …co-creation will ultimately induce firms to collaborate with customers to co-create the entire marketing program. …This is consistent with open-source innovation…and with emerging corporate practices that tap into brand communities, such as LEGO, which explicitly sought and harnessed consumer innovation to refine the successful LEGO robotic kit Mindstorms…and skinnyCorp's Threadless, which manufacturers consumer-designed and critiqued T-shirts, famously claiming that "the customer is the company."[8]

Taking this a step further, instead of thinking narrowly in terms of individual value-creation activities,[9] brand community value creation is a collective process. It is an emerging social phenomenon, developing with developments in technology, that needs to be given greater marketing consideration. The thinking behind the brand communities' research is that

value resides in the actions, interactions, and projects that acquired resources make possible and support.[10]

What this underscores is that value stems from and originates out of the *doing* and *not the things*. This suggests that value is being co-created through practices, and marketing strategies are needed to focus on the activities or practices of those consuming their products and/or services. This implies that there might be a whole lot more going on with the consumption process than the marketer is aware of. From this practices view of consumption, the meanings for things (products and services) reside within how they fit in with the activities and, in the case of brand communities, meanings are being socially derived. In other words, the practices or activities are defining the consumption, of which products and services may be a part. What is significant here is that the marketer isn't defining the consumption and may not even be defining the marketing occurring with the brand communities. So, while the marketer may choose to emphasize some aspect of quality in the marketing, it may be completely apart from what is actually significant or being consumed through the brand community via the collaborative network(s).

| Figure 7.3 | The Marketer Headed in the Opposite Direction of the Brand Community |

The questions then become, What does the co-creation process look like that is taking place through brand communities? How are brand communities consuming products or services? What are they doing with them? What are they creating with the products or services? How can the marketer participate in this co-creation process? Next, research investigating brand communities is discussed.

A Brand Community

The concept of a community generally refers to any set of social relationships that operate within certain boundaries that could be geographical (e.g., a neighborhood) and/or ideological (e.g., a religious community).[11] Social relationships create the context in which norms, practices, and behaviors develop. In other words, to understand what something means or the behavior requires knowing the social context in which it takes place. An abstract way of thinking about this would be to ask the question, Can behavior occur outside of context? The answer is no. All behaviors occur in some context or another, and to understand them requires knowing something about the context in which they take place. *Context matters.* Similarly,

> A brand community is a specialized, non-geographically bound community, based on a structured set of social relationships among admirers of a brand. It is specialized because at its center is a branded good or service. Like other communities, it is marked by a shared consciousness, rituals and traditions, and a sense of moral responsibility. Each of these qualities is, however, situated within a commercial and mass-mediated ethos.[12]

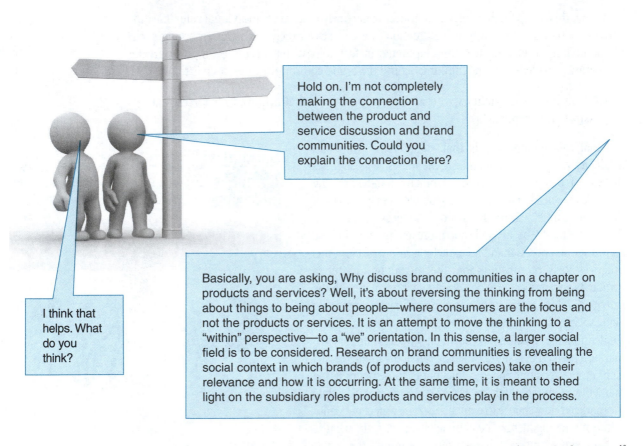

Hold on. I'm not completely making the connection between the product and service discussion and brand communities. Could you explain the connection here?

I think that helps. What do you think?

Basically, you are asking, Why discuss brand communities in a chapter on products and services? Well, it's about reversing the thinking from being about things to being about people—where consumers are the focus and not the products or services. It is an attempt to move the thinking to a "within" perspective—to a "we" orientation. In this sense, a larger social field is to be considered. Research on brand communities is revealing the social context in which brands (of products and services) take on their relevance and how it is occurring. At the same time, it is meant to shed light on the subsidiary roles products and services play in the process.

Brand communities have existed since Tupperware parties and Jeep Jamborees in the 1950s.[13] Other identified brand communities include Saab, Apple versus Microsoft versus Dell, Ford Bronco, Porsche, Lamborghini, Michelin tires, Zippo lighters, Cola-Cola, *Star Trek* (Trekkies), the *X-Files*, Harley Davidson, PlayStation versus Xbox, Republicans versus Democrats, Starbucks versus Dunkin Donuts, Oprah, Hanna Montana, Deepak Chopra, Facebook, Cancer Survivors Network, Dove ("Campaign for Real Beauty"), Red Hat Society, and Burning Man.[14, 15] The array of brands suggests that brand communities can develop around any brand, be it for a product, service, organization, or individual. As such, there are strategic opportunities to be considered.

A recent study of nine different brands investigated whether communities had developed around the brands and, if so, what practices were involved.[16] In revealing the practices associated with these potential brand communities, marketers hoped to be able to then identify strategies that would allow for their greater participation. The brands investigated included 3Con Audrey (an Internet device to check e-mail), Apple Newton (a PDA device similar to the Palm Pilot), Garmin (GPS devices—Nuvi, Quest, and Streetpilot), Jones Soda (a carbonated beverage), Lomo and Holga (cheaply made Russian and Chinese cameras), Mini Cooper (BMW Mini, a retro brand automobile), TPATH (Grammy Award–winning rock group), StriVectin (a high-end cosmetic), and *Xena: Warrior Princess* (syndicated TV melodrama with a fan fair that identifies with medieval reenactments).

The study determined that brand communities did exist around these nine brands, and 12 common value-creating practices were identified across the nine brand communities, which were grouped into four categories. See Figure 7.4. The community practices categories were (1) social networking, (2) impression management, (3) community engagement, and (4) brand use.

Figure 7.4	Brand Community Value Creation Practices

Social networking practices created, enhanced, or maintained ties with those with an interest in the brand. The practices involved welcoming, empathizing, and governing. "Examples include TPATH fans posting open invitations to community members to lifecycle celebrations, Garmin users relating road challenges and solutions to other members, StriVectin users complaining and sympathizing about aging."[17]

Impression management practices were directed toward creating positive impressions for the brand, the brand enthusiasts, and the brand community. "These included (1) evangelizing and (2) justifying."[18]

Community engagement practices pertained to reinforcing members' engagement with the brand. These practices involved documenting, badging, milestoning, and staking. It was also found that "These practices are competitive and provide members with social capital. Here, brand use is secondary to communal engagement. For example, in staking, community members delineate their specific domain of participation: The Lomo community is vast, but

I operate mostly within the groups interested in architectural lomography and within that group I spend most of my time with the German lomographers."[19]

Brand use practices involved improving or enhancing the use of the brand. These practices involved customizing, grooming, and commoditizing. An example of the brand use practice of customizing is illustrated in Figure 7.5.

| Figure 7.5 | The Mini Cooper Brand Community |

The effects from these communal practices can explain why they exist and the nature of the value generated while offering insights for marketing. We'll look at these next. See Table 7.3.

| Table 7.3 | The Effects of Brand Community Practices |

Effects	Examples
1. Endow participants with cultural capital.	Members compete on brand devotion, knowledge, and history.
2. Produce a repertoire for insider sharing.	Practices provide a source for insider jargon and modes of representation.
3. Generate consumption opportunities.	Documenting, badging, milestoning, and staking are forms of consumption.
4. Evince brand community vitality.	The existence, number, and diversity of practices are an indication for community vitality.
5. Create value.	By providing opportunities for members to demonstrate their competencies, the practices enable members to accrue social capital through adroit performances. Practices structurally add value by making actions reproducible and repeatable (e.g., how-to information). Even if the marketer has discontinued something, the practices can continue. **Value underlies all practices, and that engagement in practices is an act of value creation.**

Sources: [20]

One noteworthy observation about the practices and their effects is that, in essence, the members, the consumers, of these brand communities may be creating something entirely different than that which the marketer had perhaps envisioned or planned for, and community members can freely modify any or all aspects the brand (e.g., physically, socially). For the marketer to begin to participate in these communities, it is important to recognize the *creative will* and *social structuring* taking place through the community's practices. As such, whatever the marketer attempts to do, it can't be viewed as an attempt to impose controls on these communities. To get a better understanding of this, see the brand communities' myths presented in Table 7.4.

Table 7.4 Brand Communities—Myth vs. Reality

Myth	Reality
1. A brand community is a marketing strategy.	A brand community is a business strategy the entire organization is to be a part of.
2. A brand community exists to serve the business.	A brand community exists to serve the people in it.
3. Build the brand, and the community will follow.	Engineer the community, and the brand will be strong.
4. Brand communities should be love-fests for faithful brand advocates.	Smart companies embrace the conflicts that make communities thrive.
5. Opinion leaders build strong communities.	Communities are strongest when everyone plays a role, for example, historians, storytellers, or mentors.
6. Online social networks are the key to a community strategy.	Online networks are just one tool, not a community strategy.
7. Successful brand communities are tightly managed and controlled.	**Of and by the people, communities defy managerial control.**

Sources: [21]

Marketing Thinking in Practice: How Online Brand Communities Work

Mike Hall, a partner with online communities firm Verve, describes how online brand communities work and the role research can play. He explains the changes in thinking that involve releasing control for participation and the importance for conversation.

Getting into online brand communities may be a small step for a business, but it's one giant leap for businesskind—and researchers have the opportunity to play a central role.

Ever since the explosion of social networking, businesses have been trying to work out how online communities can be harnessed to help them grow and perform better. As with anything new, experimental activity is essential, but the varied uses of online communities, the inconclusivity of results, and practitioners' focus on the mechanism rather than the purpose mean that we are faced more with doubt and confusion than with a clear and coherent view of what their business role can be and how they work.

Verve has been working to develop a model to provide a clear discipline for how businesses can use online communities successfully. The study encompassed a review of existing literature and case studies, as well as primary interviews with a multidisciplinary group of practitioners, including clientside market insight and marketing, digital media experts, and advertising and market research agencies.

Definitions and purpose: Online brand communities are an important new development for businesses because they enhance the organisation's relationship with people. Not just with customers, but with anyone interested and active in their market—including employees, competitive brand users and market experts.

It is incorrect to call them "research communities": a brand community can work for all business disciplines, even if a company chooses to use it for only one. And over time, its value will increase with compound interest as it engages members across all the company's activities.

A new way to think of communities is as a medium, which means that (like TV as a medium, say) it carries content across multiple channels. The current channels are two: custom-built managed communities set up by or on behalf of a company, which are the main channel for research agencies and consumer insight departments; and existing open communities such as Facebook, accessed by businesses. Like all media, brand communities should be regarded as a permanent resource, which means that they are a major commitment, so it's important to understand how they work in order that there is a clear discipline for using them successfully.

The difference between a brand community and a panel is that members are allowed to have conversations of their own, on topics of their own choosing, with whomever they like, when they like—just as in real-life communities. This leads to a shift in the conventional business model of stimulus-response to a new model of stimulus-stimulus, where a more engaged community member gives the company fresh stimulus to move forward.

Participation is the new control: A huge concern for many businesses—and business people—is a perceived loss of control. It's more productive to think of a change than a loss. Our mantra is: Participation is the new control. If companies—including, especially, senior experts—engage in conversation online on member topics as well as on their own initiatives, they will be rewarded with more, better decisions, made more quickly. Stimulating wide participation of the community members is also important. Companies must give freely to ensure members feel rewarded and the community thrives. Participation is the oxygen of the community.

Researchers tend to overstate the importance of process. People do not feel more engaged because of the process, but because of the content. Information is the glue that binds a community together and keeps it participating. Content is king. It is because of the content they receive that people feel they are getting something valuable out of their involvement in the community, and it is because of the content they give, and the fact that this content is listened to and responded to, that people feel valued, which ensures their continued participation and strengthens their relationship with the organization or brand.

Research as the fusion element: The new ingredient in all of this is conversations, but managing and using them is less scary than business people think. In normal life, no one has a problem decoding, prioritizing, or acting on conversations, and there is no special trick or technique required in doing so within a community. But it does require dedicated focus and discipline, which is a skill that lies within the insight department and its agencies.

Conversations are a live current running through the use of a brand community by any business discipline, so even if a community is being used for sales, marketing, new product development in the production department, or corporate social responsibility activity by management, these conversations need to be managed, listened to, and acted upon, which puts the insight department potentially right at the center of a business in the future. And research agencies are the natural managers of communities, even when they are being used for marketing and other purposes. This is why we call research the "fusion element" of any community.

Communities for generating brand advocacy: Marketing to an online brand community also requires a big shift in the conventional business model. The stimulus of the marketing department can be broadly categorized as launches. There is a great variety of things launched: ad campaigns, new products, PR stories, beta websites, and so on. Marketing managers are used to controlling not just content but timing—launch upweights, bursts followed by gaps, and so on. Marketing to a community needs a different approach (more "drip" than "burst" for communications, for example) to replace this highly controlled old model. But the stimulus provided to the community members will also result in a more engaged brand relationship—beyond brand commitment to the golden chalice of brand advocacy—that will go some way to achieving the age-old conundrum of translating engagement into behavior. As for research, brand communities for marketing are an alternative additional medium, not a replacement for all other media in all cases, and communities are a better medium for small-scale, strong-response communications disciplines than mass market broadcasting.

What community conversations do in the marketing sphere is to initiate word-of-mouth—another target for this business discipline—which requires participation of the marketing team and management and analysis from the research department. One of the great things about how an online brand community works is that you can not only stimulate word of mouth but see what it consists of and track how it develops, particularly in the creation of company advocates, not just company advisers.

There are many other applications for every other department, best addressed individually but it's worth highlighting the huge potential for new product development and the production department. New product failure rates remain embarrassingly high and brand communities (or an elite group within them) represent a hugely exciting opportunity to improve on this, as the success of beta websites from the likes of Google have illustrated.

The trick with multidisciplinary use of a community is not to muddy the waters by using the whole community to do everything all the time and to be clear about what community members are being asked to sign up to do. Segmenting the community into general and "elite" or special interest groups makes them more manageable, confidential, and productive. Clear communication is an important part of community management by the agency that runs it.

An evolutionary process: The opportunity presented by online brand communities to businesses is well nigh unmissable. New media do not turn up often, and media that work across all business disciplines are rarer still. And embracing it need not be a daunting experience—it is important to see this as an evolutionary development for businesses. Evolution works by a series of experimental changes and that's the route for businesses to follow. Research, as the fusion element, is a good place to start, if not the only place. Taking the first step, in full knowledge of how to do it, is the important thing. In this anniversary year of the first moon landing, one might say online brand communities represent one small step for a business, but one giant leap for businesskind.[22]

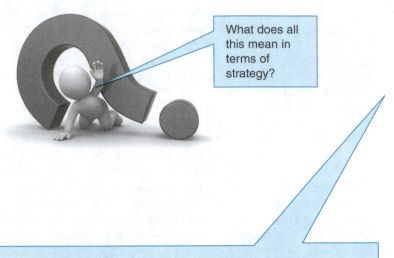

It says that the marketer needs to think about strategy in a different way. It can't simply be about creating a better thing or about controlling but, instead, needs to look more toward how to participate in the ongoing co-creation process going on all around the marketer. If you wanted to think of it in terms of innovation, those within brand communities are innovating even without the marketer. And for the marketer to be left out is an unnecessary disadvantage. New ways of thinking are called for. We'll look at these next.

Strategy Considerations

The brand community research suggests the following strategy considerations. See Table 7.5.

Table 7.5	Brand Community Strategy Ideas and More
Strategy Idea	**Explanation**
The birth	Create opportunities for consumers to construct a brand community. It could involve creating an open discussion forum with a website, supporting grass-roots activities, or offering organization activities that bring consumers together.
Releasing the reins	Encouraging consumers to modify the products or personalize services will potentially lead to evangelists, welcomers, badgers, etc., and to a stronger brand community—for example, creating website features that allow consumers to modify the brand logo or a section where consumers can list some of the changes they have made to the product itself. (This could be a potential source for product development and new innovations.)

Strategy Idea	Explanation
Welcome diversity	Develop an environment in which diversity can flourish by providing multiple forums, platforms, and situations in which different community practices could take hold. This allows for more co-creation, more value, and more opportunity for innovation.
Transparency is a mandate	Marketers need to be upfront and disclose their affiliation and not be seen as manipulative through their efforts and actions.
Greater listening	Whether it involves direct consumer contact (e.g., complaints or suggestions), following tweets, reading blogs, or tracking social network sites (e.g., Facebook), listening as a strategy is critical today. Listening allows organizations to become more responsive and able to meet changes as they are occurring.
Social themes	Here, the marketer needs to think socially to create socially themed activities. Examples might include the tribe (e.g., Harley Davidson's Brotherhood), the fort, the sewing circle, the patio, the bar, the tour group, the barn raising, or the summer camp (e.g., Harley Davidson's summer rallies). Themes can be used to create Internet or physical environments or events in which the reasons for coming together are socially thematic, with the product or service as a secondary element. **The emphasis is on people**.
Throwing open the doors	Open-market innovation involves organizations collaborating with outsiders. This could involve suppliers, channels, members, alliances, competitors, and consumers. Through increased collaboration, more and better ideas are possible, it reduces risk, is a means for assessing value, moves beyond simply the value chain, and facilitates the organization in developing a **"we"** perspective.

Sources: [23, 24, 25]

With the following Marketing Thinking Challenge, try thinking in terms of brand communities and what your marketing strategies might involve.

Marketing Thinking Challenge 7.2: Brand Communities

Go online and identify brand communities for a product, a service, and a B2B company. What types of practices can you identify with each? How are these practices defining the brands?

Also, look at the brand communities in terms of what you can identify with regard to the marketing being employed. Are they using some of the suggested strategy ideas from the chapter? If so, which ones? Are they using other strategies that weren't mentioned in the chapter? Describe them. Which strategies do you think are effective and which ones aren't? Explain why. What other ways could the marketer participate (contribute) in each of these situations?

| Figure 7.6 | Online Brand Communities |

Summary

- This chapter examines the centricity of products (or services) as a focus for marketing thinking and its influence. This form of thinking is a part of the SPOT view of marketing its related concepts. To illustrate the influence of a product focus on the marketer's thinking, the concept of quality was examined. This thinking was characterized as being thing-like and internally oriented.

- The quality orientation for products and services being based on a thing-like perspective was less about consumers and more about competing among other brands in the category.

- In contrast, the PM orientation to marketing, with its focus on participating within collaborative networks, was discussed. The thinking centers on the various ways the marketer could contribute to what might be occurring within these networks.

- To understand the context in which the marketer is potentially going to be contributing, brand communities were examined. Brand communities are a form of a collaborative network and are established and maintained through the practices of the community. Value is being created through the brand communities' practices that may or may not involve products and services. But the focus is on the practices and less about the things the practices may involve. Furthermore, the brand communities can exist without the marketer's participation and, as such, the practices and not the marketer define the consumption.

- To be able to participate, the marketer first needs to recognize the practices that are a part of the consumption and then develop ways and strategies to contribute based upon what is being created through these practices. The forms of contribution could involve process (e.g., making things more convenient), communications (e.g., listening and being more responsive), and/or creating value (e.g., providing unique benefits, enabling and/or enhancing the practices within a brand community).
- Strategy ideas were offered and discussed that were based on participation and making contributions and not on controlling the situation. There is more to be gained through releasing the reins of control to allow meaningful differences and value creation to occur, which the marketer can be a part of. What the brand community research also suggests is that, while marketers may think they are in control of their marketing and defining the consumption situation for consumers, it is quite evident that they are not. Therefore, the notion of control is a fallacy and another obstacle to thinking, similar to the diminution market parameter of difference discussed in Chapter 5.

Case: In-N-Out Burger—Keeping It Simple

In 1948, Harry and Esther Snyder decided to open a drive-thru hamburger stand in California called the In-N-Out (INO) Burger. In the 1940s, fast-food restaurants didn't exist, and the two-way communication order box (or speaker) we are familiar with today was an innovation developed by Harry and an electronic expert at that time. While he didn't have it patented, it eventually became a common feature for fast-food restaurants today. INO was built based upon a simple philosophy that has steered the company for more than 60 years.

> Give customers the freshest, highest quality foods you can buy and provide them with friendly service in a sparkling clean environment.[26]

The simplicity of the philosophy affects all aspects of the operations and marketing of the business. INO started out as a family business with Harry and his wife, and eventually their two sons got involved. The current CEO is his granddaughter, Lynsi Martinez, who took control of the business after several family members died in a plane crash.

Starting with one store in 1948, the business has grown to 420 INO locations with estimated annual profits of $420 million. In comparison, McDonald's has 31,000 locations worldwide and annual profits around $21 billion. Yet INO is estimated to be a close second with Burger King.[27]

Stacy Perman, author of the book *In-N-Out Burger: A Behind-the-Counter Look at the Fast-Food Chain That Breaks All of the Rules,* attributes INO's success to a kind of reversal, counterintuitive approach to doing business that prioritizes quality, customers, and employees over the riches that can come from rapid expansion, both geographically and through franchising. *The thinking of not expanding rapidly and franchising was based on being able to control the quality of the food.* While the philosophy may seem counterintuitive today, back in the 1940s, it wasn't. Being a product of the Depression era, these values would have been common with the times. Give people a good, healthy meal at a fair price and treat them with respect. Also, Harry never opened up a location unless he had the money and the staff fully trained. As part of this way of thinking, he paid his employees well, above the federal and state minimum wage requirements. Today, employees earn more than $10 an hour. To be consistent with his philosophy of giving customers friendly service, he knew his staff would need to feel good about themselves, and if they felt good about themselves by being paid well and working for a caring company, that they would naturally project positive, caring feelings with the customers. It was a win-win-win strategy for all parties.

What is also fundamental to the INO strategy was not to use the typical marketing hype done through traditional promotional strategies but to rely on the basics: quality, customers, and employees. "Instead of pouring hundreds of millions of dollars into ad campaigns like rivals Burger King (BKC) and McDonald's (MCD), In-N-Out relies mainly on its carefully located stores, billboards, bumper stickers, T-shirts, and its own rabid fans to broadcast its message."[28] The strategy is about word of mouth (WOM), and ultimately it resulted in an INO brand community with an ever-growing group of INO diehards.[29] Community members have even created their own "secret menu" that has gone viral on the Internet. While the INO menu is simple, only offering hamburgers, fries, and shakes, they allow customers to customize their orders to add or delete items. The "secret menu" has favorite customized options created by customers. Examples include Animal Style cheeseburger; vegetarians can order a Grilled Cheese, Double Meat (or 3 X 3 or 4 X 4), or a Protein Style burger.[30] Yet the main menu in the stores still only has hamburgers, fries, and shakes listed. Members have also taken on the responsibility of bringing in new devotees, referred to as "the conversion."[31]

The stores are simple in layout and clean. Every INO location is consistent in its décor and cleanliness. They have no freezers, heating lamps, or microwave ovens. Everything is made fresh. The fries are made with real potatoes, and customers can watch them being peeled. Fresh tomatoes come in every other day and are hand washed. The buns are made fresh on site. They have even established their own commissary to have control over the quality of the ingredients. They also created an INO "University" where new managers are trained and taught the company philosophy. The packaging (e.g., cups) has references to biblical verses (e.g., John 3:16), which stems from the family's Christian background. To give back to the community, they started a foundation in 1995 to help abused and neglected children.[32] (They had actually been helping children since the early 1980s but set up the nonprofit organization to address the issue on a larger scale.)

According to blogger Andy Beaupre, the lessons to be learned from the INO brand include being focused, differentiating, happy employees, doing good, a clear mission, staying independent, a subtle versus an overt approach, consumer loyalty, cult-like popularity, and creating an emotional connection. Accordingly, "All this adds up to a personal brand experience built on adjectives (cool, great, caring) not nouns (burgers, restaurants, revenues). It's emotional branding at its best."[33]

What other marketing lessons do you think the INO example suggests? Offer additional strategic recommendations that might be helpful. What types of changes could occur in the marketplace that would affect INO's success? How could they prepare for these changes?

References

1. Garvin, David A. (1984), "What Does 'Product Quality' Really Mean?," *Sloan Management Review*, 26 (Fall), 25, 26.
2. Garvin, David A. (1984), "What Does 'Product Quality' Really Mean?," *Sloan Management Review*, 26 (Fall), 25, 29.

3. Garvin, David A. (1984), "What Does 'Product Quality' Really Mean?," *Sloan Management Review*, 26 (Fall), 25, 29–30.

4. Zeithaml, Valarie A., A. Parasuraman, and Leaonard L. Berry (1990), *Delivering Quality Service: Balancing Customer Perceptions and Expectations*, New York: Free Press.

5. Dervitsiotis, Kostas N. (2010), "Developing Full-Spectrum Innovation Capability for Survival and Success in the Global Economy," *Total Quality Management*, 21 (2) (February), 160.

6. Dervitsiotis, Kostas N. (2010), "Developing Full-Spectrum Innovation Capability for Survival and Success in the Global Economy," *Total Quality Management*, 21 (2, February), 165.

7. Betterncourt, Lance A., and Anthony W. Ulwick (2008), "The Customer-Centered Innovation Map," *Harvard Business Review*, (May), 109.

8. Schau, Hope Jensen, Albert M. Muñiz, Jr., and Eric J. Arnould (2009), "How Brand Community Practices Create Value," *Journal of Marketing*, 73 (September), 30–1.

9. Holt, Douglas B. (1995), "How Consumers Consume: A Typology of Consumption," *Journal of Consumer Research*, 22 (June), 1–16.

10. Schau, Hope Jensen, Albert M. Muñiz, Jr., and Eric J. Arnould (2009), "How Brand Community Practices Create Value," *Journal of Marketing*, 73 (September), 31.

11. Jary, David, and Julia Jary (1991), *The HarperCollins Dictionary of Sociology*, New York: HarperPerennial, 66.

12. Muniz, Albert M., Jr., and Thomas C. Guinn (2001), "Brand Community," *Journal of Consumer Research*, 27 (March), 412.

13. Moffitt, Sean, and Alex Marshall (2009), "Brand Communities: 'It takes a community—not a campaign—raise a brand,'" *Market & Sales 2.0 Research Primer*, nGerera Corporation.

14. Muniz, Albert M., Jr., and Thomas C. Guinn (2001), "Brand Community," *Journal of Consumer Research*, 27 (March), 418.

15. Fournier, Susan, and Lara Lee (2009), "Getting Brand Communities Right," *Harvard Business Review*, (April), 105–11.

16. Schau, Hope Jensen, Albert M. Muñiz, Jr., and Eric J. Arnould (2009), "How Brand Community Practices Create Value," *Journal of Marketing*, 73 (September), 30–51.

17. Schau, Hope Jensen, Albert M. Muñiz, Jr., and Eric J. Arnould (2009), "How Brand Community Practices Create Value," *Journal of Marketing*, 73 (September), 34.

18. Schau, Hope Jensen, Albert M. Muñiz, Jr., and Eric J. Arnould (2009), "How Brand Community Practices Create Value," *Journal of Marketing*, 73 (September), 34.

19. Schau, Hope Jensen, Albert M. Muñiz, Jr., and Eric J. Arnould (2009), "How Brand Community Practices Create Value," *Journal of Marketing*, 73 (September), 34.

20. Schau, Hope Jensen, Albert M. Muñiz, Jr., and Eric J. Arnould (2009), "How Brand Community Practices Create Value," *Journal of Marketing*, 73 (September), 38–40.

21. Fournier, Susan, and Lara Lee (2009), "Getting Brand Communities Right," *Harvard Business Review*, (April), 105–11.

22. Hall, Mike (2009), "How Online Brand Communities Work," *research*, (December), www.research-live.com/magazine/how-online-brand-communities-work/4001790.article

23. Schau, Hope Jensen, Albert M. Muñiz, Jr., and Eric J. Arnould (2009), "How Brand Community Practices Create Value," *Journal of Marketing*, 73 (September), 30–51.

24. Fournier, Susan, and Lara Lee (2009), "Getting Brand Communities Right," *Harvard Business Review*, (April), 105–11.

25. Rigby, Darrell, and Chris Zook (2002), "Open-Market Innovation," *Harvard Business Review*, (October), 80–9.

26. History, In-N-Out Burger, www.in-n-out.com/history.asp

27. Wyld, David C. (2010), "Summary and Review of In-N-Out Burger: A Behind the Counter Look at the Fast Chain That Breaks All the Rules," Bizcovering, April 30, http://bizcovering.com/small-business/summary-and-review-of-in-n-out-burger-a-behind-the-counter-look-at-the-fast-chain-that-breaks-all-the-rules/

28. Perman, Stacy (2009), "In-N-Out Burger's Marketing Magic: How the restaurant chain manages its cult of popularity to encourage newbies and keep longtime customers coming back," *Bloomberg Businessweek*, April 24, www.businessweek.com/smallbiz/content/apr2009/sb20090424_877655.htm

29. Decker, Sam (2006), "4 Secrets of In-N-Out Burger's Sustained Success," *Decker Marketing*, February 7, http://decker.typepad.com/welcome/2006/02/4_secrets_of_in.html

30. Menu, In-N-Out Burger, www.in-n-out.com/secretmenu.asp

31. Perman, Stacy (2009), "In-N-Out Burger's Marketing Magic: How the restaurant chain manages its cult of popularity to encourage newbies and keep longtime customers coming back," *Bloomberg Businessweek*, April 24, www.businessweek.com/smallbiz/content/apr2009/sb20090424_877655.htm

32. Foundation History, In-N-Out Burger, www.in-n-out.com/foundation.asp

33. Beaupre, Andy (2009), "10 Branding Lessons From In-N-Out Burger," *CHECKMATE the Beaupre blog*, May 15, www.beaupre.com/blog/index.cfm/2009/5/15/10-branding-lessons-from-InNOut-Burger

CHAPTER 8

Co-creating (Co-marketing) Meaningful Differences With Marketing Communications

Decompression Exercise

Before beginning the chapter, visualize creating a picture.

Figure 8.1 Using Your Imagination

Chapter Introduction

In the last chapter, we saw how different forms of thinking about products and services affected strategy considerations—that is, a quality versus brand communities perspective. Originating out of different starting points in terms of their lines of questioning, the differences in thinking can be encapsulated in the question: *How should the marketer think about who is doing the creating—the marketer, the consumer, or the larger group (of which consumers and the marketer may be a part)?*

While collaborative networks such as brand communities suggest that the larger group is actively engaged in a *co-creation* process in which individuals, smaller groups, and/or organizations can potentially contribute through various forms of participation, there may be much more going on than what we examined so far that deserves further attention for the purposes of opening the doors for new strategies. We'll need to utilize our thinking agility here again to open these doors.

Within brand communities, we saw that the co-creation process revolves around the practices through which the communities have been erected and are maintained. It is through these practices that products and services acquire their subsidiary positions and meanings. Similarly, this co-creation process may involve marketing communications and, therefore, can be described as a *co-marketing* process. What this is referring to is that marketing can be occurring within the larger group (i.e., collaborative networks, brand communities) of which each constituent is potentially a part, contributing to the co-creation or co-marketing in which products and services, along with their marketing, may be elements of the process. It also means that the co-marketing can take place without the marketer. This situation represents a change in how we understand marketing and the role marketing is to play within contemporary times.

By examining the traditional marketing communications in contrast with developing ones via the Internet, we will be able to acquire a deeper understanding of what co-marketing means to the marketer and how it is changing our understandings associated with marketing communications and marketing in general. At the heart of the discussion is an examination of the orientations of marketing communications (e.g., a persuasive vs. a collaborative orientation) and their corresponding forms of thinking. Through this discussion, we'll identify a new form of "value" to consider as well. At the same time, we're interested in opening up new avenues and considerations for strategy. This chapter examines these issues.

Traditional vs. Contemporary Forms of Marketing Communications

There is a growing body of marketing research, both industry and academically driven, investigating the changes occurring as a result of technology and the Internet's growth and what they mean for marketing communications. To understand these changes, some have discussed the differences between inbound and outbound marketing. For example, as Rick Barnes from the HubSpot blog explains:

> Inbound Marketing is marketing focused on getting found by customers.
>
> In traditional marketing (outbound marketing), companies focus on finding customers. They use techniques that are poorly targeted and that interrupt people.

They use cold-calling, print advertising, T.V. advertising, junk mail, spam and trade shows.

Technology is making these techniques less effective and more expensive. Caller ID blocks cold calls, TiVo makes T.V. advertising less effective, spam filters block mass emails and tools like RSS are making print and display advertising less effective. It's still possible to get a message out via these channels, but it costs more.

Inbound Marketers flip outbound marketing on its head.

Instead of interrupting people with television ads, they create videos that potential customers want to see. Instead of buying display ads in print publications, they create their own blog that people subscribe to and look forward to reading. Instead of cold calling, they create useful content and tools so that people call them looking for more information.

Instead of driving their message into a crowd over and over again like a sledgehammer, they attract highly qualified customers to their business like a magnet.[1]

Figure 8.2	Outbound vs. Inbound Tactical Differences
Outbound	**Inbound**
Print Ads	Blogs, Ebooks, White Papers
Television Ads	Viral YouTube Videos
Cold Calling	Search Engine Optimization
Trade Shows	Webinars
Email Blasts	Feeds, RSS

Source: From Rick Burnes's (2008), "Inbound Marketing & the Next Phase of Marketing on the Web," Nov. 18, Hubspot Blog, http://blog.hubspot.com/blog/tabid/6307/bid/4416/Inbound-Marketing-the-Next-Phase-of-Marketing-on-the-Web.aspx[2]

Figure 8.2 illustrates the differences between the two perspectives. The problems with the traditional outbound perspective of marketing communications are highlighted further through a 2007 YouTube video parody titled the "Advertising–Customer Break Up," http://youtube.com/watch?v=DkOHsjZKBB0.

The scene is a restaurant, where a young couple is on a lunch date. The consumer character is played by a woman and the advertiser character is played by a man. The consumer is complaining that the advertiser doesn't listen to her and doesn't understand her wants and needs. He responds with one-liner messages mimicking the ways brands are typically marketed while demonstrating her point about his one-sided behavior. To illustrate how much he cares for her, he refers to the TV ad he ran along with a print campaign and a billboard in Times Square ("a 200-foot-tall declaration of love"). She also mentions that they don't meet in the same places anymore and that she has changed, yet he hasn't. At this point, he offers her "coupons!" She proceeds to say that he doesn't know her, to which he replies—What do you mean? "I know everything about you. You are 28 to 34, your online interests include music, movies, and laser hair removal. You have a modest but dependable disposable income." He continues to *talk at her,* ignoring her concerns. Sound familiar? This is an indication of how this ubiquitous perspective has become associated with marketing.

While this scenario isn't a testament to the consequences of changing technology, it does have to do with the way marketers have thought about the role of marketing and the ways they have used marketing communications to fit in with their views. As such, it represents a point of departure for marketing thinking and how changing technology is facilitating this departure. To stay current, the marketer has no choice but to reckon with these changes. The changes in technology and the contrast between inbound and outbound marketing simply highlight the issue while suggesting that the traditional outbound marketing communication approach is increasingly becoming less effective, calling for the need to rethink the role of marketing communications.

We'll look at traditional forms of marketing communications and then contrast them with contemporary forms to illustrate the ongoing transformation that is occurring in the marketplace and one in which the marketer has no choice but to participate in these changes. With this backdrop presented, marketing communication strategies follow.

Traditional Forms of Marketing Communications— Outbound and Persuasively Oriented

Marketing communications have traditionally fallen under the promotion "P" of the original marketing mix. Promotion also has its own mix, which includes advertising, sales promotions (consumer and trade), direct marketing, public relations (publicity), personal selling, packaging, and so forth, as depicted in Figure 8.3. In this context, *promotion* refers to "the coordination of all seller-initiated efforts to set up channels of information and persuasion to sell goods and services or to promote an idea." The promotion mix pertains to "the tools used to accomplish an organization's communications objectives."[3]

This view of marketing communications can be described as an outbound form of communications meant to persuade those being targeted. To understand what the objectives for these forms of communications are, one needs to consider what the marketer has in mind in terms of persuasion. In other words, what does persuasion mean in a business context?

Table 8.1 provides insight into this question through the basic characteristics of the different promotional forms of marketing communications and modes of delivery that have been developed with a persuasive perspective in mind.

Figure 8.3	The Traditional Promotion Mix (one of the 4 Ps)

Table 8.1	Marketing Communications Characteristics and Modes of Delivery
Forms of Marketing Communications	**Communication Characteristics and Modes of Delivery**
Advertising	**Characteristics:** To create awareness, affect levels of familiarity, facilitate associations (affect and/or cognitive), establish a brand, and carry sales promotions (e.g., coupons) **Modes:** TV, radio, print, billboards, transit, outdoor, Internet, etc.
Personal Selling	**Characteristics:** To develop a customer rapport, tailor information to facilitate decision making, add to a brand's meaning, and provide sales promotions **Modes:** In-person or phone
Sales Promotions (Consumer & Trade)	**Characteristics:** To temporarily change the value structure in a marketplace and provide an inducement to try a product or service, buy more of the product or service, purchase a different or complimentary product or service, or reward continuing purchasing behavior. Can also affect the brand's meaning. **Modes:** In-store, on the packaging, in the package, or the package itself; through advertising, personal sales, or direct marketing
Direct Marketing	**Characteristics:** To create ongoing interaction/dialogue to produce an immediate measureable response. Can also affect the brand's meaning. **Modes:** direct mail, telemarketing, or e-mail
Public Relations (Publicity)	**Characteristics:** To foster goodwill among customers, employees, stockholders, channel members, the government, and the general public by communicating the good things the organization is doing such as hiring more employees, providing charitable contributions, pursuing sustainable and green initiatives, new products, etc. Can also be used for damage control. Publicity via news outlets or the Internet (viral marketing) can increase credibility of the brand and/or the message. **Modes:** TV, radio, print, or the Internet
Packaging	**Characteristics:** To carry the message and the brand; provide content and regulatory information; communicate through shapes, sizes, colors, and materials; and deliver sales promotions **Mode:** Physical, as in a product, or atmospheric, as in a service context

Persuasion, in its simplest form, refers to the act of effecting a *change* in someone such as changes in beliefs, dispositions, or familiarity. Table 8.1 illustrates some of the ways marketers can engage in the act of persuasion by selectively choosing the various forms of communications called for to effect the changes that they would like to see occur among the consumers being targeted (e.g., a change in preferences).

Table 8.1 offers a formal perspective related to the characteristics associated with different forms of marketing communication. However, it doesn't fully depict other, less scrupulous communication means such as deceptive advertising, not divulging harmful product content or defects, the use of fine print or labeling that only a lawyer or scientist could read, and so forth.

On the flip side, in some sense, persuasion is similar to *learning* where learning is also about change but is grounded in a belief of egalitarianism in which inequalities can be removed. This view shows up via the need for consumer protections concerned with the potential inequalities or inequities being created in the marketplace with consumers by the marketer through various forms of marketing communications. But were the initial consumer protections actually being put in place for the consumer or for some other purpose?

Four decades ago, "consumerism" became a broadly accepted term for the political and social movements seeking to protect consumers by requiring businesses to provide nondeceptive advertising, product guarantees, honest packaging and improved safety standards.[4]

In the early stages of the *consumerism movement*, to offset inequalities purposely being created in the marketplace by businesses for their benefit, educating consumers became a priority—but not for the welfare of the consumer but, rather, for the purpose of protecting the "system of competition."[5] Consumers were secondary beneficiaries. Over the decades, as different government administrations have come and gone and economic conditions have changed, various protections and regulations have been enacted as well as eliminated. The economic conditions that began in 2008 are a result of earlier removal of marketplace regulations. For the consumer, it parallels a roller coaster ride in terms of protections and oversight. And it produced quite a ride, as captured by the following quote:

Meanwhile, my Toyota might suddenly experience runaway acceleration at any time, my bank might fail, my prescription might have hidden dangers—assuming the insurance company will allow me to buy it—and the pet food imported from China could have had a dangerous additive that killed my dog.[6]

Persuasion has always been a part of the human social **characteristic**. Perhaps the need for persuasion originated from becoming social and developing the means for getting others to see and accept one's views. The purposes for which it is used can also be interpreted in a positive or negative way depending upon the tactics used and their outcomes. For example, persuading someone to give up smoking could be seen as justifiable (e.g., advertising by the American Lung Society), leading to potentially positive outcomes (e.g., healthier consumers).

However, in the context of the tarnished side of the history of business, persuasion hasn't necessarily been driven by such noble ideas. Businesses have used questionable persuasive tactics for their benefit, and those targeted by the tactics may not have benefited, not benefited in an equal way, or actually have been harmed. It becomes an ethical issue, but to understand the logic, we'll need to look at the thinking behind it. Why had marketers been using persuasive tactics in this way? Why were the traditional outbound marketing communications developed in the way they were? What was driving their thinking? And, is this thinking still prevalent today?

Forces Driving the Persuasive Orientation

With an understanding of what has been driving marketing and its practices, along with bringing into view the changes that are taking place with the technology, we'll get a better sense of where marketing is headed and why. In the business context, the persuasion question pertains to who is benefitting—is it marketers, consumers, and/or society? Why did businesses resort to using persuasion in the way they have in the past? After all, if you had a great product or service that fulfilled consumers' needs and wants, would persuasion really be needed?

The need for persuasion or persuasive tactics in a business context perhaps originates out of different streams of thought. Some of these streams of thought are illustrated in Figure 8.4.

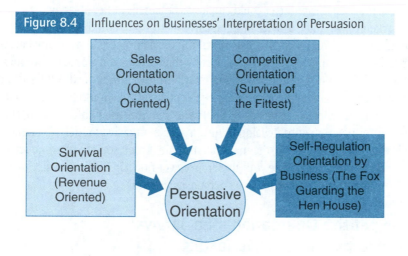

Figure 8.4   Influences on Businesses' Interpretation of Persuasion

The Survival Orientation—At the Heart of the Need for Persuasive Tactics

The survival orientation, to stay in business, is the basis or logic for the other three persuasive complementary operational orientations. For a business to exist, it must generate revenues, whether for a profit or nonprofit organization, and so the thinking centers on this very fundamental need. And, perhaps, during desperate times, the need to survive led to the view that any means to do so is acceptable. The period from the mid-1950s to the early 1970s is an example of the conditions that can lead to such thinking. During this period, the sales orientation took hold for many businesses.

The Sales Orientation and the Need for Persuasive Tactics

The sales orientation is described as follows.

The **sales orientation** era ran from the mid 1950's to the early 1970's, and is therefore after the production orientation era but before the marketing orientation era. During WWII world industry geared up for accelerated wartime production. When the war was over...[the] industrial machine turned to producing consumer products. By the mid 50's supply was starting to out-pace demand in many industries. Businesses had to concentrate on ways of selling their products. Numerous sales techniques such as closing, probing, and qualifying were all developed during this period and the sales department had an exalted position in a company's organizational structure. Other promotional techniques like advertising, and sales promotions were starting to be taken seriously. Packaging and labeling were used for promotional purposes more than protective purposes. Pricing was usually based on comparisons with competitors (called competitor indexing).[7]

With the need to generate revenues and with the buildup of supplies or products, marketers turned to their sales forces to move inventory. It became an issue of survival and searching for the means to resolve the problem of too much inventory. As such, it really didn't matter if the products would necessarily benefit the consumer. The thinking focused on simply meeting sales quotas to move product and generate revenue. The other forms of promotion techniques came along in time, filling out the promotion mix—each possessing a particular persuasive characteristic (as seen in Table 8.1) that the marketer could employ to obtain his or her objectives.

The marketer now had a tool kit of persuasive tactics that could be employed on consumers depending on the situation. It wasn't until the marketing orientation appeared that consumer needs and wants were considered. But by then, the promotional techniques had been developed and continued to influence how marketing was practiced. While the marketing orientation is concerned with consumers' needs and wants, it should be noted that the thinking behind this orientation is basically that by using consumer information, the marketer would be better positioned to develop *more effective* persuasive tactics.[8] The question again is, Who is the real beneficiary—the marketer, the consumer, society, or some relative combination? A related question is, Are your preferences your own? In other words, how much have you been influenced by marketing or its persuasive tactics?

The Competitive Orientation—The Survival of the Fittest via Persuasive Tactics

With a finite number of consumers and with increasing numbers of competitors, the survival orientation can kick in, directing the marketer's attention toward those that are seen as a threat leading to the competitive orientation. As such, another stream of thought that has had a major influence on the use of promotional techniques is the competitive orientation. If the objectives of marketing are to out-maneuver the competition to survive, then consumers are simply the means by which to get the job done, which is where the marketing orientation gains its purpose. It led to thinking in the following terms. With better consumer information at hand, the marketer can be more persuasive than his or her competitors. Competition was to be based on who was better than others at persuading consumers in the marketplace. While the marketing orientation would imply a more benevolent side to marketing, the competitive orientation seems to outweigh it and, again, disadvantages the consumer in the process.

The Self-Regulation Orientation by Business—Persuasion Can Be Beneficial (?)

The final stream of thought is driven by an economic perspective that advocates that consumers and the marketplace are best served by competition and deregulation. In its basic form, the argument is that the need for survival for businesses is a sufficient mechanism that naturally provides a certain degree of protection for consumers and the marketplace. For government to regulate the means would dampen the survival mechanism of businesses and cause a negative effect on the marketplace. From this perspective, allowing for free rein of persuasive tactics is beneficial to the nature of competition and the marketplace—or so the logic goes.

As such, "With the encouragement of Alan Greenspan, financial markets were deregulated with his stated trust that consumers would be protected adequately by self-regulation and market forces."[9] Of course, this has been vigorously argued against by consumer activists like Ralph Nader and others. "Nader himself had a strong rallying statement that with consumers against a modern corporation, you cannot trust the competitive marketplace to provide necessary protection: 'You can't have equal protection of the law when it is you versus Exxon.'"[10] Given the economic events of 2009, most would agree that some form of regulation is called for—the fox guarding the henhouse simply can't be trusted.

The streams of thought, the survival orientation, the sales orientation, the competitive orientation, and the self-regulation orientation, in essence, put the consumer's welfare down the priority pole while justifying the need for and use of persuasive or deceptive techniques that have become a normal practice of doing business. This is a case in which the marketer believes that the ends (e.g., staying in business) justify the means (e.g., persuasive tactics).

Before moving on to examine an alternative view to marketing communications, try the following Marketing Thinking Challenge.

Marketing Thinking Challenge 8.1: Persuasive Marketing Communications

Identify a product-oriented company and a service company that you believe exhibit the use of persuasive tactics in their marketing communications. For each company, explain what forms of persuasion they are they using. Then explain how you believe these practices may be contributing to or detracting from their reputations within their respective industries.

 Figure 8.5   Skeptical

An Alternative to the Persuasive Orientation

The consumer's time has arrived to change the balance of their status in the marketplace. While consumers can't depend on government to completely protect them, by becoming educated through personal experiences and/or learning from others and through technology, over time consumers have become aware of these techniques and have learned to block marketers' efforts. With use of the Internet, they may be starting to level the playing field.

As a consequence, marketers are rethinking whether to continue to use their persuasive techniques or practices. Is there an alternative way of doing business that might provide a way to repair this reputation and to establish new forms of relationships? Perhaps the new way for business, for marketing, lies within the *collaborative orientation* (CO), which leads to the *participatory marketing* (PM) perspective discussed in Chapters 6 and 7. Next, we'll look at the streams of thought driving the new collaborative orientation taking place through the different facets emerging in social media and then examine the different marketing characteristics associated with them.

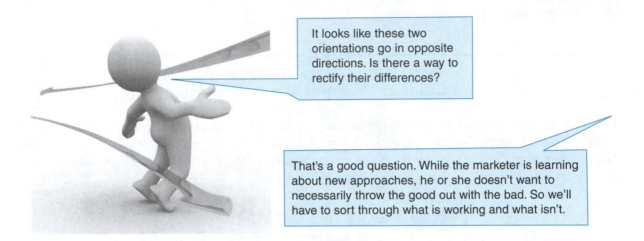

We'll see if there are points of convergence between the traditional and contemporary forms of marketing communications to develop new approaches and strategies.

The Collaborative Orientation

The collaborative orientation is driven by at least five different streams of thought: changing technology, open communicating via the Internet, a sense of community through conversing and sharing, the backlash against business, and changing world affairs. See Figure 8.6.

| Figure 8.6 | The Streams of Thought Behind the Collaborative Orientation |

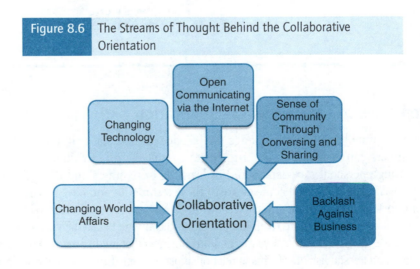

Through advances in technology, the world has become smaller and more global. What happens in one part of the world has a ripple effect throughout. The global perspective can be seen worldwide with growing interest in climate change and limited resources (e.g., oil, food). Reaching across borders to assist others in need when confronted with natural disasters or some crisis is a common occurrence today. Similarly, with the concerns over war and conflict, there is an increasing need for diplomacy and a greater interest in working out the differences. The Internet has facilitated this sense of a global community and changing world affairs. It provides and represents a forum or platform for open communications worldwide, where any one person with access to the Internet can raise the consciousness of the world to an issue. The Internet is also contributing to the sense of community by providing such means of communication built upon conversing and sharing. No other means of communication has provided such a conduit at such a grand scope.

All the while, questionable business practices have not gone unnoticed and are regularly brought to bear on the Internet. Social media are shining a bright spotlight on such practices, bringing businesses under much greater scrutiny than ever before and, hence, forcing the hand of businesses to question its own practices and to search for alternative ways.

At the same time, it is interesting that as marketers engaged in their various persuasive practices, they were creating or opening up new opportunities in the form of new businesses and technology to block marketers' efforts directed toward consumers (e.g., spam filters, TiVo, no-call lists). It is notable that out of something negative, something positive can occasionally develop.

When you think about changing world affairs, changing technology, communicating via the Internet, sense of community through conversing and sharing, and the backlash against business, what is the collaboration orientation about? Changing world affairs, open communication via the Internet, a sense of community by conversing and sharing, and the rest are all about creating a present for the future. In other words, to converse, to share, to participate, and to contribute in the present is to collaborate with the future in mind.

In this sense, collaboration pertains to a process that is in between the present and the future. It involves consuming the past and present for the future, where the future will become the present and then, the past (infinite idiom)…

While it's not exactly apparent, however, there's an opportunity here to locate another view of value, one that is more dynamic in its orientation. By applying our thinking agility and possessing a willingness to stretch our horizons, we are poised to open up a new avenue in terms of thinking about value and how it can be found within the basis of collaboration.

The Collaborative Orientation—Identifying Where the "*Value*" Resides

Several aspects are contained in this philosophical description of the collaborative orientation: the value lies in between the present and future. There is value in being a part of the process, and it is a dynamic process that can move in any direction through the participation of contributors. Perhaps what is difficult to understand is that it suggests that the *real value* resides *not* entirely in the present (e.g., what already exists, within things, products, brands) but somewhere in between the present and the future, where something is being consumed (e.g., a brand) and created (e.g., a brand community) in the process where what is being created is yet to be fully realized—the "*value*" resides in both the consuming and creating, simultaneously.

<u>Present</u> ----- *Value* ----- **Future**

In-Between…

<u>Consuming</u> ----- *Value* ----- **Creating**

This is one of the important lessons to be learned through a collaborative orientation. As such, a business would be better served by constantly focusing on creating value where the value is being developed through collaborative efforts and participation (PM) with an understanding that the value has yet to be fully realized in whatever forms it is occurring. Such collaborative efforts and participation then become the hallmark to strategy. As a consequence, the valuation process would continue indefinitely, through new forms of participation, contributions, and so on.

Next, we'll discuss the various social media tools currently available and their marketing characteristics. We will then see how they relate to this philosophical collaborative (participation) orientation for business purposes and how they play a part in the value-creation process.

Contemporary Forms of Communications—Social Media

As millions of people use the Web for conducting detailed research on products and services, getting involved in political campaigns, joining music and film fan clubs, reviewing products, and discussing hobbies and passions, they congregate in all kinds of online places. The technologies and tools, which many people now refer to collectively as "**social media**," all include ways for users to express their opinions online.[11]

Figure 8.7 illustrates the various tools available for users to express their opinions and share information, resulting in millions of online conversations taking place daily. Each tool is described in Table 8.2 along with its marketing characteristics.

| Figure 8.7 | Social Media Tools |

Table 8.2 Social Media Tools and Marketing Characteristics

Social Media Tool	Description	Characteristics
Microblog (e.g., Twitter & Tumblr)	Known as a "microblog" or "microcommunications" tool or platform that allows users to send text-based messages, known as "tweets," up to 140 characters in length to other users who have requested updates from that user. The messages can be public or private (direct).	Provides **referrals** to blogs, news sites, and company websites. Companies can **listen** in on and participate in public conversations customers are having. It can be used to **test out new products** and **create buzz**, and marketers can **track** competitors via their Twitter feeds.
Business Network (e.g., LinkedIn, Ryze, & Plaxo)	A business-oriented social networking site that allows professionals to display their credentials; connect with colleagues; keep track of job positions, promotions and accomplishments; and connect with others.	Companies can **post** job positions, **attract** prospective employees, **communicate** among professionals about organization accomplishments, and **track** competitors.
Blog	A website that discusses some topical area in which others would be interested. A blog is written by someone who is passionate about a topic or possesses an expertise in a particular area and who wishes to share information.	A blog could be a **"hub"** for a company's "content-creation wheel" by providing relevant commentary and news. Can have **links** to tweets, Facebook, or other relevant sites. Can be used to identify and develop relationships with **influencers and prospects**. Can also **track** competitors via their blog. RSS (Really Simple Syndication) readers allow you to **organize the blogs** you are following (e.g., Netvibes, Google Reader, and my6sense).
Social Network (e.g., Facebook & **Google**+)	Allows users to connect publicly and privately to share information.	Companies can create a **company profile**. **Join networks** organized by brands, celebrities, politicians, cities, workplaces, schools, etc. Can **search and add friends** and send private and public (wall) **messages**. Can **listen** in on and participate in network conversations. Can **track** competitors via their Facebook pages.
YouTube or other video (e.g., Metacafe, Vimeo, & Viddler)	A video-sharing website through which users can upload and view videos. Is available in 14 different languages and 21 countries.	Companies can **upload videos** and then **link them** in their news release. They also can be linked to via LinkedIn, Facebook, blogs, Tweets, etc. Videos can be picked up **"virally"** to create **buzz**.
Social Bookmarking Site (e.g., Diigo, Delicious, & Magnolia)	Web service that provides storage, sharing, and discovery of bookmarks. It's a way to expand computer desktops by making your bookmarks accessible from the "cloud" or the Internet. Content can be tagged with key words to be able to remember what it is for.	Companies **can learn** from how users tag different content, the descriptions they use, and what other types of content have been saved.
Forum (e.g., Yahoo!, Google Groups, Amazon reviews, GetSatisfaction, RateItAll, Yelp, TripAdvisor)	Social networks that enable members to create subgroups to host conversations around common interests and to collaborate on events, projects, and tasks.	Companies can **listen** in on and participate in public conversations participants have to **learn** about interests, experiences, and opinions. Can **track** competitors.

(Continued)

Table 8.2	(Continued)	
Social Media Tool	**Description**	**Characteristics**
Crowdsourced News (e.g., Digg, Reddit, Mixx, & StumbleUpon)	Online community networks utilizing the "wisdom of the crowd" to source, share, and showcase news, videos, pictures, music/audio, and events, voting on their popularity and visibility organized around categories.	Companies can **listen in** on these communities to find out what is **hot, interesting, or promising**. Can **track** competitive information.
DIY Site (e.g., Ning, Jive, kickAppas, & Crowdvine)	Do-it-yourself (DIY) networking sites allow businesses and individuals to initiate and host DIY services forums.	Companies can **host** and **participate** in relevant DIY forums that can be used to **learn**, **listen** in on, and **promote** products and services. Can **track** competitors.
Picture (e.g., Flickr, PhotoBucket, & SmugMug)	An online image- and video-hosting site that allows users to share and embed photos and videos in blogs and other social media.	Companies can use and provide **photos and videos**. Allowing photos and videos to be **shared**, **embedded**, and **blogged** about provides for **another way of communicating** through the social media.
Google Buzz	Started in 2010, Google Buzz is a social networking and messaging tool. It allows users to share links, photos, videos, status messages, and comments via organized "conversations" visible in the user's box.	Companies can **share messages** publicly or privately, **monitor relevant conversations** similar to Twitter, and allow for publicly **posting "buzz"** about your company and tag posts with your location. Can **track** competitors.
Geosocial Networks Site (e.g., Foursquare & Gowalla)	A social networking site with geographic services and capabilities.	Companies can **connect** and coordinate with users and events based upon the geographic location and their interests. Companies can **post** relevant information. As a participant in the network, **sales promotions** (e.g., loyalty programs) could be offered **geographically**. Can **track** competitors geographically.
Wikipedia	An online encyclopedia containing more than 15 million articles; considered to be an important reference site on the Internet.	Wikipedia articles often show up on the **first page** of a Google search. A **variety of users** rely on the articles for their research (e.g., students, journalists, and researchers). **Anyone can contribute,** which may be an opportunity for organizations to communicate with people in a different way.

Sources: [12, 13]

Several noteworthy observations can be made when comparing the differences among the traditional and more contemporary forms of communications in terms of their marketing characteristics. See the differences between Table 8.1 and 8.2. The traditional (e.g., advertising, sales promotion, etc.) tend to be one-way forms of communicating (i.e., outbound), less interactively oriented, and more intrusive versus being permission or participation oriented and more persuasive versus information or conversationally oriented. In contrast, social media forms facilitate information sharing, conversing, and community building. Such social activities have established certain social etiquettes. They also allow for creating an interactive presence online, a means for listening to others, tracking (e.g., competitors or otherwise), and developing brand communities. Additionally, it appears that social media, from a marketing perspective, are *less* about awareness as in advertising but *more* about creating advocacy (i.e., advocates, champions, and evangelists) on behalf of the company, its brand(s), product(s), or service(s).[14]

This indicates that persuasion is still important, but who is doing the persuasion has shifted. Online communities have developed their own influencers through blogs, forums, and the like. These influencers have their own followings, which can number in the millions. For example, Advertising Age provides a daily ranking of the top 150 marketing blogs/bloggers (http://adage.com/power150). Any area or topic of interest could have similar rankings of bloggers and influencers. With these differences in mind, we'll move on to discuss what this all means for marketing strategy.

Marketing Thinking Challenge 8.2: Social Media

Go online and identify a B2B industry and a product category that are heavily using social media tools. For each situation, describe the social media tools being used and then explain how they are being used as part of an online community. Also, are there facets that indicate they are listening and responding as a result of what they have learned?

Figure 8.8	Searching for Business-to-Business Social Media Use

Co-marketing Communication Strategies

"Marketers are just beginning to understand the formation, reaction, and effect of community based marketing promotions."[15] An emerging view in research, word-of-mouth marketing (WOMM), is expanding the word-of-mouth (WOM) perspective to go beyond the traditional models that involved a linear marketer influence to now consider a network coproduction model. This view recognizes that "Consumers are regarded as active co-producers of value meaning, whose WOM use of marketing communications can be idiosyncratic, creative, and even resistant."[16] Accordingly, "market messages and meanings do not flow unidirectionally but rather are exchanged among members of the consumer network."[17] This should sound familiar from our discussion of brand communities in Chapter 7. It recognizes that the production of value doesn't flow unidirectionally (or originate) from the marketer to the market but, instead, takes place within the collaborative networks among participants. In other words, consumers take what is in the marketplace and make with it whatever they see fit, which could involve the physical (e.g., modifications), the psychological (e.g., idiosyncratic meanings), and/or the social (e.g., practices). As previously discussed, the marketer doesn't have control over what happens once the marketing is out in the marketplace.

> …WOMM depends on [the] transformation from persuasion-oriented, market-generated, sales objective-oriented "hype" to relevant, useful, community desirable social information that builds individual reputations and group relationships. In this transformation of a market narrative [persuasive orientation] into a social one, the WOM communicator [the influencer(s), the evangelist(s), the advocate(s)], performs three services valuable to the marketers: (1) communicating the marketing message, (2) staking his or her reputation and trust relationships on the marketing message, and (3) converting the marketing message—through language, substance, or tone—to conform to the norms and expectations of the community has developed.[18]

Social Media—"Seeding" Strategy

The strategic implications include identifying individuals who already have an established presence online with a following (e.g., a known and respected blogger) and inviting them to try a product or service *unconditionally* with the hopes that they might become an outspoken advocate for the product or service. This strategy is called "seeding." It requires the marketer to identify relevant online communities and who might be the influencers. In this sense, the marketer is looking for a fertile site in which to plant his or her product or service "seed" within a community with the hope that it will grow with the help of the influencers as advocates.

Marketing Thinking in Practice: Ford Fiesta

Grant McCracken, a research affiliate at MIT and the author of *Chief Culture Officer*, describes how Ford used the "seeding" strategy with the Fiesta, turning narrative meanings into value through social media.[19] It represents a very powerful example of how marketing is transforming in its approach and role, capitalizing on the collaborative orientation.

How Ford Got Social Marketing Right: Ford recently wrapped the first chapter of its Fiesta Movement, leaving us distinctly wiser about marketing in the digital space.

Ford gave 100 consumers a car for six months and asked them to complete a different mission every month. And away they went. At the direction of Ford and their own imagination, "agents" used their Fiestas to deliver Meals On Wheels. They used them to take Harry & David treats to the National Guard. They went looking for adventure, some to wrestle alligators, others actually to elope. All of these stories were then lovingly documented on YouTube, Flickr, Facebook, and Twitter.

The campaign was an important moment for Ford. It wanted into the small-car market, and it hadn't sold a subcompact car in the United States since it discontinued the Aspire in 1997.

And it was an important moment for marketing. The Fiesta Movement promised to be the most visible, formative social media experiment for the automotive world. Get this right and Detroit marketing would never be the same.

I had the good fortune to interview Bud Caddell the other day and he helped me see the inner workings of the Fiesta Movement. Bud works at Undercurrent, the digital strategy firm responsible for the campaign.

Under the direction of Jim Farly, Group VP at Ford and Connie Fontaine, manager of brand content there, Undercurrent decided to depart from the viral marketing rule book. Bud told me they were not interested in the classic early adopters, the people who act as influencers for the rest of us. Undercurrent wanted to make contact with a very specific group of people, a passionate group of culture creators.

Bud said,

> The idea was: let's go find twenty-something YouTube storytellers who've learned how to earn a fan community of their own. [People] who can craft a true narrative inside video, and let's go talk to them. And let's put them inside situations that they don't get to normally experience/document. Let's add value back to their life. They're always looking, they're always hungry, they're always looking for more content to create. I think this gets things exactly right. Undercurrent grasped the underlying motive (and the real economy) at work in the digital space. People are not just telling stories for the sake of telling stories, though certainly, these stories have their own rewards. They were making narratives that would create economic value.

The digital space is an economy after all. People are creating, exchanging and capturing value, as they would in any marketplace. But this is a gift economy, where the transactions are shot through with cultural content and creation. In a gift economy, value tends to move not in little "tit for tat" transactions, but in long loops, moving between consumers before returning, augmented, to the corporation. In this case, adventures inspired by Undercurrent and Ford return as meaning for the brand and value for the corporation.

Undercurrent was reaching out to consumers not just to pitch them, but to ask them to help pitch the product. And the pitch was not merely a matter of "buzz." Undercurrent wanted consumers to help charge the Fiesta with glamour, excitement, and oddity—to complete the "meaning manufacture" normally conducted only by the agency.

This would be the usual "viral marketing" if all the consumer was called upon to do was to talk up Fiesta. But Undercurrent was proposing a richer bargain, enabling and incenting "agents" to create content for their own sakes, to feed their own networks, to build their own profiles...and in the process to contribute to the project of augmenting Fiesta's brand.

Fiesta's campaign worked because it was founded on fair trade. Both the brand and the agent were giving and getting. And this shows us a way out of the accusations that now preoccupy some discussions of social media marketing. With their gift economy approach, Ford and Undercurrent found a way to transcend all the fretting about "what bright, shining object can we invent to get the kids involved?" and, from the other side, all that "oh, there he goes again, it's the Man ripping off digital innocents." It's a happier, more productive, more symmetrical, relationship than these anxieties imply. Hat's off to Farley and Fontaine.

The effects of the campaign were sensational. Fiesta got 6.5 million YouTube views and 50,000 requests for information about the car—virtually none from people who already had a Ford in the garage.

(Continued)

(Continued)

> Ford sold 10,000 units in the first six days of sales. The results came at a relatively small cost. The Fiesta Movement is reputed to have cost a small fraction of the typical national TV campaign.
>
> There is an awful lot of aimless experiment in the digital space these days. A lot of people who appear not to have a clue are selling digital marketing advice. I think the Fiesta Movement gives us new clarity. It's a three-step process.
>
> 1. Engage culturally creative consumers to create content.
> 2. Encourage them to distribute this content on social networks and digital markets in the form of a digital currency.
> 3. Craft [it in] a way that it rebounds to the credit of the brand, turning digital currency (and narrative meaning) into a value for the brand.
>
> In effect, outsource some of our marketing work. And in the process, turn the brand itself into an "agent" and an enabler of cultural production that is interesting and fun. Now the marketer is working with contemporary culture instead of against it. And everyone is well-served." [20]
>
> ---
>
> *Source:* From "How Ford Got Social Marketing Right" by Grant McCracken reprinted with permission. Copyright © 2011 by Harvard Business Publishing; all rights reserved; www.hbr.org

The Ford Fiesta example is about moving from a "me-them" perspective to a "we" perspective, from an "outside" to a "within" perspective. It also illustrates where the value creation is occurring. The Ford example and current WOMM research suggest that "managers have an important opportunity to encourage particular narrative strategies that may be ideal for their product and/or campaign.... [For example], hard-sell offers would lend themselves to narrative strategies of explanation and evaluation, while embracing and endorsing narratives would be congruent with soft-sell, long-term brand building campaigns."[21] These strategies suggest *crossover points* (i.e., points of convergence leading into the new perspective) between the persuasive and the collaborative orientations, through the reinterpretation within a social context.

> Marketing management is just beginning to adapt to this new age of the networked coproduction of marketing message and meanings in radically altered industries, such as advertising, music production, and newspaper publishing. As it becomes increasingly recognized that few industries will remain untouched, we will increasingly understand how to supplement broadcasting of hypercommerical messages with the careful cultivation of consumers' narrative networks.[22]

Also, as mentioned in the Ford Fiesta example, an important lesson to be learned is to understand that *completing the "meaning" occurs externally*. In this sense, the "real" marketing takes place in the narrative networks.

Social Media—Listening Strategy

It is generally recommended for those just beginning with social media that an experimental approach be pursued.[23] But before getting too involved in setting up your social media strategy, a listening strategy needs to be developed. The marketer will need to identify the different communities and sites that he or she is interested in tracking. To make life easier, and to be able to track information and receive it in a more organized way, an "attention dashboard" can be set up.

A social dashboard is a dedicated microsite either within an existing corporate website or hosted at a dedicated URL that aggregates the disparate corporate social profiles and media—presenting them in one visually rich, easy-to-navigate destination that promotes outside connectivity and onsite interaction. The dashboard offers an organized view of media that's published in outside networks. Dashboards can include video from YouTube, pictures from Flickr, blog posts, pools, tweets, or other forms of updates.[24]

Examples of dashboards can be seen and set up at PeopleBrowsr, HootSuite, Collecta, Tweetdeck, and Seesmic Desktop.

The listening objectives are (1) to identify ways to become an active participant, which requires knowing the important issues and topics being discussed within the online (network) communities, and (2) to identify the influencers. Keep in mind that the marketing strategy to be developed is to take place "within" these communities.

Listening becomes fundamental to developing the social media and co-marketing strategies. The relationship is depicted in Figure 8.9.

Figure 8.9 Listening In on the Co-Marketing

Social Media Strategy

In essence, a social media strategy will have three basic facets, which are depicted in Figure 8.10.

The strategy considerations should include enabling participants to link up (to connect) and communicate (e.g., Facebook and LinkedIn); to distribute (to share) information or knowledge to their connections and the community (e.g., Twitter and slideshare); and to generate knowledge or best practice information (to collaborate) through open interaction with their connections and the community (e.g., Toolbox).[25] The listening and the social

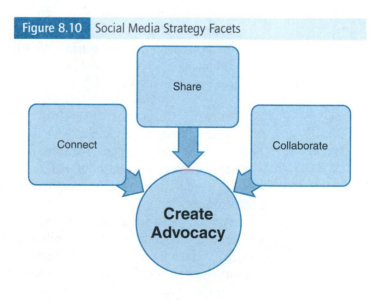

Figure 8.10 Social Media Strategy Facets

media strategies are to be complementary. The information from listening will enable the marketer to understand which connections make sense, the best ways to share information, the best platform(s) for collaboration to occur, and who the influencers are who could become advocates. It is at this point that the marketer will have a better idea of what marketing might take place within the network(s) and how to participate and contribute within the *co-marketing process.*

We have a question. What about the traditional forms of marketing communications like advertising, sales promotions, etc.? Can't we use them as well?

Yes. The crossover in terms of how they can fit in with the collaborative orientation will have to do with how they can contribute versus not using them to manipulate the process. In other words, what *value* can they contribute to the *co-marketing process*?

Regardless of industry, marketers across all sectors are increasingly making digital media a priority. Digital media presents marketers with unique opportunities to engage consumers, generate data, and establish relationships. Mass advertising will continue to have a role (albeit a declining role) in driving reach, but marketers are prioritizing channels that attract and maintain deeper consumer relationships. ...Unilever's Axe brand affiliates with prominent MySpace personalities. Procter & Gamble is building a strong online community of young girls on www.beinggirl.com. IBM has invested in blogging training for staff.[26]

In each case, whether it involves traditional or contemporary forms of marketing communications, the important issue is to understand how to reach and participate in the consumer co-marketing process. As the marketer plans his or her marketing communication strategy, each available form of marketing communication should be considered for what value it would bring to the consumer process, and the marketer should prioritize them accordingly.

For example, advertising can be used through the mass media and/or online, informing consumers about the brand while soliciting the input of their experiences and suggestions. Sales promotion can be used to reward consumers for their input and participation. Public relations can be used to communicate to the larger public the good things an organization is doing while asking for how it can help in other ways. It's not simply *taking* but *giving back* in the process that contributes. Traditional forms of marketing communications can provide value to the co-creation process if used accordingly. This then becomes a case where the means and ends are in sync, where value from both stems from contributing. In this way, marketers have the opportunity to potentially repair their reputations while facilitating the success of an organization. It becomes a win-win situation and not a win-lose, as with the persuasive orientation. See Table 8.3 for additional strategy suggestions.

Table 8.3 Social Media Marketing Strategy Suggestions

Suggestions	Explanation
Offer a peek behind the scenes.	A sneak preview of products or services can create buzz as well as be a source for feedback.
Share expertise.	Social media are about sharing. By sharing information (e.g., white papers), you'll attract more participants while boosting not only the brand but also your company's reputation.
Provide online demonstrations.	Demonstrate what your company does in an interesting way (e.g., online videos).
Link to other sites.	Help spread the word of your website by linking to other related, popular sites. You can use widgets (e.g., AddThis) that facilitate linking to other sites.
Transparency is paramount.	Openly communicate who you represent and what is going on with your company. A company blog can be used to provide the latest "scoop" with your company.
Be prepared to interact; allow others to interact and contribute.	Create the means for conversing with those interested in your website, blog, or other social media avenues. As you gain more interest, it may require a dedicated staff to keep up with the responses. The key here is to be able to respond in a timely manner. Also, you can create forums on your website to allow others to interact and, if appropriate, you could respond to some of their responses. Recognize their feedback respectfully (don't be aggressive) and give credit where it is deserved. The forums could lead to the beginnings of a brand community.
Link internally.	Set up a company network for employees to converse, share information, and contribute. This is especially important if there is more than one company location involved.
Reward contributors.	Be prepared to reward contributors, which could be other bloggers, advocates, net surfers, consumers, suppliers, channel members, or employees that participate in meaningful ways through your social network. This is where sales promotions can be used.
Listen.	Track not only what is going on online in your area of interest but also what is being said about your company.
Negative responses can be a positive.	Look at negative feedback as an opportunity to identify problems as well as a source of developing something new. Provide remedies and solutions and treat those with complaints, etc., with respect.
Communicate in real time.	Participants that have a keen interest in what you offer can be kept in the loop via microblogging (e.g., Twitter). But make sure you are communicating about things that would be of **value** to them.
Focus.	Geosocial networks can be used to be a part of different geographical networks. Can use relevant online advertising by selectively choosing the appropriate social network through which participants would find the advertising to be informative in some way.
Connect with other companies.	The business networks (e.g., LinkedIn) can be used to identify potential business partners that you might want to connect to. This could also be used to identify potential employees.
Bottom line.	To create and/or be a part of a network community, your organization needs to provide *value regularly* to participants in the form of information, knowledge, access, responsiveness, rewards, etc. Think of it in terms of participants asking, What have you done for me lately? Whatever forms of marketing communications are to be used, they themselves must also provide some value. *Never come across as being marketing aggressive.*

What is important to understand about marketing today is to appreciate where the co-marketing is actually taking place and to develop strategies that are in tune with an ever-growing online society. Marketing communication strategies need to be developed with a real-time perspective (thinking in time) and agility, to adapt to fast-changing social situations. An experimental approach (creative thinking) should be incorporated not only for entry into the social media world but also as a way to stay in sync as the tools continuously emerge.

Marketing Thinking Challenge 8.3: Creating a *Listening* Dashboard

Choose any product or service category of interest. Identify the various related online communities and sites that you think would be interesting to listen in on. Then go to one of the dashboard websites and create a listening dashboard for the product or service you have chosen. What are they talking about? How could you participate?

| Figure 8.11 | Setting Up a Listening Dashboard |

Summary

- In this chapter, we explored two different orientations—the persuasive and the collaborative orientations—in the context of marketing communications. With the advent of the Internet and social media, the persuasive orientation is becoming increasingly less attractive and less effective.
- The different forms of marketing communications—promotion mix and the social media tools—were described and contrasted in terms of their marketing characteristics.
- The social media forms of communicating were based more on conversation, sharing, and community building than the traditional promotion mix forms of communicating.
- The listening and social media strategies were offered as ways to be a part of the co-marketing that is taking place within the various social communities.

- The traditional forms of marketing communications could be used, but from the collaborative (participation) orientation perspective in which all forms of communication should be assessed based upon what value they provide in the co-marketing process.
- A new form of "value" was identified. The value was characterized with the collaboration process and viewed as a *value in process*.
- Social media marketing strategy suggestions were offered as well.

Case: Alessi—Open Innovation

Alessi is an Italian-based leading manufacturer of designer kitchen and tableware worldwide. It was started in 1921 by Giovanni Alessi in a workshop in the Italian Alps producing hand-crafted items. In the 1950s, Carlo Alessi assumed the management of the company and started hiring freelance designers to do the design work. The son of Carlo, Alberto Alessi, received his degree in law, joined the factory in July 1970 as president of the company and director of marketing strategies and design management, continued the practice of hiring freelance designers, and made it a pivotal aspect of company operations and also a means for differentiation from other companies. The traditional craftsmanship and design have always been at the core of the Alessi organization's philosophy. Today, the organization collaborates with more than 200 external designers and architects for a continued supply of ideas through its "open innovation" strategy.[i] While the core business is still stainless steel,

> Since his father's launch of famous steel products, like the "Bombe" tea and coffee set introduced in 1946, Alberto Alessi has branched out into such neighbouring fields as glassware and china, objects of plastic and wood, wall clocks, lighting fixtures and toys. He has collaborated with some iconic designers including Norman Foster, Frank Gehry, Jasper Morrison, Philippe Starck and Michael Graves.[ii]

The company mission as stated by Alberto on their website is:

> *I think that this will be the goal of design in the future (or at least, my goal for my future in the sphere of design): transforming the gadget function ascribed to objects by the consumer's society into a transitional opportunity, namely into an opportunity for consumers to improve their perception of the world.*
>
> *This kind of activity is typically paradoxical in the original meaning alongside the rule, the norm, the standard, as a means of grasping the so-called reality of the world and of life to its full extent.*
>
> *In the future most of our products will continue to be marked by a high degree of innovation and experimentation, as we believe this is the way to develop our ability to set trends, to promote our fame and to create a culture medium aimed at developing those projects we like to call Super & popular.*

Its current catalog carries more than 2,000 products offered through three different collections: the Officina Alessi (includes sophisticated, experimental, and innovative products, small-scale and limited production items), the Alessi (includes mass-produced items using premium materials, high-quality manufacturing, and sophisticated design), and the A di Alessi (includes products produced at high volumes and slightly lower prices).[27] A parallel between Alessi and Pablo Picasso has been made in which both have successfully intermixed art with business. Accordingly, Picasso's success has been attributed to understanding certain marketing fundamentals:

- Exclusive distribution (only via Gallery Kahnweiler)
- Differentiation (leveraged the use of African art styles)
- Smart Cultivation of critics "in the know" (he did portraits of collectors and "taste makers" of the day)
- Strong emotional affiliation[28]

To assess whether a product goes to market and what its potential may be, Alberto uses a kind of formula that has four basic parts. There are (1) sensoriality, memory, and imagination (SMI)—Is it pleasing? Memorable? Engender emotion? [This represents the connection between the object and the individual.]; (2) communication and language (CL)—Will it enhance position with others through communicating status or style? Is it trendy? [This represents the communication connection with others through objects.]; (3) function; and (4) price.[29, 30] The latter two are considered peripheral or having influence once the product has been available for awhile. Each is rated on a scale of 1 to 5, with a 5 representing the maximum rating of the particular element. Between Picasso's marketing fundamentals and Alberto's formula for rating a product, one can see some similarity such as differentiation, making an emotional connection, and so forth.

Alberto explains the use of his formula by contrasting it with traditional consumer testing or marketing research:

> Testing isn't really appropriate as a description. Unlike typical market research, which is often conducted by outside experts, this is organized by us, drawing on our experience. Our reactions to the test are very different too: a lot of companies would develop a prototype and test it with consumers, and, if the initial consumer reaction was negative, they would pull the plug on that product.
>
> On the other hand, we and our designers are extremely interested in understanding, in advance, what the reaction of final customers would be—but not necessarily to help us decide what to produce or not produce. If I believe it is a good project and that it has to be done, I will support it. But negative feedback can be useful in helping the designers to modify something. Not all the time, but sometimes.
>
> Fundamentally, we use the formula so we can afford more risk. I don't want to reduce the risk. Given my business, it makes no sense for me to reduce risk. I just need to determine where I am in order to have the opportunity to take a bit more risk.[31]

This suggests that traditional marketing research is characterized by being risk averse and is, perhaps, a path to meritocracy. Alternatively, Alessi values intuition and taking a chance on things that may not immediately appear to be winners. Both may be critical aspects to Alessi's innovation strategy. Alberto explains the difference between Alessi and mass production companies as follows:

> Well-organized, mass production companies try to work as far as possible from the borderline. They cannot afford to take too many risks. But by all producing the same car, the same television set, and the same fridge year after year, those companies are making products more and more boring and anonymous.
>
> The destiny of a company like Alessi is to live as close as possible to the borderline, where you are able to really explore a completely unknown area of products. The

problem is that the borderline is not clearly drawn. You cannot see with your eyes where it is. You can only sense these qualities.[32]

Given their success, it appears that Alberto and his company may be on to something. How does Alberto's thinking differ from the traditional target marketing approach? What elements do you think are critical for his strategy to continue? If you were to enter this market, how would you do so?

References

1. Burnes, Rick (2008), "Inbound Marketing & the Next Phase of Marketing on the Web," Nov. 18, *Hubspot Blog*, http://blog.hubspot.com/blog/tabid/6307/bid/4416/Inbound-Marketing-the-Next-Phase-of-Marketing-on-the-Web.aspx
2. Burnes, Rick (2008), "Inbound Marketing & the Next Phase of Marketing on the Web," Nov. 18, *Hubspot Blog*, http://blog.hubspot.com/blog/tabid/6307/bid/4416/Inbound-Marketing-the-Next-Phase-of-Marketing-on-the-Web.aspx
3. Belch, George E., and Michael A. Belch (2001), *Advertising and Promotion: An Integrated Marketing Communications Perspective*, 5th edition, New York: McGraw-Hill Irwin, GR 10.
4. Rotfeld, Jack Herbert (2010), "A Pessimist's Simplistic Historical Perspective on the Fourth Wave of Consumer Protection," *The Journal of Consumer Affairs*, 44 (2), 423.
5. Rotfeld, Jack Herbert (2010), "A Pessimist's Simplistic Historical Perspective on the Fourth Wave of Consumer Protection," *The Journal of Consumer Affairs*, 44 (2), 424.
6. Rotfeld, Jack Herbert (2010), "A Pessimist's Simplistic Historical Perspective on the Fourth Wave of Consumer Protection," *The Journal of Consumer Affairs*, 44 (2), 424.
7. Sales Orientation, NOWSELL.com, www.nowsell.com/marketing-guide/sales-orientation.html
8. Kotler, P., S. Adam, L. Brown, and G. Armstrong (2006), *Principles of Marketing*, 3rd ed., Englewood, NJ: Prentice Hall.
9. Rotfeld, Jack Herbert (2010), "A Pessimist's Simplistic Historical Perspective on the Fourth Wave of Consumer Protection," *The Journal of Consumer Affairs*, 44 (2), 427.
10. Rotfeld, Jack Herbert (2010), "A Pessimist's Simplistic Historical Perspective on the Fourth Wave of Consumer Protection," *The Journal of Consumer Affairs*, 44 (2), 425.
11. Scott, David Meerman (2010), *The New Rules of Marketing & PR: How to Use Social Media, Blogs, New Releases, Online Video, and Viral Marketing to Reach Buyers Directly*, 2nd edition, Hoboken, NJ: John Wiley & Sons, Inc., 37.
12. Jess3 and Joe Chernov (2009), *Social Media Playbook: Everything Your Company Needs to Know to Succeed on the Social Web*, Eloqua Corporation, www.eloqua.com
13. Solis, Brian (2010), *Engage! The Complete Guide for Brands and Businesses to Build, Cultivate, and Measure Success in the New Web*, Hoboken, NJ: Wiley & Sons, Inc.
14. Landry, Edward, Carolyn Ude, and Christopher Volmer (2008), "HD Marketing 2010: Sharpening the Conversation: The Team and Tools You Need to Market in an Increasingly 'Digitally Savvy' World," *Marketing & Media Ecosystem 2010*, Booz Allen Hamilton, Inc.
15. Kozients, Robert V., Kristine de Valck, Andrea C. Wojnicki, and Sarah J. S. Wilner (2010), "Networked Narratives: Understanding Word-of-Mouth Marketing in Online Communities," *Journal of Marketing*, 74 (March), 73.
16. Kozients, Robert V., Kristine de Valck, Andrea C. Wojnicki, and Sarah J. S. Wilner (2010), "Networked Narratives: Understanding Word-of-Mouth Marketing in Online Communities," *Journal of Marketing*, 74 (March), 72.
17. Kozients, Robert V., Kristine de Valck, Andrea C. Wojnicki, and Sarah J. S. Wilner (2010), "Networked Narratives: Understanding Word-of-Mouth Marketing in Online Communities," *Journal of Marketing*, 74 (March), 73.

18. Kozients, Robert V., Kristine de Valck, Andrea C. Wojnicki, and Sarah J. S. Wilner (2010), "Networked Narratives: Understanding Word-of-Mouth Marketing in Online Communities," *Journal of Marketing*, 74 (March), 83.

19. McCracken, Grant (2010), "How Ford Got Social Marketing Right," January 7, *Harvard Business Review Blog—The Conversation*, http://blogs.hbr.org/cs/2010/01/ford_recently_wrapped_the_firs.html

20. McCracken, Grant (2010), "How Ford Got Social Marketing Right," January 7, *Harvard Business Review Blog—The Conversation*, http://blogs.hbr.org/cs/2010/01/ford_recently_wrapped_the_firs.html

21. Kozients, Robert V., Kristine de Valck, Andrea C. Wojnicki, and Sarah J. S. Wilner (2010), "Networked Narratives: Understanding Word-of-Mouth Marketing in Online Communities," *Journal of Marketing*, 74 (March), 87.

22. Kozients, Robert V., Kristine de Valck, Andrea C. Wojnicki, and Sarah J. S. Wilner (2010), "Networked Narratives: Understanding Word-of-Mouth Marketing in Online Communities," *Journal of Marketing*, 74 (March), 87.

23. Scott, David Meerman (2010), *The New Rules of Marketing & PR: How to Use Social Media, Blogs, New Releases, Online Video, and Viral Marketing to Reach Buyers Directly*, 2nd edition, Hoboken, NJ: John Wiley & Sons, Inc.

24. Solis, Brian (2010), *Engage! The Complete Guide for Brands and Businesses to Build, Cultivate, and Measure Success in the New Web*, Hoboken, NJ: Wiley & Sons, Inc., 74.

25. Conn, Bill, and George Krautzel (2010), *Top 5 Trends in B2B Social Media Usage: What Every Marketer Should Know*, White Paper, www.Toolbox.com

26. Landry, Edward, Carolyn Ude, and Christopher Volmer (2008), "HD Marketing 2010: Sharpening the Conversation: The Team and Tools You Need to Market in an Increasingly 'Digitally Savvy' World," *Marketing & Media Ecosystem 2010*, Booz Allen Hamilton, Inc., 8.

    [i] Capozzi, Marla M. and Josselyn Simpson (2009), "Cultivating innovation: An interview with the CEO of a leading Italian design firm," McKinsey & Company, February, https://www.mckinseyquarterly.com/Cultivating_innovation_an_interview_with_the_CEO_of_a_leading_Italian_design_firm_2299

    [ii] www.speakerscorner.co.uk/file/44c7acecb5cbf4e61598441aae44d62b/alberto-alessi-branding-marketing-international-business-speaker-keynote-speaker-conference-speaker.html

27. *Eleven Lessons: Managing Design in Eleven Global Brands: Design at Alessi*, Design Council, www.slideshare.net/luisenrique.espinosa/design-at-alessi

28. Jones, Ryan (2009), "Picasso: Art Genius…Marketing Genius? Something in Between?," m-cause, July 15, http://m-cause.com/picasso-art-geniusmarketing-genius-something-in-between/

29. *Eleven Lessons: Managing Design in Eleven Global Brands: Design at Alessi*, Design Council, www.slideshare.net/luisenrique.espinosa/design-at-alessi

30. Capozzi, Marla M., and Josselyn Simpson (2009), "Cultivating Innovation: An Interview With the CEO of a Leading Italian Design Firm," McKinsey & Company, February, https://www.mckinseyquarterly.com/Cultivating_innovation_an_interview_with_the_CEO_of_a_leading_Italian_design_firm_2299

31. Capozzi, Marla M., and Josselyn Simpson (2009), "Cultivating Innovation: An Interview With the CEO of a Leading Italian Design Firm," McKinsey & Company, February, https://www.mckinseyquarterly.com/Cultivating_innovation_an_interview_with_the_CEO_of_a_leading_Italian_design_firm_2299

32. Capozzi, Marla M., and Josselyn Simpson (2009), "Cultivating Innovation: An Interview With the CEO of a Leading Italian Design Firm," McKinsey & Company, February, https://www.mckinseyquarterly.com/Cultivating_innovation_an_interview_with_the_CEO_of_a_leading_Italian_design_firm_2299

CHAPTER 9

The Changing Customer Interface Landscape

Decompression Exercise

Envision yourself taking a carriage ride through Central Park. What sounds do you hear and what sights do you see?

Figure 9.1 Taking a Ride in the Park

Chapter Introduction

By taking a moment to reflect upon the last eight chapters, we can map out the thinking agility course we have traversed so far. The various chapters' lines of questioning were used as a means to develop the thinking agility that is necessary to be able to see different conceptual options from which to choose and their corresponding suggested strategies. As discussed in Chapter 1, our questioning is the means by which we see. Changing lines of questioning allows us to see different things. From a thinking agility perspective, it is necessary to be able to open up these different lines of questioning to be agile in marketing thinking and, ultimately, in developing strategy. Before moving on to additional lines of questioning, let's look at some we have used so far.

We considered different ways to approach the marketplace via a situation assessment, such as whether to assume an existing market structure that strategy could be based on (a competitive orientation) or to create a new market structure through strategy (a consumer orientation based on innovation and creating new value; Chapters 3, 4, and 5).

In addition, the question of segmenting for what purpose(s) and in terms of who is doing the segmenting was considered. If we assumed the marketer was segmenting the market, this led to a pursuing/persuasive/competitive orientation—inherently, an *against* orientation operationalized by segmenting the market, leading to positioning and targeting for the purposes of being more competitive. On the other hand, if we assumed that the consumer was doing the segmenting and the marketer did not engage in the task of segmenting the marketplace, this led to a compatibility/attracting orientation—which involved a *moving-with* consumer orientation implemented by strategies of self-selection segmenting or one-to-one marketing in which the marketer is being directed by the consumers through their selections and consumption activities (Chapter 4).

By raising the question of what is fundamentally being consumed in all cases, that being difference, we were able to develop an understanding for the marketplace parameters all marketers confront (e.g., the repetition of difference) along with identifying potential contributions marketers can make through collaboration (i.e., collaborative differentiation), thereby opening up new forms of strategy considerations: collaborative offerings, collaborative pricing, collaborative segmentation (self-selection), collaborative communications (responsive communications), collaborative support (creating a community network), and collaborative platforms (means for connecting; Chapter 5).

Challenging the marketing mix concept in light of the changes taking place in the marketplace while recognizing the channeling effects associated with all concepts led to new and more open views of marketing, for example, collaborative marketing (CM) or participatory marketing (PM) that move beyond SPOT marketing (antagonistic marketing), relationship marketing (symbiotic marketing), and customer relationship management (CRM; Chapter 6).

Contrasting the traditional views of products and services from a quality perspective against a PM orientation facilitated exploration into how meaningful differences can be created through a collaborative network co-creation process (e.g., a brand community) involving community practices of which products and services may be a part (Chapter 7). In addition, the quality perspective placed the value within the products or services (a thing-like perspective), whereas the PM orientation placed the value as occurring through the ongoing practices of a brand community. In Chapter 8, comparing the traditional (e.g., advertising, sales promotions) with contemporary forms (social media) of marketing communications within a co-marketing context led to social media strategies involving connecting, sharing, collaboration, and listening along with a more dynamic view of value occurring through the collaborating process.

Each of the chapters illustrates different questioning tactics, providing a means for developing thinking agility. Good questioning leads to identifying potentially better options for strategy considerations while recognizing the limits with all forms of thinking and, hence, the need for keeping an eye open toward seeking new lines of questioning.

To continue with this development, we'll take up the task of thinking about the customer interface. We'll examine what a customer interface is, how it has been viewed, and the changes taking place at the customer interface being driven by technology. The significance of the customer interface can't be overstated. It represents the initial point in time that marketing actually takes place and where strategy plays out. As we have seen with prior concepts, the customer interface concept is evolving or transforming as well. Let's get started.

Okay, I have a question. How are the collaborative or the participatory orientations changing the customer interface? Isn't it still just about communicating with consumers? And all technology has done is create more ways in which to do this. Right?

You are partially correct in that the customer interface does involve communicating and technology has opened up more ways to interact with consumers. It has also allowed consumers to be able to freely interact among themselves *regardless* of the marketer. The collaborative or participatory orientations affect how the marketer thinks about the nature of communicating with consumers, and technology is also a part of the thinking. We'll use the following question as our starting point into the customer interface conceptual terrain.

How do you *think* about the customer interface?

Rethinking the Front Office

How you *think* about the customer interface will affect what is considered and the nature of your strategy. The days of simply interacting with customers through a simple storefront or front office seem to be a thing of the past. Today, you can serve or interact with customers through retail stores, through Web sites, through your catalog and customer service calls centers. You serve them through touch points that are human, like clerks and concierges, and you can serve them through touch points that are automated, like vending machines and voice response units. …most companies…[have] a broad collection of these interfaces and [are] investing in even more.[1]

This suggests that the nature of the customer interface is expanding in terms available options and means for interfacing with customers.

Additionally, the advances in technology are shifting marketplace dynamics more and more toward customer service and customer involvement. Both can be forms for differentiation. Some have argued that all firms in essence follow a differentiated strategy and that to effectively differentiate begins with the consumer.[2] Easy access to information on the Internet and increasing global competition are contributing to changing needs for effective customer interface. As a consequence, organizations need to be more "open, transparent and collaborative with customers."[3]

The available responses to the question of *how to think about the customer interface* are different today than they were in the past, and we should expect them to continue change in time. In other words, as a marketer, be prepared to participate and contribute to the changes in customer interface thinking.

Some are calling for an "interface imperative," suggesting that the customer interaction or experience may be the sole remaining frontier of competitive advantage.[4] The interface imperative reasoning is based upon four observations:

(1) "competitive differentiation along traditional dimensions of corporate performance is becoming largely unsustainable,"

(2) "there is longstanding evidence that quality of service matters very much—in many cases, much more than price or performance,"

(3) "given the greatly expanded scope of service work in the economy, finding appropriately skilled labor is getting harder and harder…In most developed countries today, the vast majority of jobs are service oriented and involve interaction with customers," and

(4) "new forms of interface technology that can assist frontline employees or stand in for them in customer facing roles…Customers have become more and more comfortable dealing with machines through interactions with companies' offerings, and the technology inherent in those machines has advanced."[5]

With such a changing landscape, the need to rethink the front office or the customer interface is apparent. To stay current with the momentum toward collaborative/cooperative/participatory marketing or co-marketing (see Chapters 4 through 8) along with the rapid advances taking place in new forms of customer-interface technology, organizations will need to confront how they think about organization structure in terms of where the organization boundaries begin and end (i.e., a the blurring of the organization structure), their new roles, and what to focus on to be a part of the changing consumer experience. There are many issues tied to thinking about the customer interface, suggesting its significance to marketing.

The Marketing Thinking in Practice provides a definition of a customer interface and examples of how the design of the customer interface is being strategically incorporated to create unique customer experiences.

Marketing Thinking in Practice: The Service Interface

Customer or service interface is multidimensional. It involves people and technology and, through some combination of both, customer value can be provided along at least four different dimensions. The dimensions, individually and in combination, represent means by which to differentiate in the marketplace.[6]

> "A service interface is any place at which a company seeks to manage a relationship with a customer, whether through people, technology, or some combination of the two. Be it human or machine, every service interface must deliver high levels of customer-perceived value relative to the competition, so that customer satisfaction and loyalty rise sufficiently to drive superior financial returns.
>
> To deliver that level of value, an interface must succeed along four different dimensions: [1] physical presence and appearance, [2] cognition, [3] emotion or attitude, and [4] connectedness. At the Four Seasons Hotel, the appearance of the frontline staff—uniformed, clean-cut, businesslike, courteous, individual, and authentic—is a physical differentiation.
>
> At Nordstrom, the average salesperson's ability to recognize and reward the store's best customers with appropriate service and attention is a cognitive advantage. The sense of humor and energy that Southwest's flight crews display add value on an emotional dimension. And the coordinating communications that allow the Four Seasons' staff to orchestrate a seamless hospitality experience, that enable Nordstrom's salespeople to transfer a customer gracefully from one department to the next, and that makes it possible for Southwest's crews to work as a team in flight are forms of connectedness that make a difference."

The Marketing Thinking in Practice characterizes a customer interface along the lines of how consumers may view the experience and that there are different dimensions that need to be strategically considered as to what type of consumer experience is to be potentially created at the interface. Each dimension represents a means for differentiation for an organization. Is your customer interface strategy going to be based on a physical form of differentiation, an emotional form of differentiation, or some combination of these? Later in the chapter, we will utilize this form of thinking about the customer interface for the purposes of creating the conditions for consumer value through the interface. But first, let's look at the role technology plays with developments at the interface.

Customer Interface Changing Technology

Giving such considerations to the customer interface suggests that the thinking is moving or being redirected toward a focus on greater customer service and involvement. To accomplish this, strategy can be orchestrated along the four consumer experience dimensions identified in the Marketing Thinking in Practice. While this suggests a new direction for thinking about the customer interface, a little more background is needed here to fully comprehend the significance of the changes occurring within the customer-interface frontier being driven by advances in technology.

Marketing intelligence involving technology has had a major influence on the customer interface. There have been at least three waves of change in the area of marketing intelligence over the last 25 years or so, which are briefly described next.[7]

The First Wave of Change—Leading to Product Constellations' Store Layouts

The first wave took place when retailers adopted point-of-sale (POS) systems with UPC barcode scanning. The information collected via the scanners allowed marketers to look for purchasing patterns that they could use for store layout purposes. These patterns have been described as **product constellations** such as when someone buys toothpaste and a toothbrush at the same time. To encourage sale of one item with the others, all dental products are displayed together. Scanner data can also be used in a just-in-time (JIT) manner to restock depleted inventory or to identify faster-moving items versus slower ones.

The Second Wave of Change—Leading to Customer Relationship Management (CRM)

"The second wave of change occurred when retailers began to track and analyze the purchases of individual shoppers. Some retailers, especially in the grocery industry, launched frequent shopper and customer loyalty programs to collect these data."[8] Other information was collected through "cookies" stored on individual computers. Such information was used to develop **individual profiles** involving purchase behavior and demographic information. The profiles could then be used to make **marketing offerings** on a **one-to-one basis**. In the process, customer relationships could be managed, leading to the concept of **customer relationship management** *(CRM)*. It also allowed marketers to estimate customer value and loyalty.

> Another important facet of CRM is 'customer selectivity.' …not all customers are equally profitable…The company therefore must be selective in tailoring its program and marketing efforts by segmenting and selecting appropriate customers for individual marketing programs. …the objective of a company is not really to prune its customer base but to identify the programs and methods that would be the most profitable as it creates value for the firm and the customer.[9]

The Third Wave of Change—Leading to Customer Experience Management (CEM)

The third wave of change is beginning to take hold in retail stores. The technology drivers are the digital representation of the shopping environment and the **real-time**

tracking of customers as they enter the store, walk through the aisles, and select and purchase products. Like the earlier innovations, it provides the capability to capture variations in consumer behavior over time and across people, but it adds the critical element of **context** to the mix. This new wave of marketing intelligence provides marketers with the **tools to measure consumer response to the in-store environment and manage the shopping process.** It is the foundation for *customer experience management* [CEM].[10]

A similar perspective can be applied to managing online customer experiences.

CEM is an expanded version of CRM but adds customer context or experience to the mix. For both CRM and CEM, "The core theme...is its focus on a cooperative and collaborative relationship between the firm and its customers, and/or other marketing actors."[11]

Okay. I've heard of customer relationship management (CRM) before. But I'm not sure how it is different from this customer experience management (CEM). It sounds similar.

The differences between the two stem from advances in technology that are now able to provide the marketer more detailed information about what is going on during the customer experience and enabling the marketer to act accordingly as the experiences are unfolding in real time.

Instead of simply identifying patterns of preferences at the aggregate or individual level for the purposes of store layouts or tailoring marketing offerings on a one-to-one basis as in CRM, the marketer now has the capability to manage more of the entire customer experience beyond simply offering products and services.

The focus is shifting and expanding toward *co-creating unique consumer experiences* of which products and services are a part. Yet there is another related perspective that we haven't discussed called customer interface management (CIM). It is explained in the Marketing Thinking in Practice.

Marketing Thinking in Practice: Customer Interface Management

The customer interface management (CIM) perspective is a reversal of assumptions in terms of who is defining the rules at the interface. Are the rules set by the *marketer (a product-centric view)* or by the *consumer (a customer-centric view)*? Kathryn Jackson, a representative for Response Design, in explaining CIM, describes a call center transition from a product-centric to customer-centric orientation.[12]

Now, many companies are transitioning from a product-centric to a customer-centric focus—where the customer, not the vendor, defines the rules. The company responds by designing its knowledge, processes, products and services around the customer's desired experience. This is a customer-managed relationship.

Customers make rules one at a time at the interface. Customer A may want product X just like it is. Customer B may want product X with a little of product Y thrown in. Customer C may want product X, but delivered faster than usual. Customer D may insist on a price cut if he buys products X, Y and Z.

The agent becomes a knowledge worker, able to make on-the-spot decisions that affect the outcomes. He decides, for example, that he can help customers A, C, and D; but he cannot help customer B.

You may say, "We can't put that much power at the customer interface. This will spin out of control. Agents will commit to things we can't do. We'll have to call a management committee meeting each time a customer makes a unique request." Relax. The transition won't happen overnight. You can implement customer interface management (CIM) and build processes that let agents decide wisely.

In a customer-centric organization, the steps [of]...—customer request, negotiation, commitment, acceptance of fulfillment, and satisfaction—are repeated. Customer-centric companies focus on the customer interface, defining:

- who their customers are;
- what their requests are;
- what negotiations facilitate mutually satisfying commitments;
- how the company should support the commitments; and
- how to learn from each interaction to create profitable, lasting relationships.

The components of successful customer interface management are:

- A customer-centric strategy and key performance indicators
- A learning relationship
- A system that assesses agents according to their ability to be customer-centric
- The ability to leverage investments
- A comprehensive support infrastructure
- The right tools

Let's look at each:

Customer-centric strategy and key performance indicators

...a customer-centric company builds its strategy and performance indicators on what satisfies and retains valuable customers.

A learning relationship

A company and its agents must continually learn from customers. Building and updating a knowledge database is foundational to success. Complacency has no place in customer centricity or customer relationship management. If you think your customers are the same today as they were yesterday (and you treat them so), you might as well turn off the lights and go home.

A measurement system that assesses agents according to their customer-centricity

Agents must know about, and endeavor to maximize, performance indicators. Because businesses base these indicators on strategy, and satisfying/retaining customers dictate the strategy, their metrics should show a direct correlation. For example, managers should know that the components on call monitoring sheets actually contribute to customer satisfaction. They should not monitor for certain attributes just because everyone else does.

Leverage investments

Most companies invest significantly in their people, processes, knowledge and technology. However, when Response Design performs assessments, we typically find the companies are not best leveraging their investments. We often recommend not additional investments but better utilization of existing outlays.

Building a comprehensive support infrastructure

To be customer focused—to look at each interaction as if it were the only one that mattered—you need a strong support infrastructure. We learned from our most recent benchmarking study that the linchpins to becoming customer-centric are also the most formidable obstacles to doing so: corporate culture and leadership. But there are other obstacles, too: changing the organizational structure and measurement system, and continually adapting strategy.

Implementing the right tools

There are many tools such as e-mail management software, customer and employee survey programs, benchmarking projects, employee testing software and quality monitoring software. But only certain ones are proven, of which only a subset are right for your customer-interface strategy. It's a full-time job to stay abreast of what's out there.

CULTURE AND LEADERSHIP

Making customer interface management work entails, as we mentioned, changing the corporate culture (i.e., delegating responsibility and leadership to your agents). Before undertaking this journey, consider the following:

Empowerment

How much latitude will you give agents to negotiate mutually satisfying commitments with customers…

(Continued)

(Continued)

Accountability

For what do you hold agents accountable? For the commitments they make? Do you hold others who carry out the commitments accountable? How do you develop a sense of ownership in each individual?

Feedback

How do you teach people within the organization to constructively and promptly react to colleagues who make commitments that impact fellow employees? ...Most people are uncomfortable giving feedback to peers, but this is critical if customer interface management is to be successful. We must "turn on a dime" and cannot wait until some manager finds the time to respond (by that time, we could have had thousands of other "interface moments," each of which risks a negative impact). If the agent decides poorly, then the person whom the decision directly impacted must immediately respond. If the person fulfilling the commitment falls down on the job, then the person who made the commitment must provide feedback.

Equally important, let's not forget, is feedback from customers. We have to ask the right questions, at the right time, using the right methods and media.

Learning

Much has been written about learning organizations. The most common barrier to learning is that people take things personally. People often view feedback not as a performance enhancer, but as a message that "I am defective." Rather than respond constructively to a colleague's well-intended criticism, many people become defensive or withdraw.

Learning can only take place in a culture where the truth is not hidden, and where receiving feedback is not equated with shame. Not surprisingly, a key finding of our studies is that customer-centric organizations don't hide mistakes but disclose them so they can be corrected.

Trust

If I make a commitment to a customer, do I trust the person who is to fulfill the commitment? In LeapFrog! (our call center metric database) we ask respondents to "Describe agents' confidence that the rest of the business will follow through on their promises." Only 28% of respondents say their agents are very confident by either checking an 8 or a 9 out of a possible score of 10. No respondents are 100% confident. The mean score is between five and six.

Correspondingly, does the person who is responsible for fulfilling the commitments trust the person making the commitments? More pointedly, does the company trust that agents can learn how to make empowered decisions without giving away the farm? Is this concept of empowered decisions preventing your company from becoming custom-centric?

The customer must also trust the company. As we speak at seminars, we are often surprised at the growing backlash of customers angered that companies have abused their contact information. They say, "I gave them my information, but now they spam me—I hear from them every day that they love me! I am tired of it!" In this intense learning dialogue am I still "spamming" my customers with unnecessary communication (unnecessary in the eyes of my customer)? Am I working to gain their trust and their permission to learn from them? Am I cognizant in each interaction (whether initiated by the customer or by me) that their trust is at stake. And am I doing everything to maintain or increase that trust?

Knowledge

We haven't even begun to address all the knowledge necessary to make customer centricity work. What knowledge is required to ensure the agent can negotiate the best commitment (knowledge of the customer, the product/service, how to negotiate, who the commitment is impacting, the cost of the commitment, etc.)? What knowledge is required of the people fulfilling the commitment? What about the people who are assessing the success of the interaction? What knowledge does the customer need to access? How do people discover, document and update knowledge, then make it readily accessible? How do we motivate people to document what they know? How do we motivate people to access and use invaluable insights?

SUMMARY

Before fully implementing customer interface management, expect a transition period. You cannot build accountability into your systems overnight. Many cannot place trained knowledge workers on the front lines immediately. And you cannot build empowerment parameters over the weekend.

You can, however, envision and define your destination and take steps toward it. You can look for ways to make agents accountable. And you can keep your focus on customers' acceptance of products and services.

From a customer-centric point of view, you should strive to maintain a dialog with customers. The agent, the first point of contact in this dialog, must have enough support to keep the relationship going.

CIM allows you to avoid two situations catastrophic to organizations:

- not fulfilling the commitments agents make to the customers; and
- allowing agents to make commitments that are too costly.

Accordingly, the key elements of a CIM include (1) a customer-centric perspective in which the customer is defining the consumption within certain organizational parameters; (2) customization; (3) being responsive and personable; (4) a capability for learning from customers; (5) an organizational culture based upon knowledgeable, empowered employees making decisions at the customer interface while being held accountable for them; and (6) through the CIM process, developing confidence and trust from customers.

Marketing Thinking Challenge 9.1:
Customer Interface Management (CIM)

Identify an organization that appears to be utilizing the CIM suggestions discussed in the preceding Marketing Thinking in Practice—Customer Interface Management. Then identify a related organization that isn't using the CIM suggestions and suggest how it could incorporate some of them to improve its marketing efforts. Also, describe how your suggestions will improve the customer experience.

Figure 9.2	Managing the Customer Interface

Co-marketing: Co-creating an Experience

With the customer-centric focus (through CIM and CEM), companies are taking it to a new level by providing codesigning platforms at the customer interface, utilizing mass customization systems.

An important task for firms heading toward customer centricity is to develop and operate new kinds of customer interfaces and customer interaction systems. Cooperation requires building an efficient platform…not only do the manufacturer and the customer have to collaborate, but manufacturers and intermediaries, especially retailers, must collaborate as well.

This generates its own complexity: Traditionally, the competitive advantage of a retailer is based on the ability to provide an appropriate assortment of goods for the targeted market that falls within its capabilities for connecting with one or more distribution chains. This traditional approach lowers transaction costs by bundling supply and demand. Customized solutions, in contrast, mean that assortment, efficient stock-keeping, and distribution are no longer the driving sources of competitive advantage. On the contrary, interaction skills and matching customization possibilities with the needs of a specific customer during the process of co-design are becoming the primary sources of competitive advantage…

In traditional mass production, retailers are acting as a buffer between customers and manufacturers. In a co-design system, the manufacturer has to get access to information on each single customer in order to fulfill the customer's order, and potentially can match the retailer's advantage. As a result, there is a new demand for interaction and cooperation between customers, retailers and manufacturers.[13]

Figure 9.3	Working With Customers to Get Their Design Details

Co-design platforms provide for mass customization and represent the next stage in collaboration. Here, customization technology is required both at the platform or interface (e.g., a website) and throughout the manufacturing and delivery process.

A number of companies are incorporating collaborative means through their websites such as Cisco (technology), Procter & Gamble (consumer goods), Sony (electronics), Starbucks (coffee), and Unilever (consumer goods); Adidas provides an example of a codesign customer interface through which consumers can actually codesign shoes by going to their website *mi adidas* to design shoes to their specifications and receive them by mail. Other co-design examples include Dell Computers (PCs), NikeID (shoes), Interactive Custom Clothes (jeans), Land's End (khakis), Reflect (cosmetics), and Lego (toy kits).

Venturing further into the collaborative horizon, Second Life (www.secondlife.com) offers insight to where things might be headed. Second Life represents a *metaverse*—an Internet-based virtual world—where consumers can create their own communities, take on virtual personalities via avatars, and modify products to their specifications.

…metaverse marketing paved the way for a new phase in marketing and retailing. Specifically, …consumers have been traditionally looking for products that could fulfill their needs. Retailers responded to demand by initially offering the right product for the right consumer (segmentation strategy), which then gradually developed to a customer-oriented strategy. Electronic retailers were partially successful when it came to developing customer relationship management tools using the Web extensively and by targeting specific customers via the use of e-mails…Nowadays, …we are going through the next step of this gradual transformation, with consumers seeking not only to consume a product or service, but to interact and experience it.[14]

In traditional retailing, customers are generally looking for convenience, customer service, product availability, social interaction and atmosphere, competitive prices and product choice…while in electronic retailing consumers are looking for excellent prices, as they have the ability to run online price checks, a plethora of product choice, satisfactory product/service delivery at the consumer's home and user friendliness/ease of Web site navigation…For example, when it comes to grocery shopping and consumers selecting a transacting space, they face the dilemma of selecting the atmospherics and interaction of the real space over the convenience of the electronic space and vice versa. Metaverse retailing has the capability to put back the context and enrich the environment, while at the same time maintaining the convenience factor.[15]

Metaverses allow consumers to create their own virtual worlds, to interact with others, and to purchase products or services within a self-created enriched environment. What is also occurring is a shift in orientation in terms of where the value resides. As you may recall, we raised the *value* question in previous chapters. For example, does the value reside in products (or services) or in the practices within brand communities (Chapter 7), or is it to be thought of in static terms or more dynamically through an understanding of collaboration (Chapter 8)?

We can now take up the question again and approach it from a customer interface perspective to obtain further insight into where the value is for the purposes of understanding what strategy we might focus on.

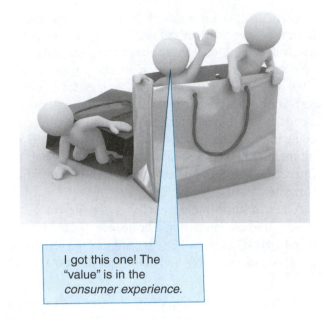

Where is the "value"? In products or services or elsewhere?

I got this one! The "value" is in the *consumer experience.*

Creating *Value*—An Expanding View

Co-marketing recognizes that there is more to what is being marketed than simply products and services. *What is pivotal to the co-marketing thinking is that the marketing function is larger than the organization itself.* The thinking involves an understanding of the broader picture in what is taking place with products and services in the marketplace—that is, products and services simply represent elements to be taken up, to be used as a part of *the collaboration of difference creation.*

As we saw in Chapter 5, the repetition of *difference* in the marketplace involves constant *change* and the element of chance. Accordingly, marketing is not to be thought of narrowly in terms of some dyadic relationship only involving the consumer and marketer (e.g., CRM) but actually involves many other entities that have influence on what is being created through products and services. These other entities include consumers, conversations taking place on the Internet, contributing channel members, complementary marketing through partnerships, competitors, governments, and so forth. This broader view now assesses that the "value is centered in the experiences of consumers and not just embedded in products and services."[16] It is the *value in experience.*

Within a hyperreality or metaverse context, some have conceptualized the *co-creating* customer experiences phenomenon by centering on creating *experience rooms.*[17] At the same time, the value in experience also involves the value in experience by the other collaborating entities as well. For example, as a strategy, the value in experience can also be developed throughout channels to create trust, openness, and sharing to provide greater flexibility, customization, and responsiveness, contributing to the customer experience. This is taken up further in Chapter 10 in discussing distribution considerations and strategies.

Similarly, by providing platforms for consumers, channel members, and so on for the purposes of sharing information and assisting each other, the marketer is opening up additional dimensions, potentially contributing to the value in experience for all entities involved. The benefits include *being open* to the repetition of difference and *being available* to participate in *the ongoing collaboration of difference creation among all*. It is a way to "*move with*" consumers through the various means for collaboration and participation. The differences between the traditional SPOT marketing and co-marketing are presented in Table 9.1 and depicted in Figures 9.4 and 9.5.

Table 9.1	SPOT Marketing vs. Co-Marketing
SPOT Marketing	**Co-Marketing**
Fixed Assortments	Customized /Flexible/Real-Time
Bundling Supply and Demand—Aligning Distribution Capabilities	Unbundling Supply & Demand—Opening Up New Channel Relationships
Emphasis on Efficiencies—Lower Transaction Costs	Emphasis on Interaction/Co-Design/ Collaboration/Participation
Selling Product	*Co-Creating an Experience*

Figure 9.4   Traditional Axes

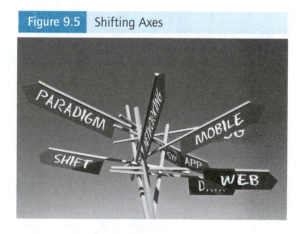

Figure 9.5   Shifting Axes

The advantage of co-marketing (i.e., a sustainable form of collaborative differentiating as mentioned in Chapter 5) does not necessarily come from the first purchase but through subsequent purchases as an individual's purchasing information is used to personalize subsequent co-design experiences through a company's interactive platform(s).[18]

The co-influences that are bringing co-marketing and CEM to the center stage of marketing thinking are (1) the Internet and social media, (2) marketing intelligence technology, and (3) mass customization technology. See Figure 9.6 on the next page.

Figure 9.6   The Co-Influences Leading to Co-Marketing and Customer Experience Management (CEM)

Returning to an Earlier Form of Thinking—The "Artisan"

While it may appear that we are advancing in our thinking in terms of our understanding of the customer–supplier (marketer) relationship, we may actually be reverting to an earlier relationship form of thinking described as the "artisan," which was prevalent before the advent of technology (before 1850 CE) and was characterized as customer-centric, local, personal, and responsive.[19] As discussed in Chapter 1, thinking can move in any direction spherically and, as such, isn't necessarily progressive. The circling back to the earlier form of thinking in this case can be attributed in part to technology.

With the advent of technology (1850–1930), the division in labor propagated along with layers of management. Standardization appeared, along with greater person-to-person separation between the consumer and supplier (marketer) in the forms of voice mail, pagers, automated phone systems, e-mail, and the like.

In time and with the arrival of the Internet, technology has also caused a shift in power within the consumer–suppler (marketer) relationship by providing consumers easy access to information and the ability to freely communicate among themselves. It is within this power shift that the corridors for a new era are appearing in which the marketer has to reconsider past business practices and think more about developing stronger, more personalized relationships with customers. Ironically, this new era can be characterized as a return to the artisan values in which companies are moving back to developing ways for a more personal relationship with customers and recognizing the value in doing so. This waking up, so to speak, by organizations to try to capture the *artisan sense* to build individual consumer relationships stems from not only the changes in consumer behavior attributed to the Internet but also the advances in marketing intelligence and customization technology that enable marketers to participate in consumers' experiences as they unfold.

In essence, as we have seen in previous chapters, marketing thinking has been evolving through different orientations. And through the customer interface, another shift is emerging that moves beyond customer relationship management (CRM) to customer interface management (CIM) and customer experience management (CEM) that culminate into co-marketing. The movement in thought is depicted in Figure 9.7.

Figure 9.7 Changing Marketing Thinking Orientations

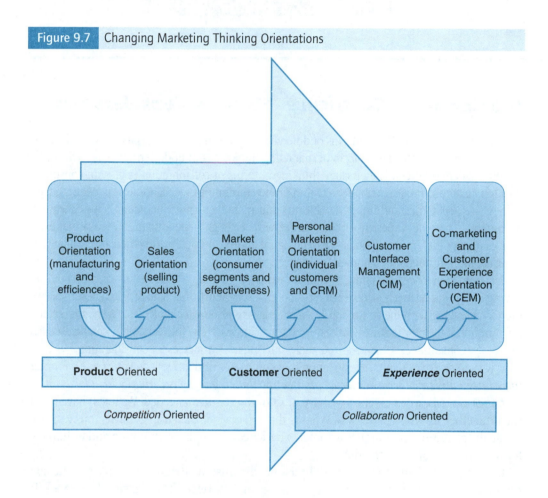

Marketing Thinking Challenge 9.2:
Co-marketing and Customer Experience Management (CEM)

Identify an organization that provides a platform(s) for co-creating and what you believe to be an excellent customer experience as a result. Describe the various facets that are contributing to the quality of the customer experience. What other facets could they consider that would make the experience even better?

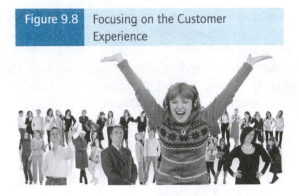

Figure 9.8   Focusing on the Customer Experience

The Consumer *Experience*–Strategy Considerations

Marketers today are thinking in terms of different dimensions than in the past, as with the competitive orientation. This newer form of marketing thinking is multidimensional as well, but the dimensions are different. They include thinking in terms of collaboration (e.g., with consumers through customization, contributions within brand communities, collaborative networks); technology (e.g., customization through platforms and manufacturing, interacting with consumers during their customer experience); customer experience (e.g., facilitating unique customer experiences along different dimensions—psychological and/or physical); and co-creating value (e.g., value creation through the customer experience).

Technology has been changing consumers' experiences and, as a consequence, marketers are having to climb a relatively steep learning curve in a very short time. The problem becomes even more challenging with the continuously increasing rate of new technologies. As the marketer is learning about the new technology, the thinking also involves how the technology can be used as a part of the consumer experience—potentially offering new strategies for consideration.

With such developments, the question that comes to mind is, *How do you create a marketing strategy utilizing the newer form of marketing thinking (co-marketing) with a focus on the customer experience?* In essence, we have most of the elements needed. We'll just have to put them together in a systematic way. What is the objective of the strategy? The objective is to create the conditions for unique customer experiences through collaboration and technology for the purposes of value creation.

Earlier in the chapter, we discussed possible dimensions that can be a part of the customer interface (see the Marketing Thinking in Practice—The Service Interface). In Chapter 3, we used the Strategy Canvas and Four Actions Framework as means for creating unique value. We can use them again here, but now from the customer-experience perspective in terms of which dimensions are going to be emphasized at the interface. We are appropriating the Strategy Canvas and Four Actions Framework by focusing on the customer experience and considering the different customer-experience dimensions for purposes of value creation. You could think of it as creating a **Blue Ocean** strategy based upon unique customer experience. In addition, we'll need to discuss some other customer interface dimensions that haven't been mentioned. Finally, in Chapter 8, we also discussed the marketing communications and social media characteristics that can be considered in terms of which are to be a part of the interface to facilitate the chosen customer-experience dimensions. To approach the consumer experience challenge, the streams of thought that come together representing a new canvas for developing strategy are depicted in Figure 9.9.

- The *first stream* of thought involves the different dimensions that can be associated with consumer experiences, for example, the entertainment, information, or emotional.
- The *second stream* of thought is about *co-creating value*. Here, we can appropriate the Strategy Canvas and Four Actions Framework discussed in Chapter 3 for this purpose.
- The *third stream* of thought to consider is thinking through the various dimensions of the customer interface available.
- The *fourth and final stream* of thought pertains to the array of available means that marketers have available today to not only communicate with consumers but also affect the nature of their experiences.

Figure 9.9 Four Streams of Thought—Consumer Experience Strategy Considerations

Consumer Experience			
(1) Consumer Experience Dimensions	(2) Creating Value	(3) Consumer Interface Dimensions	(4) Communication Options

The First Stream of Thought—The Dimensions of Consumer Experience

This is the starting point for developing a customer-experience strategy. The dimensions of consumer experiences vary from one situation to the next. This will require some thought and research to open up a sufficient array of dimensions for consideration.

For example, in a financial context, the dimensions might include transaction efficiency, value for cost, 24/7 availability, ethical and compliant partnership, a constant stream of new solutions, security, and a customer centric platform.[20] In a hotel setting, the dimensions of a hotel guest experience could include amenities (benefits), convenience, incentives, and environment.[21] Or, in a more general context, the dimensions of customer service may involve convenience and accessibility (e.g., Dell), environment (e.g., Estée Lauder), self-help tools and support (e.g., Nike), product and service availability, attitudes and friendliness (e.g., Southwest Airlines), competence and expertise (e.g., Netjets), speed and responsiveness (e.g., Tesco), personal(ized) attention (e.g., Nordstrom), community (e.g., Harley Davidson), and links to related suppliers (e.g., Apple).[22] Other potential dimensions could include social, emotional, entertainment, information, pragmatic, vicarious, contextual, and so on.

It's important to keep in mind that depending on their situation, each consumer will perceive the event differently and create a unique experience of his or her own (i.e., his or her own path of difference creation). The array of potential consumer experience dimensions is an opportunity to think through how you might create or facilitate the conditions for a particular customer experience and cast a wide enough set of dimensions to allow for different consumer situations. *The focus here is on creating the context or the conditions* that consumers would want to utilize in their own difference-creation process or consumption. Figure 9.10 illustrates a framework to think through the different dimensions that could be associated with a consumer experience and idiosyncratic nature of their consumption.

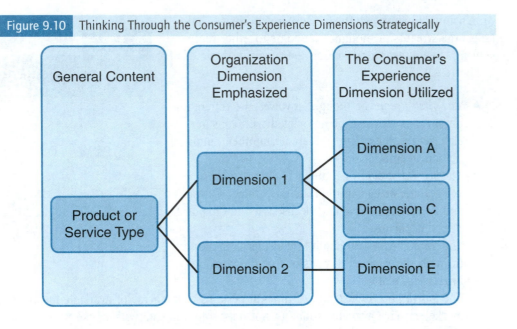

Figure 9.10   Thinking Through the Consumer's Experience Dimensions Strategically

The Second Stream of Thought—Value Creation Through the Customer Experience

The focus here is on value creation operationalized through appropriating the Strategy Canvas and the Four Actions Framework. The Strategy Canvas can be used to map out the different experience dimensions associated with relevant brands. This represents what is currently available to consumers in terms of consumer experiences. It also conceptually represents a stepping-away point from what others are providing so as to provide something unique (i.e., unique customer experiences) and, potentially, more valuable to consumers. See Figure 9.11 as an example.

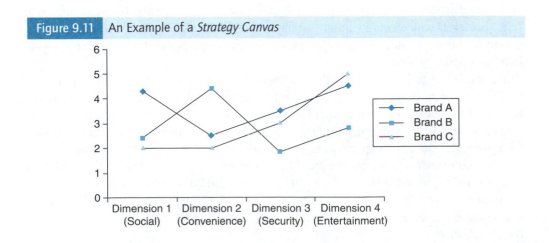

Figure 9.11   An Example of a *Strategy Canvas*

Based upon the different dimensions identified, the Four Actions Framework questions can then be used to strategically think through the process of facilitating unique value through the consumer experience. See Figure 9.12.

Figure 9.12   Using the Four Actions Framework to Create Unique Consumer Experience Value

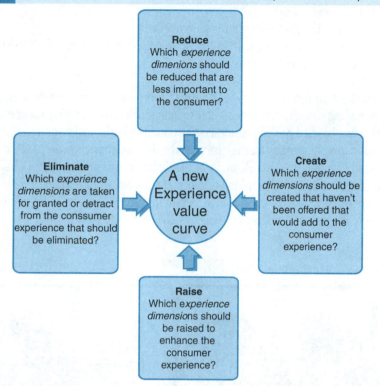

Both of the dimensions identified with the first stream of thought and the Strategy Canvas should be examined through the Four Actions Framework. Some of the dimensions identified with the first stream of thought may not yet have been utilized by others in the marketplace but may represent a means for a meaningful departure from what is currently available. The Strategy Canvas simply presents the backdrop for what is currently being offered in terms of customer experiences. As such, our thinking shouldn't be bound by these dimensions. Here, creative thinking can be utilized as well.

The Third Stream of Thought—Interface Dimensions From a Customer-Experience Perspective

The third stream of thought to consider looks at the customer interface options. Figure 9.13 presents an array of customer interface dimensions. These dimensions were originally conceived around an online environment, but with the retail and online environments becoming increasingly intertwined through technology, the dimensions can be appropriated for in-store considerations as well, or the ways in which the two environments are to be connected. Each of the dimensions represents lines of questions that can be applied for the purpose of creating value through the consumer experience. For example,

- What type of interface context is best for the customer-experience dimensions you are trying to facilitate? Aesthetically or functionally oriented?

- What type of interface content supports your customer-experience dimensions?
- What type of interface theme(s) do you want to associate with your customer-experience dimensions?
- How much customization should occur at the interface and by whom?
- What forms of communications at the interface will facilitate your customer-experience dimensions?
- What forms of interface connections are needed?
- What forms of commerce will you provide through your interface to support your customer-experience dimensions?

At the same time, *co-marketing* involves creating the broader template for the consumer experience while providing ways the consumer is able to individualize the experience. For example, codesign platforms can be used provide customers the option to individualize orders and to name the price they would be willing to pay for the customized order (i.e., copricing setup). (Pricing strategies are discussed in Chapter 11.) Also, elements of the different mixes discussed in Chapter 6 can be appropriated for the purpose of thinking of other potential customer-interface options by using them as lines of questioning that could lead to identifying other means by which to create different/unique forms of customer experiences through the customer interface.

| Figure 9.13 | Seven Design Elements of the Customer Interface |

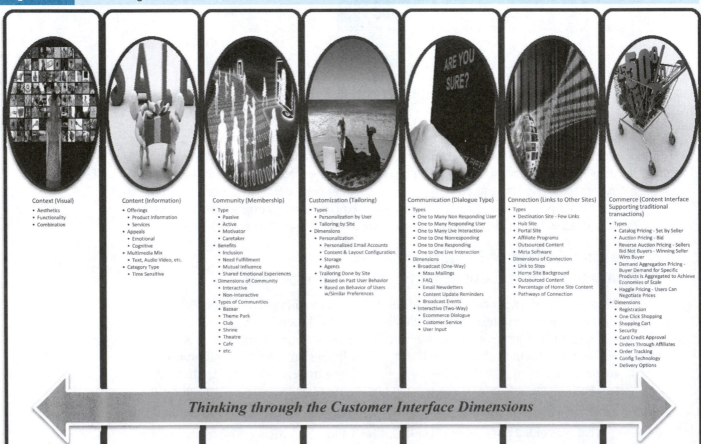

The Fourth Stream of Thought—Marketing Communications From a Customer-Experience Perspective

In thinking through the various ways to create conditions for creating consumer value through their experiences, we also need to consider the various means the marketer has available to communicate with consumers that potentially affect or facilitate the desired experience dimensions. This represents the fourth stream of thought. Each of the means present in Figure 9.14 should be thought of in terms of how they can either contribute to or detract from a particular type of consumer experience to be facilitated. For example, various in-store electronics such as handheld scanners and interactive kiosks can provide information, incentives, and convenience. The Internet e-mail option can be used, in which consumers can sign up to be on the list for alerts (e.g., travel), new deals, or the availability of new items.

The characteristics of the different forms of marketing communications discussed in Chapter 8 can be used here as well. See Tables 8.1, 8.2, and 8.3. The questions to consider include, How will the characteristics of different marketing communications either add to or detract from the unique consumer experience you are trying to facilitate? And how might their effects vary by context?

Both Figures 9.13 and 9.14 are simply meant to suggest things to consider and aren't meant to be exhaustive lists or mutually exclusive. Here, you'll need to be resourceful in outwardly expanding your interface options and marketing communications that you consider, and some may have overlapping characteristics that also need to be taken into account.

Figure 9.14 The Customer Experience Viewed through Available Customer Interfacing Options

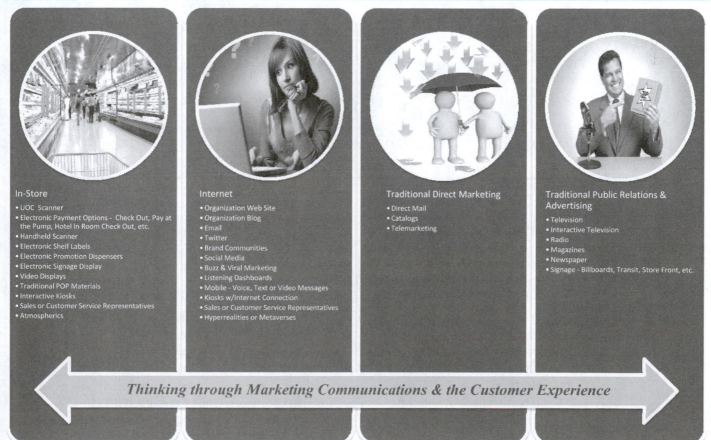

In-Store
- UOC Scanner
- Electronic Payment Options - Check Out, Pay at the Pump, Hotel In Room Check Out, etc.
- Handheld Scanner
- Electronic Shelf Labels
- Electronic Promotion Dispensers
- Electronic Signage Display
- Video Displays
- Traditional POP Materials
- Interactive Kiosks
- Sales or Customer Service Representatives
- Atmospherics

Internet
- Organization Web Site
- Organization Blog
- Email
- Twitter
- Brand Communities
- Social Media
- Buzz & Viral Marketing
- Listening Dashboards
- Mobile - Voice, Text or Video Messages
- Kiosks w/Internet Connection
- Sales or Customer Service Representatives
- Hyperrealities or Metaverses

Traditional Direct Marketing
- Direct Mail
- Catalogs
- Telemarketing

Traditional Public Relations & Advertising
- Television
- Interactive Television
- Radio
- Magazines
- Newspaper
- Signage - Billboards, Transit, Store Front, etc.

Thinking through Marketing Communications & the Customer Experience

---

Marketing Thinking Challenge 9.3:
Co-creating Value Through the Customer Interface

Identify a company of interest and then, using the Four Streams of Thought approach discussed in the chapter and depicted in Figure 9.8, develop a detailed strategy for your chosen company to create a unique experience for customers. Explain the logic behind your strategy and the value to be co-created through the customer experience.

(Hint: Think in terms of the types of dimensions that could be associated with the customer experience. You'll need to do some research to understand the context for the company you have chosen for your MT Challenge. Use the Strategy Canvas as means to think through these customer-experience dimensions and then use your chosen customer-experience dimensions as a basis for thinking through the available marketing communications and interface options. Present your rationale for choosing your marketing communications and interface options based on how their characteristics support your customer-experience dimensions.)

Figure 9.15	Creating a Unique Experience

Summary

- The *customer interface* was defined as "any place at which a company seeks to manage a relationship with a customer, whether through people, technology, or some combination of the two."[23] It is where consumer value can be created.
- Technology is playing an ever-increasing role in changing the nature and ways in which the marketer can interface with customers. Over time, we have gone from a simple storefront or front office view of customer interface to thinking in terms of facilitating and being a part of *consumer experiences* through the customer interface.
- Consequently, technology has also had the effect of inadvertently causing a return to an artisan form of thinking and marketing, which involves much more customer-centric,

local, personal, and responsive marketing. This has become achievable as a result of advances in marketing intelligence and mass customization technology, which are allowing a refocusing of the customer orientations toward the more informed, expanded, and collaborative orientation of the customer experience.

- From a co-marketing perspective, the value at the interface was identified as a *value in experience* that is customer experience. As such, strategy could be developed with a focus on co-creating value at the interface through *value in customer experience*.

- A systematic approach was offered in the chapter, illustrating how to develop a *value-in-customer-experience* strategy. This approach involved considering (1) the various potential dimensions of consumer experience that could be used to create the conditions for facilitating unique consumer experiences at the interface, (2) how the dimensions either contribute to or detract from the desired consumer experience, affecting the value of the experience, (3) the customer interface dimensions that can also have an effect on the experience, and (4) the available marketing communications and their characteristics, which can play a role in affecting the consumer experience.

Case: Four Seasons Hotel and Resorts—Getting It Right

The Four Seasons Hotels and Resorts story is perhaps an example of the American dream, but it begins in Canada in 1961. It started as a modest motel, the Four Seasons Motel Hotel, "with 125 affordable rooms in a rather seedy area outside of the core of downtown Toronto" by Isadore (Issy) Sharp, a Polish immigrant.[24] By the time Sharp opened his fourth hotel in 1972, the Four Seasons Sheraton, he had combined two hotel models into one by "combining 'the best of the small hotel with the best of the large hotel.' He envisioned a medium-sized hotel—big enough to afford an extensive array of amenities, but small enough to maintain a sense of intimacy and personalized service."[25] A significant part of his new hotel concept involved redefining the luxury hotel experience as superior services over and beyond décor.[26] Atmospherics and amenities were important, but superior service was going to be what the Four Seasons Hotel customer experience was all about. His logic was that it would be a means of differentiating while supporting the basis for charging premium prices for accommodations.

> How could Sharp attain that level of service? By seeing the causal link between the way a hotel treated its employees and the way employees treated guests. Rather than treating its employees as disposable, Four Seasons distinguished itself, in Sharp's words "by hiring more attitude than experience, by establishing career paths and promotion from within, by paying as much attention to employee complaints as guest complaints…by pushing responsibility down and encouraging self-discipline, by setting performance high and holding people accountable, and most of all, adhering to our credo, generating trust."

To take the Four Seasons Hotel into the future, Sharp and his management team in 1972 implemented four key strategic decisions that were set into place by four milestone objectives that played out over the next 25 years—each to support the existing one before the next could occur. In Sharp's words, the four milestone objectives were:

1. Only operate medium size hotels with exceptional quality and to be the best in each city.

2. How to be the best? Quality of service is to be their competitive advantage.

3. To achieve quality of service they would have to rely on their people—all of the people in the company. They would need to create a committed and superior workforce that would differentiate them from competitors based upon an ethical credo—The Golden Rule.

4. To invest in the brand name so that it would be synonymous with quality and to be more valuable then ownership of real estate. [27]

Today, the Four Seasons Hotel continues its strategy of people first in its "3 Ps"—people, product, and profit.

Their philosophy is that people come first. If the employees focus on service, then they will have a good product which will bring profit. …Everything they do is driven by the customer and for the customer. In fact, they strive to go beyond expectations—and beyond what training can deliver. Some stories told include:

- A guest left their luggage in a taxi and did not realize it until the taxi had taken off. Although the customer did not know which taxi company, let alone which cab, the bell-man tracked down the luggage and had it delivered to the customer…without the guest ever asking for this to be done.
- While checking out of the Four Seasons Paris, a couple was asked by the front desk clerk if everything was okay (supposedly she could tell something was wrong). The guests told her that their stay was perfect. However their daughter was staying in Paris for a few months and they were a little concerned about leaving her behind. The clerk pulled out a business card and wrote her personal cell phone on the back saying, 'Call me from the States if you ever need anything.'"[28]

The Four Seasons staff is known for paying attention to customer details such as remembering customers' names and for setting up a "Teen Concierge" in recognizing that teens have different needs. "This concierge is closer in age to teenagers and is there to serve the needs of these younger guests."[29] It is also branching out into social media as a part of its emerging strategy. It recently launched a new family blog—The Have Family Will Travel blog at http://family.fourseasons.com/. The site provides holiday video creation, access to trip advice and perspectives, customer stories, and more.[30] Four Seasons also has a presence on Twitter, Facebook, YouTube, and mobile/web applications.[31]

As Four Seasons Hotels and Resorts continues to incorporate social media into its day-to-day business, the company sees real time interactions as a natural extension of its service model. From virtual wine tastings on Twitter to Facebook pages awash with visitor images and timely conversations, to active participation in location-based apps such as Foursquare and Gowalla, Four Seasons has its finger solidly on the pulse of the modern traveller.[32]

The key factor to Four Seasons's success has been its focus on quality through its employees. As such, the customer interface is a critical factor to the strategy.

Research Four Seasons's online forms of customer interface from its website to its social media usage and assess the company's performance from what you can see. Is the quality of service apparent via these online forms of customer interface? What problems to you see? What recommendations would you offer?

References

1. Rayport, Jeffrey F., and Bernard J. Jaworski (2004), "Best Face Forward," *Harvard Business Review*, December, 47.
2. Fulmer, William E., and Jack Goodwin (2001), "Differentiation: Begin With the Consumer," *Business Horizons*, September–October, 55–63.
3. McCauley, Cindy, and Amy Kates (2009), "The Organization-Customer Interface," *Entrepreneur*, June, www.entrepreneur.com/tradejournals/article/205989751.html
4. Rayport, Jeffrey F., and Bernard J. Jaworski (2004), "Best Face Forward," *Harvard Business Review*, December, 48.
5. Rayport, Jeffrey F., and Bernard J. Jaworski (2004), "Best Face Forward," *Harvard Business Review*, December, 48.
6. Rayport, Jeffrey F., and Bernard J. Jaworski (2004), "Best Face Forward," *Harvard Business Review*, December, 49.
7. Burke, Raymond R. (2006), "The Third Wave of Marketing Intelligence," in *Retailing in the 21st Century: Current and Future Trends*, ed. Manfred Krafft and Murali Mantrala, Springer, 113–125.
8. Burke, Raymond R. (2006), "The Third Wave of Marketing Intelligence," in *Retailing in the 21st Century: Current and Future Trends*, ed. Manfred Krafft and Murali Mantrala, Springer, 113.
9. Parvatiyar, Atul, and Jagdish N. Sheth (2001), "Customer Relationship Management: Emerging Practice, Process, and Discipline," *Journal of Economic and Social Research*, 3 (2), 5.
10. Burke, Raymond R. (2006), "The Third Wave of Marketing Intelligence," in *Retailing in the 21st Century: Current and Future Trends*, ed. Manfred Krafft and Murali Mantrala, Springer, 114.
11. Parvatiyar, Atul, and Jagdish N. Sheth (2001), "Customer Relationship Management: Emerging Practice, Process, and Discipline," *Journal of Economic and Social Research*, 3 (2), 4.
12. Jackson, Kathryn E. (2001), "Empowerment at the Customer Interface," Customer Management Interface, September 5, www.callcentermagazine.com/shared/article/showArticle.jhtml?articleId=8701843
13. Berger, Christoph, Kathrin Möslein, Frank Piller, and Ralf Reichwald (2005), "Co-Designing Modes of Cooperation at the Customer Interface: Learning From Exploratory Research," *European Management Review*, 2, 71.
14. Papagiannidis, Savvas, and Michael Bourlakis (2010), "Staging the New Retail Drama: At a Metaverse Near You!," *Journal of Virtual Worlds Research*, 2 (5), 5.
15. Papagiannidis, Savvas, and Michael Bourlakis (2010), "Staging the New Retail Drama: At a Metaverse Near You!," *Journal of Virtual Worlds Research*, 2 (5), 6.
16. Edvardsson, Bo, Bo Enquist, and Robert Jonston (2003), "Co-creating Customer Value Through Hyperreality in the Prepurchase Service Experience," *Journal of Service Research*.
17. Edvardsson, Bo, Bo Enquist, and Robert Jonston (2003), "Co-creating Customer Value Through Hyperreality in the Prepurchase Service Experience," *Journal of Service Research*.
18. Berger, Christoph, Kathrin Möslein, Frank Piller, and Ralf Reichwald (2005), "Co-Designing Modes of Cooperation at the Customer Interface: Learning From Exploratory Research," *European Management Review*, 2, 70–87.

19. Jackson, Kathryn E. (2001), "As The World Turns…From Artisan to Ginger," *Customer Management Interface*, July 5th, www.callcentermagazine.com/article/CCM20010627S0001

20. "The Eight Dimensions of Customer Experience for Financial Services," White Paper: Financial Services, *CA Transforming IT Management*, October 2007, www.ca.com/files/whitepapers/eight_dimensions_customer_exp.pdf

21. Knutson, Bonnie J., Jeffrey A. Beck, Seunghyun Kim, and Jaemin Cha (2009), "Identifying the Dimensions of the Guest's Hotel Experience (Hotel Experience Index)," *Entrepreneur*, February, www.entrepreneur.com/tradejournals/article/193406678.html

22. Cross, Stuart (2009), "10 Dimensions of Great Customer Service," *BNET*, November 19, www.bnet.com/blog/customer-service/10-dimensions-of-great-customer-service/587

23. Rayport, Jeffrey F., and Bernard J. Jaworski (2004), "Best Face Forward," *Harvard Business Review*, December, 49.

24. Marin, Roger (2007), "Isadore Sharp: Creating the Four Seasons Difference," www.rotman.utoronto.ca/rogermartin/OM_Excerpt2.pdf

25. Marin, Roger (2007), "Isadore Sharp: Creating the Four Seasons Difference," www.rotman.utoronto.ca/rogermartin/OM_Excerpt2.pdf

26. Marin, Roger (2007), "Isadore Sharp: Creating the Four Seasons Difference," www.rotman.utoronto.ca/rogermartin/OM_Excerpt2.pdf

27. www.fourseasons.com/about_us/corporate_bios/isadore_sharp/#multimedia

28. Shapiro, Stephen (2008), "Innovation at the Four Seasons Hotel," www.steveshapiro.com/2008/02/26/innovation-at-the-four-seasons-hotel/

29. Shapiro, Stephen (2008), "Innovation at the Four Seasons Hotel," www.steveshapiro.com/2008/02/26/innovation-at-the-four-seasons-hotel/

30. (2011), "Four Seasons Hotels and Resorts Launches New Family Blog as Part of Expanding Social Media Strategy," *Hospitality Net*, February 8, www.hospitalitynet.org/news/154000320/4050125.search?query=four+seasons+hotel+strategy

31. Brown, Danny (2010), "Four Seasons, Four Outposts," *The Human Side of Social Media and the Social Side of Marketing*, May 10, http://dannybrown.me/2010/05/10/four-seasons-hotels-art-of-social-media/

32. (2011), "Four Seasons Hotels and Resorts Launches New Family Blog as Part of Expanding Social Media Strategy," *Hospitality Net*, February 8, www.hospitalitynet.org/news/154000320/4050125.search?query=four+seasons+hotel+strategy

CHAPTER 10 Thinking Beyond Logistics

Decompression Exercise

Visualize taking a mental balloon ride. What sights do you see?

Figure 10.1 Take a Balloon Ride

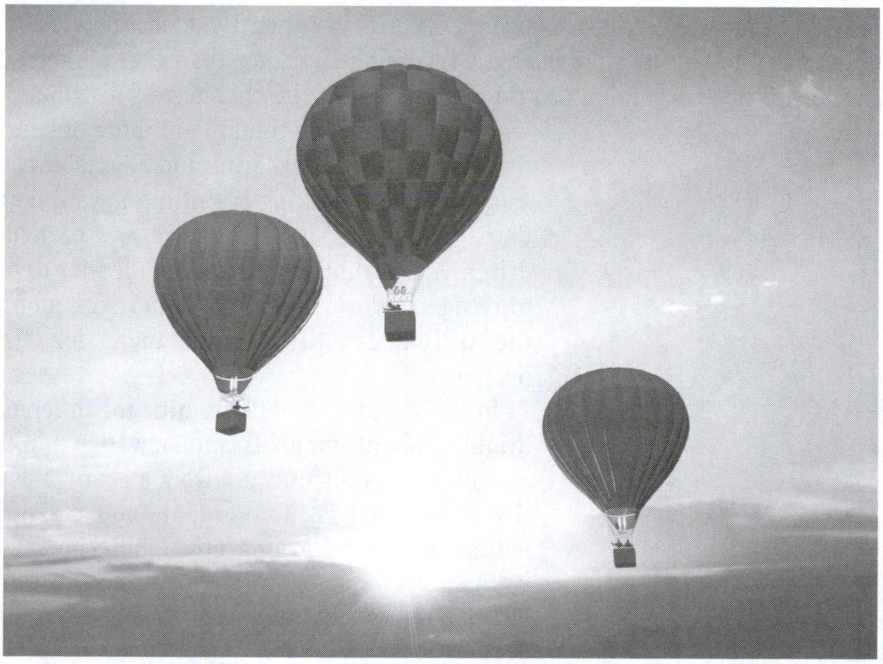

Chapter Introduction

In the previous chapters, we have seen significant changes occurring in marketing thinking that result in new concepts and different forms of strategy. On one level, the thinking is shifting from a command-and-control perspective (an inside-outside perspective) to one that develops its sensibilities from within the process of participating with others (a within perspective). On a more fundamental level, the marketers' thinking is changing through their participation by acquiring and recognizing the strategic value found within the sensibilities that include an awareness beyond oneself, empathy, vigilance, openness, being a part of ongoing change, a willingness to work with others, drawing on the resources of others, reducing risk through collaboration, mutually beneficial relationships, value creation, and a more organic view of marketing in the form of co-marketing (collaborative or participatory marketing). As discussed in Chapter 6, the Vulnerability Paradox plays out when marketers recognize the *strengths within the sense of vulnerability*.

Similar changes are also taking place in terms of how marketers think about logistics and channel management. An issue for the marketer has always been how to determine the best way to get products (or services) to consumers. As such, the marketer could simply view the issue by thinking in terms of it as a delivery function. This *functional perspective* is the basis of the traditional logistics/channels perspective found in marketing. As an alternative, the marketer could reconsider this view and look at it in terms of thinking of the process from a *value creation perspective*. This can be done by examining the activities comprising the process (internally and externally) and assessing their value contributions by the way products (or services) are being made available to consumers. Beneficiaries could include the manufacturer, channel members, and the consumer. This is characteristic of thinking along the lines of value chains. The marketer could expand his or her thinking even further by examining the process by thinking less in terms of a linear and fixed process/structure but, rather, one that is more organic, nonlinear, flexible, and agile, which creates value in the process. This more *organic value-creation perspective* is associated with value nets.

Another way to consider the changes occurring is, rather than the marketer solely thinking in terms of assuming control or oversight of the channels of distribution, the marketer can also be thinking in more organic ways that allow for greater sharing and adaptability. At the same time, the thinking is shifting toward networks that are nonlinear, more inclusive, and participation driven. Again, thinking agility is called for to be able to recognize these different perspectives, along with the willingness to consider them for strategy purposes.

In this chapter, we will examine the differences in thinking about channels and how the thinking is actually expanding outward from a channel perspective to one that is more organic and biological in nature, involving learning, adaptability, and flexibility. As a consequence of the expansion in thinking, new strategies and value aspects are emerging that need to be considered. To understand the new strategies, we will start by looking at the different forms of thinking associated with logistics and channels of distribution.

Let's take on the *channel concept*. How is the channel concept *channeling* marketing thinking? How has the concept affected strategy? And what is emerging as an alternative perspective?

Thinking Through the Channel Concept

Traditionally, marketing channels have been defined as follows: "**marketing channels** are sets of interdependent organizations involved in the process of making a product or service available for use or consumption. They are the set of pathways a product or service follows after production, culminating in purchase and use by the final end user."[1,2] Accordingly, a marketing channel is a pathway through which a product or service passes on its way to the consumer. Or, "marketing channels can be compared with a pipeline through which water flows from a source to terminus. Marketing channels make possible the flow of goods from a producer, through intermediaries, to a buyer....Some intermediaries actually purchase items from the seller, store them, and resell them to buyers."[3] By these definitions, a marketing channel is a *thing* in the form of a supply channel, a pathway, or a pipeline.

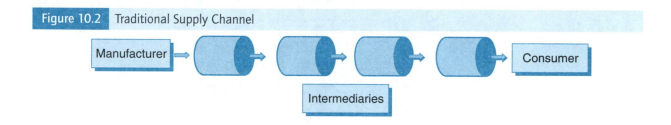

Figure 10.2   Traditional Supply Channel

Implicit, if not explicit, within this thinking is a channeling effect caused by the channel concept that involves a linear sense to the pathway to the consumer. The pathway starts with the manufacturer and then proceeds on its way to the consumer. Here we see that the doing or the act is being initiated by the manufacturer or marketer. It is an inside-outside perspective, which inherently possesses the marketer–consumer dualistic thinking characteristic as exemplified in Figure 10.2 and that was previously discussed in Chapter 6. The focus of the thinking is on creating and controlling a structure to deliver products and/or services to the consumer, which may involve a direct or an indirect path through intermediaries. As such, the *delivery function* itself can then be performed exclusively by the manufacturer or divided up among the intermediaries in terms of the various functions that comprise the overall delivery of products and/or services to the consumer or customer. In either case, it involves a *linear-pathway form of thinking* in which the pathway is a delivery function that can be done by one or multiple entities. Inherent in this form of thinking is an emphasis on creating efficiencies throughout the delivery function in terms of assortment bundling, functional expertise, and so forth.

Considerations of costs, exclusivity, and/or consumer access may be used in the development of the channel structure. However, the greater number of intermediaries that are involved increases the stages or levels associated with the pathway to the consumer, as well as the changing of hands through which the product(s) or service(s) pass, which may actually lead to greater inefficiencies. Once established, the structure has the tendency to take on the characteristics of one-size-fits-all(no customization), becoming rigid, creating greater separation or distancing from the consumer, increasing the potential for inefficiencies and costs, and a place for product to build up. Figure 10.3 illustrates traditional consumer channel structural pathways and the various functions to be carried out.

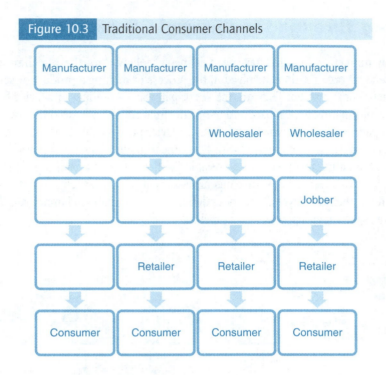

Figure 10.3   Traditional Consumer Channels

Channel Structures and Functions

The first column shows a *direct channel* structure and the other columns represent *indirect channels* utilizing intermediaries, with the last column being a three-stage or -level channel structure. The *intermediaries* in Figure 10.3 include wholesalers, jobbers, and/or retailers that each carry out particular functions within the channel. For both the consumer and B2B channel situations, the various *functions* being carried out up and down the channels include physical movement of products or services (transportation and storing), matching (sorting and packaging), transferring of merchandise title, financial arrangements being made along with payments, channel and market information being communicated, promotional activities being performed, and risk taking.

Wholesale organizations buy products or services to be resold to other businesses. Wholesalers provide a series of functions, including selling and promoting, forming assortments, bulk breaking, warehousing, transportation, financing, risk bearing, providing information, and management services. *Jobbers* represent limited-service wholesalers. They can provide the racks or shelves to retailers (rack jobber), purchase merchandise and then sell it to those paying cash and providing merchandise transport (cash-and-carry jobber), take ownership but not possession of the merchandise and simply solicit orders from wholesalers and retailers to have the merchandise sent directly from the manufacturer (drop shippers), or provide truck services to retailers (truck jobber).[4]*Retailers* sell directly to consumers.

In similar way, business-to-business (B2B) channel structures can also be set up. For example,

An industrial-goods manufacturer can use its sales force to sell directly to industrial customers [a direct channel]; or it can sell to industrial distributors, who sell to the industrial customers [a one stage or level channel]; or it can sell through manufacturer's representatives or its own sales branches directly to industrial customers [a two stage or level channel], or indirectly to industrial customer through industrial distributors [a three stage or level channel].[5]

Channel Distribution Strategies

From this traditional channel perspective, the marketer has several different *consumer access options* available. The three general distribution strategies include intensive, exclusive, or selective. The *intensive distribution strategy* involves having as many pathways as possible availing products in as many places as needed, such as with vending machine items (e.g., snacks, soft drinks). The *exclusive distribution strategy* utilizes only one means through which the product or service would be made available (e.g., a designer's cologne sold exclusively through Neimen Marcus). The *selective* is some combination of the two.

A Shift in Channel Thinking

In the early 1980s, there was a shift in thinking about channels from a functional perspective to thinking about value creation through the channel structure. In essence, the functional form of thinking had led to a thinking obstacle in the form of viewing the channel as a series of functions for the purpose of moving product to the consumer. In the process, the functions became defined (e.g., a wholesaler or a jobber) and, as such, they had their boundaries as to what consisted the function and what didn't. The thinking became more rigid, which obscured thinking of them in different ways and/or configurations. It led to what can be described as "silo" thinking—similar to when organizations are structured by function (e.g., marketing, accounting, finance, etc.). Silo thinking can lead to less communications across functions and inefficiencies internally and externally to an organization. Also, the focus was more on the movement of products and less about the value associated with how the products and/or services were to be moved. The value-creation perspective instead involves thinking about how what is being performed within the channel is contributing to value creation for those involved within the channel and, ultimately, for the consumer.

While the thinking is shifting toward value creation, it inherently still possesses the channel concept structural characteristics—that is, thinking in terms of pathways and the various functions being carried out but further thinking of them as chains in which value can be transferred or created along the way—a *value chain*. As we will discuss later, the channel structural characteristics will be seen as a limitation of this form of thinking. Within value chain thinking, different chain configurations and arrangements within the channel can result in differences in value for the consumer.

Here, a value chain is a way of rethinking the functions being traditionally carried out and considering them at a more fundamental level in terms of the activities that comprise the functions being performed. The activities can then be viewed from a value-creation perspective individually and collectively. We'll examine the value-chain perspective in more detail next.

A Value-Chain Perspective

The shift toward value creation can be tied to the concept of a *value chain*. In 1985, Michael Porter, a Harvard professor, introduced his value chain concept.[6] It was conceived as a conceptual and analysis tool to identify competitive advantages by creating unique forms of value through either lower costs or differentiation. This thinking involves viewing the organization as a series of activities that can be mapped out and their contributions assessed in regard to buyer value. Through the analysis, a series of considerations come into view in terms of how to best configure the organization's activities to produce unique buyer value. Figure 10.4 (on the next page) presents an organization's value chain and its general categories of activities.

Figure 10.4   The Value Chain

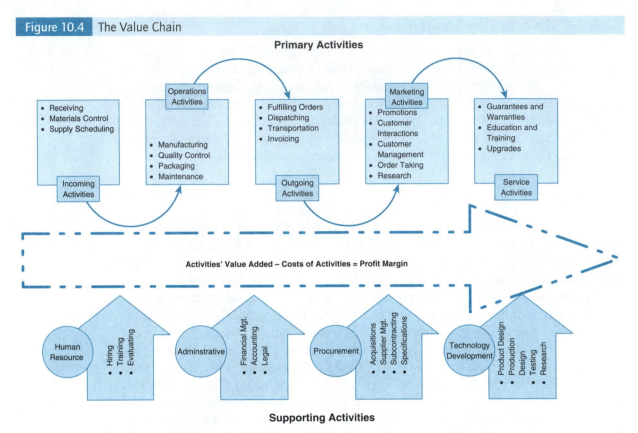

According to value chain theory,

> Competitive advantage grows out of the way firms organize and perform discrete activities. The operations of any firm can be divided into a series of activities such as salespeople making sales calls, service technicians performing repairs, scientists in the laboratory designing products or processes, and treasurers raising capital.
>
> Firms create value for their buyers through performing these activities. The ultimate value a firm creates is measured by the amount buyers are willing to pay for its product or service. A firm is profitable if this value exceeds the collective costs of performing all of the required activities. To gain competitive advantage over its rivals, a firm must either provide comparable buyer value but perform activities more efficiently than its competitors (lower cost), or perform activities in a unique way that creates greater buyer value and commands a premium price (differentiation).
>
> …Firms gain competitive advantage from conceiving of new ways to conduct activities, employ new procedures, new technologies, or different inputs.
>
> …A company's value chain for competing in a particular industry is embedded in a larger stream of activities…term[ed] the value system…The value system includes suppliers, who provide inputs (such as raw materials, components, machinery, and purchase services) to the firm's value chain. On its way to the ultimate buyer, a firm's product often passes through the value chains of the distribution channels. Ultimately, products become purchased inputs to the value chains of their buyer, who use the products in performing activities of their own.[7]

The value system is depicted in Figure 10.5.

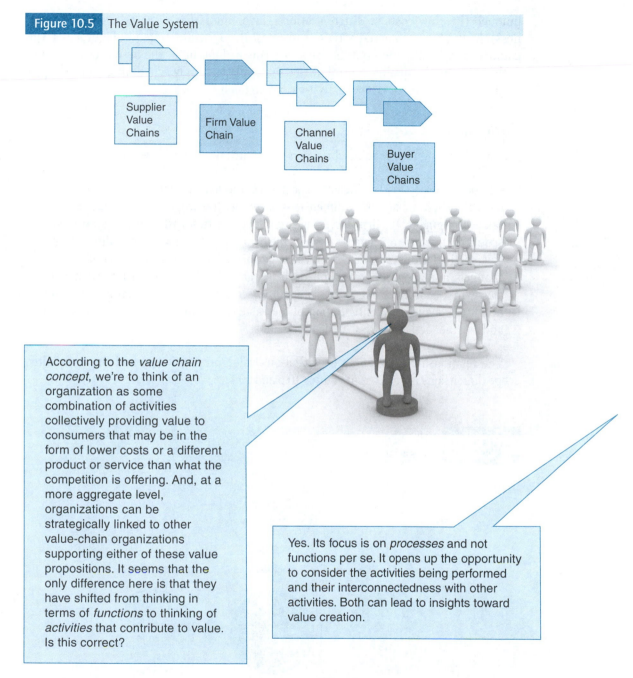

Figure 10.5 The Value System

Supplier Value Chains

Firm Value Chain

Channel Value Chains

Buyer Value Chains

According to the *value chain concept*, we're to think of an organization as some combination of activities collectively providing value to consumers that may be in the form of lower costs or a different product or service than what the competition is offering. And, at a more aggregate level, organizations can be strategically linked to other value-chain organizations supporting either of these value propositions. It seems that the only difference here is that they have shifted from thinking in terms of *functions* to thinking of *activities* that contribute to value. Is this correct?

Yes. Its focus is on *processes* and not functions per se. It opens up the opportunity to consider the activities being performed and their interconnectedness with other activities. Both can lead to insights toward value creation.

At the same time, the value-chain perspective focuses on creating an organization that is configured more advantageously than the competition through its activities that lead to either lower costs or a differentiated product or service at a premium price. Both create meaningful differences in the marketplace in the forms of obtaining a low-cost position or a unique form of differentiation different than what is available elsewhere by way of the configuration of the organization and/or interorganizational activities.

As such, the value-chain perspective involves assessing the individual activities that are to be performed, eliminated, changed, or created along with assessing how the activities link up with other activities contributing to the value proposition being pursued (i.e., low costs or differentiation—involving issues of costs and/or effectiveness). Examples of potential activities to be assessed are illustrated in Figure 10.4. One could start with the inbound logistics in terms of looking at the activities associated with assessing the quality control of raw materials to supply scheduling and then proceed to analyze the operations activities and so forth.

Competitive Scope

Another dimension to the value-chain perspective involves *competitive scope*.

> Competitive scope is the breadth of activities the firm performs to compete in an industry. There are four basic dimensions of competitive scope: **segment scope,** or the range of segments the firm serves (e.g., product varieties, customer types); **industry scope,** or the range of related industries the firm competes in with a coordinated strategy; **vertical scope,** or what activities are performed by the firm versus suppliers and channels; and **geographical scope,** or the geographic regions in which the firm operates with a coordinated strategy. Competitive scope is vital to competitive advantage because it shapes the configuration of the value chain, how activities are performed and whether activities are shared among units.[8]

The relationship between an organization's value proposition(s) and the competitive scope dimensions is depicted in Figures 10.6 and 10.7.

Figure 10.6	Value Chain Considerations—Value Propositions and Competitive Scope Dimensions

| Figure 10.7 | Competitive Scope and Value Propositions |

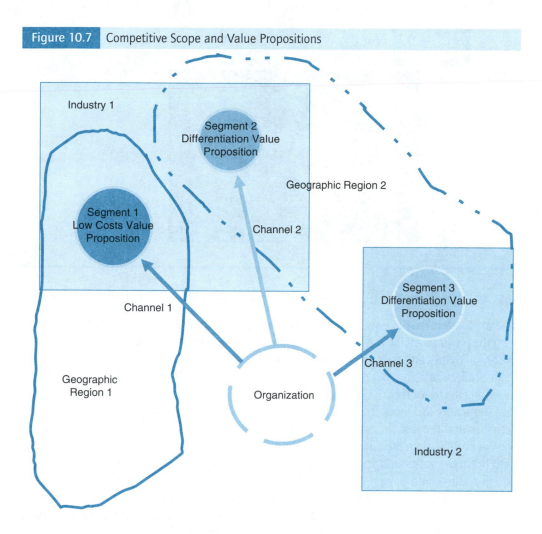

Before moving on, try the following Value Chain Marketing Thinking Challenge.

Marketing Thinking Challenge 10.1:
Analyzing an Organization as a Value Chain

Choose any organization of interest. It could be an organization you work for or one that you find interesting. (1) Research the organization and identify its *competitive scope*. (2) Based on its competitive scope, is it pursuing a cost or a differentiation value strategy? (3) Using the value chain categories of activities identified in Figure 10.4, try to find out as much information as you can on these activities that are being performed by the organization. Then estimate how much value these activities contribute (lowering costs or differentiation, e.g., increasing effectiveness) to the value strategy you initially identified in Part 2. (4) What did you learn from this challenge?

Figure 10.8	Analyzing an Organization From a Value-Chain Perspective

Issues With the Value-Chain Perspective

There are several issues associated with a value-chain approach that you may have encountered with the previous Marketing Thinking Challenge. It is very difficult to map out all of an organization's activities and their interlinkages and to assess their individual contributions of value to the overall value being offered to consumers (i.e., their costs and the amount consumers would be willing to pay for them). The complexities of the analysis also include the size of an organization (larger organizations increase the complexity) and how to assign a value to the individual activities and the issue of assigning a value to the interlinkages of activities while taking into consideration competitive scope. Additionally, the value-chain perspective or thinking starts with the organization and, hence, is an inside-outside (command-and-control) perspective.

The value-chain perspective is a competitive perspective that also inherently possesses the same characteristics associated with a **Red Ocean** strategy, which involves *exploitation* (discussed in Chapter 3). In this case, it is exploitation through the conceptual value lens (i.e., to get the most consumer value out of an organization's activities). An exploitation perspective doesn't take into account innovation and leads to rigidness through investment and ownership in the value-chain structure internally and externally. The following Marketing Thinking in Practice discusses further the issue of innovation with the value-chain perspective.

> ## Marketing Thinking in Practice:
> ## The Value Chain
>
> Jeffrey Phillips, V. P. of Marketing and Sales at OVO Innovate on Purpose, raises an interesting observation about Porter's Value Chain in its omission for considering innovation. His argument is presented below.[9]
>
> > ...In the 1980s, Michael Porter wrote a number of books about corporate strategy that became the basis for much of the education of MBAs, at least where strategy was concerned. Few MBAs in the 80s and 90s failed to study Porter's Five Forces or Value Chain Analysis. Since many of those MBAs minted in that period are now in leadership positions in their firms, it behooves us to understand the models they carry around with them, and whether or not those models are open and extensible where innovation is concerned, or whether they ignore or resist innovation.

...Porter's insight was to identify all the primary functions of a business and all the support functions of a business and seek to understand what the firm did exceptionally well, and what it must do at least moderately well. While other strategists had thought and written about the linkages between internal operations, Porter was one of the first to create the concept of the Value Chain. Today we often think of the value chain as extending "upstream" to suppliers and "downstream" to distribution channels and even to customers or consumers. The tool is a powerful metaphor when thinking about where and how a firm adds value.

Primary activities are the ones we usually think of as distinct operations or departments and are the "direct" costs in a business—inbound and outbound logistics, "operations" which could be manufacturing or development, marketing and sales, and service. Support activities are those that we traditionally think of as "overhead"—Human Resources, Information Technology, Procurement, and what Porter called Firm Infrastructure—legal, financial, management and so forth.

The model, once again, does not explicitly call out innovation, and in this breakdown of the organization it is hard to decide where and how innovation should add value. Clearly innovation can play a role in any of the primary functions. Innovation can improve the way we make things, or the way we distribute products and services, or the customer support and service we offer. Conversely, innovation could be considered a "supporting" capability that improves all functions from an enabling perspective. It's possible that innovation exists in both locations. However, there are two other items to consider when thinking about innovation and the Value Chain analysis.

First, the model describes a business operating at peak efficiency turning out products and services, but doesn't do such a great job describing where in the business new ideas, new products and services are originating. It's hard to pinpoint where the "R&D" function is within this model, and whether that is a primary function or a support function. Second, as we've already noted, when Porter built the model it reflected the operations within the context of the business. Given the integrated nature of most organizations and their upstream suppliers and downstream partners, we typically think of the "value chain" as reaching from the companies and individuals that provide raw materials and inputs, to the end consumer on the "downstream" side. The same is true for innovation. Good ideas may come from anywhere, not just within the context of the firm.

Like many organizations today, the concept of innovation is important, but as in the Value Chain model it is not clear where it should reside, or how it should be considered, as a primary function or a support function. In almost 30 years we've yet to answer that question successfully. Perhaps the Value Chain Model and our existing corporate hierarchies need to be rethought in the context of innovation.

Challenges to the Value-Chain Perspective

As described in the following quote, the value-chain thinking is also being challenged by the changes occurring in the marketplace.

The argument developing here is that corporate structures (as well as decision-making processes) are changing. The point may be made a little stronger: it is becoming very clear that "value" is migrating in many industries. For example, the automotive industry is experiencing a shift in value profile. Hitherto, value was maximized in the production process, current indications and expectations for the future are this will migrate toward the marketing and service processes.

Three major changes are suggested. The first concerns the emphasis on performance. Currently many organizations emphasize cost-led efficiency as a primary objective. Not only is this constraining, but also it has to be shown not to be in the shareholders' interests: cost reductions typically have a negative impact on customer service and this, in turn, has the same impact on revenues. The second change involves a switch from an internal focus in which assets and resources must be owned to one of cooperation and collaboration in which assets and resources are managed. The third shift is one in which the organization becomes proactive in its operations and this [pertains to] both customer and supply markets. Market responsive organizations tend to be inflexible and typically have very slow "time-to-market" responses. In other words, they are imitators rather than innovators![10]

In addition, these changes affect how management thinks about organizational structure and issues of ownership versus managing assets. The following quote characterizes the changes taking place in business:

Toward the end of the twentieth century a number of changes occurred that suggest that organizational structures and management attitudes and behavior in the foreseeable future will differ markedly from the traditional model. Not only had business become global in every respect, but in almost all markets end-user expectations were undergoing significant change which were forcing business to come to terms with demands for increased choice and quality, flexible ordering and servicing systems, on-line accessibility to suppliers and competitive prices. The response by business has been equally dramatic. Large organizations have reduced their activities down to core processes and capabilities, adopting the view that astute asset management and risk management are more about managing assets than ownership. Consequently the largest international corporations can be seen divesting their non-core businesses and adopting holonic structures…[developing] mutually supporting clusters of interdependent interorganizational business systems.[11]

Marketplace changes are commanding organizations to reconsider at a very fundamental level how they think about organization structure, issues of ownership versus managing assets, and moving from a command-and-control perspective to one that involves thinking in terms of systems of interdependent businesses that require greater cooperation and collaboration to be successful in these very dynamic environments. As the thinking shifts farther out from a channel perspective of interdependent interorganizational business systems, the linear view of the channel and simply the movement of product or services start to dissipate toward something that appears to be similar to some biological or organic formation. The lines of questioning are also changing, leading to new approaches and strategies to consider. Examples of the changing lines of questioning include, Which is better:

(1) To manage or own assets?

(2) Traditional business configurations or organic business models that are multidimensional, interdependent, interorganizational, and adaptive, involving learning systems?

(3) A reactive market-response perspective (imitators) or proactive operations (innovators)?

At the same time, the thinking has migrated toward considering different modes of collaboration and, ultimately, toward thinking in terms of value nets. Next, we'll discuss forms of collaborative distribution that include modes of collaboration and values nets.

Forms of Collaborative Distribution

As discussed in Chapter 9, with the advent of the Internet, social media, marketing intelligence and mass customization technology, the codesign, co-creation, or co-marketing perspectives have made their way into marketing thinking. What has been ushered in is a greater sense of focusing in on the co-creation process with consumers.

Traditionally, the competitive advantage of a retailer is based on its ability to provide a fitting assortment for the targeted market segment and its capabilities in distribution. By bundling supply and demand, retail is lowering transaction costs. When providing customized solutions, however, assortment, efficient stock keeping, and distribution are no longer the driving sources of competitive advantage.

On the contrary, interaction skills and matching the customization possibilities with the needs of a specific customer during the process of co-design are becoming the prime sources of competitive advantage....at the end each order has to be transmitted separately to the corresponding manufacturer, and as the manufacturer gets access to information for every single customer, the relationship between suppliers and retailers change when introducing mass customization.

In the same manner, as transaction marketing is supplemented (or even substituted) by relationship marketing, transaction based relationships between suppliers and retailers are being replaced by collaborative relationships between these two parties.[12]

Thinking in competitive advantage terms, the advantage in a codesign consumer collaborative scenario doesn't come from the first purchase per se but by way of the subsequent purchases.[13] This is due to the advantage of having customer customized portfolio information that can be used in the subsequent purchases to make a more personalized customer experience. This characterizes a return to the artisan view of thinking along with co-marketing, as discussed in Chapter 9. The collaborative initiative has lead to four potential modes of collaboration. They can be described as consumer direct, manufacturer driven, retail driven, and intermediary based.[14]

Consumer-Direct Mode of Collaboration

The consumer-direct mode of collaboration, as it suggests, is where the organization has setup means for customers to place orders to their specifications through a codesign platform (e.g., a website). There is no channel per se, and a retailer isn't involved. Without a channel, there isn't the opportunity for channel conflict. But there could be a conflict if another channel (a traditional channel) is being used as well. Also, for this mode of collaboration, organizations would need to possess the necessary customer-interface skills. Examples of companies utilizing this mode of collaboration as a part of their marketing strategy include Dell Computers, Nike (e.g., NikeID), and Lego.

Figure 10.9 The Consumer Codesigns Directly With the Marketer

The Manufacturer-Driven Mode of Collaboration

The manufacturer-driven mode of collaboration is characterized by utilizing retail partners. The retailer's role is to provide customer access and the means/platform for the codesign process. The bundling of customer specifications at the retail setting can reduce internal complexities for the manufacturer.

Figure 10.10 A Consumer in a Retail Environment Codesigning an Order to the Manufacturer

In this mode, the collaboration is dominated by the manufacturer (mass customizer). Especially from the perspective of a customer, the manufacturer is the provider of the customized product and main interaction partner. The retailer just provides access and infrastructure for the codesign process. Customer data and customer relationships are within the ownership of the supplier.[15]

To utilize this mode of collaboration effectively, manufacturers would need the necessary customer-interface skills along with motivating sales personnel. An example of this mode of collaboration is Bali Today, a window blinds manufacturer that utilizes Home Depot for access to consumers and provides a platform for customizing blinds.

The Retail-Driven Mode of Collaboration

The retail-driven mode of collaboration is initiated by the retailer in an effort to become more service oriented as a means of differentiating. The retailer has the customer-interface expertise and, as such, reduces the manufacturer's marketplace risk. It is the retailer that possesses the full customer information. The retailer sends the customer's specifications to the supplier to have the order fulfilled. The manufacturer acts as a traditional supplier, providing the customized goods to the retailer. The difficulties with this mode of collaboration involve arrangements for reliability, consistency, and responsiveness from the suppliers and manufacturer. In this scenario, the consumer views the retailer as the supplier. Examples include Custom Foot and Land's End.

Figure 10.11   Consumers Going to a Retailer to Codesign an Order

The Intermediary-Based Collaboration Mode

The intermediary-based collaboration mode centers around an intermediary working between the retailer and the manufacturer to achieve customization.

> … established retailers are sometimes neither willing nor able to deliver the new capabilities required for customization. But at the same time, many manufacturers are typically not set up for close contact with end-consumers. Here the inclusion of an intermediary may avoid channel conflicts if this broker acts as the visible market player. The same is true for internal conflicts between the individualization processes, the old sales force or between business units. The inner structure of many manufacturers often impedes a seamless and comfortable interaction process, since customer-orientation is not anchored in the company's culture. It took mass customization pioneer Levi Strauss four years to establish a relationship management program for its "Original Spin" program in order to lockin first-time customers into its system. Here, the collaboration with a specialized intermediary who understands the relationship processes of individualization could have sped-up this practice.[16]

Figure 10.12 An Intermediary Assisting With the Collaborative Transition Process

The intermediary mode of collaboration could be used transitionally as a way to move into one of the other forms of collaboration. The difficulties for this mode of collaboration include requiring a comprehensive understanding of the customization process, added costs, and that it creates greater degrees of complexity in terms of information (e.g., sharing, miscommunications). Real Age is an example of this mode of collaboration.

Marketing Thinking Challenge 10.2:
Modes of Collaboration

With the four different modes of collaboration in mind, identify organizations that are examples of each (other than the ones mentioned in the chapter). Provide a detailed description of their modes of collaboration. What advantages and disadvantages do you see with each example identified? In what ways could they improve their modes of collaboration?

Figure 10.13 Thinking About Different Modes of Collaboration

Inherent in the modes of collaboration previously discussed is a one-to-one, linear form of thinking that can be attributed to the channel concept. The many-to-one thinking as with collaborative networks (Chapter 5) and brand communities (Chapter 7), along with the advances in technology, are expanding collaborative thinking outward from a channel perspective per se to "value nets" that are discussed next.

Value Nets—A New View of Collaboration

A **value net** is not what the term supply chain conjures up. It is no longer about supply; it's about creating value for customers, the company, and its suppliers. Nor is it a sequential, rigid chain. Instead, it is a dynamic, high-performance network of customer/supplier partnerships and information flows. The traditional supply chain manufactures products and pushes them through distribution.…In value nets, information is moving in real-time across the cooperating businesses, the relationships among the partners is dynamic and varies with changing conditions, and the operating targets of the business include not just efficiency but also agility. In value nets, the business value is created by businesses and their suppliers, buyers, and partners through the combination and enhancement of services by all participants.[17]

Several streams of thought come together to fill in what these value nets might look like. The thinking involves an organic view of the networks, an on-demand feature, and componentization. We'll start with the organic view.

The Holonic Perspective. The organic view of a value net is referred to as a "holonic" net, which is described as follows:

… a set of companies that acts integratedly and organically; it is constantly re-configured to manage each business opportunity a customer presents. Each company in the network provides a different process capability and is called a holon…

Holonic networks are not hierarchical structures—rather, each business within the structure is equal to each of the others. The network is in dynamic equilibrium and it is self-regulating. Access to, and exchange of, information throughout the network is open, as is access to and exchange of information across the network boundaries. The network is evolutionary and is constantly interacting with its environment. It is a knowledge network, a learning organization.[18]

The characteristics of a holonic (value) net (HVN) are presented in Table 10.1.

Table 10.1	Holonic (Value) Net Characteristics

Characteristics	Explanation
Customer Aligned	Customer expectations initiate sourcing, building, and delivery activities in the net. "The customer commands the net."
Collaborative and Systemic	Companies engage suppliers, customers, and possibly competitors in a unique network of value-creating relationships. "Each activity is assigned to the partner best able to perform it."
Agile and Scalable	Flexible manufacturing and distribution enhanced by information-flow design facilitates responsiveness. "Everything in the value net, physical or virtual, is scalable."
Fast Flow	Lead times are rapid and compressed. "Rapid delivery goes hand in hand with reliable and convenient delivery."
Digital	E-commerce is a key enabler. However, it is the flow of information and its intelligence use that drives the value net. "Rule-based, event-driven tools take over many operational decisions. Distilled real-time analysis enables rapid executive decision making."

Source: [19]

The "On-Demand Business" Perspective. In essence, the holonic (value) net is about creating a new business model that is being referred to as an "on-demand business."

> …is a business that is able to recognize change as it is occurring and react appropriately, ahead of the competition, and keep pace with the demands of its customers, value-net partners, and employees alike. In trying to achieve this state, the business will need to leverage technology to the fullest.…Fundamentally, becoming an on demand business is equivalent to achieving total business flexibility. Two important enablers contribute to the realization by an enterprise of this vision of on demand—componentization and service orientation.[20]

Componentization, or the modularity design, allows for the necessary flexibility within the holonic (value) net. As such, the net can be constructed, deconstructed, and reconstructed as the demand calls for.

> The process of deconstruction/construction is realized through business components, which correspond to distinct business functions. In the on demand environment, the component-based firm links its components efficiently and seamlessly both internally and across the firm's boundaries with the best-of-breed components provided by external partners.[21]

The holonic (value) net also suggests a newform of value—that is a "*value in orchestration*."[22] The life of the holonic (value) net, the organic nature of the net, will depend upon the means or mechanisms within the net, across businesses, and within organizations to efficiently and effectively reconfigure in the on-demand environment. It will require "rapid adaptation."[23] As such, greater communications, access and the flow of real-time information, cooperation and collaboration, and thinking in dynamic terms are required. Examples of companies using value nets include Apple, Cisco, and Dell.[24] The rapid adaptation of a holonic (value) net is illustrated in Figure 10.14.

Figure 10.14	Holonic (Value) Net—Rapid Adaptation in an On-Demand-Business Environment

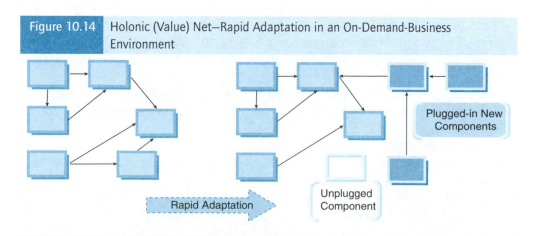

Graphic Source: [25]

Marketing Thinking Challenge 10.3:
Orchestrating a Holonic (Value) Net

Identify an organization(s) that you believe exemplifies the adaptive holonic (value) net thinking. Explain how it has set up its net. From what you have found, does it appear that the net is achieving the goals of rapid adaptation and mass customization?

Figure 10.15   Rapid Adaptation and Mass Customization

Summary

- In this chapter, we examined the effects of the channel concept on marketing thinking. The concept possesses an inside-outside, command-and-control perspective, one-size-fits-all, linear, functional view for providing products and/or services to consumers.

- Thinking of the supply channel as a series of functions is being succeeded by thinking in terms of organizational activities directed toward creating consumer value, either in the form of lower costs or differentiation from what is currently available. As such, the two competitive value propositions were to be pursued through configuring unique value chains.

- The concept of the value chain included linking up with other organizations' value chains up and down the channel to organize the activities in pursuit of the value propositions.

- At the same time, the value chain thinking is being challenged by dynamic marketplace conditions and advances in technology, which have led to a new form of thinking.

- Instead of thinking in terms of the channel concept, which was still inherent in the value-chain perspective, the thinking is shifting again toward a more organic view in the form of rapid adaptive holonic (value) nets. Within this view, the "value in orchestration" of the net is recognized.

Case: Zara Retailing—What's on the Shelf Today?

ZARA

Zara designs, manufactures, and sells clothing worldwide throughout its many retail stores. It is a part of the retailing Inditex Group owned by Spanish tycoon Amancio Ortega. Inditex brands include Massimo Dutti, Pull and Bear, Stradivarius, and Bershka. The headquarters is located in A Coruña, Spain. According to WorldLingo.com, Zara has stores in Spain (364), France (103), Italy (59), Portugal (57), Germany (56), the United Kingdom (50), Mexico (47), Greece (43), Japan (29), China (8), Sweden (10), Venezuela (9), Indonesia (7), Lebanon (6), Chile (6), Uruguay (2), and Morocco (2).[26] The list continues to grow every year as it expands into other parts of the world. The United States had 19 stores in 2006[27] and expanded to 49 stores in 2010.[28] It also launched its online retail store in 2010 with websites for Spain, the United Kingdom, Portugal, Italy, Germany, and France.[29,30]

Its competitors include Hennes and Mauritz (H&M), the Gap, Benetton, and Chico's.

Normally the [fashion] retail industry takes about three to five months to develop a new seasonal collection. Experts need to guess on the fashion trends people want, and failure means markdowns, write offs, and most importantly, low revenues. Zara takes a counter-intuitive approach made possible by their speed. Instead of guessing on the fashion, they ask and monitor what the customer wants and is able to distribute the product within two weeks to the consumers. It follows trends that are successful with other retailers and delivers an imitation. So how does Zara know what the customers want?[31]

This question gets ahead of the Zara's story. The real insight into its strategic thinking has to do with how it is able to be faster and more agile and, at the same time to deliver what consumers want throughout the season. It has also been capitalizing on the formula of success through rapid expansion.

By the early 1980s, Ortega had begun formulating a new type of design and distribution model. The clothing industry followed design and production processes that required long lead times, often up to six months, between the initial design of a garment and its delivery to retailers. This model effectively limited manufacturers and distributors to just two or three collections per year. Predicting consumer tastes ahead of time presented inherent difficulties, and producers and distributors faced the constant risk of becoming saddled with unsold inventory.[32]

The way the clothing industry traditionally operated involved questioning what will be the next fashion trend. Its focus was trying to set the next fashion trend, and with a fickle consumer, it is always a gamble as to the degree of getting it right. Also, with a six-month or more lead time, many things can change within. Ortega wanted to eliminate the long lead time, so instead of predicting what consumers might want so far out in the future, he established his business model around a shorter cycle driven by consumers' wants and preferences.

In contrast, the competitors were driven by a cost model in which they had most, if not all, of their clothing outsourced to manufacturers in Asia, where the labor costs are substantially lower. The disadvantages include longer lead times and less flexibility. Once the orders were placed, the companies had put their money on the table, so to speak, setting the stage for the gamble to play out one way or the other. Zara also outsources around 50 to 60% of its production, but it was done more locally.[33] Zara decided it needed more control over the design, manufacture, distribution, and selling of it products to be able to be faster to the market and more responsive to consumers. The first component of its strategy was to build state-of-the-art facilities for dyeing, processing, cutting, and garment finishing. The dyeing process was seen as a bottleneck that needed to be overcome for Ortega's vision to come true.[34] This key component represented the building block for speed and flexibility. Instead of having to order already-dyed fabric, Zara could create the colors needed on the spot. In essence, it was creating an on-demand production system.[35]

The second component involved information technology (IT). "Poor communication is often the culprit of bottlenecks. Zara invested in information technology (IT) early on."[36]

> Ortega sought a means of breaking the model by creating what he called "instant fashions" that allowed him to respond quickly to shifts in consumer tastes and to newly emerging trends. Ortega's dream remained unfulfilled, however, until he met up with José Maria Castellano. A computer expert, Castellano had worked in Aegon Espana's information technology department before becoming chief financial officer for a Spanish subsidiary of ConAgra. Castellano joined Ortega in 1984 and set to work developing a distribution model that revolutionized the global clothing industry. Under Castellano's computerized system, the company reduced its design to distribution process to just 10 to 15 days. . . . State-of-the-art production and warehousing procedures, as well as the installation of computerized inventory systems linking stores to the company's growing number of factories, enabled the company to avoid taking on the risk and capital outlay of developing and maintaining a large back inventory.[37]

> Their in-house IT is simple and effective. Vendors and suppliers report that people are accessible and answers can be obtained quickly. Internal communication is maximized by housing the designers, pattern makers, and merchandisers on one floor, as well as everyone else involved in getting the product completed.[38]

A third component of Zara's strategy involved changing the clothing design process.

> Rather than placing the design burden on a single designer, the company developed its own in-house team of designers—more than 200 by the turn of the 21st century—who began developing clothes based on popular fashions, while at the same time producing the company's own designs. In this way, the team was able to respond almost immediately to emerging consumer trends as well as to the demands of the company's own customers—for instance, by adding new colors or patterns to existing designs.[39]

Later, this concept of a team of designers expanded out to be referred to as a creative team.

> Design collections are not developed by small elite groups of designers but by creative teams. Teams consist of designers, sourcing specialists, and product development personnel. The teams work simultaneously on different products, expanding on styles that were previously successful. Designers are trained to limit the number of reviews and changes, speeding up the development process and minimizing the number of samples to be made.[40]

Return to the question of how Zara knows what the customers want. While it uses point-of-sale information to determine which items are selling and which aren't, it also relies heavily on word-of-mouth communications with employees. "Empowered store managers report to headquarters what real customers are saying. Products that are not selling well are quickly pulled and hot items quickly replenished. Their quick turn around on merchandise helps generate cash which eliminates the need for significant debt."[41] Zara also restocks stores every two weeks. Additionally,

> Every Zara employee has a PDA which is used to gather customer opinions about its products and what they want to see in the store. This kind of data is extensively gathered on a daily basis and sent directly to headquarters. Then recent graduates from fashion schools are employed to design the clothes that the consumers suggest. These designs are manufactured and shipped out to the retail stores in as little as ten days.[42]

The entire operation is built around vertical integration involving a centralized distribution system to create the speed and flexibility needed. From a marketing perspective, it has created "a consumer climate of scarcity and opportunity in the Zara's retail stores."[43]As a result, "Zara's global average of 17 visits per customer per year is considerably higher than the three visits to its competitors."[44] Consumers know that what they see today in the store may not be there tomorrow. What keeps them coming back is to see what is new.

Research the company to see its current status. Is it using a traditional channel perspective, a value-chain perspective, or a collaboration perspective as discussed in the chapter? As it continues to expand, will its formula for success continue to work? What are the limits to this strategy? What recommendations would you make guiding Zara into the future?

References

1. Kotler, Philip, and Kevin Lane (2009), *Marketing Management*, Upper Saddle River, NJ: Pearson Prentice Hall, 410.
2. Coughlan, Anne T., Erin Anderson, Lois W. Stern, and Adel I. El-Ansary (2001), *Marketing Channels*, 6th ed., Upper Saddle River, NJ: Prentice Hall.
3. Berkowitz, Eric N., Roger A. Kerin, Steven W. Hartley, and William Rudelius (2000), *Marketing*, 6th ed., New York: Irwin McGraw-Hill, 420.
4. Berkowitz, Eric N., Roger A. Kerin, Steven W. Hartley, and William Rudelius (2000), *Marketing*, 6th ed., New York: Irwin McGraw-Hill, 427.
5. Kotler, Philip, and Kevin Lane (2009), *Marketing Management*, Upper Saddle River, NJ: Pearson Prentice Hall, 416–417.
6. Porter, Michael E. (1985), *Competitive Advantage: Creating and Sustaining Superior Performance*, New York: The Free Press.
7. Porter, Michael E. (1990), *The Competitive Advantage of Nations*, New York: The Free Press, 42–43.
8. Porter, Michael E. (1986), *Competition in Global Industries*, Boston: Harvard Business School Press, 22.
9. Phillips, Jeffrey (2010), "Innovation and Porter's Value Chain," *Innovate on Purpose*, September, http://innovateonpurpose.blogspot.com/2010/09/innovation-and-porters-value-chain.html
10. Walters, David (2004), "New Economy—New Business Models—New Approaches," *International Journal of Physical Distribution & Logistics Management*, 34 (3/4), 227.
11. Walters, David (2004), "New Economy—New Business Models—New Approaches," *International Journal of Physical Distribution & Logistics Management*, 34 (3/4), 219.
12. Piller, Frank, Christopher Berger, Kathrin Möslein, and Ralf Reichwald (2003), "Co-Designing the Customer Interface: Learning from Exploratory Research," Arbeitsbericht Nr. 37 (März) des lehrstuhls für Betriebswirtschaftslehre—Information, Organization und Management der Technischen Universität München, 5.
13. Piller, Frank, Christopher Berger, Kathrin Möslein, and Ralf Reichwald (2003), "Co-Designing the Customer Interface: Learning from Exploratory Research," Arbeitsbericht Nr. 37 (März) des lehrstuhls für Betriebswirtschaftslehre—Information, Organization und Management der Technischen Universität München, 1–34.
14. Piller, Frank, Christopher Berger, Kathrin Möslein, and Ralf Reichwald (2003), "Co-Designing the Customer Interface: Learning from Exploratory Research," Arbeitsbericht Nr. 37 (März) des lehrstuhls für Betriebswirtschaftslehre—Information, Organization und Management der Technischen Universität München, 25.
15. Piller, Frank, Christopher Berger, Kathrin Möslein, and Ralf Reichwald (2003), "Co-Designing the Customer Interface: Learning from Exploratory Research," Arbeitsbericht Nr. 37 (März) des lehrstuhls für Betriebswirtschaftslehre—Information, Organization und Management der Technischen Universität München, 21.
16. Piller, Frank, Christopher Berger, Kathrin Möslein, and Ralf Reichwald (2003), "Co-Designing the Customer Interface: Learning from Exploratory Research," Arbeitsbericht Nr. 37 (März) des lehrstuhls für Betriebswirtschaftslehre—Information, Organization und Management der Technischen Universität München, 22.

17. Brown, George W. (2009), "Value Chains, Value Streams, Value Nets, and Value Delivery Chains," April, www.bptrends.com, 8–9.
18. Walters, David (2004), "New Economy—New Business Models—New Approaches," *International Journal of Physical Distribution & Logistics Management*, 34 (3/4), 220.
19. Walters, David (2004), "New Economy—New Business Models—New Approaches," *International Journal of Physical Distribution & Logistics Management*, 34 (3/4), 223.
20. Cherbakov, L., G. Galambos, R. Harishankar, S. Kalyana, and G. Rackham (2005), "Impact of Service Orientation at the Business Level," *IMB Systems Journal*, 44 (4), 654.
21. Cherbakov, L., G. Galambos, R. Harishankar, S. Kalyana, and G. Rackham (2005), "Impact of Service Orientation at the Business Level," *IMB Systems Journal*, 44 (4), 654.
22. Walters, David (2004), "New Economy—New Business Models—New Approaches," *International Journal of Physical Distribution & Logistics Management*, 34 (3/4), 224.
23. Cherbakov, L., G. Galambos, R. Harishankar, S. Kalyana, and G. Rackham (2005), "Impact of Service Orientation at the Business Level," *IMB Systems Journal*, 44 (4), 655.
24. Bovet, David (2000), *Value Nets: Breaking the Supply Chain to Unlock Hidden Profits*, New York: John Wiley & Sons, Inc., 14.
25. Cherbakov, L., G. Galambos, R. Harishankar, S. Kalyana, and G. Rackham (2005), "Impact of Service Orientation at the Business Level," *IMB Systems Journal*, 44 (4), 655.
26. www.worldlingo.com/ma/enwiki/en/Zara_%28clothing%29
27. Tiplady, Rachel (2006), "Zara: Taking the Lead in Fast-Fashion," *Bloomberg Business Week*, April 4, www.businessweek.com/globalbiz/content/apr2006/gb20060404_167078.htm
28. http://en.wikipedia.org/wiki/Zara_%28clothing%29
29. Caesar, Julia (2010), "Zara Launches Online Retail Store," *BBC News*, September 2, www.bbc.co.uk/news/business-11155437
30. http://en.wikipedia.org/wiki/Zara_%28clothing%29
31. Mital, Tuschar (2009), "Zara," *KnowTheCo*, January 16, www.knowtheco.com/index.php?news=20
32. www.worldlingo.com/ma/enwiki/en/Zara_%28clothing%29
33. Anderson, Kim, and Jim Lovejoy (2007), "The Speeding Bullet: Zara's Apparel Supply Chain," *Techexchange*, March, www.scribd.com/doc/37281774/Zara
34. Anderson, Kim, and Jim Lovejoy (2007), "The Speeding Bullet: Zara's Apparel Supply Chain," *Techexchange*, March, www.scribd.com/doc/37281774/Zara
35. Dutta, Devangshu (2002), "retail @ the speed of fashion," *Third Eyesight*, www.3isite.com/articles/ImagesFashion_Zara_Part_I.pdf
36. Anderson, Kim, and Jim Lovejoy (2007), "The Speeding Bullet: Zara's Apparel Supply Chain," *Techexchange*, March, www.scribd.com/doc/37281774/Zara
37. www.worldlingo.com/ma/enwiki/en/Zara_%28clothing%29
38. Anderson, Kim, and Jim Lovejoy (2007), "The Speeding Bullet: Zara's Apparel Supply Chain," *Techexchange*, March, www.scribd.com/doc/37281774/Zara
39. www.worldlingo.com/ma/enwiki/en/Zara_%28clothing%29
40. Anderson, Kim, and Jim Lovejoy (2007), "The Speeding Bullet: Zara's Apparel Supply Chain," *Techexchange*, March, www.techexchange.com/thelibrary/speeding.html
41. Anderson, Kim, and Jim Lovejoy (2007), "The Speeding Bullet: Zara's Apparel Supply Chain," *Techexchange*, March, www.scribd.com/doc/37281774/Zara
42. Anderson, Kim, and Jim Lovejoy (2007), "The Speeding Bullet: Zara's Apparel Supply Chain," *Techexchange*, March, www.techexchange.com/thelibrary/speeding.html
43. Craig, Amanda, Charlese Jones, and Martha Nieto (2004), "ZARA: Fashion Follower, Industry Leader," Case Study, Philadelphia University, April 2, www.philau.edu/sba/news/zarareport.pdf
44. www.uniquebusinessstrategies.co.uk/pdfs/case%20studies/zarathespeedingbullet.pdf

CHAPTER 11 The Question of Price

Decompression Exercise

Daydream awhile before starting.

Chapter Introduction

The changes in marketing thinking we have seen across the chapters are also prevalent with the question of price. From the marketer's initial perspective, price may primarily represent income.[1] However, on deeper examination of the ways in which it functions in the marketplace, price holds a much wider scope of meaning, which this chapter examines.

While it may seem straightforward, the setting of the price for products and services isn't. Many considerations need to be taken into account that we will examine throughout this chapter. Some of the issues involve the following.

If the marketer's price is set incorrectly, results can be low sales, a less-than-desirable rate of return, a loss, and/or a wrong brand image. A question that comes to mind is what makes setting the price for products and services so challenging? Perhaps it has to do with how it is used by consumers, the role price plays in strategy, and the dynamics of the marketplace, which are integral to a price. For example, price can be the basis for competition, such as with the airline industry or among gas stations. Or consumers can use price as a heuristic for quality—higher prices suggest higher quality, for example, the difference between a Rolex and a Timex. In such situations, price finds itself in a dynamic, relative frame of reference in which it is constantly being cast about, affecting its position and meaning.

Another problem in setting the price is that the relationship between costs and the price is inherently reciprocal. You can't know the costs for a product without knowing the volume to be sold, and the volume to be sold is dependent upon the price. Further, you need to understand the costs to be able to set the price to achieve a profitable level, or a loss might occur. It's a kind of Catch-22 situation in that you need to know one to know the other and vice versa. Where do you start?

Furthermore, is setting the price for a product the same as for a service? How do they differ, and how do these differences affect the pricing of them?

To take up the question of price, we'll start with the question, What is price? Then, we'll explore, What role does price play in strategy? We'll look at the various perspectives and means for setting a price. Examining price in this way will allow for a more in-depth exploration into the thinking involved in pricing while providing a frame of reference for understanding the reasoning behind pricing strategies.

This price thing seems like a puzzle. I like a good puzzle that makes you think.

It's good to see that you're up for the challenge. Let's get started with the first question.

I agree. If we can identify the pieces, we'll be able figure out the pricing puzzle and offer our own strategies.

What is price?

The Origins of Price

The question of price stems from earlier forms of economic systems. It originates from the difficulties associated with the barter system. Before our current monetary system, the economic system was based upon goods being exchanged for other goods—that is, "pure barter." With such a system, a number of problems and inefficiencies can arise. Some of the problems include transporting (e.g., having to carry around a product to acquire another—carrying around a chicken, for example), spoilage, value comparison (e.g., How do you compare the value of eggs against the value of a bale of hay?), and timing issues (e.g., perhaps you're not interested in what another merchant has at that time).

To deal with these issues, the idea of an intermediate medium was needed as a kind of community that could be used for exchange purposes. Early forms of such a commodity included salt, tea, tobacco, cattle, and seeds.[2] While these were steps toward creating a more standardized medium for exchange, issues remained with transporting, storage, and spoilage (or perishing). This is where the need for the concept of money came into view. The exact means and timing of when money appeared on the scene are and continues to be controversial. Various different theories have been advanced, including (1) the Carl Menger (1909) market theory that "postulates that money evolved spontaneously from the logic of the market," (2) religious and/or state explanations, or (3) cultural justifications in which money is defined "as a system of symbols that make exchanges independent of time, persons, and particular situations."[3] For example, according to Menger's theory:

> ...it follows that money comes about through a process of selection performed by the market forces, on the basis of which the commodity that proves the most saleable is chosen to take on the function of exchange intermediary. Thus money is seen to be a commodity like all other commodities, deriving its value for the same reasons as do the other goods traded. Logically, as trade evolves, any commodity chosen by the agents as exchange medium may be transformed into money within certain limits of time and space.
>
> This was a theory in sharp contrast with the then prevailing ideas according to which money was seen as a mere token of value whose role in trade was specifically ascribed to a convention among economic agents or legal rules. Thus, as Menger saw it, money stood out from other commodities in that it played the role of intermediary in exchanges, but such a role could only be traced back to the fact that, to begin with, money itself was constituted by a commodity with its own intrinsic value.[4]

The intrinsic value of money can be tied to the functions that it plays in the marketplace. Its adoption has transformed the merchant's exchange process. The properties of money include that it can easily be transferable, doesn't spoil or perish, has an unlimited space and time associated with it, is divisible, can increase in value over time, is a commodity used as a medium for the exchange for other items, and is used as the means for establishing what something is to be exchanged for—that is, its price. In this sense, price is the monetary amount for which a product or service will potentially be exchanged. The significance is that price, being based upon a monetary system, is tied into a larger frame of reference from which it acquires its meaning as well as its strategic roles. This frame of reference allows for comparisons between dissimilar products and services as it reorients the focus away from the products or services per se and toward price. The reorientation occurs as a result of money having its own intrinsic value. In essence, the exchange involves two aspects—one, money via the price and two, the product and/or service. It is within the reorientation that price has taken on its significant position and in which pricing strategies play out. Next, we'll turn our attention toward understanding the strategy roles of price.

Marketing Thinking Challenge 11.1: A Return to the Bartering System

To get a better understanding of the role money plays in terms of price and today's marketplace, consider how things would be different if all exchanges took place based on bartering and that money didn't exist. What would be the differences in the marketplace both small and large? How would marketing be different? What would strategy involve in a bartering system?

| Figure 11.2 | A Marketplace Where "Pure Bartering" Takes Place |

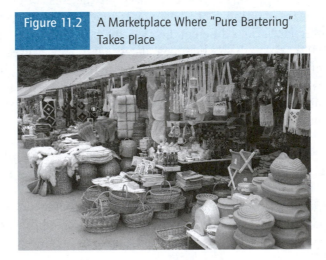

The Strategy Roles of Price

Price, in many ways, acts as a cue for consumers to assess the relative value across the array of products and services found in the marketplace. As a cue, price may initially act as a means for getting consumer attention that many products and services are competing for. It can also be used for comparison purposes to evaluate one product against the rest. It may further be used as a means to set up consumers' expectations in interpreting the consumption experience. This suggests that the role price plays for strategy purposes can be multifaceted. Based upon this understanding, marketers have developed a number of pricing strategies that are based upon the price cue perspective.

The Marketer's Perspective

Setting the initial price for a product or service is a very important decision. It sets the initial reference price suggesting what something is worth, but it also establishes a parameter that affects subsequent pricing. Initially, the pricing question asks, *At what level should the price be set—high or low(or somewhere in between)?* Setting the price high allows the opportunity to lower it in time, which can affect demand. Setting it low restricts the strategy options. It's easier to lower prices than to raise them. Consistent with the high or low responses to the pricing question, marketers have utilized two different pricing strategies that are based on different situations and reasoning, which are discussed next.

Perceptually, high price suggests higher quality, prestige, style, and/or something new to the market (e.g., a new innovation). For example, Apple consistently sets its prices high, such as with the iPhone and iPad, and then gradually lowers the price incrementally over time. This is a *skimming strategy*. Apple's strategy capitalizes on being first to the market and is based upon projecting an image of high quality and style. A skimming strategy can also be applied across multiple channels, starting with one that is less price sensitive to capitalize on the premium pricing and to build up sales volume to the point at which the marketer can lower the price, which then would be of interest to another channel. The lowering of price is achieved by being able to lower costs as a result of economies of scale and the experience curve through the increased sales volume.

In contrast to the skimming perspective, the marketer could set the price purposely low to pursue a high-sales-volume strategy. This approach is based upon a *penetration pricing strategy*. Once employed, it sets the image for the brand in the marketplace as being a low-cost brand. In this case, it is not attempting to use price to facilitate a high-quality brand image but is instead trying to establish a low price point position in the market (e.g., the lowest-priced product available). It is a competitive focus on price. From the consumer's perspective, this has the advantage of reducing risk and involvement on their part. And it may very well be the case that marketers have resorted to competing against each other on price.

However, perceptually, there is a lot more going on than the skimming and penetration pricing strategies suggest. The consumer's perspective has led to a number of pricing strategies. These strategies also illustrate the level of detail and thought required in thinking through pricing strategies. We'll examine these next.

The Consumer's Perspective

There are two general perspectives on how consumers use price. Both are based on a cue perspective. The first perspective views price as an *information cue*. Using the price-quality heuristic as an example, the consumer might use price as a segregator to interpret the quality of the product or service. Higher prices suggest higher quality and vice versa with lower prices. As such, this represents a *price-quality strategy*.

The second perspective considers a broader context that includes other marketing information of which price is a part. "We refer to the pieces of information that surround the actual selling price as **semantic cues** because the consumer's interpretation or judgment of the selling price depends on how he or she interprets this information (semantics!)."[5] Accordingly, other pricing information is needed to facilitate the consumer's interpretation of the value suggested through the price. This is where the marketer would utilize a *reference pricing strategy*. A reference price is included with the selling price. Examples of reference prices are the "regular price," "compare-at price," or "MSLP" (manufacturer's suggested list price). In this case, the value is to be interpreted via the difference between the reference price and the selling price. Implicitly, this strategy also focuses the consumer's attention on the price of the product being considered while diverting attention from competitive comparisons.

Figure 11.3 Consumers Excited Over a Sale

Drawing on the reference pricing strategy by adding the word "sale" to it can significantly increase demand by as much as 50% or more.[6] The *sale price strategy* can be very effective if used appropriately. However, overuse of the "sale" tag and/or deceptive practices can have the opposite effect as well. To protect consumers from such practices, various government acts (e.g., the Sherman Antitrust Act covers price fixing, the Robinson-Patman Act outlaws price discrimination, and the Consumer Goods Pricing Act prevents manufacturers from requiring a set retail price) and local regulations that businesses must follow have been put into place. In a similar way, pricing products with a price ending in a 9 implicitly implies a sale. This is a *price ending in 9 strategy*.

A *discount pricing strategy* is based upon a sales perspective. There are many ways to incorporate discounts into a pricing strategy. In general, discounts are used as incentives to promote sales volume or to reward some form of behavior (e.g., paying on time). Discounts can be based upon quantities purchased (e.g., 10% break for purchasing 100 units), seasonal discounts (e.g., Black Friday—the Friday after Thanksgiving for retail stores in the United States—and Black Monday for online sales), and/or a bundling discounts (e.g., McDonald's Family Fun Pack). Discounts can also be used throughout the channel, which may involve volume discounts, early-payment discounts, and/or sales prices (e.g., introductory prices, promotional prices).

Decoy pricing involves purposely using a third priced option as a "decoy" as a means to draw out the more attractive option available when two other options are also presented. The third priced option is designed purposely in terms of its pricing and its attributes to be inferior on both accounts (i.e., asymmetrically dominant) compared to the one option the marketer wants the consumer to purchase while being only partially inferior in respect to the second option also available.[7] Table 11.1 illustrates this pricing strategy using a cell phone example.

Table 11.1

Cell Phones	Option 1	Option 2	Option 3
Flash Memory	8GB	3GB	6GB
Price	$700	$500	$800

The third option makes the first option appear better in all respects, while the second option is only better with respect to one aspect: price. Here, the consumer looking for the best deal would most likely choose the first option, and this can be attributed as a result of the decoy option (the third option) being made available for comparison purposes. Apple is a good example of a company that uses this pricing strategy.

…Apple often sells each gadget in a pricing series, such as the new iPod Touch's $199, $299, and $399 price points for different storage capacities. You may gladly spend $229 to get a hot media player, thinking it's a deal vs. the highest-priced version…and not blink that you could instead buy an iPhone 4 at the lower price of $199 with more features. The

$399 "decoy" has clouded your judgment. Apple wins the best of both worlds—stoking demand for products that look like bargains and for all the decoys it sells at much higher prices. Yes, some people will spend $399 for a music player with slightly better technology—and Apple makes even fatter margins.[8]

The *bundle pricing strategy* is similar to decoy pricing. Here, the marketer has two options—to offer a la carte or package (bundled) prices. Package pricing gives the impression to consumers that they are getting a deal with everything all included, while in most cases they are paying more. The consumer doesn't know how much the individual items in the package actually cost, and some of the aspects of the package may not be of interest to the consumer. Hence, the consumers may actually be paying more for what they consume than if they had purchased the items a la carte. *A la carte pricing* provides greater transparency yet may also lead to more negotiation by the consumer looking for a deal.[9] It can also increase marketing costs. The Internet has also had an impact on price transparency through the various websites that offer comparison of companies' offerings. *Price transparency* allows the consumer to make more informed decisions while potentially impacting the marketer's margins through being compared and revealing what the consumer is actually getting and paying for. This perspective ultimately takes on a competitive aspect through the comparison platform provided through the Internet. Price transparency has had a major impact on the airline and hotel industries.

Consumers are familiar with certain items they purchase on a regular basis. As such, they may use these known prices as a "signpost" for comparison purposes.

Research suggests that customers use the prices of signpost items to form an overall impression of a store's prices. That impression then guides their purchases of other items for which they have less knowledge. While very few customers know the price of baking soda (around 70 cents for 16 ounces), they do realize that if the store charges more than $1 for a can of Coke it is probably also charging a premium on its baking soda.... The implications for retailers are important, and many already act accordingly. Supermarkets often take a loss on a Coke or Pepsi.[10]

The implications for using a *signpost strategy* are to identify the products about which consumers have accurate knowledge, are popular, and are complementary and then price them accordingly to project the appropriate store pricing theme.[11]

To give consumers the sense that they are getting the best price for the product or service, marketers will sometimes use a *price guarantee strategy*. If they find another store selling the item for less within a certain period of purchasing the product, the store with the price guarantee will reimburse the customer for the difference or refund his or her money. This strategy is meant to reduce the likelihood of consumers making comparisons among stores. They can simply rely on the guarantee, knowing they are getting the best price. Many electronics stores, such as Best Buy, use this strategy.

Another interesting pricing cue strategy involves purposely overpricing. Consumers have a tendency to develop a means by which to not have to devote a lot of effort toward deliberating on every or typical purchase decisions. Accordingly,

If the price associated with a unique additional benefit is low enough, consumers will buy without further questioning of their prior impressions. An excessively high price, on the other hand, will discourage purchasing in a blink because it is apparent that additional deliberation could reveal nothing that would overcome the budgetary downside....[However] there often exists between these no-brainer extremes a range of prices that should induce consumers to think and gain clarity regarding the personal relevance of the offered benefit....the amount of consumer deliberation triggered by the posted price is influenced by the effort of thinking, the potential (maximum) usage value of the benefit, and the consumer's prior belief about the personal relevance of that potential.[12]

The *willful overpricing strategy* (a transgressive pricing strategy) provokes consumers to deliberate further than they normally would on the material difference(s) among the overpriced item and others in the product category. In contrast, to stay within the typical price range of the product category is a regressive pricing strategy (staying close to the market average price). In essence, the willful overpricing strategy is the marketer's attempt to utilize price as a means to provoke consumer thinking—that is, it is a consumer thinking strategy orchestrated by creating a contrast between the average price found in the marketplace for a product with a price above this point to get them to consider the additional benefit(s) being offered at a premium price.

[T]he effect of a higher price is not to select less-price-sensitive or higher-income consumers, as in existing models of vertical differentiation..., but to trigger a polarization of demand that induces a split between enthusiasts and the indifferent.[13]

Apple's pricing is an example of separating the enthusiasts from the indifferent. The willful overpricing strategy is a differentiation strategy that is meant to provoke consumers to consider the differences among available products.

A more recent pricing strategy gaining interest is participative pricing.[14,15] A *participative pricing strategy* is consistent with a co-marketing perspective in which the consumer is able to participate in establishing the price (e.g., Progressive Insurance's "name your price"). While various forms of participative pricing have been around for a while such as with auctions, reverse auctions, negotiating on a purchase such as with a car, garage sales, or flea markets, the concept has been extended to a pay-what-you-want (PWYW) approach. In the PWYW situation, it is the consumer that has total control over what is to be paid for an item.

The most prominent, recent example of an application of PWYW is that of the rock band Radiohead. For two months, the band offered fans the chance to download its new album from its Web site and to pay as much as they wanted. The album was downloaded more than two million times, and the band reported afterward that this price format was profitable. Among other online downloads (e.g., www.sheeba.ca, open-source software), PWYW is also applied in areas such as gastronomy and hotel industries. For example, the Pakistani restaurant Wiener Deewan, in Vienna, has allowed clients to self-determine the prices for their meals since opening in 2005. Prices for drinks are fixed, but customers can decide how much they want to pay for the food. According to press reports and direct interviews with the owner, the business model has been successfully established, and the restaurant even expanded just two months after opening. Similar concepts can be found worldwide, such as in Berlin (www.weinerei.com), Seattle (www.terrabite.org), and Melbourne (www.lentilasanything.com).[16]

Other examples of PWYW include websites like Priceline.com. The participative pricing strategy also has the effect of shifting consumers' attention toward setting the deal price and away from evaluating the deal, which can lead to higher intent to purchase.[17] From the above pricing strategy descriptions, we can see price is a significant consumer cue used to signal the suggested worth for something, to facilitate certain meanings to be associated with a brand (e.g., high quality or low cost), as an incentive to purchase, and/or to either decrease consumer involvement (e.g., through a low-price offer, reducing risk and thinking) or increase involvement (e.g., through participative pricing). The Table 11.2 summarizes the pricing cue strategies.

Table 11.2 Pricing Strategies	
Pricing Cue Strategy	**Applicable Situation**
Skimming	First to market with a new innovation and differentiate on quality, prestige, and/or style.
Penetration	The ability to capitalize on economies of scale to be able to obtain a low cost level to set price low. A low cost position could discourage competition.
Price-Quality	To differentiate based upon some unique benefit.
Reference Pricing "regular price," "compare-at price," or MSLP Sales Ending in "9"	To provide a means for consumers to interpret an increase in value. Could be directed toward new and/or existing customers.

Discount Pricing
    Quantity
    Seasonal
    Bundling
	Similar to a sales situation, an incentive is being offered for the purposes of increasing sales and/or rewarding a particular purchasing behavior.

Decoy Pricing	Using a third priced option for comparison purposes for making one of the other two choices available appear superior on all accounts. The decoy option is an unattractive option, both on price and attributes.
Bundle Pricing	Offering a package deal with a single price.
A La Carte Pricing	Each attribute and/or amenity is priced individually. Provides for greater transparency and can lead to being viewed as more credible and competitive by comparison.
Signpost	For new or infrequent customers of a store.
Price Guarantee	To compete with other stores by ensuring the consumer is getting the lowest possible price and need not look elsewhere.
Willful Overpricing	To further differentiate from the others in the marketplace by getting consumers to deliberate on the differences in a product category.

Participative Pricing
    Auctions
    Negotiations
    PWYW
	To increase consumer involvement and to use pricing as an additional means for differentiation.

In looking over the pricing strategies, it seems that price can be used for a number of different strategic roles including competing, establishing value, encouraging purchases, and even for diverting attention from the product itself to focus on the deal. And, if I'm following the logic correctly, this all fundamentally stems from adoption of money as the commodity medium for exchanges.

Yes. Without the medium of money, the concept of price wouldn't exist as we know it, and the pricing strategy roles are based in part on the functions money provides. Think about it. What is price?

Marketing Thinking Challenge 11.2: Participative Pricing

Identify three different organizations that are using a PWYW pricing strategy. Try identifying ones that haven't been mentioned in the chapter. Describe how they promote this pricing feature. See if you can find out through your research whether their pricing strategy has been profitable. Explain whether you think their strategy is effective. What other pricing considerations and/or suggestions would you offer that could enhance their efforts even more?

Figure 11.4 A Consumer Deciding How He/She Will Pay

Marketing Thinking in Practice: Raise Your Prices!

A recent article posted in the *Wall Street Journal* discusses reasons for not pursuing a low-cost strategy but, instead, competing based on performance. It raises questions that can be used for the purposes of developing a price-performance strategy through identifying value opportunities, setting priorities, and aligning price with value. It also highlights the need for customer cooperation to create an effective pricing strategy.[18]

By now, we're all aware of the slash-your-prices scenario many companies take as a given these days: Your customers demand more and have online access to product comparisons from multiple sellers; you face global competition from rivals that have labor-cost advantages; and the financial crisis has accelerated the commoditization of more and more markets.

The solution? Cut your prices to gain volume and scale.

That definitely works for a few companies. But the reality is a very few—think Wal-Mart or Costco or Southwest Airlines. In fact, the very success of these business models makes it difficult for their competitors to duplicate—think Kmart or Sears, or any number of bankrupt budget airlines.

This article is for everybody else: those who choose not to compete on the basis of cost and low price. This article is for companies that can and should compete on the basis of performance, for which their customers willingly pay higher prices.

By competing on performance instead of price, you shift the battle to where your company's strengths lie—in the ability to deliver unique benefits. So-called performance pricers are adept at three core activities: identifying where they can do a superior job of meeting customers' needs and preferences; shaping their products and their business to dominate these segments; and managing cost and price in those areas to maximize profits.

If you can find these performance segments, manage them cost-effectively, and communicate to the customer the extra value being delivered, then as long as your offering is superior to the competition or other alternatives, you will be able to boost both prices and profits.

For an idea of how to become a master of performance pricing, let's consider a global chemical company we studied.

For years the company had a pretty typical sales rule: It would take any order at any acceptable price. That sounds familiar, no doubt. But by 2003, it had recognized this wouldn't generate acceptable shareholder returns or growth.

So the company switched to performance pricing, using a continuing four-step process that any company can duplicate: Identify value opportunities, choose which ones to prioritize, align their value and price, and constantly communicate to customers the value being provided. Here's a look at each of their four steps.

Identify Value Opportunities

The leaders of the company started out by repeatedly asking in meetings across functions: What can we do to help our customers succeed or be happier? Every product, service and benefit the company delivered to its customers was examined to better understand all of the ways in which it had some impact on the customer, and how the offering could be improved.

Take a simple example: The company sells rubber stoppers to packagers of pharmaceuticals that use the stoppers to cap containers of injectable drugs. The company had long viewed the stoppers as a commodity. They're easy to make, perform a simple function and cost very little. But looking at them afresh, from the customers' perspective, it recognized that the stoppers could deliver multiple benefits to customers, and that these benefits could be quantified and ranked in terms of the value they produced for the customer.

(Continued)

(Continued)

The stoppers' low price was only the first benefit. Their design could be tweaked to improve customers' packaging-line speeds, lowering their operating costs. And because the customers used the stoppers to seal vials with different contents, making stoppers in different colors was recognized as a way to help hospitals and doctors reduce errors by making each vial more recognizable, and thus lower their insurance costs.

Set Priorities

After detailing the benefits, the company had to decide which products to develop further and how to invest its resources accordingly.

To be considered for performance pricing, an offering had to meet two basic tests. First, it had to have either a strong competitive position in its market or a highly ranked benefit to the customer (benefits were ranked, from low to high, in three groups: offering low acquisition price, helping reduce operating costs, and improving sales by enhancing quality). And second, the product had to be manufacturable at a cost that yielded attractive profit margins.

Thus, any product whose main benefit was its low sale price was likely to be rejected. But so were premium products if their costs were high and their projected total market too small. For example, the company had done well with a certain dental-filling product, but the total potential market was extremely limited and the investment costs would have included long, expensive testing of the product on people.

The stoppers, by comparison, looked promising. They offered highly valued benefits to customers, and could be produced at low cost.

Align Price and Value

The next step was to set higher prices in line with what the customer was willing to pay.

The key here is being able to document and quantify the precise nature of the benefits that your products offer, and to figure out what their tangible value is to the customer, in terms of acquisition cost, operating cost and added value to the end user. Once the supporting data are in hand, then you sit down with the customer to discuss what the new price should be.

In the case of the rubber stoppers, the company used the data to successfully argue to a customer that two products, while nearly identical in appearance, should be priced very differently because of the different ways they were used. One stopper sealed vials of a vaccine for chickens that the customer sold for less than $5 a vial; the other sealed vials of an anticancer medication that sold for more than $1,000.

While the stoppers looked alike, the higher-value application had tighter tolerances and came with significantly more technical assistance, service responsiveness and quality-control data, due to the difference in the costs and risks associated with the two stoppers. Indeed, failure of the seals on a few of the anticancer vials would have far greater impact on the customer's bottom line than a few ruined vials of the chicken vaccine. And, while both kinds of stoppers helped production—in terms of high packaging-line run efficiency and low scrap rates—higher efficiency for the anticancer vials, resulting from the technical assistance and tighter tolerances, translated into increased profits for the customer.

Thus the chemical company proposed a significantly higher price for the anticancer-vial stopper, and presented reams of data from the tracking system to support its argument. The customer later came back with figures of its own that painted a lesser impact than the company had suggested. But the customer's figures were in the ball park, the chemical company said. The two companies agreed on a new price for the anticancer stoppers that was a multiple of the price for the chicken-vaccine stoppers, and both parties felt like winners.

Get Cooperation

Such a system relies on a lot of help from the customer, and getting that cooperation takes work. The chemical company had to display a thorough understanding of all the issues the packager faced to win its case for the differently priced stoppers. After such increases are won, continuing efforts to communicate why higher prices are justified can bring other benefits as well.

By adopting performance pricing throughout the firm, over the next five years, the chemical company's profits grew 10% annually in a market growing less than 2% a year.

The approach also provided a strategy that allowed the company to weather the recession better than competitors: In 2009, industry volume declined more than 20%, compared with 14% for the company. But, despite lower volume, the company's return on sales increased by more than 40% due to its ability to identify value opportunities, prioritize requirements, align value and price, and communicate value to cost-conscious customers.

Questions to Ask Yourself

1. Does your company continuously focus on improving its products and services in ways that are important to customers and that allow you to raise prices and increase profits?

2. Do you communicate regularly with customers to find out how you can improve your offerings, and to make sure they're aware of any unique value you provide?

3. Do your salespeople speak to the right decision makers and others who care about these value benefits in the customer's organization?

4. Does your company involve every department in discussions about product development and pricing strategy in order to maximize efficiency, quality and profits?

5. Does your company consider pricing when it's still developing a new service or product instead of when the product or service is introduced to the market?

If you answered no to any of these questions, your company is probably not doing enough to maximize profits in line with products and services that customers want and are willing to pay more for. And if you lack a repeatable process for doing these things internally at your company, it is unlikely that you will effectively identify and communicate value externally with your customers: Like so many other important things in business, pricing and leadership begin at home.

Price Determination

With the above pricing strategies in mind, let's turn our attention toward the issues of understanding the fundamentals associated with price determination. Pricing strategies and price determination go hand in hand. Also, the choosing of a pricing strategy must also be aligned with the overall marketing strategy. As mentioned in the introduction, price determination is not necessarily a straightforward process. Three different approaches could be utilized. Each has its own perspective and, hence, is grounded in a unique perspective of the situation. Figure 11.5 illustrates the approaches to price determination. We'll examine each and also look at pricing services.

Figure 11.5   Price Determination Approaches

Cost-Based Price Determination

The cost-based approach is a typical means to start with since somewhere along the price determination process, the marketer needs to have an understanding of the costs that are involved and the relationship between price and costs. There are three general perspectives within the cost-based approach: cost-plus pricing, markup pricing, and experience curving pricing.

The *cost-plus pricing* approach utilizes three types of information to determine a price. These are fixed costs, variable costs, and profit margin. *Fixed costs* are expenses that don't fluctuate with production or sales. They are generally referred to as an organization's overhead costs that include electricity to heat the building, salaries, office furniture, facility maintenance, and the like. *Variable costs*, on the other hand, as suggested by their name, vary as production levels increase or decrease. These costs are typically calculated by unit costs. Decreases in per-unit costs can come from economies of scale (e.g., price discounts in buying in bulk) and from becoming more proficient in the manufacturing process in time (i.e., the experience or learning curve). The *profit margin* is the desired dollar amount to be received after the total costs have been factored in. As such, the cost-based price determination approach is primarily an internal perspective.

$$\text{Price/unit} = \text{Function } \{[(\text{Fixed \$ Costs}) + (\text{Variable \$ Costs}) + (\text{Profit \$ Margin})] \: / \: \text{\# of Units}\}$$

As an example,

Fixed Costs = $200,000

Variable Costs/Unit = $500

Profit Margin = $100,000

Number of Units Project to be Sold = 3000

Price/Unit = $200,000 + ($500 x 3000) + $100,000 = $1,800,000/3000 = $600/Unit
    Fixed Costs   Variable Costs   Profit Margin.

A variation to the cost-plus pricing approach is *markup pricing.* It works in a similar way but focuses on the variable costs in determining price. This could be used when an organization has many products or items to sell, and it can be used by any of the channel members.

Price/Unit = Function [(Variable $ Cost/Unit) x (1+ Markup %)]

Continuing the example above with markup pricing,

Variable Costs/Unit = $500

Markup % = 15

Price/Unit = $500 x 1.15 = $575.

The third approach to cost-based pricing involves *experience curve pricing.* Here, instead of using the average costs per unit based upon existing cost figures, the marketer uses a lower-than-average cost per unit to base his or her price on. The lower-than-average cost per unit is based upon an understanding that costs will decrease as production experience increases.[19]

However, in general, the difficulty with the cost-based approach is knowing whether the calculated price would actually lead to the number of estimated units to be sold. The cost-based approach doesn't explicitly take this into account. Another perspective is needed. To have a better idea of whether the above prices would work in terms of the number of units to be sold at the determined price, the marketer has to have an understanding of the consumer's price sensitivity associated with the product or service. In doing so, the marketer has to consider how many consumers would be willing to pay for the product at a certain price point. This can be captured through the *price elasticity function,* which is a function of price versus demand. This function can be determined by marketing research or as a surrogate means by assessing the existing prices in the marketplace and their relative market share. Figure 11.6 illustrates a typical price elasticity demand function.

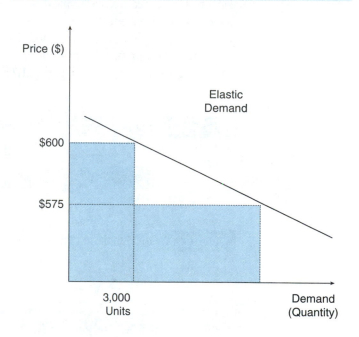

Figure 11.6 A Price Elasticity Demand Function

In essence, this approach provides the marketer a sense of the possible range of prices and what could be expected from the prices in terms of sales. However, many factors can significantly affect what might actually occur once the price of a product or service is set and then marketed accordingly. For example, the consumer's perspective pricing strategies discussed previously suggest a number of other considerations would need to be taken into account. In addition, the competitive reaction may also have a significant effect on the outcome of sales. In setting the initial price, the marketer needs to consider how the pricing strategy is to play out over time as well (thinking in time). As mentioned previously, setting the price too low restricts the marketer's options. Furthermore, a low-price strategy is grounded in a competitive orientation as in the **Red Ocean** strategy discussed in Chapter 3. Next, we'll examine the competitive-based pricing approach.

Competitive-Based Price Determination

Instead of determining price based upon costs, competitive-based price determination focuses on what the competition may do (a proactive posture) or is currently doing (a reactive posture, *parity strategy*) in terms of their prices. A competitive approach may utilize either the *skimming* or *penetration strategy* as a way to combat the competition. From this perspective, the marketer's thinking is drawn (channeled) into the existing marketplace pricing parameters in terms of its anchors (i.e., the low and high prices) and the average.

Several aspects can be noted about this channeling effect. As a result of their size, larger organizations are more able and apt to take up the low-cost position (e.g., Wal-Mart). Also, there is a tendency to use competitive-based pricing for product categories that have become established and, in the process of becoming established, a number of brands may be found competing within the product category. It is through the process of becoming established that there is the tendency to utilize the competitive-based pricing. This has the result of affecting the marketplace price parameters by narrowing the difference between the range anchors by gravitating toward the low price in the range. The low price may also move to an even lower position as a result of the competition. Both come about as a consequence of competitive rivalry. From the consumer's perspective, marketing that is directed toward a focus on price results in the brands becoming perceived as more and more similar with the only difference being price—that is, the products are simply viewed as commodities. In the end, this only contributes to the momentum of the migration toward the lower price point affecting the average and the high price point. These changes are depicted in Figures 11.7 and 11.8.

| Figure 11.7 | The Beginning of Product Category—A Wider Range in Prices |

Lowest Price   Average Price   Highest Price

| Figure 11.8 | An Established Product Category—The Narrowing of the Range in Prices |

A Narrowing Range   The Price Migration

Lowest Price   Average Price   Highest Price

A competitive-based price determination doesn't take into account the consumer's perspective in terms of value or price sensitivity. The focus is on the competition, and the consumer is simply the medium in which the competition plays out by way of the ongoing price wars. Next, we'll examine price determination by considering the consumer's perspective.

Market-Based Price Determination

Instead of focusing on costs (an internal perspective) or on the competition (an external perspective focused on competition), the third approach to price determination involves concentrating on the potential value a product or service can provide to consumers and setting the price based upon its value to consumers. Market-based price determination is based on a value-based perspective. Value-based price determination is less straightforward than the other two methods. The reasons include the difficulties in assessing value in that value can come in many different forms, as we have seen throughout the chapters, in terms of the value in products and service, value in practices, value in use, value in experience, and value in orchestration. As such, value is idiosyncratically determined by consumers and changes across situations and by events in time. Given these difficulties, the value approach to price is consistent with the movement in marketing thinking toward a co-marketing perspective. Before discussing the co-marketing perspective to value-based pricing, we'll discuss some of the ways that have been used to attempt to assess market value.

Different methods have been utilized for the purposes of value determination.[20]They include expert interviews, focus groups, conjoint (or tradeoff) analysis, and value-in-use assessments.

The *expert interviews* approach draws on the expertise of company personnel to provide their perspective in setting the price. Such company personnel may include marketing as well as finance professionals. The difficulty with this approach is that it inherently has an internal perspective, which is also further evident through the process of trying to get a consensus among the experts.

Focus groups are another method available. The marketer solicits groups of 10 to 12 consumers to come together to discuss various aspects of the product for the purposes of determining how they view the product and its value. This method attempts to obtain information from consumers and, as such, is externally oriented. However, the difficulty with this approach is with the focus-group setting and the type of information that comes from this form of research, along with issues (problems) of being able to generalize the results to a larger consumer population. A focus-group setting can be characterized as an artificial setting in that it is different than the actual consumption context in which the consumers would be purchasing and consuming the products and/or services. It is preferable to study consumers in their natural environments and to not create confounding effects or misinformation found in an artificial setting.

Conjoint analysis is another form of marketing research that asks a sample of consumers to respond to a series of paired choices. It has been widely used in industry to determine which set of product attributes would be the most attractive to potentially different consumer groups. The marketer uses the consumer information for the purposes of configuring the most appropriate offering via the research results. It has been suggested that

> It has the advantage of enabling firms to capture the value of intangible product features (brand names, reputation, and so on) and the value of features about which direct questioning might lead to unreliable results (such as value of superior delivery, superior service, and so on). However, it has the disadvantage of failing to ascertain the value of features that are not included in the design of the questionnaire.[21]

The research is typically done in a setting different than the actual consumption context and, as such, affects the nature of the information being obtained. Also, the paired-choice format of the questioning may have its own confounding affects, as well as potentially causing an additional distortion in the information.

The *value-in-use assessment* takes into account the consumption context and proceeds to observe and interview consumers as they are using the products and/or services.

> Such value-in-use assessments enable assessment of customer satisfaction and customer dissatisfaction (in terms of product and service dimensions) as customers experience them in their daily use. These assessments are useful for uncovering unmet customer needs or problems that customers would not voice in laboratory tests or in response to direct questioning.[22]

In essence, the research involves relating consumers' degree of (dis)satisfaction to the value of the consumption of the product and/or service. This requires an interpretation of the consumer's interpretation of the consumption, which presents its own difficulties. However, what is noteworthy with this approach is that it is attempting to assess the value within the context in which the value is derived by the consumer. This represents an important step toward obtaining a better understanding for market value from the consumer's perspective.

Included in the market-based approach to price determination are the *participative pricing* approaches. They include auctions, reverse auctions, purchase negotiations (cars, garage sales, or flea markets), and PWYW. These approaches transcend the others in that it is the consumer that is directly affecting the price for a product or service. In the case of PWYW, the consumer dictates the price, thereby setting the value for the marketer in terms of what the marketer will receive from the exchange. This represents a reversal in roles while potentially creating a riskier situation for the marketer. Yet if the marketer is really providing consumer value, research has shown that this price approach can be profitable.[23]

Services Pricing

Services represent a unique challenge to marketers in terms of setting the appropriate price.

> The good news is you have a great deal of flexibility in how you set your prices. The bad news is there is no surefire, formula-based approach you can pull off the shelf and apply in your business. Pricing services is more difficult than pricing products because you can often pinpoint the cost of making a physical product but it's more subjective to calculate the worth of your counsel, your staff's expertise, and the value of your time.[24]

The three perspectives previously discussed (cost-based, competitive-based, and market-based) can also be considered here, along with a yield-management perspective. These are discussed next.

For example, from a *cost-based perspective,* the costs to account for include material costs that might be used in the service, labor costs, and overhead costs. Here, a cost-plus approach could be used. Using a *competitive-based perspective* involves setting the service(s) pricing based upon what others are charging. The *market-based perspective* is going to be based upon setting the price according to the perceived value of what you are offering. This will require market research to develop a better understanding as to how consumers perceive similar services in the market and on what they are basing their interpretation of value. For example, returning to the discussion in Chapter 2 on the concept of satisfaction, with knowledge of consumer expectations pertaining to the service being offered, the marketer is in a better position to understand how value is being derived and then is able to set the price(s) accordingly.

"Yield management is the umbrella term for a set of strategies that enable capacity-constrained service industries to realize optimum revenue from operations. The core concept of yield management is to provide the right service to the right customer at the right time for the right price."[25]With limited seats and rooms, airlines and hotels utilize this pricing approach.

> The strategic levers of yield management can be summarized as four Cs: namely, calendar, clock, capacity, and cost. They are bound together by a fifth C: the customer. The strategic levers of yield management are geared to matching service timing and pricing to customers' willingness to pay for service in relation to its timing. Based on customers' demand levels and characteristics, management can shift the

demand of those customers who are relatively price sensitive but time insensitive to off-peak times. Shifting that demand clears prime times for customers who are relatively time sensitive but price insensitive.[26]

Using an airline example, if you book early when plenty of seats are available, you'd get a better price. As the window closes and the time for departure approaches and the number of seats available becomes increasingly limited, the prices will increase accordingly.

Forms of Pricing: In addition to the previous pricing approaches is the actual form of the pricing. Three different forms of pricing can be used with services: hourly rate, flat fee, and variable pricing. The *hourly rate*

ensures that you are achieving a rate of return on the actual time and labor you invest in servicing each customer. Hourly rates are often used when you are pricing your own consulting services, instead of pricing a service that uses labor and materials from others. Your rate should be determined by your amount of expertise and seniority; a more senior consultant will generally be paid a higher hourly rate than a less experienced or junior consultant.[27]

The *flat fee* covers the entire services. For consumers who want to know up front how much the service is going to cost, this is an appropriate pricing strategy. The *variable pricing* form involves bargaining and negotiations with each customer. This may increase customer involvement and the perception that, as a result of the negotiations, they have gotten a good deal.

In any case, pricing services will require some experimentation and constant monitoring. The things to look for include what your customers are saying about your service, your ongoing profitability, how the competition is setting or changing its prices, and what new services are being offered.[28]

Marketing Thinking Challenge 11.3: Price Determination

Identify organizations that you believe are using the three different pricing approaches (i.e., cost-based, competitive-based, and market-based pricing). How did you determine their pricing methods? What effects do you see playing out in their respective markets stemming from their pricing approaches/strategies? What would you recommend?

Figure 11.9 Price Determination Playing Out in the Market

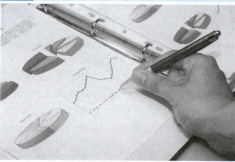

Summary

- We began our discussion by examining the origins of the price concept. The price concept is a result of the concept of money being adopted to alleviate the difficulties with the barter system. Furthermore, price gets its meaning by way of a monetary understanding. The strategic role(s) price plays is inherently found in the functions of money. Without the monetary system as we know it, the price concept and strategies would not exist.

- As such, we saw that price can be used to signal the worth for something (e.g., how much will it be exchanged for), it can facilitate the meaning for a product or service (e.g., high vs. low quality), it can be used as an incentive to encourage purchases (e.g., through a sale), it can potentially increase or decrease consumer involvement (e.g., participative pricing vs. a low price), it can be the basis for competition or differentiation, and it is the organization's primary means for income and profitability.

- The three different price-determination approaches were discussed, including cost-based, competitive-based, and market-based. The cost-based approach is an internal perspective, whereas the other two approaches are externally oriented, focusing on different entities. The competitive-based approach sets price based upon the competition, and the market-based approach sets price based upon a consumer valuation assessment.

- Service pricing can also utilize the three price-determination approaches (cost, competitive, and/or market) along with considering a yield-management approach. These were discussed within a service context.

- The price strategy and determination must also be considered within the marketer's overall strategy for consistency and to increase effectiveness.

Case: Panera Bread Company—Believing in Reciprocity

WE ARE PANERA. We are bakers of bread. We are fresh from the oven. We are a symbol of warmth and welcome. We are a simple pleasure, honest and genuine. We are a life story told over dinner. We are a long lunch with an old friend. We are your weekday morning ritual. We are the kindest gesture of neighbors. We are home. We are family. We are friends.[29]

Panera is a bakery-café organization, and as of September 28, 2010, had 1,421 bakery-cafes in 40 states and in Ontario, Canada, "operating under the Panera Bread®, Saint Louis

Bread Co.® and Paradise Bakery & Café® names, delivering fresh, authentic artisan bread served in a warm environment by engaging associates."[30] Panera

> offer[s] made-to-order sandwiches using a variety of artisan breads, including Asiago cheese bread, focaccia, and its classic sourdough bread. The chain's menu also features soups, salads, and gourmet coffees. In addition, Panera sells its bread, bagels, and pastries to go. More than 580 of its locations are company-operated, while the rest are run by franchisees.[31]

The Panera Bread® legacy began in 1981 as Au Bon Pain Co., Inc. Founded by Louis Kane and Ron Shaich, the company prospered along the east coast of the United States and internationally throughout the 1980s and 1990s and became the dominant operator within the bakery-cafe category.[32]

However, it wasn't until 1993, when the Au Bon Pain company acquired a chain of bakery-cafes under the name of the St. Louis Bread company, that the Panera concept would start to take shape.

A major opportunity came in 1993, when Au Bon Pain acquired the St. Louis Bread Company. At the time the deal was struck, St. Louis Bread had 19 company-owned and operated bakery-cafés and one franchised outlet. Thereafter, Au Bon Pain continued to expand the purchased company, introducing the bakery-café concept into new markets. In its home area in Missouri, the new franchised units were opened as St. Louis Bread bakery-cafés, but elsewhere they opened under a different name—Panera Bread. Over the course of its ownership by Au Bon Pain Co., Inc., the Panera/St. Louis Bread division would enter new markets and continue to grow at a solid clip.

By the end of 1996, Au Bon Pain had grown to 231 company-run and 58 franchised bakery-cafés. Of the 231 company-operated units, 177 were Au Bon Pain owned and operated outlets and 54 were Au Bon Pain franchise-operated bakery-cafés. The remaining 54 company-owned bakery-cafés and 10 franchise units were St. Louis Bakery Company units. As concepts, the Au Bon Pain and St. Louis Bakery Company stores were very similar. Both specialized in high quality foods served for breakfast and lunch. Their menus included fresh baked goods, made-to-order sandwiches, soups, salads, and custom-roasted coffees as well as other beverages. The company's targeted customers were principally urban white-collar workers, suburban residents, and shoppers, students, and travelers with busy schedules to keep. The company's chief strategy was to provide high quality, fresh foods at reasonable prices and with greater variety than its chief market competitors. Most of the bakery-cafés were located in and around major urban centers, including Boston, other New England cities, New York, Philadelphia, Pittsburgh, Washington, D. C., Columbus, Cleveland, Cincinnati, Chicago, St. Louis, Minneapolis, Los Angeles, Atlanta, and outside the United States in Santiago, Chile. For the 1996 fiscal year, total sales generated by the company-owned stores and its franchised units reached approximately $259 million. On the average, company-owned Au Bon Pain bakery-cafés generated about $940,000 each, while the Panera/St. Louis Bakery units generated about $1.1 million per outlet.[33]

Under the new management, the St. Louis Bread company was repositioned, including changing its name to Panera, and from 1993 to 1997 saw a 75% increase in volume while outpacing its Au Bon Pain bakery-cafes counterpart. It was during this period that the Panera concept had been realized. As a result of its success, the owners decided to gamble on the Panera concept by taking it to an even grander scale. To do this required focusing all of it resources behind the Panera bakery-café concept.

In May 1999, all of Au Bon Pain Co., Inc.'s business units were sold, with the exception of Panera Bread, and the company was renamed Panera Bread. Since those transactions were completed, the company's stock has grown thirteen-fold and over $1 billion in shareholder value has been created. Panera Bread has been recognized as one of *Business Week's* "100 Hot Growth Companies." As reported by *The Wall St. Journal's* Shareholder Scorecard in 2006, Panera Bread was recognized as the top performer in the restaurant category for one-, five- and ten-year returns to shareholders.

What seems to be behind the Panera success story is an organization centered on values of quality of food ingredients; using old-style artisan bakery methods; providing a friendly, warm, and clean restaurant atmosphere; hiring and training personable employees; being a good corporate neighbor; and consistently adhering to these values even in hard times.

At Panera Bread®, we believe in giving back to local communities. We show our appreciation for customers not only within our bakery-cafes but also throughout the communities we serve by sponsoring special events open to the neighborhood, participating in charitable events and offering various Operation Dough-Nation® programs.[34]

The Operation Dough-Nation® programs include providing charity to those in need, daily donations of unsold products to local food banks, and participating in various fundraising events. For example, the company has been a strong advocate in the fight against breast cancer.[35] Recently, it has been experimenting with a new nonprofit business model that utilizes PWYW pricing.

Panera Bread Co. is asking customers at a new restaurant to pay what they want. The national bakery and restaurant chain launched a new nonprofit store here this week that has the same menu as its other 1,400 locations. But the prices are a little different—there aren't any. Customers are told to donate what they want for a meal, whether it's the full suggested price, a penny or $100. The new store in the upscale St. Louis suburb of Clayton is the first of what Panera hopes will be many around the country. Ronald Shaich, Panera's CEO until last week, was on hand at the new bakery Monday to explain the system to customers. The pilot restaurant is run by a nonprofit foundation. If it can sustain itself financially, Panera will expand the model around the country within months. It all depends on whether customers will abide by the motto that hangs above the deli counter: "Take what you need, leave your fair share." Panera hopes to open a similar location in every community where it operates. Other nonprofits have opened community kitchens, where customers set the price, and the idea has spread among food enthusiasts and philanthropists. But Panera brings new scale to the idea—its community restaurants will use the company's distribution system and have access to its national food suppliers.[36]

If Panera Clayton's restaurant can sustain itself, the net proceeds will be donated to community groups.

The downtown Clayton store's menu items are the same as at other Panera outlets. But instead of prices, there are "suggested funding levels" on its menu board. After placing their orders, customers are handed a receipt with a suggested price—which doesn't include any sales tax—and they're told to pay what they think is appropriate. There are still cash registers, but they are used to provide change or to take payment with credit cards. Customers are encouraged to pay more. And the cafe asks customers who can't pay to volunteer an hour of their time at the store at a later date, but it was unclear Monday how exactly that system would work. "You're on your honor," a sign by the menu board said. The proceeds will pay for the store's operations, and remaining money will go to community groups that have not yet been disclosed.[37] With the 2008 recession, the Panera restaurant is not only about donating to community groups but also is able to help individuals that have hit hard times and need a meal. As stated by Chairman Shaich, "I have long harbored desires to contribute to the broader world beyond Panera."[38] Panera executives have indicated that they are pleased with the initial experiment, reporting that customers had been paying 85% of the retail price, and are planning on opening other nonprofit stores utilizing the PWYW pricing.[39]

Research Panera and find out how the PWYW pricing is working. If it is working, explain why you believe this form of pricing works. What suggestions would you make and when would this type of pricing be appropriate?

References

1. Hansen, Torben, and Hans Stubbe Solgaard (2004), "Strategic Pricing: Fundamental Considerations and Future Perspectives," *The Marketing Review*, 4, 99–111.
2. Bellis, Mary, "The History of Money," http://inventors.about.com/od/mstartinventions/a/money.htm
3. "The Origin of Money," ONB—Oesterreichische National Bank, http://inventors.about.com/od/mstartinventions/a/money.htm
4. Mastrommatteo, Giuseppe, and Luigi Ventura (2007), "The Origin of Money: A Survey of the Contemporary Literature," *Int. Rev. Econ.*, 54, 198.
5. Solomon, Michael R. (2011), *Consumer Behavior: Buying, Having, and Being*, Upper Saddle River, NJ: Prentice Hall, 69.
6. Anderson, Eric, and Duncan Simester (2003), "Mind Your Pricing Cues," *Harvard Business Review*, 81 (9) 98.
7. Decoy effects, http://en.wikipedia.org/wiki/Decoy_effect
8. Kunz, Ben (2010), "Apple's Pricing Decoys: Rumor Says a Small, 7-inch iPad Is Coming. It's a Ploy to Help Apple Defend Margins," Business Week, September 1, www.businessweek.com/technology/content/sep2010/tc2010091_060916.htm
9. Tjan, Anthony (2010), "The Pros and Cons of Bundled Pricing," *Harvard Business Review*, HBR Blog Network, February 26, http://blogs.hbr.org/tjan/2010/02/the-pros-and-cons-of-bundled-p.html
10. Anderson, Eric, and Duncan Simester (2003), "Mind Your Pricing Cues," *Harvard Business Review*, 81 (9) 99–100.
11. Anderson, Eric, and Duncan Simester (2003), "Mind Your Pricing Cues," *Harvard Business Review*, 81 (9) 100.
12. Wathieu, Luc, and Marco Bertini (2007), "Price as a Stimulus to Think: The Case for Willful Overpricing," *Marketing Science*, 26 (1), 126.
13. Wathieu, Luc, and Marco Bertini (2007), "Price as a Stimulus to Think: The Case for Willful Overpricing," *Marketing Science*, 26 (1), 127.
14. Chandran, Sucharita, and Vicki G. Morwitz (2005), "Effects of Participative Pricing on Consumers' Cognitions and Actions: A Goal Theoretic Perspective," *Journal of Consumer Research*, 32 (September), 249–259.

15. Kim, Ju-Young, Martin Natter, and Martin Spann (2009), "Pay What You Want: A New Participative Pricing Mechanism," *Journal of Marketing*, 73 (January), 44–45.

16. Kim, Ju-Young, Martin Natter, and Martin Spann (2009), "Pay What You Want: A New Participative Pricing Mechanism," *Journal of Marketing*, 73 (January), 44–45.

17. Chandran, Sucharita, and Vicki G. Morwitz (2005), "Effects of Participative Pricing on Consumers' Cognitions and Actions: A Goal Theoretic Perspective," *Journal of Consumer Research*, 32 (September), 257.

18. Cespedes, Frank V., Elliot B. Ross, and Benson P. Shapiro (2010), "Raise Your Prices! Face It: Most Companies Can't Compete on Price. And the Good News Is They Don't Have To," *Wall Street Journal*, May 24, http://online.wsj.com/article/SB10001424052748704240004575085513717202 880.html

19. http://en.wikipedia.org/wiki/Experience_curve_effects

20. Hinterhuber, Andreas (2008), "Customer Value-Based Pricing Strategies: Why Companies Resist," *Journal of Business Strategy*, 29 (4), 41–50.

21. Hinterhuber, Andreas (2008), "Customer Value-Based Pricing Strategies: Why Companies Resist," *Journal of Business Strategy*, 29 (4), 45.

22. Hinterhuber, Andreas (2008), "Customer Value-Based Pricing Strategies: Why Companies Resist," *Journal of Business Strategy*, 29 (4), 45.

23. Kim, Ju-Young, Martin Natter, and Martin Spann (2009), "Pay What You Want: A New Participative Pricing Mechanism," *Journal of Marketing*, 73 (January), 44–45.

24. Wasserman, Elizabeth (2009), "How to Price Business Services," *Inc.*, November 1, www.inc.com/guides/price-your-services.html

25. Withiam, Glen (2001), "Yield Management," *Center for Hospitality Research*, Cornel University of Hotel Administration, www.hotelschool.cornell.edu/research/chr/pubs/reports/abstract-13622.html

26. Withiam, Glen (2001), "Yield Management," *Center for Hospitality Research*, Cornel University of Hotel Administration, www.hotelschool.cornell.edu/research/chr/pubs/reports/abstract-13622.html

27. Wasserman, Elizabeth (2009), "How to Price Business Services," *Inc.*, November 1, www.inc.com/guides/price-your-services.html

28. Wasserman, Elizabeth (2009), "How to Price Business Services," *Inc.*, November 1, www.inc.com/guides/price-your-services.html

29. www.panerabread.com/about/

30. www.panerabread.com/about/company/history.php

31. www.answers.com/topic/panera-bread-company

32. www.panerabread.com/about/company/history.php

33. www.answers.com/topic/panera-bread-company

34. www.panerabread.com/about/community/

35. Cornell, Scott (2011), "Panera Raises Money for Breast Cancer," *NCNLocal*, February 2, http://ncnlocal.com/ncnlocal_mall/article_31b614ca-2ee7-11e0-9e74-001cc4c03286.html

36. "Panera Bread Co. Opens Nonprofit Location Where Customers Can Pay What They Want." May 19, 2011. New York Daily News. Used with permission of The Associated Press Copyright © 2011. All rights reserved.

37. Kumar, Kavita (2010), "Customers Pick Their Own Price at Panera," *SunNews*, May 22, www.thesunnews.com/2010/05/22/1488263/customers-pick-their-price-at.html

38. Kumar, Kavita (2010), "Customers Pick Their Own Price at Panera," *SunNews*, May 22, www.thesunnews.com/2010/05/22/1488263/customers-pick-their-price-at.html

39. Kumar, Kavita (2010), "Customers Pick Their Own Price at Panera," *SunNews*, May 22, www.thesunnews.com/2010/05/22/1488263/customers-pick-their-price-at.html

Reflective vs. Forward-Looking Sides of Marketing Thinking

CHAPTER 12

Assessment vs. *Navigating* Strategy–Using Metrics

Chapter Introduction

Across the chapters, we have seen marketing thinking play out in many different ways, creating conceptual tools along the way. As should be expected, traditional forms of marketing thinking are being challenged and making way for newer ways of thinking and conceiving of marketing that result in different strategy considerations. This is a positive development of any healthy discipline that continues to breathe in new life through its main lifeline (that being the thinking capacity of its constituents, which allows for the ability to learn and adapt), all the while contributing to the practices found in marketing. As a marketer, you will also contribute by developing new marketing practices and strategies. A rich source for developing new ways of marketing thinking can be found within the vulnerabilities you'll face as a marketer.

Vulnerabilities Marketers Face. The changes in marketing thinking can be characterized as a willingness to recognize and consider the vulnerabilities all organizations are exposed to in various degrees. Within this awakening, the marketer is recognizing that there are strategic avenues to pursue within the various vulnerabilities that can improve an organization's position. To ignore them is a nonthinking position and potentially exposes the organization to greater risks. This refers to the *vulnerability paradox* discussed in Chapter 6 as played out through the collaborative and participatory forms of marketing thinking expressed in the following observation:

> As exchange becomes more relational, at an instant one or another party may be receiving more than the other and so either party is vulnerable to loss. …strong relationships are often ones of mutual vulnerability.[1]

This suggests that relationships are characterized by the state of being vulnerable— whether symmetrical or asymmetrical and in one form or another. An extreme position would suggest that the only way to eliminate the state or condition of vulnerability is to discontinue the relationship(s). However, businesses are dependent upon relationships; hence, this isn't a viable choice. Businesses must recognize the inherent vulnerabilities within their relationships. Organizations large and small are dependent upon their customers. Therefore, there are vulnerabilities to be found within these relationships as well as with alliances, channel members, and so forth. According to the *vulnerability paradox,* strength lies within the sense of vulnerability in the forms of greater vigilance, awareness, proneness for change, empathy, openness, and a willingness to work with others.

Vulnerability comes in many different forms. The *relational vulnerability* described above, while significant, represents only one form. Applying our thinking agility skills, the marketer should look for other forms as well. Each organization finds itself in a unique situation and, as a result, confronts different vulnerabilities. In general, each form of vulnerability represents an opportunity through which the marketer can develop strengths. The key is first to recognize the vulnerabilities that lead to developing the sense of vulnerability described above, which then opens the doors or questioning (thinking) leading to the strengths.

Another vulnerability all marketers confront is the *navigational vulnerability*. The navigational vulnerability stems from the organization's interest in controlling the outcomes of its strategy and not recognizing it has limited control due to the complexity of the marketplace and that it is working with incomplete information. As discussed in Chapter 5, the parameters of difference (e.g., the repetition of difference) occurring throughout the marketplace contribute to this state of vulnerability. The difficulties in understanding the marketplace were also highlighted, for example, in Chapters 3 and 4 with the situation assessment and market segmentation.

Marketers have always been interested in assessing the outcomes of their strategies in one form or another—whether it has to do with efficiencies, effectiveness, and/or accountability. The beginnings of this interest lie within the origins of strategy as conceived through the military's command-and-control perspective (discussed in Chapter 3) and operationalized through the formal planning process in which goals and objectives are established in the context of strategy development. From the onset, this creates a *post hoc* assessment perspective of determining the success of a strategy via its objectives. This has led to what is referred to as rear-view-mirror (lagging) measures or metrics that have been heavily used by companies.[2] It should be noted that the *post hoc* perspective represents a thinking obstacle that is inherent in this way of thinking and use of these metrics. This obstacle is explained in discussing the different scenarios within the strategy/objective relationship that follows.

In Chapter 1, strategy was defined as the marketer's way to be different in the marketplace. In this context, strategy represents the way (or the means) to accomplish the desired form of difference, the objective(s) (or the ends). Strategy and objectives go hand in hand in that a strategy is established to obtain a particular set of objectives. Inherent in this view is the integral roles strategy and objectives play together.

Three different scenarios are possible within the strategy/objective relationship. The *first scenario* is that both are established in time period one (T1) and do not vary from their originally conceived perspective. The *second scenario* involves maintaining the objective(s) established in T1 but allowing the strategy to vary to accomplish the objectives to be assessed in time period two (T2). The *third scenario* is one in which both the strategy and objectives are allowed to vary as conditions are changing between T1 and T2 and beyond.

The first two scenarios are driven by the command-and-control perspective and inherently possess the *post hoc* perspective. The third scenario differs by taking on a more adaptive, forward-looking perspective. It also recognizes that the marketer doesn't have complete control over the situation and that changes to the strategy and/or objectives may be necessary as marketplace conditions change. This also suggests the changing role(s) and thinking associated with objectives within the strategy context.

The problem with the first two scenarios involves the role of the objective. The issue lies within setting a strategy objective in T1 to be accomplished and assessed later in T2. In essence, it assumes that the known conditions in T1 will be consistent throughout until T2. In other words, the marketer is using the known information in T1 (via the objectives established in T1) to assess the strategy outcome in T2's conditions. What is to be questioned here is the rigidity of the role of an objective and the assumptions that have led to this rigidity. This has several effects. It assumes static directional and evaluative roles by not taking into consideration the possibility for changing conditions. *It also has the potential to channel the marketer's perspective within the strategy perspective, which leads to an internal perspective.* In contrast, as in the third scenario, if strategy is to be adaptive, then so should the objective(s) as needed. Juxtaposed, instead of thinking in terms of the *post hoc*, rear-view-mirror perspective, an alternative analogy of headlights comes into view—a forward-looking perspective of *developing adaptive foresight.*[3] Using the analogy, the headlights allow the driver to see far enough ahead to make necessary changes to avoid an unnecessary event—for example, running into a deer. Here, forward-looking (leading) metrics are being developed that facilitate the adaptive capability to change course as characterized in the third scenario.

Applying 4-DS thinking to the three strategy/objectives scenarios. Returning to our 4-DS thinking perspective, the marketer in the first scenario isn't utilizing the thinking time dimension (characterized by *change* and *chance*) and assumes the static perspective. A similar argument could be made in regard to the second scenario as well. The result is that the marketer is put in the position of always having to look in the rear-view mirror to see where he or she has been.[4] It is an after-the-fact orientation. As such, the marketer is over utilizing the *reflective* 4-DS dimension at the expense of the forward-looking time dimension. In contrast, the marketer in the third scenario is utilizing a forward-looking, *time* dimension over the *reflective* dimension. These scenarios implicitly raise a corresponding issue between assessment (a *post hoc*, rear-view, *reflective* perspective) and navigating (a forward-looking, thinking-in-time perspective).

The difference between the time and creative dimensions of the 4-DS thinking. Before moving on to consider the different perspectives, it is a good opportunity to further explicate the differences between the *time* and *creative* dimensions of the 4-DS thinking. The time dimension involves thinking in terms of *change* and the element of *chance* that is present with all change. It recognizes the inevitability of *change* and *chance* and considers possibilities of *change* that may be on the horizon. It is a *forward-looking form of thinking* about one's environment or situation. It is being prone for *change* to anticipate its occurrence. In contrast, *creative* thinking, while also a *forward-looking form of thinking,* involves the marketer's capacity to create new differences that would be a part of change and chance. The marketer is thinking in terms of how to participate in the ongoing change(s) by creating change through new forms of difference. As such, the marketer is actively participating in the repetition difference as described in Chapter 5.

In this chapter, we will explore the differences between the assessment and navigation perspectives and the metrics (rear-view vs. forward-looking) that are associated with the two different views. In addition, we will also consider an in-between perspective in the form of a balance scorecard.

Figure 12.2   Rear-View vs. Forward-Looking Perspective

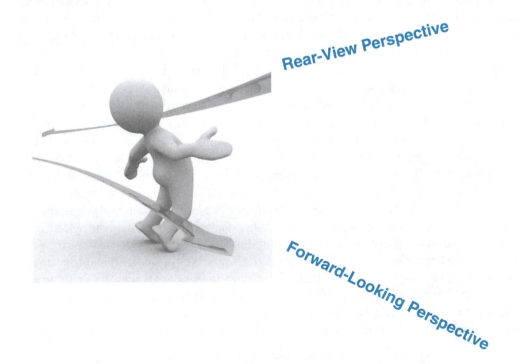

Returning to Chapter 2, we discussed the idea of strategy as a question. It seems that we are back to this issue in terms of thinking of our strategy as an *answer* or as a *question*. If we think of our strategy as an answer, then we'd be interested in assessing whether we got it right in terms of our objectives (the rear-view-mirror perspective). On the other hand, if we think of strategy as a question, then we'd be interested in the navigating perspective, which is a forward-looking view. Correct?

Yes, that is correct. Once again, you have to look at the thinking behind what is being presented. An *assessment perspective* focuses on determining whether the strategy achieved its objectives. As you might already be thinking, there are issues with this view. On the other hand, the *navigating perspective* is about *moving* forward by recognizing that *change* and *chance* are inevitable and keeping strategy open to adapt accordingly, which may require changing objectives (or directions) as needed. In other words, instead of thinking in terms of a fixed target as in the assessment perspective, it's about a moving target. As such, the roles of objectives are different and lead to different types of metrics.

The Backward-Looking Perspective and Rear-View Metrics

As previously mentioned, the rear-view (backward-looking) orientation originates out of the command-and-control perspective. It assumes that from known information acquired in T1, the organization can command future events through its strategy and that the control of these events can be evaluated in T2 through assessment using information acquired in T2 (outcomes) to be compared with the objectives developed in T1. From this perspective, the success of a strategy is assessed by the degree of control it had over the situation measured through the degree of obtainment of the objectives established in T1. It should be noted that *navigational vulnerability* previously discussed is not recognized within the command-and-control perspective. As the labeling of the perspective implies, it assumes otherwise.

Assessment is critical to this backward-looking orientation involving rear-view metrics. One such view of a metric is as follows:

A "***metric***" is a performance measure that top management should review. It is a measure that matters to the whole business. The term comes from music and implies regularity:

the reviews should typically take place yearly or half-yearly. A metric is not just another word for measure—while all metrics are measures, not all measures are metrics. Metrics should be *necessary*, *precise*, *consistent* and *sufficient* (i.e., comprehensive) for review purposes. Metrics may be financial (usually from the profit and loss account), from the marketplace, or from non-financial internal sources (innovation and employee).[5]

Another view of metrics is as follows:

> Metrics that capture the past are rear-view mirrors, retrospective snapshots of the ways customers have evaluated the company, its employees, or its products and services in the past. Customers' perceptions and overall judgments are the rear-view-mirror measures…
>
> Perceptions are customer beliefs about the attributes and performance of products and services. Customer judgments are overall assessments, such as customer satisfaction, perceived quality, perceived value, loyalty, or attitudes toward the brand or organization.[6]

Rear-View Metrics

Reasons for adopting rear-view metrics include ease of obtaining customer information through surveys, determining key strategy drivers, and tracking performance.[7] Rear-view-mirror metrics have also been developed around three main categories: psychological, behavioral, and operational.

Psychological metrics measure customers' awareness levels and/or how they are assessing an organization's products and/or services. For example, they can indicate how satisfied customers are with the organization's products.

Behavioral metrics measure customer behavior and may be a part of a customer relationship management (CRM) program. For example, loyalty (reward) programs can be implemented based on purchases. Or, based on purchasing patterns identifying product constellations, the retail setting can be designed to facilitate such purchases.

Operations metrics measure the internal activities of an organization associated with customer behavior. For example, these metrics can be used to improve operation efficiencies. Examples of rear-view metrics are presented in Table 12.1.

Table 12.1	Rear-View (Backward-Looking) Customer Metrics

Category	Metric	Description	Perspective
Psychological	Perceptions	About attributes and performance of products, services, and/or brand.	Retrospective and focuses on current customers.
	Awareness		
	Image		
	Reputation		
	Beliefs		
	Judgments	Overall assessments of product, services, brands, and/or organizations.	Retrospective and focuses on current customers.
	Satisfaction		
	Perceived Quality		
	Perceived Value		
	Loyalty		
	Attitudes		

Category	Metric	Description	Perspective
Behavior	Customer Relation Management (CRM)	Assesses customers' behavior on what, when, how much, and how long to continue to buy a product or service.	Retrospective and focuses on current customers.
	Number of Customers Acquired		
	Percentage of Customers Retained		
	Dollar Value of Cross-Selling		
	Percentage Increase in Customer Migration to Higher Margin Products or Services		
	Percentage of Multi-Channel Shopping		
	Individual Customer's Percentage of Returned Products		
	Word of Mouth Activity		
Operational	Complaints	These represent internal assessments related to customer activities.	Retrospective from an internal perspective of current customers' activities.
	Response Times		
	Resolution Times		
	Waiting Times		
	Returns		
	Capacity Measures		
	Engineering Measures		

Source(s): [8, 9]

Issues With Rear-View Metrics

From Table 12.1, we can see that all of the metrics are retrospective and customer focused, whether externally or internally. From the *psychological metrics* category, strategy is focused on creating awareness, satisfaction, perceived quality or value, or positive attitudes. As such, a company's strategy that emphasizes satisfaction, for example, possesses a rear-view perspective and is being operationalized through the satisfaction metric.

Behavioral metrics suggest that strategy pertains to the acquisition and/or retention of customers; to cross-selling, to customer migration to higher margin products, or to multichannel customers; and/or to the percentage of purchases returned. For example, a focus on the percentage of purchases returned may lead the marketer toward pursuing an objective of decreasing the percentage as far as possible—similar to a zero-defect objective. However, the predictive element is missing from looking at the percentage of purchases returned in this way. Later, we'll see how, from a forward-looking metrics perspective, this information can be used differently for predictive purposes. Here, a company's strategy that focuses on behavioral outcomes—for example, customer retention—possesses a rear-view perspective and is being operationalized through the retention metric.

Strategy from an *operational metrics* perspective is focused on decreasing response times, reducing potential customer interface issues, tracking returns to address potential product defects, and managing capacity levels to ensure maximum customer-related performance. Likewise, a company's strategy that emphasizes quality control, for example, possesses a rear-view perspective and is being operationalized through the quality-control metric.

Using Single vs. Multiple Metrics

The presentation of rear-view metrics raises several issues. With so many metrics to choose from, the complexity may discourage their use. There may be a tendency to try to develop a single metric, a "silver metric," to assess marketing performance.[10] However, a single measure isn't able to capture marketing performance well enough because marketing and strategy are multidimensional. Also, the list of metrics doesn't provide a means to interrelate the multiple dimensions or perspectives.

What is needed is something that addresses the complexity of available metrics while providing a means to interrelate multiple dimensions (or perspectives) and an adaptive platform. What has been called a Balanced Scorecard has been offered to address these issues. It is discussed in the next section. Before moving on, try the following rear-view-metrics Marketing Thinking Challenge.

Marketing Thinking Challenge 12.1: Rear-View Metrics in Use

Identify an organization that you believe is using rear-view metrics. Describe its marketing strategy and the rear-view metrics it is using to assess its strategy. Then explain how its use of these metrics is influencing (positively and/or negatively) that strategy.

| Figure 12.3 | Assessing Strategy—Did it work? |

Marketing Thinking in Practice: Rear-View Metrics

On a small-business website, the question of whether your organization is using rear-view metrics is discussed. It is suggested that lagging indicators (rear-view metrics) are not enough and that leading indicators are necessary as well.[11]

Are Your Business Metrics a Rearview Mirror?

Probably one of the most overused buzzwords in business today is the word, metrics. When someone first asked me about metrics, I thought they were trying to discuss the difference of meters versus yards! Metrics has become a catchall for any measure or indicator we use to determine if our business is succeeding or not.

Every organization I have been in has struggled with the decision of what to measure, and how to measure it.

Performance metrics are a necessity to managing an organization. The old slogan, "If I can measure it, I can manage it" is as true today as it ever was. Not all measures are good. If we measure the effectiveness of our sales staff on how many calls they make and reward based on that measure, we may be rewarding unsuccessful calls and not rewarding closed sales. What brings in the income, sales calls or closed sales? Our metrics (and the corresponding rewards) will have a positive or negative impact on our organization.

One management tool, the Balanced Scorecard, is an effective tool for developing the right metrics to measure the right performance. In its simplest description, the Balanced Scorecard is a series of measures that are all related to the key drivers of the business in terms of financial, customer, business process, and learning and growth results.

To develop effective metrics, you start with the business goals and strategy of the company. From there you will define what are the measures of success in this strategy. As Stephen Covey teaches us, "Begin with the end in mind!"

Once the measures of success are determined, we identify what actions must be taken to achieve those measures. We then determine what measures will tell us if we have been successful in taking those actions. We refer to these measures as lagging indicators.

Lagging indicators are like your rearview mirror. However, they do not tell you early on if your strategy is being implemented as designed and taking you in the direction that you want to go. We need to establish other measures that will tell us if the strategy is being implemented as planned, these are leading indicators.

Obviously we cannot drive our car by only using the rearview mirror, we need to look through the windshield as well to make sure the car is headed in the right direction. Leading indicators are our business drivers and our metrics should be biased toward business drivers that will help us to steer our company, rather than outcome measures that will only tell us where we have been.

It's important to have a mix of leading and lagging indicators with the proper balance so you can know you are headed in the right direction and that you have achieved your goal.

In addition to the right mix of metrics, the metrics must be available to the people who have the authority to act on it, so communication and dissemination of the data is essential. Don't limit the methods of communicating these data, use all of the modes available to you. If only the navigator knows where you are going but never tells the driver, the data is useless.

It's an old adage in business, "If you can't measure it, you can't manage it." Are you measuring the right things and are you looking forward and not through your rearview mirror?

The Balanced Scorecard Perspective

"The balanced scorecard is like the dials in an airplane cockpit: it gives managers complex information at a glance."[12] As originally conceived, the balanced scorecard provides a means to balance four different perspectives by combining them into one scorecard. The four different perspectives include the customer perspective, the financial perspective, the internal business perspective, and the growth perspective (innovation and learning). The interrelations of the perspectives are illustrated in Figure 12.4, (on the next page), and an example of how to translate a strategy into a balanced scorecard is presented in Figure 12.5.

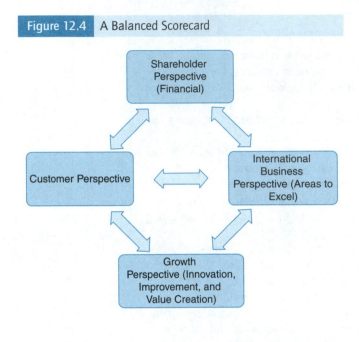

Figure 12.4   A Balanced Scorecard

Figure 12.5   An Example of Linking Strategy to a Balanced Scorecard

Vision	Strategy	Scorecard
• Be the preferred provider • Be the industry leader	• Services that surpass needs • Customer satisfaction • Continuous improvement • Quality of employees • Shareholder expectations	• **Financial**—Return on capital, cash flow, project profitability,and reliability of performance • **Customer**—Value for money, competitive price, hassle-free relationship, high-performance professionals, and innovation • **Internal**—Shape customer requirement, tender effectiveness, quality service, and superior project management • **Growth**—Continuous, product and service innovation,and empowered workforce

Source: [14]

Figure 12.5 illustrates an example presented in the *Harvard Business Review*. The senior management's vision at Rockwater, a global engineering and construction company, was as follows: "As our customers' preferred provider, we shall be the industry leader in providing the highest standards of safety and quality to our clients."[13] To pursue this vision, they developed a multidimensional strategy focusing on five interrelated elements. By providing (1) services beyond customer expectations, they could obtain (2) customer satisfaction. To be more responsive to customer needs, (3) continuous improvements were needed in terms of equipment and so forth. (4) High-quality employees were also needed in terms of operations and in serving customers. These strategy elements were to culminate into (5) greater shareholder returns. Based upon these strategy objectives, they translated to the scorecard more concrete and measureable objectives (goals) and actions within each of the respective areas of responsibility. These are presented in Figure 12.5.

Issues With the Balanced Scorecard

The balanced scorecard was conceived to illustrate how different perspectives can be managed to work together versus conflicting with each other or splitting off into different directions. It is a way of getting the various entities of an organization to pursue a common vision while illustrating their strategic role in the pursuit. It is also a means to provide a way for the different entities to communicate among themselves and to pull people together under one vision, one strategy. It attempts to put vision and strategy front and center while releasing the reins of control to allow adaptation as things change through employee empowerment.

The scorecard puts strategy and vision, not control, at the center. It establishes goals but assumes that people will adopt whatever behaviors and take whatever actions are necessary to arrive at those goals. The measures are designed to pull people toward the overall vision. Senior management may know what the end result should be, but they cannot tell employees exactly how to achieve that result, if only because the conditions in which employees operate are constantly changing.[15]

The balanced scorecard illustrates the importance of an integrated perspective while recognizing that adaption is important as well. In addition, it illustrates the second scenario previously discussed in the introduction in which strategy is allowed to vary to achieve fixed objectives. From Table 12.2, we can see that the metrics associated with three out of the four perspectives are retrospective (or rear-view metrics), with the Growth perspective being the only one possessing metrics that are more future or forward oriented.

Table 12.2   Balanced Scorecard Metrics (Combination)

Category	Metric	Description	Perspective
Financial	Return on Capital	Assesses profitability, growth, and shareholders' value.	Retrospective and doesn't reflect contemporary value-creating actions.
	Cash Flow		
	Quarterly Sales		
	Profitability		
	Market Share		
	Etc.		
Customer	Lead Time (e.g., Time to fulfill an order or time to market with a new product.)	How well the organization is performing from the customers' perspective.	Retrospective externally oriented focusing on current customers.
	Quality (e.g., Defect rate or the accuracy of delivery.)		
	Performance & Service (e.g., Creating value for customers.)		
	Costs (e.g., Coming in within an acceptable customer cost range.)		
Internal	Cycle Time	How well an organization's internal operations are able to meet customer expectations.	Retrospective internal perspective processes assessed against customers' expectations.
	Quality Control		
	Productivity		
	Employee Skills		
	Etc.		
Growth	Continuous Improvement	Assesses the organization's ability to innovate, improve, and learn.	Future oriented internally and externally toward value creation.
	Product and Service Innovation		
	Empowered Workforce		
	Etc.		

Sources: [16, 17]

A Future-Oriented Scorecard

To address the retrospective aspect of the balanced scorecard, an alternative approach involves developing *strategic foresight* by creating what is called a "Future Scorecard," which envisions multiple possible views of the future by considering different scenarios (combining internal, resource-based with external, market-based scenarios) and their probable occurrence.[18]

The development of a future scorecard needs to be based on a creative learning culture and on experiences in the fields of future thinking and strategic management (Van der Heijden 2002). One core element is open dialogues about the perspectives and strategies of the company (Zohar 1997). The future scorecard overcomes traditional limits in thinking, leads the decision makers to new questions and increases the tolerance of different points of view. Scenarios...enable the decision makers who are "trapped in operative daily business" to free themselves and systematically broaden their perspectives.[19]

The Future Scorecard adds to the mix of considerations of multiple views of the future while still incorporating an integrated perspectives platform, as with the original scorecard. This involves *thinking in time* and facilitating thinking beyond the familiar. It is also using scenarios as a means to work around the familiarity obstacle to thinking (discussed in Chapter 2) to generate new questions and new ways of seeing things and to be forward thinking in strategy development. Before moving on to discussing forward-looking metrics, try the following balanced-scorecard Marketing Thinking Challenge.

Marketing Thinking Challenge 12.2: Creating a Scorecard

Choose an organization you are interested in and identify what you believe to be its strategy. Then, using the four different perspectives described in Figure 12.4, create a scorecard by providing the different objectives (goals) that would be associated with the different perspectives and describe how they would be measured. Also, explain how the identified objectives relate to each other across the different perspectives.

Figure 12.6	Combining Multiple Perspectives Under One Strategy

The Forward-Looking Perspective and Metrics

As previously discussed, *forward-looking metrics* are indicators that are meant to shed light on the potential for future events or behavior. They are indicators for the potential of future occurrences to develop an *adaptive foresight* capability in terms of where things are headed.[20] While these forward-looking metrics still involve information on past or present events (or what is known), they are using this information to predict future events. The difference with forward-looking versus rear-view metrics is with the orientation as to how the known information is to be used. In other words,

> Is the information to be used in an **assessment** way, to determine the degree of control (success) achieved by the employed strategy using rear-view metrics to evaluate the degree of obtainment of the objective(s)? Or is the information to be used to **navigate** strategy using forward-looking metrics to adjust the course (direction and/or means) in a constantly changing, turbulent business environment?

Since forward-looking metrics and the interest in them are a more recent development, there aren't as many examples as there are rear-view metrics, which have been around a lot longer. However, there are two general categories of forward-looking metrics that are based on level of aggregation: at the individual customer level and at an aggregated customer level.

Forward-Looking Metrics—At the Individual Level

At the individual customer level, examples of forward-looking metrics include customer lifetime value (CLV), average interpurchase time, cross-buying behavior, expected future contribution margin, purchase returns, and customer referral value (CRV). See Table 12.3. The customer lifetime value (CLV) metric is based on customer-generated revenue minus the costs in maintaining the relationship.[21]

$$CLV = Revenue_{(Lifetime\ Customer\ Generated)} - Costs_{(To\ Acquire\ \&\ Maintain\ the\ Relationship)}$$

A CLV perspective "uses behavioral information about past customer interactions with the firm to predict future customer behavior and customer value."[22] This information allows the marketer to manage customer value by determining which customers are creating the most value for an organization and to direct the marketing accordingly.

Other behavioral variables can also be used to predict future customer behavior and value, such as average interpurchase time, cross-buying, purchase returns, and RFV (recency of last purchase, frequency of purchase, and the value of amount spent). Customers demonstrating shorter interpurchase time periods, greater cross-buying behavior, and higher RFVs represent greater potential value to an organization.

The percentage of purchases returned was also used as a rear-view metric. However, the way in which it was being used—that is, retrospectively—didn't provide the predictive capability. In contrast, using it as forward-looking metric, the percentage of purchases returned can be associated with different customer value. "For example, customers who return a moderate amount of purchases, 10–15% in total, have been shown on average to purchase more into the future than any other customer."[23] This suggests that some level of returns is not necessarily a negative and that to identify customers based on their percentage of products return may lead to greater profits. Therefore, instead of focusing on reducing the percentage of returns to some minimum acceptable level as in a rear-view-metrics perspective, the forward-looking-metric focus is on identifying the potential associated within the return behavior and identifying the predictive capability within the metric. Again, the differences in the metrics have to do with the orientation being applied (i.e., backward vs. forward, assessment vs. navigating).

It has also been found that multichannel shoppers are more profitable.[24, 25, 26] Potential growth areas can be identified by looking at the "share of wallet" metric, which is the percentage of a customer's purchases compared to the amounts being spent with competitors.[27] With the Internet, social media, and brand communities (as discussed in Chapter 8), another way of looking predicting customer behavior and value is through the customer referral value (CRV) metric. CRV is calculated by subtracting the marketing costs used to prompt a customer to make a referral.[28]

$$CRV = \text{Revenue}_{\text{(Estimated Revenue based upon the \# of Successful Referrals per Incentive)}}$$

$$- \text{Costs}_{\text{(Incentive Costs to Prompt Referrals)}}$$

This metric may take on an even more significant role with advances in the Internet and other technology.

| Table 12.3 | Forward-Looking Customer Value Metrics | | |

Category	Metric	Description	Perspective
Individual Customer Value	Customer Lifetime Value (CLV)	Assesses the customer value to the organization by calculating the customer generated revenue minus the company's costs in maintaining the relationship. [It's an estimation of the expected cash flow (adjusting for risk) from an individual customer based upon known characteristics.]	Future and predictive oriented.
	Average Inter-Purchase Time		
	Cross-Buying Behavior		
	Brand Switching		
	Expected Future Purchase Frequencies		
	Expected Future Contribution Margins		
	Purchase Returns		
	RFV – **R**ecency of last purchase, **F**requency of purchases, and **V**alue ($) of amount spent.		
	Share of Wallet – Percentage of customer's purchases compared to what is being spent with competitors.		
	Customer Referral Value (CRV) – The value the customer brings in minus the marketing costs that prompted the referral.		
Aggregated Customers' Value	Customer Equity (CE)	Aggregately assesses the cumulative expected value of the total customer base.	Future and predictive oriented.
	Segment or Cohort Levels		
	Aggregate Acquisition and Retention Rates		

Sources: [29, 30, 31]

Forward-Looking Metrics—At the Aggregate Level

Table 12.3 also presents the aggregate level forward-looking metrics. At the customer aggregate level, the customer equity (CE) metric can be calculated by assessing the cumulative expected value of the entire total customer base for an organization.[32] This will require examining the number of purchases being made by each customer and their margin contributions and then aggregating this information as an estimate for the future value of the organization's customer base behavior. It can also be calculated by customer segment or cohort. Other aggregate metrics can include customer acquisition and retention rates.

However, when it comes to pursuing customer acquisition or retention, research has shown that it is not preferable to pursue one over the other.[33]

The firm would never want to only maximize acquisition rates or maximize retention rates to maximize profitability since customer retention relies directly on which customers were acquired. This would only lead to acquiring and retaining customers who are not profitable in the long term.[34]

With time, more and more forward-looking metrics will be developed that may be even more insightful for predicting future behavior and customer value.

Issues With Forward-Looking Metrics

Since forward-looking metrics are just beginning to be a part of the marketer's repertoire of available tools, there are a limited number of them so far, as seen in Table 12.3. New ones will need to be developed to expand marketing thinking outward into different directions while affecting strategy along the way. They require a greater degree of thinking agility at this stage in time since the thinking is relatively new and more abstract, being less familiar. Also, ones like CLV, CRV, and CE all possess elements of future value, which involves speculation. As such, they need to be used with this in mind while recognizing that the time elements of change and chance are always on the horizon.

Differences Between Assessment and Navigating

We have seen that assessment is a *post hoc* perspective and has its corresponding rear-view metrics. The information that comes from assessment is from events that have already taken place and, as such, it is descriptive. *Assessment* also has the tendency to channel the marketer's focus within the strategy and, hence, causes an obstacle to thinking. See Figure 12.7. From this perspective, strategy is viewed as an answer and possesses a more closed posture as a consequence.

The alternative to assessment is a *navigating perspective* that is forward looking. It's not about looking backward in terms of prior failures and/or successes but about navigating the future. Navigating strategy is accomplished by developing strategic or adaptive foresight through developing and using future scorecards and/or forward-looking metrics.

With advances in technology, strategy navigation will benefit not only from the development of forward-looking metrics but also from technology that scans the environment (e.g., social media) and is capable of detecting developing differences. Such technologies are already coming into view, as with listening dashboards and software (e.g., Voicescape) that are able to detect weak signals (see Chapters 3 and 8). As such, the marketer's perspective has to be larger in scope than that of his or her strategy and forward-looking as indicated in Figure 12.7. To accomplish this, monitoring and adaptive difference detection need to be incorporated.

Figure 12.7 Assessment vs. Navigating Perspectives

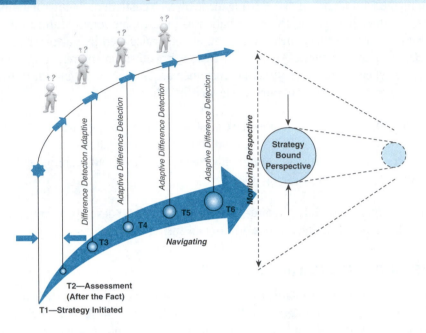

**Marketing Thinking Challenge 12.3:
Creating a Forward-Looking Metric**

Based upon your understanding of forward-looking metrics, create a new forward-looking metric that is different from the ones identified in the chapter. Explain how it is forward looking and how it should be used for strategy purposes.

Figure 12.8 Creating a Forward-Looking Metric

Summary

- The chapter's focus was on the different perspectives available to guide strategy. They included a rear-view, balanced-scorecard, and forward-looking view. Also, inherent within these views was the issue of assessment versus navigating strategy.

- The assessment perspective was viewed as being *post hoc* or retrospective and, consistent with this perspective, rear-view metrics were used for the purposes of evaluating strategy. In contrast, the navigating perspective was forward looking, utilizing forward-looking metrics for the purposes of developing strategic or adaptive foresight. The balanced scorecard was offered as an in-between approach, that is, using retrospective and forward-looking metrics while adding an integrated perspective. The Future Scorecard contribution included using a scenario approach to envision multiple views of the future while providing a means for identifying new questions and new ways of thinking.

- Assessment, while grounded in a command-and-control orientation, also led to a strategy-bound view, resulting in a thinking obstacle for the marketer. Navigating via forward-looking metrics along with advances in technology is expanding this strategy-bound view to include a wider and more dynamic orientation, utilizing technology for monitoring and adaptive difference-detection purposes.

Case: Best Buy—Looking Forward—A New Way

The Best Buy Company, Inc., started out in 1907 in St. Paul, Minnesota, under the name Sound of Music and specialized in audio equipment.[35] It wasn't until 1983 that the company changed its name to Best Buy. This represented a strategy shift to expand its operations into a wider assortment of discounted brand-name goods (e.g., appliances, videocassette recorders), central service, and warehouse distribution. "Despite rapid growth, Best Buy had become barely profitable in 1997 when the stock price bottomed out. …Management implemented changes throughout the retail stores that returned the chain to a position as a market leader."[36] Its expansion continued well into 2003. Along the way, it had expanded geographically throughout the United States and Canada; added DVD hardware and software to its line of products; launched its Bestbuy.com website and Redline Entertainment (an independent music label and action-sports video distributor); and acquired Magnolia Hi-Fi (a high-end electronics retailer), Future Shop (a Canadian electronics chain), Musicland (a music and entertainment software retailer), and Geek Squad (a 24-hour computer support taskforce). By the end of 2003, it had more than 600 stores.[37]

Parallel to the company's expansion was the rise of employee Brad Anderson. Anderson joined the company in 1973 as an audio-components salesperson when it was still named Sound of Music. He had an Associate of Arts degree from Waldorf College, a Bachelor's in sociology from the University of Denver, and had attended Northwestern Seminary for one year.[38, 39] He worked his way up by starting in sales (1973 to 1981), moving up to store manager (1981 to 1986), vice president (1986 to 1991), executive vice president (1991 to 2001), president (2001 to 2002), and CEO and vice chairman (2002 to present).[40] It was when cofounder Richard M. Schulze promoted Anderson to vice president that he began to help shape the direction of the company. Anderson became Schulze's right-hand man, and they both transformed the "chain from a commission-driven store to a discount store, warehouse-style format."[41]

In 2002, Brad Anderson succeeded Richard M. Schulze as CEO. This represented a pivotal point for Best Buy. At the time, competition was heating up in the electronics retail arena with competitors like Circuit City, Wal-Mart, and Costco. Price had become a main means for competition and, as a consequence, a shakeout was looming in the future. (Ultimately, it would be Circuit City that lost out, but this did not occur until 2009.) At about the same time,

> Best Buy ran into difficulties stemming from the 2001 acquisition of the Musicland chain. Through the Musicland acquisition, Best Buy was attempting to reach new customers and to increase sales of consumer electronics at Musicland stores. However, there were overall declines in mall traffic and in CD sales, partially due to music piracy, and Musicland customers did not purchase more electronics. Anderson developed a new company strategy focusing on existing Best Buy customers and sold the money-losing Musicland group in 2003.[42]

Meanwhile, Anderson had become aware of research by Columbia Professor Larry Selden that showed that

> unprofitable customers can wreak havoc on a customer's bottom line and stock price. …The notion of analyzing customer profitability and adopting strategies to either shed ones deemed unprofitable or change pricing, services or policies to improve their economics has been around for awhile—though few companies have had the [courage] to actually execute such strategies. Those that have, generally are manufacturers or distributors, who in most cases can simply cut off unprofitable customers/channels if they want. It's quite another thing for a retailer to do so, given retail price transparency, generally homogeneous service policies, and open door access to all customers. … Despite resistance from his leadership team, CEO Anderson [had] forced through [the] changes that cater to the most profitable customers and discourage the devils.[43]

This had become known as the "angels-devils" strategy.[44] Perhaps it also has some reference to Anderson's seminary background.

In essence, Anderson's strategy is utilizing the customer lifetime value (CLV) metric for the purposes of navigating Best Buy's strategy. He is attempting to use a forward-looking metric for strategy purposes. Anderson referred to his initiative as "customer centricity."

> The idea…was to create new stores that reflected the shopping patterns of local communities. Customer centricity was described in *Forbes* as involving "a massive effort to identify and serve the company's most profitable shoppers by rebuilding stores, adding to staff, and upgrading wares." Best Buy management reviewed products "to see what sold and what didn't in order to adjust merchandise according to the income level and buying habits of shoppers at every location."[45]

> Best Buy estimates that as many as a fifth of 500 million customer visits each year are undesirable. And the CEO wants to be rid of them. He says the strategy is based on a theory that advocates rating customers according to profitability, then dumping the up to 20% who are unprofitable. The new approach upends standard practice among mass merchants, who typically seek to maximize customer traffic.[46]

"To deter the undesirables, it is cutting back on promotions and sales tactics that tend to draw them, and trimming them from marketing mailing lists."[47]

…Best Buy also started new restocking fees on returns, ended relationships with many shopping [the] Web, started selling returned merchandise only over the web, not in the same store where it was returned, policies all designed to thwart the devils.[48]

As part of its research, for example, Best Buy discovered that 55 percent of its customers were women, and that for the most part they loathed their shopping experience at the retailer. Men look for a specific product at a discount price. Women want not just a digital camera, but a printer, cable, and other accessories— and they care far more about these things than price. Equally important, they want help with installation, while most men prefer to try to put things together themselves. Accordingly, Best Buy adopted mostly common-sense solutions once it understood the issues involved. Related products were bundled together. In many stores, kids now have special play areas while their moms browse. To help with installation, the company acquired Geek Squad. Buy a flat screen TV and they'll have it running before your favorite show airs.[49]

Best Buy has applied the "customer centricity" theme to the point of even conceptualized store layouts and amenities along the lines of customer profiles. For example,

Jill stores feature personal shopping assistants (PSAs) who know how to steer a homemaker to the right digital camera for her family. Buzz stores have broad assortments of video games. Stores can target more than one segment…"Centrizing" a store is a big investment—a typical Barry department alone requires as much as $600,000 for lighting and fixtures. Best Buy also invests in schooling employees in financial metrics such as return on invested capital so that they can gauge for themselves the effectiveness of merchandising displays. (Recent example: Buzz departments have an area where kids can try out Dance Pads, a video game accessory you activate with your feet.) Specialized salespeople, such as PSAs and home-theater experts, get additional training that may last weeks.[50]

Initially, the stock market didn't react well to Best Buy's strategy, with a 12% plunge in its stock price. But once the strategy started to play out, its stock price quickly rebounded in 2006.[51] As of 2011,

As the world's leading consumer electronics specialty retailer, Best Buy would appear to be well positioned to capitalize on improving discretionary consumer spending patterns. However, …the fall of Circuit City and other industry participants has invited increased competition from mass merchants, warehouse clubs, and online retailers, changing the economics of the consumer electronics retail category in the process. Although Best Buy's customer-centric shopping environment and service offerings provide some differentiation, [the financial markets may not be]…convinced that the firm has enough of an economic moat to fend off its encroaching rivals over time.[52]

Its competitors today include Wal-Mart, Costco, Amazon.com, RadioShack, and HHGregg Incorporated.

Research the current Best Buy situation. Based upon the information provided in the case and what you find out from your research, what would you recommend Best Buy do? What would a CLV perspective suggest it do? How well do you think Best Buy will do in this market? Explain your rationale.

References

1. Zeithaml, Valarie A., Ruth N. Bolton, John Deighton, Timothy L. Keiningham, Katherine N. Lemon, and J. Andrew Petersen (2006), "Forward-Looking Focus: Can Firms Have Adaptive Foresight?," *Journal of Service Research*, 9 (2), 175.
2. Zeithaml, Valarie A., Ruth N. Bolton, John Deighton, Timothy L. Keiningham, Katherine N. Lemon, and J. Andrew Petersen (2006), "Forward-Looking Focus: Can Firms Have Adaptive Foresight?," *Journal of Service Research*, 9 (2), 170.
3. Zeithaml, Valarie A., Ruth N. Bolton, John Deighton, Timothy L. Keiningham, Katherine N. Lemon, and J. Andrew Petersen (2006), "Forward-Looking Focus: Can Firms Have Adaptive Foresight?," *Journal of Service Research*, 9 (2), 168–183.
4. Zeithaml, Valarie A., Ruth N. Bolton, John Deighton, Timothy L. Keiningham, Katherine N. Lemon, and J. Andrew Petersen (2006), "Forward-Looking Focus: Can Firms Have Adaptive Foresight?," *Journal of Service Research*, 9 (2), 170.
5. Ambler, Tim (2000), "Marketing Metrics," *Business Strategy Review*, 11 (2), 61.
6. Zeithaml, Valarie A., Ruth N. Bolton, John Deighton, Timothy L. Keiningham, Katherine N. Lemon, and J. Andrew Petersen (2006), "Forward-Looking Focus: Can Firms Have Adaptive Foresight?," *Journal of Service Research*, 9 (2), 170.
7. Zeithaml, Valarie A., Ruth N. Bolton, John Deighton, Timothy L. Keiningham, Katherine N. Lemon, and J. Andrew Petersen (2006), "Forward-Looking Focus: Can Firms Have Adaptive Foresight?," *Journal of Service Research*, 9 (2), 170.
8. Zeithaml, Valarie A., Ruth N. Bolton, John Deighton, Timothy L. Keiningham, Katherine N. Lemon, and J. Andrew Petersen (2006), "Forward-Looking Focus: Can Firms Have Adaptive Foresight?," *Journal of Service Research*, 9 (2), 168–183.
9. Petersen, J. Andrew, Leigh McAlister, David J. Reibstein, Russell S. Winer, V. Kumar, and Geoff Atkinson (2009), "Choosing the Right Metrics to Maximize Profitability and Shareholder Value," *Journal of Retailing*, 85 (1), 95–111.
10. Ambler, Tim, and John Roberts (2005), "Beware the Silver Metric: Marketing Performance Measurement Has to Be Multidimensional," Centre for Marketing Working Paper, No. 05-709.
11. Wangen, R. (2009), "Are Your Business Metrics a Rearview Mirror?," *Implement Improvement*, June 24, http://implementimprovement.com/?p=575
12. Kaplan, Robert S., and David P. Norton (1992), "The Balanced Scorecard—Measures That Drive Performance," *Harvard Business Review*, January–February, 71.
13. Kaplan, Robert S., and David P. Norton (2009), "Putting the Balanced Scorecard to Work," in the 10 Must From HBR Reads, *Harvard Business Review*, 56.
14. Kaplan, Robert S., and David P. Norton (2009), "Putting the Balanced Scorecard to Work," in the 10 Must From HBR Reads, *Harvard Business Review*, 56.
15. Kaplan, Robert S., and David P. Norton (1992), "The Balanced Scorecard—Measures That Drive Performance," *Harvard Business Review*, January–February, 79.
16. Kaplan, Robert S., and David P. Norton (1992), "The Balanced Scorecard—Measures That Drive Performance," *Harvard Business Review*, January–February, 71–79.
17. Kaplan, Robert S., and David P. Norton (2009), "Putting the Balanced Scorecard to Work," in the 10 Must From HBR Reads, *Harvard Business Review*, 54–67.

18. Fink, Alexander, and Bernard Marr (2005), "The Future Scorecard: Combining External and Internal Scenarios to Create Strategic Foresight," *Management Decision*, 43 (3), 360–381.

19. Fink, Alexander, and Bernard Marr (2005), "The Future Scorecard: Combining External and Internal Scenarios to Create Strategic Foresight," *Management Decision*, 43 (3), 379.

20. Zeithaml, Valarie A., Ruth N. Bolton, John Deighton, Timothy L. Keiningham, Katherine N. Lemon, and J. Andrew Petersen (2006), "Forward-Looking Focus: Can Firms Have Adaptive Foresight?," *Journal of Service Research*, 9 (2), 168–183.

21. Kumar, V., Katherine N. Lemon, and A. Parasuraman (2006), "Managing Customers for Value: An Overview and Research Agenda," *Journal of Service Research*, 9 (2), 88.

22. Petersen, J. Andrew, Leigh McAlister, David J. Reibstein, Russell S. Winer, V. Kumar, and Geoff Atkinson (2009), "Choosing the Right Metrics to Maximize Profitability and Shareholder Value," *Journal of Retailing*, 85 (1), 102.

23. Petersen, J. Andrew, Leigh McAlister, David J. Reibstein, Russell S. Winer, V. Kumar, and Geoff Atkinson (2009), "Choosing the Right Metrics to Maximize Profitability and Shareholder Value," *Journal of Retailing*, 85 (1), 104.

24. Petersen, J. Andrew, Leigh McAlister, David J. Reibstein, Russell S. Winer, V. Kumar, and Geoff Atkinson (2009), "Choosing the Right Metrics to Maximize Profitability and Shareholder Value," *Journal of Retailing*, 85 (1), 95–111.

25. Kumar, V., and Rajkumar Venkatesan (2005), "Who Are Multi-Channel Shoppers and How Do They Perform?: Correlates of Multichannel Shopping Behavior," *Journal of Interactive Marketing*, 19 (2), 44–62.

26. Peterson, J. Andrew, and V. Kumar (2009), "Are Product Returns a Necessary Evil? The Antecedents and Consequences of Product Returns," *Journal of Marketing*, 73 (3), 35–51.

27. Petersen, J. Andrew, Leigh McAlister, David J. Reibstein, Russell S. Winer, V. Kumar, and Geoff Atkinson (2009), "Choosing the Right Metrics to Maximize Profitability and Shareholder Value," *Journal of Retailing*, 85 (1), 104.

28. Petersen, J. Andrew, Leigh McAlister, David J. Reibstein, Russell S. Winer, V. Kumar, and Geoff Atkinson (2009), "Choosing the Right Metrics to Maximize Profitability and Shareholder Value," *Journal of Retailing*, 85 (1), 104.

29. Zeithaml, Valarie A., Ruth N. Bolton, John Deighton, Timothy L. Keiningham, Katherine N. Lemon, and J. Andrew Petersen (2006), "Forward-Looking Focus: Can Firms Have Adaptive Foresight?," *Journal of Service Research*, 9 (2), 168–183.

30. Petersen, J. Andrew, Leigh McAlister, David J. Reibstein, Russell S. Winer, V. Kumar, and Geoff Atkinson (2009), "Choosing the Right Metrics to Maximize Profitability and Shareholder Value," *Journal of Retailing*, 85 (1), 95–111.

31. Kumar, V., Katherine N. Lemon, and A. Parasuraman (2006), "Managing Customer for Value: An Overview and Research Agenda," *Journal of Service Research*, 9 (2), 87–94.

32. Kumar, V., Katherine N. Lemon, and A. Parasuraman (2006), "Managing Customer for Value: An Overview and Research Agenda," *Journal of Service Research*, 9 (2), 88.

33. Reinartz, Werner, Jacquelyn S. Thomas, and V. Kumar (2005), "Balancing Acquisition and Retention Resources to Maximize Customer Profitability," *Journal of Marketing*, 69 (1), 63–79.

34. Petersen, J. Andrew, Leigh McAlister, David J. Reibstein, Russell S. Winer, V. Kumar, and Geoff Atkinson (2009), "Choosing the Right Metrics to Maximize Profitability and Shareholder Value," *Journal of Retailing*, 85 (1), 101.

35. Best Buy, Wikipedia, http://en.wikipedia.org/wiki/Best_Buy

36. "Brad Anderson 1949–," Reference for Business, Encyclopedia of Business, 2nd ed., www.referenceforbusiness.com/biography/A-E/Anderson-Brad-1949.html

37. http://en.wikipedia.org/wiki/Best_Buy

38. Holm, Sheri Booms (2003), "Best Buy CEO Contemplates Faith and Leadership in the Workplace," *Story Magazine*, Luther Seminary, 4th Quarter, www.luthersem.edu/story/default.aspx?article_id=67&issue_id=10

39. "Brad Anderson 1949–," Reference for Business, Encyclopedia of Business, 2nd ed., www .referenceforbusiness.com/biography/A-E/Anderson-Brad-1949.html

40. "Brad Anderson 1949–," Reference for Business, Encyclopedia of Business, 2nd ed., www .referenceforbusiness.com/biography/A-E/Anderson-Brad-1949.html

41. "Brad Anderson (executive)," http://en.wikipedia.org/wiki/Brad_Anderson_%28executive%29

42. "Brad Anderson 1949–," Reference for Business, Encyclopedia of Business, 2nd ed., www .referenceforbusiness.com/biography/A-E/Anderson-Brad-1949.html

43. (2004) "Best Buy Uses New Customer Analysis and Segmentation Strategy," *News and Views*, November 18, www.scdigest.com/assets/NewsViews/04-11-18-1.cfm?cid=403&ctype=content

44. McWilliams, Gary (2005), "The Customer Isn't Always Right: Best Buy Wants to Keep the Wrong Kind of Shopper Out of Its Stores," *The Wall Street Journal*, January 2005, www.wsjclassroomedition .com/archive/05jan/bigb_bestbuy.htm

45. "Brad Anderson 1949–," Reference for Business, Encyclopedia of Business, 2nd ed., www .referenceforbusiness.com/biography/A-E/Anderson-Brad-1949.html

46. McWilliams, Gary (2005), "The Customer Isn't Always Right: Best Buy Wants to Keep the Wrong Kind of Shopper Out of Its Stores," *The Wall Street Journal*, January 2005, www.wsjclassroomedition .com/archive/05jan/bigb_bestbuy.htm

47. McWilliams, Gary (2005), "The Customer Isn't Always Right: Best Buy Wants to Keep the Wrong Kind of Shopper Out of Its Stores," *The Wall Street Journal*, January 2005, www.wsjclassroomedition .com/archive/05jan/bigb_bestbuy.htm

48. "Best Buy Uses New Customer Analysis and Segmentation Strategy," (2004), *News and Views*, November 18, www.scdigest.com/assets/NewsViews/04-11-18-1.cfm?cid=403&ctype=content

49. Gulati, Ranjay (2010), "Inside Best Buy's Customer-Centric Strategy," April 12th, HBR Faculty, *Harvard Business Review*, http://blogs.hbr.org/hbsfaculty/2010/04/inside-best-buys-customer-cent.html

50. McWilliams, Gary (2005), "The Customer Isn't Always Right: Best Buy Wants to Keep the Wrong Kind of Shopper Out of Its Stores," *The Wall Street Journal*, January 2005, www.wsjclassroom edition.com/archive/05jan/bigb_bestbuy.htm

51. Bolye, Matthew (2006), "Best Buy's Giant Gamble: Brad Anderson's Consumer Electronics Superstore Rules the Market. So Why Is He Messing With His Business Model?," March 29, *Fortune*, http://money.cnn.com/magazines/fortune/fortune_archive/2006/04/03/8373034/ index.htm

52. "Best Buy Co. Inc., BBY," (2011), Morningstar, February 11, http://quote.morningstar.com/ Stock/s.aspx?t=BBY&culture=en-US&region=USA&r=992394&byrefresh=yes

SECTION 4

A Thinking Organization

CHAPTER 13 Cultivating a Thinking Culture

Decompression Exercise

Take a moment to gaze into the candlelight.

Figure 13.1 The Intrigue of Fire

Chapter Introduction

Throughout the text, we have examined the thinking behind different marketing concepts, theories, and their associated strategies for the purpose of developing our thinking agility. At the same time, the focus of this development has been at the individual level through the Marketing Challenges and cases. Strategy benefits to the degree the marketer is able to continuously utilize and develop his or her 4-DS thinking capabilities. In addition, the environment can significantly influence the marketer's thinking. Typically, the marketer's focus is on the external environment in terms of the changes taking place in the marketplace. This is to be expected given the nature of marketing. However, the internal environment shouldn't be overlooked, as the workplace also has the potential to affect the marketer's thinking. Some environments are more conducive to a thinking environment than others are. As such, this chapter's focus is on examining the characteristics of workplace environments that value and promote thinking at the individual and organization levels.

Changes external to the marketer's organization are constantly occurring in terms of new technologies, Internet developments, increasing innovation rates, new competitors, and so on. To stay abreast of external changes, the organization has to internally adapt at least at an equal pace. The *"living organization"* metaphor has been used to characterize such necessary organizational changes and to study the factors that lead to organizational longevity.

> Many people naturally think and speak about a company as if they were speaking about an organic, living creature with a mind and character of its own. This common use of the language is not surprising. All companies exhibit the behavior and certain characteristics of living entities. All companies learn. All companies, whether explicitly or not, have an identity that determines their coherence. All companies build relationships with other entities, and all companies grow and develop until they die. To manage a "living company" is to manage with more or less consistent, more or less explicit appreciation for these facts of corporate life, instead of ignoring them.[1]

Since the late 1980s and early 1990s, studies have been conducted on *organizational learning* and the benefits from developing this capability. Such benefits for organizations include being able to develop a sustainable competitive advantage,[2] to create or charter their own future,[3] or to be able to adapt in changing environments.[4] At the same time, some have argued that the focus on learning may not be adequate under certain circumstances, for example, in turbulent environments that are characterized by rapid change, uncertainty, and complexity.[5,6,7,8]

It was recognized as early as the mid-1970s that *thinking* is required for situations that aren't characterized by the past, as in unexpected or novel situations.[9,10] Learning benefits from the experiences of the past. *Thinking* also utilizes the past with its *reflective* dimension and, to various degrees, the *critical* dimension, but *thinking is also about creating a future that may not resemble the past*. The *creative* and *time* dimensions of 4-DS thinking extend beyond a learning perspective.

In the following example, a thinking perspective is applied in a manufacturing context by using the brain as a metaphor to model flexible production systems.

> Manufacturing flexibility is critical for survival in industries characterized by rapid change and diverse product markets. Although new manufacturing technologies make it possible to accomplish flexibility, their potential remains unrealized by firms whose organizational elements do not possess adaptive capabilities. We use the brain as a metaphor to generate insights on how firms might design flexible production systems. We chose the brain as a metaphor because it is a self-organizing system capable of responding rapidly to a broad range of external stimuli.[11]

Beyond focusing on learning, organizations are starting to consider the broader, more encompassing thinking perspective and to conceptualize the organization not as a learning organization but as a *thinking organization*.[12, 13]

Additionally, it is recognized that learning is evidenced by some form of psychological, behavioral, and/or social change, and one source for these changes is thinking. *As such, thinking is a prerequisite for learning at either the individual or group level.* Whether the interest is in improving an organization's capability to learn and/or to be more proactive (through developing the creative and TIME dimensions of 4-DS thinking at the organizational level), the concept of a *thinking organization* encompasses both aspects. With a constantly changing marketplace, organizations need to be agile, that is, agile in their strategy. This agility stems from thinking agility within the organization.

The interest in developing thinking within organizations is highlighted in the following quote from the *New York Times*:

> Jump's work has elements of management consulting and a bit of design-firm draftsmanship, but its specialty is conceiving new businesses, and what it sells is really the art of innovation. The company is built on the premise that creative thinking is a kind of expertise. Like P&G and Mars, you can hire Jump on your behalf, for somewhere between $200,000 and $500,000 a month, depending on the complexity and ambiguity of the question you need answered. Or you can ask Jump to teach your corporation how to generate better ideas on its own; Jump imparts that expertise in one- and five-day how-to-brainstorm training sessions that can cost $200,000 for a one-day session for 25 employees.

This was a pretty exotic business model when Jump opened in 1998, but it isn't today. In the last decade, a quirky legion of idea peddlers has quietly invented what might be a new discipline and is certainly an expanding niche. How and why this happened is, naturally, a subject that everyone in the field theories about. What's clear is that in recent years, much of corporate America has gone meta—it has started thinking about thinking. And all that thinking has led many executives to the same conclusions: We need help thinking.[14]

In this chapter, we will broaden our thinking agility and 4-DS thinking to an organization level. There are several reasons for doing this. It should be recognized that there is a reciprocal relationship between thinking and one's environment(s), as depicted in Figure 13.2. Through thinking, the marketer can affect his or her environment and, at the same time, the environment has the potential to influence the marketer's thinking. Similarly, this relationship occurs between the marketer and his or her organization and, likewise, between the organization and its environment. If the organization's culture is conducive to thinking, that is, in terms of possessing a culture valuing, supporting, and facilitating thinking, then accordingly, the organization will potentially be more poised for an adaptive, agile, and proactive strategic posture with its environment.

To elevate our thinking agility to the organization level, we'll examine different types of organizational cultures, organizational barriers to forward- (future-) oriented thinking dimensions (*creative* and *time*), and the characteristics of a thinking culture that are

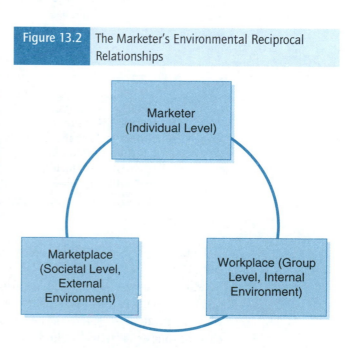

Figure 13.2   The Marketer's Environmental Reciprocal Relationships

Marketer (Individual Level)

Marketplace (Societal Level, External Environment)

Workplace (Group Level, Internal Environment)

conducive to opening up the doors to these dimensions of our 4-DS thinking while creating an environment that promotes thinking agility.

Organizational Cultures

Across the chapters, the traditional marketing perspectives have been contrasted with emerging contemporary ones. The traditional perspectives can be described as focusing on controlling and competing, whereas the contemporary perspectives focus on collaborating and creating. For example, as discussed in Chapter 4, Red Ocean strategies compete and control through exploitation. Blue Ocean strategies pertain to creating new markets. The persuasive forms of marketing involve competing, and the collaborative/participative forms of marketing (co-marketing) focus on co-creation. It can also be observed that such strategies or forms of marketing reflect their organization's culture. For example, if the culture of an organization revolves around an internal perspective of control, then it would value hierarchies, standardization, efficiencies, and structure. In contrast, if the culture of an organization were externally oriented to creating, then it would value creativity, innovation, differentiation, and be focused on the future.

This seems to suggest that an organization's culture has the effect of predetermining the direction and scope of your strategy. What do you think?

It could be described as a chicken-and-egg issue: What came first? But to your point, the effects that organizational culture have on the marketer's thinking are real and significant.

Figure 13.3 presents four types of organizational culture and their respective values.[15] The culture types are based upon bipolar, two-dimensional axes. The figure presents two basic questions that, when combined, describe an organization's culture. For example, is your organization internally or externally oriented? What level of stability versus flexibility does your organization strive for? The answers to these questions can be used to characterize the basis of your organization's culture.

Figure 13.3   Organizational Culture Types

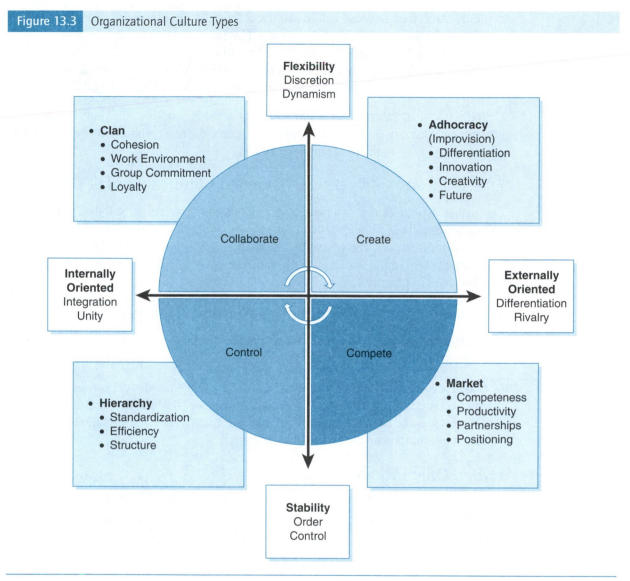

Source: [16]

Internally and Controlling-Oriented Cultures (Hierarchical Cultures)

Companies that have an internal orientation and seek a high level of stability in terms of order through standardization and structure (e.g., hierarchies) are grounded in an internal controlling culture (e.g., McDonald's, Ford). Fast-food organizations such as McDonald's utilize standardization to achieve efficiencies in their operations to be fast and consistent. Large manufacturers, because of their size, typically use structure as in hierarchies (layers of management) for control purposes while striving to capitalize on standardization and the learning curve.

Internally and Collaboratively Oriented Cultures (Clan Cultures)

Companies that are internally oriented, emphasizing cohesion, a good work environment, and employee loyalty, possess an internal collaborating culture (e.g., Tom's of Maine, In-N-Out Burger).

Unlike American national culture, which is founded upon individualism, Japanese firms had a more team-centered approach. This basic understanding affected the way that Japanese companies structured their companies and approached problems. Their Collaborate (clan) organizations operated more like families—hence the name—they valued cohesion, a humane working environment, group commitment, and loyalty.[17]

Companies that value employees by creating rewarding working environments strive for greater employee satisfaction, which they believe leads to greater productivity and customers satisfaction (e.g., as in the In-N-Out Burger case).

Externally and Competitively Oriented Cultures (Market Cultures)

Companies that are externally oriented and strive for higher levels of stability, productivity, partnerships, and positioning exemplify an external competing culture (e.g., General Electric, Citigroup, universities). The competing orientation tends to focus on taking away market share from others in the marketplace. It is an example of a *moving-against orientation* that was discussed in Chapter 4.

Externally and Creating-Oriented Cultures (Adhocracy Cultures)

Companies that are externally oriented and pursue differentiation in the marketplace through differentiation, innovation, and creativity typify an external creating culture (e.g., Google).

Google develops innovative web tools, taking advantage of entrepreneurial software engineers and cutting-edge processes and technologies. Their ability to quickly develop new services and capture market share has made them leaders in the marketplace and forced less nimble competition to play catch-up.[18]

Hybrid Orientations

While these four types of organizational cultures represent the extremes, hybrid cultures are possible as well. For example, a company that is pursuing collaboration (internally and externally) and differentiation in the marketplace represents a co-creation culture (e.g., Mini-Cooper, Adidas). Organizations that pursue internal and external (e.g., open-source innovation, alliances, etc.) sources for innovations while embracing brand communities typify co-creation cultures (e.g., Apple) and can be characterized as possessing a *moving-with orientation* as discussed in Chapter 4.

Significance of Organizational Culture

Each of the cultures described can serve different organizational situations and, hence, one isn't seen as being necessarily preferable to the others. They are simply different strategic elements to consider. At the same time, it is suggested that the organization's culture can have a significant influence on the marketer's thinking in terms of what strategies would fit in or be acceptable within the culture. In this context, organizational culture has a channeling affect, which may also lead to groupthink and, as such, is seen as a thinking obstacle at the individual and organizational levels. The more entrenched the cultural values, the more they increase the level of difficulty in avoiding or working through this thinking obstacle at the expense of strategy.

Before we move on to discuss potential barriers to organizational thinking, try the following organizational culture and strategy Marketing Thinking Challenge.

Marketing Thinking Challenge 13.1: Organizational Culture and Strategy

Identify companies that exemplify the four different organization cultures represented in Figure 13.2 and any hybrids. From what you can identify, do their marketing strategies reflect their organization cultures? What observations can you make from what you have found?

| Figure 13.4 | Different Cultures, Different Strategies |

Barriers to Organizational Thinking

By examining what impedes creative thinking, we can identify organizational barriers that can potentially extend into all of the 4-DS of thinking. Since creative thinking involves a forward form of differentiation, it represents a departure from current forms of thinking within the organization. As such, it can be viewed by those that have established their positions within the organization along current forms of thinking as being threatening in one form or another. At the same time, some have even referred to creative thinking as the "game changer."[19]

> Creativity is the driver of global competitive advantage. What sets companies apart from the crowd isn't just that they're playing the game well; they're redefining what it means to play the game.[20]

While the strategic importance of creativity is becoming more recognized, there continues to be resistance to investing in organizational creativity. Reasons include that creativity is messy, inefficient and imprecise. There is no formula that guarantees the successful generation, let alone implementation of a creative idea. Creativity involves false starts, misfires and failures. Consequently, predicting how much time or money the development and execution of a creative idea requires is difficult. As a result many companies invest in creativity only when they have slack resources.[21]

This suggests that those adhering to this perspective see creativity as a luxury and not as a necessity. Yet the future of an organization lies within the realm of creative thinking. To not invest in an organization's creative capacity is to confine the organization to the past. And, as we have seen, an organization's culture is based upon what it values. To develop a "thinking organization" requires *a culture for thinking* in which creativity is a part.

As we have already discussed, creativity is about creating something different, something new. The process isn't linear or straight forward. It can be messy and time consuming. And there aren't any guarantees as to what the process will produce and whether what comes from the process will be successful. At the same time, the process involves people—not only those engaging in creativity but also those that will be affected by the potential change(s) represented by the new ideas. Figure 13.5 brings into focus some of the issues that would need to be dealt with to move toward a thinking culture and make room for *creative thinking*.

Figure 13.5	Organizational Barriers to Creative Thinking

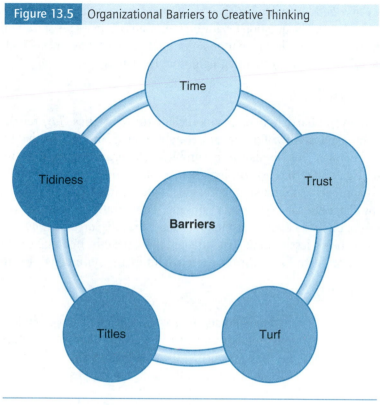

Sources: [22]

Allocating Time

To make room for creativity, it has to be valued, and as such, time needs to be allocated for it. Marketing as an occupation is a very demanding profession, with the pressures of daily activities including meetings, monitoring changes, and dealing with issues as they arise. *Thinking organizations* value thinking and provide for it (e.g., time, resources) as with any other activity that is valued by and needed for the organization to be successful. Perhaps a hallmark of a thinking organization is the degree to which time and resources are allocated toward creative thinking.

Establishing Trust

With the uncertainty associated with *creativity*, it is necessary to allocate not only time but also a nourishing and supportive environment. From the employee's perspective, such environments translate into an element of trust. For *creative thinking* to have an opportunity to breathe and take hold within the organization, there has to be an element of trust. Yet trust isn't sufficient for *creativity* to flourish. *Creative thinking* can easily be squelched by organizational norms and practices. Hence, the fragility of creativity needs to be recognized and protected before trust can be established. Trust is just the beginning.

At the same time, the organization needs to bring to the foreground the issue of its predisposition toward answers instead of questions. A culture built on valuing answers will have the tendency to blame those that make mistakes and come up short. In contrast, a culture that is built upon valuing questioning views mistakes and failures as opportunities to pursue different lines of questioning that have the potential to lead to new paths of success.

Fundamental to a thinking organization is the element of trust that supports a questioning, inquiring environment. The question for any organization is, Can we resist the temptation for the quick answer(s) while allowing our organization to explore new, unexplored conceptual frontiers that might not lead to anything significant right away?

The Issue of Turf

Two equally powerful barriers to creativity include turf and titles. *Turf* refers to an individual's area of responsibility. It is similar to establishing a familiar box that the marketer sees as his or her own. This has also been a problem with organizations that are structured functionally (e.g., marketing, accounting, finance, etc.) versus being organized via some flexible team approach. As discussed in Chapter 10, functional structural designs, organizational or by channels, can lead to "silo thinking." Organization structures and, similarly, turfs impede creativity by being resistant to change. *Thinking organizations* attempt to be more organic by being less rigid in structure and more flexible. In doing so, they have the tendency to reduce the turf issue, as the responsibilities are continuously being redefined.

The Issue of Titles

Titles play out in a similar manner if status and recognition are tied to one's title.[23] *Thinking organizations* instead focus on promoting a nourishing and supportive environment by recognizing people for their ideas and supporting them while they are working on their ideas. Ideas are to be valued over titles and, as such, titles lose their purposes.

Tidiness Is a Problem

Then there is the messiness of creativity. Tidiness isn't a virtue of creativity, given its unconstrained nature. Thinking organizations loosen the reins to the unstructured process of creativity. Another way of thinking about the issues of tidiness and how it relates to thinking is to compare the differences between conventional and integrated thinking. Creativity isn't described as *conventional thinking* in terms of being linear or involving either-or choices, which tends to be more associated with critical and/or reflective thinking. *Integrated thinking* benefits from creativity by being multidimensional and nonlinear to be able to generate new choices. This more complex or abstract thinking isn't as straightforward as conventional thinking and can be described as being more messy. Yet it is through this messy process that new forms of thinking or ideas can flow. The differences between the two forms of thinking are presented in Figure 13.6.[24]

Additionally, as discussed in Chapter 1, contributing to the success of thinkers like Steve Jobs of Apple, Jeff Bezos of Amazon, and others was a questioning nature that constantly sought new associations that hadn't yet been formed.

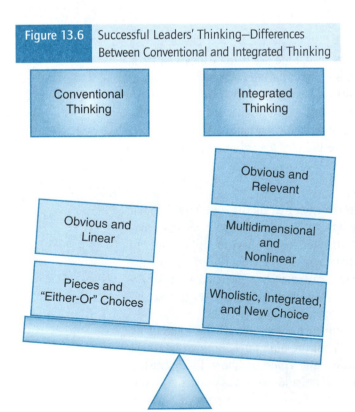

Figure 13.6 Successful Leaders' Thinking—Differences Between Conventional and Integrated Thinking

Conventional Thinking

Integrated Thinking

Obvious and Relevant

Obvious and Linear

Multidimensional and Nonlinear

Pieces and "Either-Or" Choices

Wholistic, Integrated, and New Choice

Their "innovator's DNA" involved the inclination to seek new associations, which is also a characteristic of integrated thinking and its element of creativity.

With these organizational barriers (time, trust, turf, title, and tidiness) in mind, we'll turn our attention to examining the characteristics that promote thinking within an organization.

Marketing Thinking Challenge 13.2: Barriers to a Thinking Organization

Identify an organization that you believe has its potential limited by its culture's barriers to thinking. What thinking barriers were you able to identify? What recommendations would you make to improve the situation?

Figure 13.7   Organizational Barriers to Thinking

Marketing Thinking in Practice: Creativity Is the New Style in Leadership!

Blogger Connie Harryman comments on why creativity is becoming increasingly important and how creative leadership can lead to greater organizational creativity.[25] Creative leadership is characterized by being forward looking, experimenting, and co-creating.

> Competency in creative leadership leads the list for standout CEOs according to the IBM 2010 Global CEO Study. The survey included over 1,500 Chief Executive Officers from 60 countries and 33 industries.
>
> Creativity is more important than rigor, management discipline, integrity or vision. Creativity is identified as the leading competency. Our world is becoming incredibly complex and dealing with ambiguity in this complex world requires creativity.
>
> I listened to a webinar sponsored by *Harvard Business Review*. IBM's Saul Berman and Peter J. Korsten shared some insights on standout companies in today's ambiguous environment.

(Continued)

(Continued)

> As we come out of the worst recession in 50 years, the new economic environment is viewed as structurally different, with more complexity, more uncertainty, and more volatility. However, standout companies (the top 25%) are turning complexity to their advantage with creative leadership.
>
> There are three different ways that standout companies achieve success and capitalize on complexity. They embody creative leadership, they reinvent customer relationships, and they build operating dexterity.
>
> A speedy decision is valued over a correct decision. There is a philosophy of correcting things as they move forward.
>
> Creativity is the leading indicator of leadership quality. Creative leadership drives the change needed in the organization to stay ahead of the market. Creative leaders use different communication styles and tools.
>
> They are more open to experimentation with Twitter, Facebook, LinkedIn and other social media. Standout companies break with the status quo of industry, enterprise, and revenue models.
>
> Chief executives believe that to navigate an increasingly complex world will require creativity. They will co-create with their clients. They will globalize what is possible due to standardization and localize what is necessary and whatever needs local tuning. Think "glocal."
>
> When creativity is implemented within an organization, then it is better prepared to deal with some of the massive shifts taking place, such as new government regulations, changes in global economic power centers, accelerated industry transformation, growing volumes of data, and rapidly evolving customer preferences.
>
> Clearly creativity is the new leadership differentiator for standout companies. You must ask yourself, what tools are you providing to your organization to unleash the creativity of your employees?

Characteristics of Thinking Organizations

A thinking organization is built upon a paradoxical relationship between the individual and the group. This can be attributed to the reciprocal relationship involving the individual and her or his environment, as previously discussed. What this means is thinking at the individual and organization (group) levels are codependent upon on this relationship. A thinking organization is built upon the thinking of the individual, yet the individual's thinking is influenced by the degree of explicit thinking occurring throughout the organization by others. In others words, you can't have a thinking organization without the thinking of the individual (the employee) and the individual's thinking is influenced or dependent upon the organization's thinking culture (other employees). This suggests that consideration has to be given to both the individual and the group to strike the right mix to achieve thinking throughout.

The Question of Control and Thinking

We'll discuss a number of elements that relate to the individual and the group. Fundamental to this is an understanding that control, that is, management control needs to be rethought in terms of its effects and subsequent consequences on thinking within the organization. Thinking, especially creative thinking, doesn't flourish under constraints. *This means thinking and control are at odds with each other.* Managing thinking is an oxymoron. Therefore,

> Perhaps, instead of thinking in terms of managing thinking by attempting to control it, it would be better from a thinking organization's perspective to think in terms of managing for thinking.[26]

Elements of a Thinking Organization

Roughly four groups of elements are associated with thinking organizations: *play*, collaborating (internally and externally), *questioning*, and supportive open environments. These elements can also be the basis for promoting thinking agility within the organization. See Figure 13.8 (on page 313). The classification is not meant to be an exhaustive list but is simply intended to be suggestive.

Play: We'll start with the element of *play*, which represents a significant element to a thinking organization. *Play* seems counterintuitive to a business environment, but it is vital to creativity and *thinking in time*. Within the element of *play*, the possibilities for new associations appear and can be toyed with through experimentation, which can potentially lead to other forms of associations. This process is important to an organization for identifying future innovations. *Play* also brings in the element of fun that promotes the intrinsic motivation of the individual.

In time and through incubation, the ideas and the thinking can develop into even farther-reaching advances. *Play* represents a major resource for the advancement of an organization that shouldn't be overlooked. Organizations like Apple, Google, advertising agencies, and many other organizations have capitalized on this element, which is evidenced through their continuing launch of new innovations.

Questioning: Questioning is another vital element to any thinking organization. It represents the hallmark of a thinking organization in that we have defined *thinking as questioning*. Questioning, in essence, represents that step away from the *status quo* toward something new and different. It is through questioning that differences are created, and questioning is the way in which difference plays out within an organization and throughout the marketplace.

As we discussed in Chapter 5, difference repeats, and the repetition is occurring through questioning. If the organization wishes to actively participate in the difference-creation process, then the organization must develop its questioning capabilities and a culture for questioning (thinking). Without this vital questioning capability, the organization is to be destined to the past and potentially disadvantaged from others that take a *more active strategic questioning status*.

Supportive and Open Environments: In discussing the trust barrier to a thinking organization, norms and practices should be examined in terms of their effects on thinking.

As previously mentioned, it's important to take steps toward protecting the fragility of creativity. Supportive and open environments are conducive for creative organizational environments. Leadership in terms of modeling thinking can be used to initiate the type of thinking environment desired and to develop an appreciation for differing perspectives. The organization needs to establish as one of its central values the valuing of differing perspectives and to avoid the opposite, as in the groupthink phenomenon.[27] *Making thinking explicit within an organization is vital.*

For example, "Bring in expert thinkers (consultants) into an organization, display quotations, cartoons, (such as Dilbert), puzzles and inspirational tools in the halls and waiting rooms to help explicit thinking."[28] More and more consulting firms specializing in organizational thinking, such as Jump, are available that can be used to help in the process. As a part of the thinking leadership, it is important for management to carry through their support and keep the environment open when failures occur.

Consistent with this view, failures are recognized not as some end but simply steps within an ongoing inquiring process. Some insights can only come from failures and, hence, the value of failures needs to be recognized and understood throughout the organization. The advances in thinking being made should also be recognized throughout the organization. Accomplishments need to be recognized.

Collaboration: Collaboration in the forms of networking and teaming is also integral to a thinking organization.[29] Networking through open-source innovation and external partnerships provides for a means of drawing on the expertise of others outside of the organization. It is a means to expanding the borders of an organization outward. Companies like Unilever, Apple, Google, and others utilize open-source innovation as a means for expanding their organizational thinking capabilities externally.

Teaming is another form of collaboration (an internal form) and can be used to work around functional organizational structures. Teaming individuals with different areas of expertise to work together can be a catalyst for an environment that leads to synergies in thinking in which the combined ideas (thinking) are greater (e.g., in terms of uniqueness, scope, and/or depth) than the individuals' ideas considered separately.

The elements of a thinking organization (*play*, *questioning*, collaborating, and a supportive open environment) work together, promoting thinking at the individual level, which aggregates to the organizational level and reciprocally promotes greater thinking at the individual level and vice versa. It becomes a reciprocating thinking engine fueling both the individual's and the group's (organization's) thinking.

Try the following thinking organization Marketing Thinking Challenge 13.3. There are two additional challenges, 13.3 and 13.4, that you can use to see how your marketing thinking has developed over the course of the chapters. Challenge 13.4 puts you in the role of writing a Marketing Thinking Challenge. It is a challenge on thinking about thinking. Challenge 13.5 asks you to generate 10 additional interesting marketing questions. This challenge is meant to be used in conjunction with Challenge 1.1, which also asked for 10 interesting questions. After completing Challenge 13.5, compare your two lists of questions. Do you see any differences? Has your marketing thinking changed? How?

| Figure 13.8 | Elements of a Thinking Organization Culture |

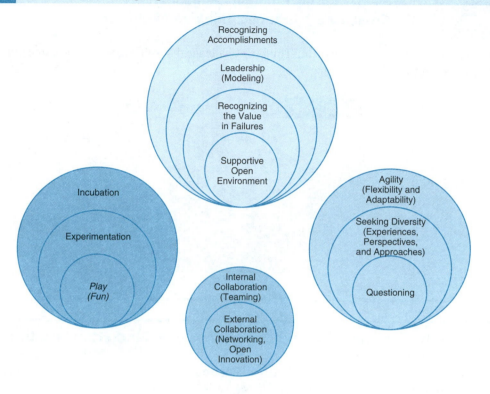

Recognizing Accomplishments
Leadership (Modeling)
Recognizing the Value in Failures
Supportive Open Environment

Incubation
Experimentation
Play (Fun)

Agility (Flexibility and Adaptability)
Seeking Diversity (Experiences, Perspectives, and Approaches)
Questioning

Internal Collaboration (Teaming)
External Collaboration (Networking, Open Innovation)

Marketing Thinking Challenge 13.3: Identifying Thinking Organizations

Identify several organizations that you believe would qualify as thinking organizations and explain how they are using these characteristics as a part of their strategies.

| Figure 13.9 | A Thinking Organization |

Marketing Thinking Challenge 13.4: Creating a Marketing Thinking Challenge

It's your turn to create an interesting Marketing Thinking Challenge that you believe will promote thinking. Create an interesting Marketing Thinking Challenge.

Figure 13.10 Creating a Thinking Challenge

Marketing Thinking Challenge 13.5: Interesting Marketing Questions

Reflecting over the chapters, generate 10 interesting marketing questions that would be useful to a marketer. Then compare these questions to the ones you generated in Marketing Thinking Challenge 1.1. What insights can you see between the two lists of questions?

Figure 13.11 Question Marks

Your list of 10 interesting marketing questions:

1. _____

2. _____

3. _____

4. _____

5. _____

6. _____

7. _____

8. _____

9. _____

10. _____

Summary

- In this chapter, we examined the relationship between thinking at the individual and organizational levels. This relationship was described as reciprocal in that each had the potential to affect the other.
- A thinking organization was distinguished from a learning organization by being able to deal with situations that aren't characterized by the past. Organizations' cultures were found to have the potential to influence the marketer's thinking, affecting (e.g., channeling) the nature of their strategies.
- Four main cultures were identified: controlling, competing, collaborating, and creating. Hybrids are also possible.
- Barriers to organizational thinking were identified in the form of time, trust, turf, title, and tidiness. To be able to develop a thinking organization, these barriers need to be recognized and resolved.
- At the same time, the following elements were found to promote a thinking organization: *play*, *questioning*, *collaboration*, and a *supportive open environment*. To the degree to which one is able to develop a thinking organization, strategy ultimately benefits.

Case: Google, Inc.—Seeking the Fun in Innovation

Google Inc. prides itself on nurturing a special type of work environment—a culture that breeds innovation and one that is meant to be fun. To a Googler, work isn't to be interpreted as some hardship but, instead, as something one would want to do—similar to having a particular interest such as a hobby and looking forward to being able to pursue it and explore all its aspects. As a result, Google has been ranked among the top five companies to work for by *Fortune Magazine* for the last five consecutive years since 2007.[30, 31, 32, 33, 34] In 2010, *Universum* conducted its first global employer attractiveness survey. "From the world's leading economies, nearly 130,000 students at top academic institutions chose their ideal companies to work for."[35] Google was ranked number one. What is Google doing to make it such an attractive place to work?

Google's website provides a list for the *Top 10 Reasons to Work at Google* (presented below):[36]

1. **Lend a helping hand.** With millions of visitors every month, Google has become an essential part of everyday life—like a good friend—connecting people with the information they need to live great lives.

2. **Life is beautiful.** Being a part of something that matters and working on products in which you can believe is remarkably fulfilling.

3. **Appreciation is the best motivation**, so we've created a fun and inspiring workspace you'll be glad to be a part of, including an on-site doctor; massage and yoga; professional development opportunities; shoreline running trails; and plenty of snacks to get you through the day.

4. **Work and play are not mutually exclusive.** It is possible to code and pass the puck at the same time.

5. **We love our employees, and we want them to know it.** Google offers a variety of benefits, including a choice of medical programs, company-matched 401(k), stock options, maternity and paternity leave, and much more.

6. **Innovation is our bloodline.** Even the best technology can be improved. We see endless opportunity to create even more relevant, more useful, and faster products for our users. Google is the technology leader in organizing the world's information.

7. **Good company everywhere you look.** Googlers range from former neurosurgeons, CEOs, and U. S. puzzle champions to alligator wrestlers and Marines. No matter what their backgrounds, Googlers make for interesting cube mates.

8. **Uniting the world, one user at a time.** People in every country and every language use our products. As such we think, act, and work globally—just our little contribution to making the world a better place.

9. **Boldly go where no one has gone before.** There are hundreds of challenges yet to solve. Your creative ideas matter here and are worth exploring. You'll have the opportunity to develop innovative new products that millions of people will find useful.

10. **There is such a thing as a free lunch after all.** In fact we have them every day: healthy, yummy, and made with love.

The list provides insight into the types of people they are looking for. Their ideal candidate is someone they would describe as being "Googley."

It's an ill-defined term—we intentionally don't define that term, but it's…not someone too traditional or stuck in ways done traditionally by other companies, …Each prospective hire is interviewed by at least five staff members, who ask a series of questions intended to make them understand how the candidate thinks about solving a problem. Getting the right answer is not necessary.[37]

The list also suggests an understanding of the nature from which innovation comes— that is, from people and the environments they interact within. These are two critical elements to the Google pursuit.

Accordingly, having the right people isn't sufficient; Google's recipe also involves creating an environment that stimulates thinking and the sharing of ideas.

Google maintains a casual and democratic atmosphere, resulting in its distinction as a "Flat" company. The company does not boast a large middle management, and upper management is so hands on, it's hard to qualify them in a separate category. Teams are made up of members with equal authority and a certain level of autonomy is maintained. "We're a highly collaborative culture," said Karen Godwin, the office's online sales and operations manager and a former Kodak executive. "There's no top-down hierarchy."

This techno-democracy takes a good deal of effort to maintain. In order to secure it, a sort of bread and circuses environment is created. Google boasts some unique cultural aspects:

- Local touches like ski gondolas in Zurich, expressing each office's unique location and personality.
- Dogs, lava lamps, and massage chairs.
- Double rooms (few single offices!) with three or four team members.
- Foozball, darts, assorted video games, pianos, ping pong tables, lap pools, gyms that include yoga and dance classes.
- Social groups of all kinds, such as meditation classes, film clubs, wine tasting groups, and salsa dance clubs.
- Health food at a wide variety of cafés, and outdoor seating for sunshine brainstorming.
- Snacks and drinks to keep Googlers going throughout the day.[38]

All aspects of the Google work environment represent opportunities to promote thinking. For example,

Every bathroom stall on the company campus holds a Japanese high-tech commode with a heated seat. If a flush is not enough, a wireless button on the door activates a bidet and drying.

Yet even while they are being pampered with high-tech toiletry, Google employees are encouraged to make good use of their downtime: A flier tacked inside each stall bears the title, "Testing on the Toilet, Testing code that uses databases." It features a geek quiz that changes every few weeks and asks technical questions about testing programming code for bugs.

The toilets reflect Google's general philosophy of work: Generous, quirky perks keep employees happy and thinking in unconventional ways, helping Google innovate as it rapidly expands into new lines of business.[39]

At Google, innovation is an ongoing process. As such, success and failures go hand-in-hand. Google has an interesting take on the role failures play in the innovation process.

"If you're not failing enough, you're not trying hard enough," said Richard Holden, product management director for Google's AdWords service, in which advertisers bid to place text ads next to search results. "The stigma [for failure] is less because we staff projects leanly and encourage them to just move, move, move. If it doesn't work, move on."[40]

The Google culture values collaboration internally and externally. They have constructed a corporate culture that deeply believes in delegation. Individual employees are encouraged to speak their mind from the first day, and even decisions classically reserved for management, such as hiring, are done through a collaborative process. ... The result of their efforts is perhaps the best example of a Loose-Tight company; one where the core employees have autonomy, but under the regime of a single unifying philosophy. ... Google is, and will likely remain, one of the most dynamic and competitive firms in the world today. Its willingness to learn from its experiments and learn from its mistakes compliment perfectly its internal collaborative structure.[41] Google also pursues external collaboration by supporting the open-source developer community.[42] For example, Google launched its Summer of Code mentoring program in 2005. It's a program for students 18 and older to get involved in free and open-source software while "providing a sustainable stream of new contributions to the open source community."[43]

Levity is also important component to the Google culture. Examples include:

> ...creating April Fools' Day jokes. For example, Google MentalPlex allegedly featured the use of mental power to search the web. In 2007, Google announced a free Internet service called TiSP, or Toilet Internet Service Provider, where one obtained a connection by flushing one end of a fiber-optic cable down their toilet. Also in 2007, Google's Gmail page displayed an announcement for Gmail Paper, allowing users to have email messages printed and shipped to them. In 2010, Google jokingly changed its company name to Topeka in honor of Topeka, Kansas, whose mayor actually changed the city's name to Google for a short amount of time in an attempt to sway Google's decision in its new Google Fiber Project.

> In addition to April Fools' Day jokes, Google's services contain a number of Easter eggs. For instance, Google included the Swedish Chef's "Bork bork bork," Pig Latin, "Hacker" or leetspeak, Elmer Fudd, and Klingon as language selections for its search engine. In addition, the search engine calculator provides the Answer to the Ultimate Question of Life, the Universe, and Everything from Douglas Adams' *The Hitchhiker's Guide to the Galaxy.* Furthermore, when searching the word "recursion," the spell-checker's result for the properly spelled word is exactly the same word, creating a recursive link. Likewise, when searching for the word "anagram," meaning a rearrangement of letters from one word to form other valid words, Google's suggestion feature displays "Did you mean: nag a ram?" In Google Maps, searching for directions between places separated by large bodies of water, such as Los Angeles and Tokyo, results in instructions to "kayak across the Pacific Ocean." During FIFA World Cup 2010, search queries like "World Cup," "FIFA," etc. will cause the "Goooo...gle" page indicator at the bottom of every result page to read "Goooo...al!" instead.[44]

From what is described above and from what you can find out about Google, would you characterize Google as a thinking organization? If so, what are its thinking characteristics? If it is not a thinking organization, what would be needed to elevate it to a thinking organization? What suggestions would you offer to Google to create an even better environment for thinking? Explain the role Google's culture plays in its strategy.

References

1. De Geus, Arie (1997), *The Living Company*, Boston, MA: Harvard Business Press, 9.
2. Stata, Ray (1989), "Organizational Learning—The Key to Management Innovation," *Sloan Management Review*, 30 (3), 63–74.

3. Senge, Peter M. (1994), *The Fifth Discipline: The Art and Practice of the Learning Organization*, New York: Doubleday Business Press.

4. Dodgson, Mark (1993), "Organizational Learning: A Review of Some Literatures," *Organization Studies*, 14 (3), 375–394.

5. Weick, Karl E. (1991), "The Nontraditional Quality of Organizational Learning," *Organization Science*, 2 (1), 116–124.

6. McMaster, Michael (1996), *The Intelligence Advantage: Organization for Complexity*, Newton, MA: Butterworth-Heinemann.

7. Sorrento, Mark, and Mary Crossan (1997), "Making Sense of Improvisation: Spontaneous Action, Strategy, and Management Behaviour," Working Paper, University of Western Ontario, No.95-11.

8. Moorman, Christine, and Anne S. Miner (1998), "The Convergence of Planning and Execution: Improvisation in the New Product Development," *Journal of Marketing*, 62 (3), 1–20.

9. Langer, E. J. (1978), "Rethinking the Role of Thought in Social Interactions," in *New Directions in Attribution Research*, 2, ed. J. Harvey, W. Ickes, and R. Kidd, Hillsdale, NJ: Lawrence Erlbaum Associates, 35–58.

10. Abelson, R. P. (1976), "Script Processing in Attitude Formation and Decision Making," in *Cognition and Social Behavior*, ed. J. Carroll and J. Payne, Hillsdale, NJ: Lawrence Erlbaum Associates, 33–46.

11. Garud, Raghu, and Suresh Kotha (1994), "Using the Brain as a Metaphor to Model Flexible Production Systems," *Academy of Management Review*, 19 (4), 671.

12. Akgun, Ali E., and Gary S. Lynn, "Thinking Organization," Working Paper, Stevens Institute of Technology, www.iamot.org/paperarchive/155C. PDF

13. Hunt, Rikki, and Tony Buzan (1999), *Creating a Thinking Organization: Ground Rules for Success*, Surrey, UK: Gower Publishing Company.

14. Segal, David (2010), "In Pursuit of the Perfect Brainstorm," *New York Times*, December 16, www .nytimes.com/2010/12/19/magazine/19Industry-t.html

15. Tharp, Bruce M. (2009), "Four Organizational Culture Types," White Paper, *Haworth – Organizational Culture*, April, www.haworth.com/en-us/Knowledge/Workplace-Library/ Documents/Four-Organizational-Culture-Types_6.pdf, 1–6.

16. Tharp, Bruce M. (2009), "Four Organizational Culture Types," White Paper, *Haworth – Organizational Culture*, April, www.haworth.com/en-us/Knowledge/Workplace-Library/ Documents/Four-Organizational-Culture-Types_6.pdf, 1–6.

17. Tharp, Bruce M. (2009), "Four Organizational Culture Types," White Paper, *Haworth – Organizational Culture*, April, www.haworth.com/en-us/Knowledge/Workplace-Library/ Documents/Four-Organizational-Culture-Types_6.pdf, 4.

18. Tharp, Bruce M. (2009), "Four Organizational Culture Types," White Paper, *Haworth – Organizational Culture*, April, www.haworth.com/en-us/Knowledge/Workplace-Library/ Documents/Four-Organizational-Culture-Types_6.pdf, 4.

19. "Creative Thinking: The Game Changer" (2010–2011), in *OlinBusinessMagazine*, Washington University in St. Lois, Olin Business School, www.olin.wustl.edu/docs/Communication/ OlinBusinessMagazine_2010-11.pdf, 11–15.

20. "Creative Thinking: The Game Changer" (2010–2011), in *OlinBusinessMagazine*, Washington University in St. Lois, Olin Business School, www.olin.wustl.edu/docs/Communication/ OlinBusinessMagazine_2010-11.pdf, 11.

21. "Creative Thinking: The Game Changer" (2010–2011), in *OlinBusinessMagazine*, Washington University in St. Lois, Olin Business School, www.olin.wustl.edu/docs/Communication/ OlinBusinessMagazine_2010-11.pdf, 12.

22. "Creative Thinking: The Game Changer" (2010–2011), in *OlinBusinessMagazine*, Washington University in St. Lois, Olin Business School, www.olin.wustl.edu/docs/Communication/ OlinBusinessMagazine_2010-11.pdf, 14.

23. "Creative Thinking: The Game Changer" (2010–2011), in *OlinBusiness Magazine*, Washington University in St. Lois, Olin Business School, www.olin.wustl.edu/docs/Communication/ OlinBusinessMagazine_2010-11.pdf, 14.

24. Martin, Roger (2007), "How Successful Leaders Think," *Harvard Business Review*, June, 60–76.

25. Harryman, Connie (2010), "Creativity Is the New Style of Leadership!," June 16, www .developyourcreativethinking.com/index.php/2010/06/16/creativity-is-the-new-style-of-leadership/

26. Akgun, Ali E., and Gary S. Lynn, "Thinking Organization," Working Paper, Stevens Institute of Technology, www.google.com/search?q=%22thinking+organization%22&ie=utf-8&oe=utf-8&aq=t&rls=org.mozilla:en-US:official&client=firefox-a

27. McFadzean, Elspeth (1998), "Enhancing Creative Thinking Within Organizations," *Management Decision*, 36 (5), 309–315.

28. Akgun, Ali E., and Gary S. Lynn, "Thinking Organization," Working Paper, Stevens Institute of Technology, www.google.com/search?q=%22thinking+organization%22&ie=utf-8&oe=utf-8&aq=t&rls=org.mozilla:en-US:official&client=firefox-a

29. "Creative Thinking: The Game Changer" (2010–2011), in *OlinBusinessMagazine*, Washington University in St. Lois, Olin Business School, www.olin.wustl.edu/docs/Communication/OlinBusinessMagazine_2010-11.pdf, 13.

30. Levering, Robert, and Milton Moskowitz (2007), "In Good Company: The Full List of *Fortune*'s 100 Best Companies to Work for 2007," *Fortune Magazine*, January 29, http://money.cnn.com/magazines/fortune/fortune_archive/2007/01/22/8398125/index.htm

31. Levering, Robert, and Milton Moskowitz (2008), "100 Best Companies to Work for 2008," *Fortune Magazine*, February 4, http://money.cnn.com/magazines/fortune/bestcompanies/2008/index .html

32. Levering, Robert, and Milton Moskowitz (2009), "100 Best Companies to Work for 2009," *Fortune Magazine*, February 2, http://money.cnn.com/magazines/fortune/bestcompanies/2009/index .html

33. Levering, Robert, and Milton Moskowitz (2010), "100 Best Companies to Work for 2010," *Fortune Magazine*, February 8, http://money.cnn.com/magazines/fortune/bestcompanies/2010/index .html

34. Levering, Robert, and Milton Moskowitz (2011), "100 Best Companies to Work for 2011," *Fortune Magazine*, February 7, http://money.cnn.com/magazines/fortune/bestcompanies/2011/index .html

35. "The World's Most Attractive Employers 2010," *Universum*, www.universumglobal.com/IDEAL-Employer-Rankings/Global-Top-50

36. "Top 10 Reasons to Work at Google," www.google.com/intl/en/jobs/lifeatgoogle/toptenreasons/index.html

37. Goo, Sara Kehaulani (2006), "Building a 'Googley' Workforce," *Washington Post*, October 21, www .washingtonpost.com/wp-dyn/content/article/2006/10/20/AR2006102001461.html

38. Johansson, Greg (2010), "The World's Most Successful Corporate Culture," May 29, *suite101*, www .suite101.com/content/google-the-worlds-most-successful-corporate-culture-a242303

39. Goo, Sara Kehaulani (2006), "Building a 'Googley' Workforce," *Washington Post*, October 21, www .washingtonpost.com/wp-dyn/content/article/2006/10/20/AR2006102001461.html

40. Goo, Sara Kehaulani (2006), "Building a 'Googley' Workforce," *Washington Post*, October 21, www .washingtonpost.com/wp-dyn/content/article/2006/10/20/AR2006102001461.html

41. Johansson, Greg (2010), "The World's Most Successful Corporate Culture," May 29th, *suite101*, www.suite101.com/content/google-the-worlds-most-successful-corporate-culture-a242303

42. Hibbets, Jason (2010), "Google and the Culture of Participation," August 2, *opensource*, http://opensource.com/life/10/8/google-and-culture-participation

43. Hibbets, Jason (2010), "Google and the Culture of Participation," August 2, *opensource*, http://opensource.com/life/10/8/google-and-culture-participation

44. Google, Wikipedia, http://en.wikipedia.org/wiki/Google

Index

CREDITS

Figure 1.1, page 4: © Hawaya/Shutterstock.com

Character with question marks over head, page 6: © Ramin Khojasteh/Shutterstock.com

Character sitting on a question mark, page 7: © Ramin Khojasteh/Shutterstock.com

Figure 1.3, page 8: © Hank Frentz/Shutterstock.com

Figure 1.4, page 9: © Jamie Roach/Shutterstock.com

Figure 1.5, page 10: © ronfromyork/Shutterstock.com

Characters with chess pieces, page 10: © Lukiyanova Natalia/frenta/Shutterstock.com

Character watering the word "Success", page 11: © Apostol_8/Shutterstock.com

Characters standing by signpost, page 12: © Reji/Shutterstock.com

Figure 1.7, pages 12–13: Sphere with two rings © ngirl/Shutterstock.com; Sphere with four arrows pointing to the center © almagami/Shutterstock.com; "The particular 4-DS view represents a perspective" © Handy Widiyanto/Shutterstock.com

Figure 1.8, page 13: © KOUNADEAS IOANNHS/Shutterstock.com

Figure 1.9, page 14: © suravid/Shutterstock.com

Figure 1.10, page 14: © KOUNADEAS IOANNHS/Shutterstock.com

Figure 1.11, page 15: © Galushko Sergey/Shutterstock.com

Figure 1.12, page 15: © immrchris/Shutterstock.com

Figure 1.13, page 15: © KOUNADEAS IOANNHS/Shutterstock.com

Figure 1.14, page 16: © Bruce Rolff/Shutterstock.com

Figure 1.15, page 17: © R.T. Wohlstadter/Shutterstock.com

Figure 1.16, page 17: © Vicente Barcelo Varona/Shutterstock.com

Figure 1.17, page 18: © argus/Shutterstock.com; Character with Binoculars © KOUNADEAS IOANNHS/Shutterstock.com

Figure 1.18, page 18: © Jiri Flogel/Shutterstock.com

Figure 1.19, page 19: © Monkey Business Images/Shutterstock.com

Figures 2.1, page 21: © Michael G. Smith/Shutterstock.com

Figure 10.9, page 239: © Ramin Khojasteh/ Shutterstock.com

Figure 10.10, page 240: © Volodymyr Vasylkiv/Shutterstock.com

Figure 10.11, page 240: © Losevsky Pavel/ Shutterstock.com

Figure 10.12, page 241: © Reji/Shutterstock.com

Figure 10.13, page 241: © LadyLyonnesse/ Shutterstock.com

Figure 10.15, page 244: © kentoh/ Shutterstock.com

Figure 11.1, page 249: © Vladimir Nikulin/ Shutterstock.com

Character with two puzzle pieces fitting together, page 250: © Kirsty Pargeter/ Shutterstock.com

Figure 11.2, page 252: © Alin Popescu/ Shutterstock.com

Figure 11.3, page 254: © Kirsty Pargeter/ Shutterstock.com

Character sitting on a big question mark, page 258: © apostol_8/Shutterstock.com

Figure 11.4, page 258: © Ilin Sergey/ Shutterstock.com

Figure 11.9, page 267: © janprchal/ Shutterstock.com

Panera Logo, page 268: http://www.panera-bread.com/about/

Figure 12.1, page 275: © paul prescott/ Shutterstock.com

Figure 12.2, page 278: © Volodymyr Vasylkiv /Shutterstock.com

Photo of man with binoculars, page 279: © Andresr/Shutterstock.com

Figure 12.3, page 282: © Reji/Shutterstock .com

Figure 12.6, page 286: © Ford Prefect/ Shutterstock.com

Figure 12.8, page 290: © Sarah Nicholl/ Shutterstock.com

Figure 13.1, page 299: © Kiseleva Olga/ Shutterstock.com

Characters standing together, one with hand up, page 302: © Volodymyr Vasylkiv/ Shutterstock.com

Figure 13.4, page 305: © Dmitriy Shironosov/Shutterstock.com

Character with hard hat and roadwork equipment, oage 306: © KOUNADEAS IOANNHS/Shutterstock.com

Figure 13.7, page 309: © Konstantinos Kokkinis/Shutterstock.com

Figure 13.9, page 313: © Wavebreakmedia ltd /Shutterstock.com

Figure 13.10, page 314: © Ramin Khojasteh/ Shutterstock.com

Figure 13.11, page 314: © Wooden headWorld/Shutterstock.com

Google Screenshot, page 315: http://www .google.com/

SAGE research**methods**
The Essential Online Tool for Researchers

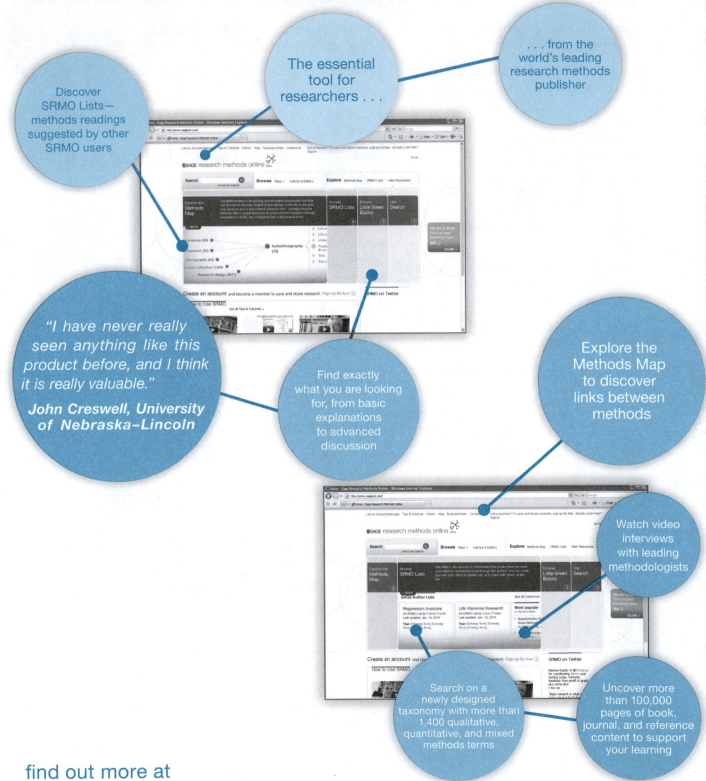

The essential tool for researchers . . .

. . . from the world's leading research methods publisher

Discover SRMO Lists—methods readings suggested by other SRMO users

"I have never really seen anything like this product before, and I think it is really valuable."

John Creswell, University of Nebraska–Lincoln

Find exactly what you are looking for, from basic explanations to advanced discussion

Explore the Methods Map to discover links between methods

Watch video interviews with leading methodologists

Search on a newly designed taxonomy with more than 1,400 qualitative, quantitative, and mixed methods terms

Uncover more than 100,000 pages of book, journal, and reference content to support your learning

find out more at
srmo.sagepub.com